KU-421-450

Daniel Finkelstein is a British journalist and opinion writer. A former executive editor of *The Times*, he continues to write for the paper. He has been Political Columnist of the Year four times and recently joined the board of Chelsea Football Club. He was appointed to the House of Lords in 2013.

A *Sunday Times* Bestseller

Book of the Year in *The Times*, *Guardian*, *Financial Times*, *Economist*, *New Statesman*, *Spectator*, *Daily Express*, *Evening Standard*, *Times Literary Supplement*, *Aspects of History*, *BBC History Magazine* and Waterstones.

Winner of the Slightly Foxed Best First Biography Prize 2023

Winner of the Parliamentary Book Award for Best Memoir/Autobiography 2023

'Danny Finkelstein has written an elegant, moving account of the history of one family, and in doing so shines light on the history of the twentieth century. If you want to understand Hitler and Stalin, read this book about people whose lives were upended by both of them' **Anne Applebaum**

'A terrific piece of work, epic, moving and important, the grim history of twentieth century Europe encapsulated in one extra-ordinary, ordinary family' **Robert Harris**

'Powerful and beautifully written. Once the Second World War breaks out the book works like a thriller, as both families race against the clock to escape certain death. But there are bigger themes running through Finkelstein's writing, elevating *Hitler, Stalin, Mum and Dad* to the status of a modern classic – and just as deserving of acclaim as Philippe Sands's *East West Street* or

Edmund de Waal's *The Hare With Amber Eyes*, both of which used inventive ways to examine the Holocaust afresh' **Observer**

'Superb book on the histories of [Daniel Finkelstien's] parents in Nazi and Stalin's murderous tyrannies' **Simon Schama**

'A staggeringly good book: beautifully written and painfully gripping . . . you have to read it!' **Nigella Lawson**

'*Hitler, Stalin, Mum and Dad* is an extraordinarily powerful and moving book, which is both an unremitting chronicle of suffering and torture, and uplifting in the way it reveals the human will to survive unimaginable hardship. The subtitle does not do justice to the depth of the story since it is, of course, about much more than one family. But, thanks to Finkelstein's skill as a storyteller, it always has the family at its heart and is, despite the sombre subject matter, immensely readable. This should be compulsory reading for anyone who wants to try to understand the dark twentieth century; it reminds us that murderous depravity was not the preserve of Nazism alone but rivalled – and sometimes surpassed – by Stalinism' **Anna Sebba, *Spectator*, Books of the Year**

'Superb. Finkelstein is a versatile writer who has delivered an exciting story of courage and persistence, powered by a sense of filial duty and engagingly sustained over its hundreds of pages'

Daily Telegraph

'Carefully researched and beautifully written; as gripping as any thriller and in places so overwhelming that I had to stop to compose myself. I've been moved to tears by books before, but never from page three and then consistently throughout' **Guardian**

'An unflinching and gripping family history . . . Finkelstein has written an indelible chronicle of both historical and personal significance'   ***The Washington Post***

'I have read countless accounts of the Holocaust. This one is particularly distinguished. Through his ancestors, Finkelstein describes the geographic sweep of the crimes. This is a masterful tale, haunting, elegiac, at times joyful and humorous. It is a history, a commentary and a thriller, alternating between the suffering at the hands of the Germans and the Soviets'   ***Financial Times***

'Captivating . . . Superb. This is a beautiful book about a horrific time when life was cheap and cruelty abundant. It took possession of me. I read it quickly, but then couldn't stop thinking or talking about the Finkelstein and Wiener families'   ***The Times***

'An unforgettable epic of a book'   ***Daily Mail***

'I was also deeply moved by Daniel Finkelstein's *Hitler, Stalin, Mum and Dad*, [a] book about the precarity of life and the rise of unreason . . . It's shattering – up there with the memoirs of Edmund de Waal and Philippe Sands in terms of moral power'   **Jessie Childs, *Spectator*, Books of the Year**

'A breathless, brilliant memoir. What makes *Hitler, Stalin, Mum and Dad* remarkable is not simply the story, the detail and the historical records to which the author has access. But, with two of every three European Jews dead by 1945, that anyone was left to tell it at all'   ***Evening Standard***

'A masterpiece . . . At once an epic tale on the scale of *War and Peace*, an intimate portrait of his family and its traumas and a book of compelling urgency, with a vital political message at its heart . . . This book will be read for generations as a classic, a work of truth and history but with the emotional power of the most searing novel' **_Jewish Chronicle_**

'Finkelstein has written a remarkable book, an extraordinary testimony to love and hate, in which the voice of every family member speaks clearly from the past. It is essential reading for our troubled present' **_Irish Times_**

'A profoundly moving family memoir. To read Finkelstein, one of our great thinkers and writers, on the precise nature of those two versions of earthly hell and the exact process by which people came to be in them, is an unforgettable experience . . . This is a vital addition to the literature of two catastrophes of the twentieth century. With great clarity and wisdom he demonstrates what evil politics can do. There is not a word of padding. The prose, distilled into what is both true and interesting, can sometimes be disarmingly simple' **_Spectator_**

'Hair-raising . . . The tales he tells are so overflowing with cruelty and loss that Mr. Finkelstein's prose needs only to be spare and plain for us to be scorched by his narrative, which includes not just Hitler's depredations but Stalin's too – a double measure of evil'
Wall Street Journal

'A tale of survival, eloquently told' **_Economist_**

'Unforgettable . . . He tells the traumatic story of what happened to his German and Polish grandparents and parents before and during World War Two with his trademark mixture of deep thoughtfulness and non-dressy prose'
Ysenda Maxtone Graham, _Spectator_, Books of the Year

'It is rare to find a book that succeeds on so many levels'
Jewish News

'This truly remarkable book brings vividly home the horrors perpetrated against one family by Adolf Hitler and Joseph Stalin, serving as an indictment of their crimes against millions. Diligently researched, beautifully written and on occasion unbearably moving, this is a powerful moral work about political extremism and the importance of bearing witness, but at the heart of it is love'
Andrew Roberts

'Superb. An extraordinary story: moving and terrible but redemptive'
Jonathan Dimbleby

'A tale of survival and humanity surrounded by death and brutality. At a time when Holocaust denial is on the rise among the young, and people talk fondly again of communism, it is a reminder that for all their problems, our wonderful, messy democracy and our great shared European civilisation must be constantly defended'
George Osborne

'An extraordinary story – both horrifying and inspiring – that grips you completely from start to finish.'   **Gyles Brandreth**

'By far the best book published this year . . . superb'
Peter Hitchens

'This is a powerful and moving account of one family's story of resilience and survival during one of the most terrible periods of human history. It will never not be acutely relevant. Everyone should read it'   **Sonia Sodha**

'Daniel Finkelstein movingly weaves together the personal and the historical, including many lesser known events, to create this compelling, propulsive and eye-opening account of World War II. Deeply researched and chillingly relevant'   **Judy Batalion**

'A beautiful tale of tragedy and astonishing survival, a riveting and deeply affecting saga from a fantastic writer' **Alex Kershaw**

'Finkelstein writes about the dual distinct, horrific paths taken during [the 1930s and 1940s] by his German-born mother, Mirjam Weiner, and his Polish-born father, Ludwik Finkelstein . . . Two riveting stories' ***Washington Independent Review of Books***

'Drawing on oral history, letters, diaries and government records, *Hitler, Stalin, Mum and Dad* [is] by turns, sobering, suspenseful, and inspiring . . . Finkelstein captures the lived experiences of these two families in often haunting detail' ***The Jerusalem Post***

'Against a backdrop of mounting repression and horror . . . Finkelstein details [his family's] sufferings with immersive precision' ***The Forward***

'An extraordinary narrative . . . An excellent contribution to the literature of the Shoah and a moving homage to the will to endure' ***Kirkus Reviews, starred review***

Also by Daniel Finkelstein:

Everything in Moderation

HITLER, STALIN, MUM AND DAD

A FAMILY MEMOIR OF
MIRACULOUS SURVIVAL

DANIEL FINKELSTEIN

WILLIAM
COLLINS

William Collins
An imprint of HarperCollins*Publishers*
1 London Bridge Street
London SE1 9GF

WilliamCollinsBooks.com

HarperCollins*Publishers*
Macken House, 39/40 Mayor Street Upper,
Dublin 1, D01 C9W, Ireland

First published in Great Britain in 2023 by William Collins
This William Collins paperback edition published in 2024

1

Copyright © Daniel Finkelstein 2023

Daniel Finkelstein asserts the moral right to be identified as the author of this work
in accordance with the Copyright, Designs and Patents Act 1988

A catalogue record for this book is available from the British Library

ISBN 978-0-00-848389-0

All rights reserved. No part of this publication may be reproduced,
stored in a retrieval system, or transmitted, in any form or by any means,
electronic, mechanical, photocopying, recording or otherwise,
without the prior permission of the publishers.

This book is sold subject to the condition that it shall not, by way of trade or
otherwise, be lent, re-sold, hired out or otherwise circulated without the publisher's
prior consent in any form of binding or cover other than that in which it is
published and without a similar condition including this condition being imposed
on the subsequent purchaser.

Typeset in Adobe Garamond Pro
by Palimpsest Book Production Ltd, Falkirk, Stirlingshire

Printed and bound in the UK using
100% renewable electricity at CPI Group (UK) Ltd

This book contains FSC™ certified paper and other controlled sources
to ensure responsible forest management.

For more information visit: www.harpercollins.co.uk/green

To Anthony and Tamara

To Sam, Aron and Isaac

And to Nicky, of course

I'm prepared to forget, as long as everyone else remembers.
-Alfred Wiener

Contents

Map   xviii
Family trees   xx
Introduction   1

Part One: Before

Mum
Alfred and Grete   17

Dad
Dolu and Lusia   45

Mum
An Amsterdam Childhood   65
The Truth on Trial   78
Trapped   88

Part Two: During

Dad
A Knife in the Back   105

Mum
Overrun   125
Joy and Glee   132
The Departing   143
Betty from Nottingham   161

Dad
Into Exile   177
The Island of Hunger and Death   187

Mum

Alfred's War   207
Citizens of Paraguay   217

Dad

Amnesty   229
What Happened to Dolu   242
Reunion and Freedom   253

Mum

Westerbork   267
The Transfer   282
Camille   293
Belsen   299
The Exchange   314

Dad

The Dock at Southampton   333

Mum

Three Skeletons   347

Part Three: After

Dad

The Lady of Hendon Central   357

Mum

The Man on the President's Conscience   363

Mum & Dad

Friday Evening   379

Acknowledgements   389
Notes   395
List of illustrations   443
Index   445

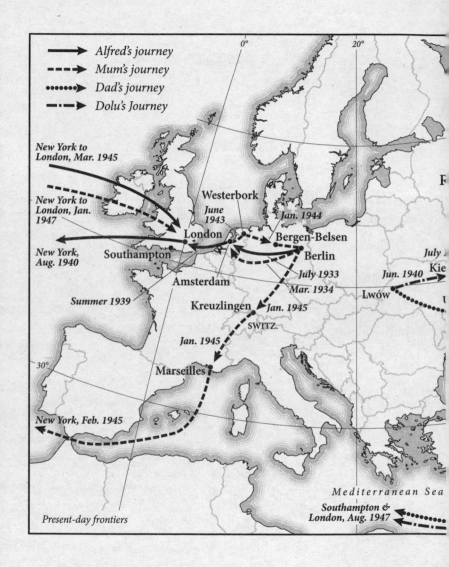

Alfred's journey
Mum's journey
Dad's journey
Dolu's Journey

New York to
London, Mar. 1945

New York to
London, Jan.
1947

New York,
Aug. 1940

Westerbork
June
1943

Jan. 1944

Bergen-Belsen

Berlin

London

Southampton

Amsterdam

July 1933

July

Jun. 1940   Kie

July 1933

Mar. 1934   Lwów

Kreuzlingen   Jan. 1945

Summer 1939

SWITZ.

Jan. 1945

30°

Marseilles

New York, Feb. 1945

0°   20°

Present-day frontiers

Mediterranean Sea

Southampton &
London, Aug. 1947

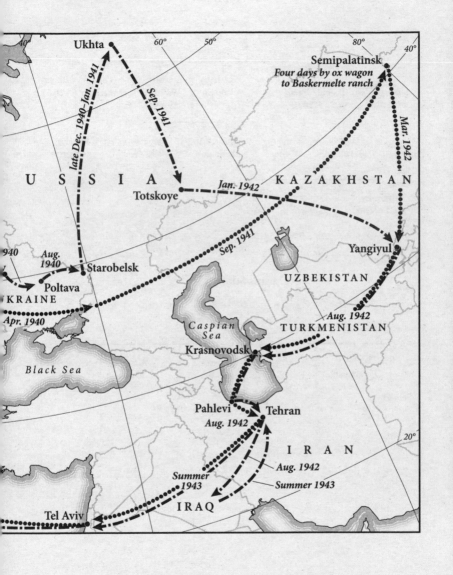

Dolu's family

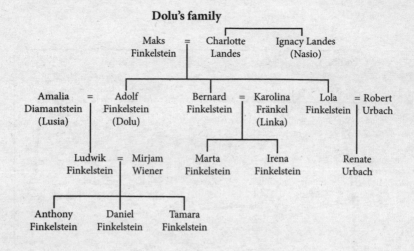

Maks Finkelstein = Charlotte Landes — Ignacy Landes (Nasio)

Amalia Diamantstein (Lusia) = Adolf Finkelstein (Dolu)

Bernard Finkelstein = Karolina Fränkel (Linka)

Lola Finkelstein = Robert Urbach

Ludwik Finkelstein = Mirjam Wiener

Marta Finkelstein

Irena Finkelstein

Renate Urbach

Anthony Finkelstein

Daniel Finkelstein

Tamara Finkelstein

Lusia's family

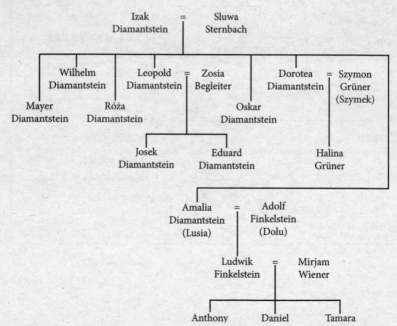

Izak Diamantstein = Sluwa Sternbach

Wilhelm Diamantstein

Leopold Diamantstein = Zosia Begleiter

Dorotea Diamantstein = Szymon Grüner (Szymek)

Mayer Diamantstein

Róża Diamantstein

Oskar Diamantstein

Josek Diamantstein

Eduard Diamantstein

Halina Grüner

Amalia Diamantstein (Lusia) = Adolf Finkelstein (Dolu)

Ludwik Finkelstein = Mirjam Wiener

Anthony

Daniel

Tamara

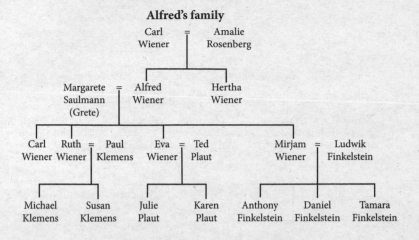

Alfred's family

Carl Wiener = Amalie Rosenberg

Margarete Saulmann (Grete) = Alfred Wiener | Hertha Wiener

Carl Wiener | Ruth Wiener = Paul Klemens | Eva Wiener = Ted Plaut | Mirjam Wiener = Ludwik Finkelstein

Michael Klemens | Susan Klemens | Julie Plaut | Karen Plaut | Anthony Finkelstein | Daniel Finkelstein | Tamara Finkelstein

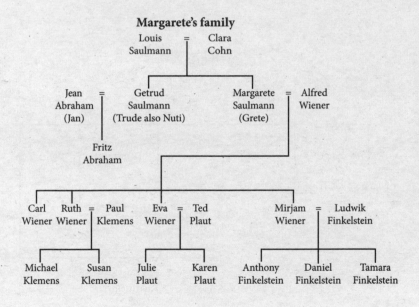

Margarete's family

Louis Saulmann = Clara Cohn

Jean Abraham (Jan) = Getrud Saulmann (Trude also Nuti) | Margarete Saulmann (Grete) = Alfred Wiener

Fritz Abraham

Carl Wiener | Ruth Wiener = Paul Klemens | Eva Wiener = Ted Plaut | Mirjam Wiener = Ludwik Finkelstein

Michael Klemens | Susan Klemens | Julie Plaut | Karen Plaut | Anthony Finkelstein | Daniel Finkelstein | Tamara Finkelstein

Introduction

Truth lies at the feet of Liberty.

When I'm in New York, I always stay in Midtown, picking a hotel a block or two away from where my grandfather lived during the war, when he was working for British intelligence and the American government. On the second or third day of my visit, I'll get on the subway at Grand Central and 42nd Street and travel for fifteen minutes or so down to Bowling Green. From there, it's a short walk to the Staten Island Ferry terminal.

Before long, I am seeing what my mother saw as she came up on deck on the Red Cross ship that bore her to safety. I'm experiencing the moment she described shortly afterwards in a school essay, taking among her earliest, erratically spelled, but still remarkably confident, steps in English. 'The very first of America that I saw were some huge skyscrapers in New York, the next thing was the Statue of Liberty which welcome the newcommers, when I saw this beautiful symbol I felt that I was realy in "the Land of the Free and the Home of the Brave".'

Yet moving though this always is, it's not actually why I make the pilgrimage. I go because this is where the truth lies. I go because this is where Auntie Ruth threw my grandfather's medals into the water.

In the autumn of 2012, we tidied the lounge, hired a party tent from some people we found on the internet, and asked a man from that place round the corner to supply some food. And then we held a party for my fiftieth birthday.

On the guest list were the people who mattered most to me. My family, of course. And some friends from work. But most of the crowd were from the group my wife Nicky calls 'Everyone'. People she got to know when she was in the sixth form, and who became my friends because my sister was part of 'Everyone' too. That's how Nicky and I met. Through Tamara.

There were differences between us all, naturally. But what was the same about us was more important. We were living happy, stable, safe, reasonably prosperous lives in the suburbs. We were also mostly Jews, many of us members of families who had been here for no more than two generations.

When she was young, my sister was startled to be asked by another child she met at a swimming gala: 'Where does your Mum come from?' It had never occurred to Tamara that our mother had a foreign accent. Or that anyone else might notice we didn't 'come' from Hendon. And if you asked most of my birthday guests where they came from, they might have said, 'London', or, 'just north of London'. But most of them didn't really 'come' from there at all.

So I thought this was the right audience for what I had to say.

We cut the cake that had been ordered by Nicky from the baker on the High Street, and which featured a marzipan representation of me sitting on a sofa with a can of Diet Coke while watching television. And then I gave a short speech to thank everyone for being there.

I told Nicky I loved her; my friends and family how much they meant to me; said how grateful I was for my presents; and then added this:

I'm grateful for one other thing. By time they were my age, my parents and my grandparents had lost everything they had. Their country, their home, their property. They'd been forced to start again in a foreign land and a foreign language.

We live here in peace and we don't stay up at night fearing we will be woken by a knock on the door. We don't fear our children will be sent to fight in a faraway war. We don't fear arrest or exile.

So here's to the Sunrise Cafe in North Harrow and the tube station and Brent Cross Shopping Centre and the local dry cleaner's. Here's to all of us who love this country and its small ideas and don't want it swept away in a fit of popular enthusiasm or revolutionary zeal.

Here's to the places that took in my family and yours. Here's to the suburbs and all of you who live in them.

I don't think, if I was having this birthday party now, that I'd make the same speech.

It's not that I believe we're on the verge of social collapse. But the last decade – uncomfortable as it is to admit – has dented my confidence. There are too many places in the world where such a collapse has already happened and too many people who've been its victims. Something about the confidence I showed that night seems to me like smugness now. The idea that the value of liberal democracy, and law, and liberty, and tolerance, is a lesson that has been learned and can't be unlearned seems hopelessly overoptimistic.

What happened to my parents isn't about to happen to me. It isn't about to happen to my children. But could it? It could. Absolutely, it could.

———

So I think it's time that I told the story of my Mum and my Dad and their parents. To describe what happened to them; why it happened; and why it matters.

My parents – Mirjam* and Ludwik† – didn't wallow in their experiences, but nor were they secretive about them. I could ask them whatever I liked, and I did. At the same time, my mother, in particular, took the view that she had suffered so we didn't have to.

Shortly before Mum died, a book was published called *Survivor*, which features pictures by the photographer Harry Borden of people who had lived through the Holocaust. The pictures are accompanied by short handwritten notes by the portrait subjects. One of the photographs is of my mother standing at the door of our dining room. The note on the opposite page in Mum's big neat lettering reads: 'I think of myself as a person, a wife and mother first, and a survivor last.'

And she was true to this, always remaining on top of what had happened rather than letting what had happened get on top of her.

When, in 1985, Ronald Reagan planned a presidential visit to the Bitburg cemetery in West Germany, a controversy arose because SS officers were buried there. Sitting in my bedroom, I heard on the radio that it had been decided that Reagan would deal with the fuss by also visiting the site where the Bergen-Belsen concentration camp had been. I went downstairs to the kitchen, where Mum was doing some washing up. Excitedly I told her: 'Mum, President Reagan's going to Belsen.' Without turning round, she calmly replied: 'So what? I've been.'

My father was also capable of gentle humour about what he had suffered. So much so, that occasionally I mistook his jokes for reality. Had he and my grandmother really bribed a Soviet train guard with a bottle of scent called 'The Breath of Stalin'? In the stories they told us when we were young, their Russian captors were always portrayed as bungling bureaucrats and fools, unable to cope with my grandmother's defiance. Is that truly what happened?

My parents' approach meant that little about their stories was

---

* Pronounced *Miriam*.

† Pronounced *Lud* [rhymes with good]-*vik*.

withheld from me. But it did still leave a mystery of its own. Why were they like this? How had they managed to emerge from such trauma and be so *normal*?

Why weren't they angrier? More hostile? When my father, lecturing in East Germany, was told it was election day, how could he smile and reply: 'If it's all right with you, I won't stay up for the results'? Why did they bring their children up like they did?

I am only just beginning to understand this as an adult would understand it. Because when you are young, you don't ask all that many questions about your parents. They just are.

———————

I see entirely why my sister had been startled to hear someone describing the way our mother talked as being in some way foreign. The slight note of Dutch (or was it German?) in her perfect English, that sort of gentle intonation, wasn't that just the way Mums spoke?

And yes, my father could be a little formal. He'd wear a jacket at the weekend, and straighten his tie to answer the telephone. When on holiday in the United States with my uncle, who lived there, they all agreed to eat in a Denny's roadside diner. My uncle, wearing fairly casual clothes, proposed that they quickly get changed before dinner. When they met later, Ted had changed into a tracksuit, while my father had changed from his customary jacket and tie into an even more formal business suit. Even on the beach, Dad would remain fully clothed, making the concession only of wearing an anorak and hiking boots.

His formality was never coldness to anybody, least of all to his children. And he never minded being teased, since he was able to laugh at himself. He admitted that when he was young, he had been the most solemn of his peers; a girl once asked to sit on his lap, he got up and gave her his seat. But he claimed with some justice that, as he got older, others gradually overtook him in solemnity, until in his old age he was the life and soul of the party, while everyone else only wanted to talk about their latest hospital procedure.

Qualities I now understand were really just his prewar Polishness we put down to his general mild eccentricity. In other words to the same bundle of idiosyncrasies that also meant that he would absentmindedly put on the coffee maker in the morning without emptying it first, so that it would spill everywhere. And then get up the next morning and do exactly the same again. The eccentricity that meant that if you asked him a question while walking, he would stop to ponder his answer, requiring two of us to stand behind him and push before we could get going again.

Even as children, we did realise that Dad was unusually preoccupied with intellectual matters. More so than other Dads. He was, after all, a university professor, and a pioneer in his field of measurement engineering. But learning was more than his career, it was his essence. He would raise questions of philosophy or politics at breakfast, and then at supper he would respond to the points you had made, having in the meantime consulted some printed authority in his large library. For his birthdays we would buy him encyclopedias – of mechanics, or ancient civilisations, or political thought – and he would read them like novels, progressing from A to Z.

His stock of knowledge was consequently vast. When a newspaper quiz asked for the date of the construction of London's Admiralty Arch, he calculated the answer by recalling the entire Latin inscription off by heart. Then he translated the Latin and gave me the date. When Dad died, one of his grandchildren observed that 'now we will have to use Google'.

He also spoke nine languages. As a child I didn't reflect on how he had acquired them. I rather embarrassed myself once, enthusiastically telling a political delegation from Russia that my father spoke Russian. When they equally enthusiastically asked how he had learned, I had to explain that he picked it up from those who had imprisoned him.

Yet there were gaps. He had thousands of books, but only six records (and one of those was a Sooty and Sweep show, so I'm pretty sure it was mine). He had no interest in organised sports or in any kind of celebrity, even those from his own era. It wasn't that he was contemptuous of popular culture, it was just that it was a bit of a blank.

I can see now the obvious reason for this. He had never really been a teenager, spending almost all those years struggling to survive and establish himself in a new country. When I asked him which football team he supported, he pretended that he followed Pipidówka United and had been checking on their progress. It was only many years later that I realised that Pipidówka was a Polish joke denoting a generic and undistinguished small town.

There was, by the way, one exception to his indifference to pop culture. He liked to watch really terrible television. He would ask Mum whether she minded him leaving the kitchen table before everyone had finished supper so that he wouldn't miss the beginning of *Kojak*, a programme featuring a bald detective who sucked a lollipop. I once came into the lounge to find him watching the denouement of an episode of *Quincy, M.E.* in which there had been a murder perpetrated by poisoning the snacks on a luxury yacht. The cry, 'Find me every tortilla chip on this boat', became a family joke. As did Dad's enjoyment of John Wayne films. He liked dramas in which good confronts evil, and good prevails. Of course he did.

And then there was Granny. During my childhood, before going to Hendon Central underground station and journeying on the Northern Line to City University every morning, Dad would drop in on his mother Lusia,* who lived around the corner. Since they had first acquired a permanent home on the Hendon Way in the late 1940s, neither Dad nor Lusia had moved more than 300 metres from it or from each other. We all, my mother and my siblings, accepted this close relationship, and this aversion to moving, for

---

* Pronounced *Lush* [rhymes with *Bush*]-*aah*.

what it was, without spending undue time pondering its origin. Dad's close relationship had become my Mum's and then ours.

After Dad went to work, my grandmother would set off to shop at the local Express Dairy and the butcher's, dressed immaculately in white gloves, a beautiful cloth coat and a smart hat. The incongruity was to us a source of amusement, but also a little pride. She was known by every shopkeeper as the Lady of Hendon Central.

To her grandchildren she was endlessly indulgent, but we were aware of her frankness and toughness too. Once, when I was canvassing the local streets in an election campaign, a fellow activist related to me that he had just met a lady who wouldn't vote for us because of our candidate's 'stupid hairstyle'. I knew immediately, and without further inquiry, that the lady had been Granny. She had many friends and would talk to them happily on the phone, mostly in Polish, but if they bored her she would put the phone receiver down on the table, and go and make herself a cup of coffee while they nattered on. She was entirely unconcerned that they might notice she wasn't there.

When we went on holiday, Granny would often come too. My sister recalls one country walk – Dad with his tie, Granny with her hat – when a cow started towards the family. Granny stepped forward and hit it on the nose with her handbag until it changed course. It took Tamara rather by surprise, but it is less surprising once you know a bit more about Lusia.

I think this setup – my cerebral father; his mother, the Lady of Hendon Central, living round the corner; the Polish talk and Polish food; the absence of a wider family living nearby – might have felt, might indeed have been, quite an odd one if it hadn't been for my mother.

My father was professionally successful, and not in the slightest insular. He had worked in the coal mines and the laboratory as well as the lecture room, and was popular with his colleagues in these varied places, whatever their background. Yet it was Mum, I think, who was most responsible for anchoring our family in modern Britain, seeing ourselves as part of something new rather than as the last stranded remnant of a dying continental Jewish culture.

In some ways, my mother was very conventional. She saw it as her job to keep the household running and support my father in his career. She did almost all the cooking, and prided herself on being able to lay her hands on a protractor or a missing sock or last-minute fancy dress when a panicking child was about to leave for school or a party. ('A green camel suit? Sure. One hump or two?' was her joke on these occasions.) She did the driving as well, as Dad was too absentminded to be trusted with a car. She was almost always there at teatime and available to assist with homework.

Yet this is very far from a full description of who she was, and the impact she made upon her children. After starting as an industrial chemist (whenever I said that an item had the aroma of real leather, she would remind me that she used to create fake-leather smells for a living) she became a maths teacher. She took maths very seriously. Sometimes we would spend forty-five minutes at dinner working out how many cans of drink you could fit in a fridge of a particular cubic volume. Despite my father's expertise in measurement, it was Mum who initiated such conversations. I recall that while they were both quite irritated that people do not appreciate that centimetres are not a proper measurement according to the International System of Units (or perhaps that they did not appreciate that they are, I forget), Mum's indignation was greater.

Her scientific training was accompanied by an open mind. She was excited by the modern world, young people, new technologies. She would buy new gadgets because she enjoyed reading the instructions and finding out how they worked. She had me take her to a pop concert to see what it was like and, when she was seventy-four years old, asked me to go with her to see Chelsea play West Ham United because she had never been to a professional football match. In the last year of her life, when she couldn't get out much any more, she would ring me up and ask me to challenge some political opinion she'd picked up in the newspapers, so that she wouldn't succumb to lazy prejudice. She also deliberately selected books that argued against positions that she held, or that might be held by people of her age.

Perhaps her most striking feature was her sense of proportion. She would never allow herself to have a petty row with the neighbours, or resign from the synagogue council, or disapprove of one of her children's choice of partner. She accepted the eccentricities of others with the words, 'We all have our own meshugas', a Yiddish word for craziness. It was, to her, out of the question that one member of the family would fall out with another, and it was made clear to all of us that saying – thinking, in fact – disobliging things about a relative was unacceptable.

This was allied to her sense of humour. Her favourite joke was 'Apart from that, Mrs Lincoln, how did you enjoy the theatre?' as it expressed perfectly what she found ridiculous. She thought it absurd as well as tragic that people would try to outbid each other when relating their wartime suffering. 'It's not a competition,' she would say. This is one of the reasons she didn't talk about the Holocaust unless she was asked to. The other is that she worried she might bore people. Before giving one of her first talks on the subject, she asked me whether she should mention having known Anne Frank, and having seen her in Belsen. 'Do you think they'd be interested in that?'

So my mother set the tone for our home, inventing a family life and happy childhood that she hadn't herself been able to enjoy. She adored my father, but there was no sense that he ruled. She made sure Dad never took himself too seriously, should he ever be tempted to do so. And he had the same respect for her. When, in their later years, they served together as chairs of a voluntary association, my father said to the members: 'You will find that Mirjam is the lion, and I only provide the roar.'

Even our Jewish life, which as children we ascribed to my father's strong intellectual interest in Judaic studies (in retirement he studied at a rabbinical school and wrote a doctoral thesis on the progressive rabbinate of Warsaw), I can see now was at least equally my mother's creation.

A belief in the value of belonging was the core of her Judaism. When asked if the Holocaust had shaken her faith, she always replied that it hadn't, because she didn't believe in the sort of supernatural God who would intervene in the world anyway. 'People have to intervene in the world,' she said. But this didn't make her any less Jewish.

The centre of our family life was the Friday evening meal in my parents' dining room in Hendon. Even as adults with children of our own, we very rarely missed it, and while Lusia was alive she was always there too. My father would work his way round the table blessing his children and grandchildren, before we cut the plaited loaves of challah, and then would come, inevitably, my mother's chicken soup with matzo balls and a main course which might be goulash, or another dish with a continental influence. Mum found it hard work, but also profoundly worthwhile. She certainly saw it as a triumph over Hitler; while Lusia and my Dad felt it a restoration of the Finkelstein family after the catastrophe that had almost destroyed it.

———

This, then, is how we were brought up, my older brother Anthony, my younger sister Tamara and me. A Hendon childhood, buying records in Hounsom's on the Watford Way and stationery in Batty's nearby; playing tennis and mini golf in Shirehall Park; going camping with the 7th Hendon Scout Troop; holidaying in British seaside towns and in cottages on windy moors; learning about British kings and queens; having Mum read us stories about Paddington and Winnie-the-Pooh.

My parents had a full social life, but also a simple one – once a week or so, a couple of friends round for dinner or cake. The company they most enjoyed was each other's. An evening in, eating (inexplicably) boiled eggs in tinned curry sauce with rice; a morning trip in the car to the coffee bar attached to the local supermarket. Suburban life.

But there had once been a life elsewhere, tranquillity in different suburbs, childhood literature in other languages, and kings and queens who ruled foreign lands and not ours. This is the story of how that life was destroyed and how it came to be remade.

This is a story of love and murder. A story of how the great forces of history crashed down in a terrible wave on two happy families; of how it tossed them and turned them, and finally returned what was left to dry land. It's a story of brilliant ingenuity, great bravery and almost unbelievable coincidences.

It's a story of secret archives and freezing wastelands; of forgery and theft; concentration camps and the Gulag. Of evil and the consequences of evil. And of freedom, and freedom's reward.

It's the story of how my family took a journey which ended happily in Hendon, eating crusty bread rolls with butter in the Tesco café near the M1, but on the way took a detour through hell.

PART ONE

BEFORE

MUM

Alfred and Grete

On a March weekend in 1920, a car flying a diplomatic flag set off towards the Reich Chancellery in Berlin for a meeting with the Chancellor of Germany. Only the man heading to the meeting wasn't a diplomat, no meeting had been scheduled, and the Chancellor of Germany wasn't really Chancellor, he just said that he was.

In the turbulent hours before this strange incident, there had been a coup in Berlin. As columns of troopers wearing jackboots, and helmets with swastikas on them took over government buildings, the Cabinet fled, leaving in convoy for Dresden. In their place was installed an administration headed by a portly, bull-necked, shaven-headed man called Wolfgang Kapp, the head of the Fatherland Party and the creature of militant right-wing soldiers.

The causes of the coup were various, the programme of the plotters confused, but Alfred Wiener, my maternal grandfather, was certain the takeover could only mean trouble. The men taking over were exactly the sort he'd been warning people about ever since he came back from the war. Extreme, in the grip of conspiracy theories about the betrayal of Germany, and, worst of all from Alfred's point of view, convinced that the Jews were at the root of the country's troubles.

So, he reasoned, he'd have to do something about it. He persuaded a friend – he was very good at persuading people – to

17

lend him his diplomatic car, drove straight through the armed ranks of the rebels and stopped at the Reich Chancellery. Then he got out, demanded to see Kapp, somehow succeeded in doing so, and remonstrated with him about antisemitism.

In the circumstances, Alfred was perhaps fortunate that within a couple of days the putsch had collapsed, with Kapp fleeing in a taxi with a knotted sheet containing his belongings secured to its roof. If the plotters had succeeded, it's unlikely Alfred would have survived very long.

The confrontation with Kapp was classic Alfred behaviour. It was physically brave, almost foolhardy; it was clear-sighted, understanding the threat the extremists posed to Germany's Jews; it was prescient, seeing before others did what might lie ahead for Jews; it took personal responsibility for the fate of his fellow Jews; and it represented his almost limitless faith, his almost boundless optimism, that rational argument and insisting on the truth could change things.

These characteristics were responsible for taking him in his life and career from triumph to disaster before triumph again. They were to be praised as the qualities of a great man and criticised as the beliefs and behaviour of a naif. They saw him rise to become one of the leaders of German Jewry and to hold that position through the tumultuous twenties and into the thirties as the Nazi threat grew. And he took them with him into exile when a meeting with Hermann Göring and its menacing aftermath made it obvious he would have to leave Germany.

———

At the end of 1918, Alfred Wiener had returned to Berlin after more than three years of fighting in the war, to the realisation that his battles were just beginning.

He had responded to his army call-up in April 1915 without the slightest hesitation or reservation. He felt a strong sense of national attachment and duty, a view reinforced among many

German Jews by a desire for the defeat of Russia, the country of barbaric pogroms. He had fought on both the Western and Eastern Fronts, waged war with heavy artillery and armoured vehicles, acted as an interpreter in the German-Turkish campaign, and edited the army newspaper in Jerusalem and Damascus. And he had almost died. A severe bout of dysentery came close to ending his campaign, and his life, at the beginning of 1917. For his gallantry he was awarded two medals – the Iron Cross (second class) and the Iron Crescent. Both these accolades were solid rather than spectacular, but Alfred was proud of his service.

There were lots of things people said about Alfred – that he was humorous, that he was bookish, that he was bald from a young age, that he made friends easily, that he was hard working, that he was opinionated; after his death, newspapers were full of attempts to capture his looks and his personality and what made him so beguiling. But if he were asked, he would have wanted any description to start with the fact that he was German.

He was born in 1885 in Potsdam, and one of his closest associates, the great sociologist Eva Reichmann, remarked after his death that:

When he pronounced the very name 'Potsdam' you could hear in his sonorous voice the distant echo of a clarion call. He loved Potsdam and was imbued with its historical tradition. Up to his last years, he used to meet some of his former classmates once a year; so convinced was he of the mysterious 'spirit of Potsdam' as he conceived it, that when I once asked him if he was not afraid that there might be Nazis among the old boys, he replied without hesitation, as if stating an indisputable maxim: 'Of course not, they are from the Potsdam Gymnasium.'

He maintained throughout his life, this strong feeling of belonging to his country and his culture. This romantic idea of his nation made what happened to him – his exile, the loss of his nationality, the way the Holocaust engulfed his family, the destruction of the liberal values he associated with his country's better nature – a particularly poignant tragedy.

But Alfred was, of course, a particular sort of German. He was a German Jew, words he thought went together naturally. When he was three, Alfred had moved to Bentschen, a small market town near the Polish border, where his father had established a haberdashery. It was in these years, before returning to Potsdam when he was twelve, that Alfred's rather singular Judaism took shape.

Bentschen, Alfred later recalled, 'had a nice synagogue, which was beautifully renewed and solemnly inaugurated with the help of my blessed father during the years when I lived there', but 'Jewish life was expressed by the so-called modern part of the community, who did not visit the place of worship, except on high festival days'.

Alfred's Judaism would always remain an idiosyncratic mixture of the modern and the orthodox. He was a religious traditionalist who did not keep the dietary laws or often go to the synagogue. His commitment was a serious one – he studied at the Academy for the Science of Judaism in Berlin and at one point planned to become a rabbi – but at its heart was Jewish learning and belonging rather than observance. At home, the family would always have a Sabbath meal on a Friday evening, but the food would not necessarily be kosher. He took a close interest in the Jewish education of his children, ensuring that they received special tuition, but he would stay at home when they went to services.

Alfred was not a conventional person, in many ways. The depth and intensity of his intellectual interests was unusual. A friend said of him, years later, that 'he was driven by a veritable awe for the power, almost the magic, of the printed word; anything printed was to him sacred, and the waste paper basket was sparingly used'. He was 'pre-occupied with books, of which he knew well nigh all there is to be known'.

In his early twenties, he had spent time travelling and studying in Egypt, Syria and Palestine, and fallen in love with the Middle

East, returning to Germany to write a doctoral thesis on Arabic stories of relief from hardship. At my parents' wedding, a couple of sentences in to the standard speech of the father of the bride, he noticed his friend, the Hebrew Bible scholar Paul Kahle, among the guests. He switched to the subject of Egyptology and remained there for the rest of his address.

Yet although all this may not have been common, it was not unique. Alfred belonged to a small but recognisable group, the German Jewish intellectuals – the philosophers and lawyers and doctors and physicists and psychoanalysts – that Hitler would seek to destroy, and largely succeed in destroying. And this group was part of the larger Jewish middle class, who, having finally been granted citizenship as the first half of the nineteenth century advanced, wanted to realise the promise of civic and social emancipation that had been made to them.

The Jews of Germany had moved into the big cities, established themselves as the creators and consumers of culture and art, built businesses and educated their children as professionals, and become well-represented in the ranks of the wealthiest and most cultivated members of Berlin society. All this was progress, and now before them was the prospect of the full social and civic equality, the full acceptance, that still eluded them.

On his return from military service, Alfred saw less reason for optimism. For all the comradeship he had enjoyed during the war, and his fondness for the veterans with whom he had shared tanks and trenches, he realised what defeat had done to his fellow soldiers, how it had embittered them, spurred them to search for someone to blame. And he could see that the future for German Jews might not be acceptance as equals, it might be intimidation and death. The struggle against this would be his new battle.

'A mighty antisemitic storm has broken over us, a storm that has not come about according to the laws of physics, but rather by means of unlimited funds in the hands of skilfully led organizations, which have stimulated and promoted it and are zealously seeking to further it,' read the opening words of *Prelude to Pogroms?*, the tract he published in 1919 as his first major contribution to the fight.

It was, scholars agree, an uncannily farsighted publication, seeing the disaster to come before almost anyone else did. It gives Alfred good claim to be the first person in Europe to sound the alarm.

Even twenty years later, there were many people who did not appreciate the seriousness of antisemitism in Germany and what it might mean. Yet only a few months after the First World War Armistice, this was Alfred's warning:

> It may be that our 'decent antisemites' disdain to solve the Jewish problem with shotguns and cudgels, but what does that matter to the 'men of action' who state more or less openly in leaflets – and quite fearlessly at secret meetings – that they envy the Poles and Romanians their pogroms, and who work systematically to imitate them in our dear fatherland? This is why we describe the antisemitic rabble-rousing of our day as agitation for pogroms.

He noted the signs. The speakers on the streets talking of 'the desirability of plundering Jewish businesses, of murder and manslaughter'; the leaflets in which 'we Jews are once again being burdened with the accusation of ritual murder for the purpose of manufacturing goat sausages' and which warn against 'sexual intercourse with Jews and other roundheads'; the campaigns to boycott Jewish shops; the public letters that announce that the Jews deserve death; the public promises that 'we will shortly free ourselves, completely and mercilessly, from these bloodsuckers, the Jews'. And he noted behind it all, the money financing antisemitic militia and the targeting of workers' councils by paid agitators.

Is this, he asked, 'the thanks of the fatherland to the thousands upon thousands of Jewish soldiers who shed their life's blood for us all, without considering religion or origins, and who are now beneath cemetery lawns'? He resists adding, as he might have done, how near he came to lying beneath the cemetery lawn himself.

And he finished with an appeal to the decent Germans, whom all his life he believed he lived among, to see what was happening and to act.

The morality of any decent human being demands that the good be encouraged and the evil resisted. Anyone who does not wish to see the blood of citizens flowing in the streets, or that history should report bestial murders and violence to our descendants must be prepared to fight pogrom antisemitism. Antisemitic rabble-rousing is the precursor of anarchy.

But good was not encouraged, and evil was not resisted, and history did indeed report bestial murders and violence to Alfred's descendants.

———

Underneath the words *Prelude to Pogroms?*, the title page of Alfred's publication featured a subtitle, *Facts for Thoughtful People*. It was always his approach to try to dispel lies and misunderstandings with truth, carefully taking apart the arguments and slanders of his opponents. Yet his writing was often passionate, and deeply personal. This reflected his political commitment to liberal ideas, his belief in the emancipated German Jew, but also something else – a concern for his own security and that of his family.

Alfred Wiener's struggle was not just for the advancement of civil rights, or, as he saw it, the protection of civilisation against barbarism, it was also a much simpler one. It was a struggle to be allowed to live in peace with his books and his research and his scholarly debates with his friends. To live in peace with his wife and his children.

Because although he may have encountered hatred on returning from the Front, he also found love. And in the summer of 1921 my grandparents were married.

Alfred had been introduced to his future wife by one of his army friends, Jan Abraham, who had asked him to his home and to meet the woman, Gertrud Saulmann, whom Jan was courting. Trude's younger sister Margarete was there, and soon she and Alfred were together.

In certain superficial respects, Alfred and Grete appeared incongruous. She was almost exactly ten years younger than him, and a fair bit taller (Grete was nearly six foot while Alfred was more like five foot seven). Intellectually and culturally, however, they were very well-suited indeed.

Born in Hamburg in 1895, the daughter of a factory owner and businessman, Grete had soon shown her academic ability, mastering four languages before the war interrupted her education. She had then spent the years between 1914 and 1917 in her home city, working for the Red Cross at the railway station as troops set off for war and the wounded came home. Later, she started on the sort of work in which she engaged for the rest of her life, helping families made destitute by conflict. As a volunteer for Hamburg War Aid, Grete helped run kitchens supplying cheap food, and a central warehouse which redistributed donated items – clothes, shoes and household goods. It served as rehearsal for the days when she would herself be a refugee, helping others in the same position.

In 1917, she had resumed her education, studying economics in Bonn, Berlin and Freiburg, and eventually achieving a PhD. It was a rare distinction for a woman in the early 1920s, and made her an ideal partner for Alfred, sharing his scholastic inclination and quite possibly surpassing his academic ability. She went on to be the secretary of the professional association of women economists in Germany, to attend the congress of the German Women's Associations, and to write articles and papers reviewing Nazi economics.

The subject of Grete's PhD was the thinking of a group of extreme German free marketeers who had formed their own political party in the late nineteenth century. She contrasted their libertarianism with the work of English classical economists. Grete argued that the extremists had distorted economics for their ideological purposes. And this was also her attack on national socialist economics. Grete's preference, in other words, was for rigorous and evidence-based thinking that rejected extremes – an intellectual approach that was similar to Alfred's.

Two other things helped cement Grete and Alfred's partnership. The first is that Alfred's army friend Jan married Grete's sister Trude. The two sisters were born less than ten months apart and were exceptionally close. The four of them – Jan and Trude, Alfred and Grete – lived almost as a unit, and when one couple moved home, the other would move nearby. The second is that the Wieners shared a strong commitment to Judaism and a determination to maintain proud German and Jewish identities, without compromising either. Grete was less inclined to orthodoxy than Alfred, but more obser-vant. In this respect, they balanced each other perfectly.

Grete and Alfred's marriage may have been a partnership, but it wasn't entirely one of equals. Both the age gap and traditional views of the role of men and women saw to that. Grete shared the burden of Alfred's work and supported his ideals and causes, but as his aide and his secretary. And as the couple began to have children, it was Grete who would do most of the child rearing and the housework. And the cooking. My mother used to say that her father couldn't even boil an egg, and when I laughed, she assured me that 'no, seriously, he could not'.

The pair had their first child quite quickly. An only son, named Carl after Alfred's father, was born in 1922, but tragically died following a burst appendix, aged five. The first to survive childhood, Ruth, was not born until 1927, with a younger sister, Eva, following in 1930. Consequently, the girls did not remember much of their home and life in the Charlottenburg district of Berlin, where Grete and Alfred had settled, but which they had to leave in 1934.

Save for a few fragments: that they lived in an apartment and not on the ground floor; that they would take trips to the beach, including one when Ruth almost drowned and Alfred had to rescue her from the sea while fully clothed; that (inevitably) Jan and Trude, and in time their son Fritz, lived nearby; that the Wiener home was full of heavy continental furniture and even more full of books; and that the typical pose of their father was in his study chair, smoking a cigar, surrounded by pieces of paper.

That's when he was there at all. For the other thing the girls remembered was how much their father was away. They were enjoying an ordinary middle-class family life, but Alfred spent most of his time out in the world protecting this life rather than living it.

———

A huge mass meeting to brand the ritual murder accusation against Jews as a libel was held last night at Würzburg. The meeting was called under the auspices of the Central Union [Association] of German Citizens of the Jewish Faith.

Alfred Wiener, leader of the Union, Mayor Löffler, and the Rev. Winkelmann, Evangelical pastor, spoke on the falsity of the libel and the outrages perpetrated in spreading it. Herr Holz, editor of the anti-Semitic journal, *Der Stürmer*, a member of the National Socialist party, was given the floor to state the case for the anti-Semites.

Several hundred Hitlerites who crowded into the hall, apparently not to seek enlightenment but to cause trouble, raised a tumult, compelling the police to close the meeting.

In 1919, Alfred had gone to work for the largest and most influential organisation representing Jewish interests in Germany, and within a few years became one of its leaders, as General Secretary. It meant a life of constant argument, turbulent meetings and some personal danger. The meeting in Würzburg – away from his family, arguing directly with the enemy, trying to hold back lies with truth – was typical of many of his nights in the 1920s.

Alfred's employer, the Centralverein deutscher Staatsbürger jüdischen Glaubens (usually referred to as the CV by Germans, and, in English, as the Central Association of German Citizens of the Jewish Faith), calculated that by the time Hitler came to power, its followers numbered three quarters of the 600,000 Jews living in Germany. With sixty members of staff based in Berlin, and a similar number in regional offices all over the country, the CV was one of the few organisations to span the whole of the country's Jewish community, a community which was religiously and politically disparate. As the 1920s progressed, the need for such breadth became increasingly apparent.

In the early part of the decade, Germany had been highly politically unstable, as factions from the left and right tried to seize power and settle their disputes with violence. And that was even before hyperinflation, with its devastating impact on the livelihoods of everyone, the poor, pensioners, small businesses, the middle class. (Grete's PhD, which was scheduled for publication, was one of the victims. Printers diverted their resources to printing banknotes rather than books.) Even as circumstances began to improve, the atmosphere remained febrile.

And the supposed power of the Jews, the subject of suspicion and prejudice for hundreds of years, provided a convenient explanation for the sorrows of modern Germany.

The CV sought to fight this prejudice in a number of ways: it held hundreds and hundreds of meetings, some of them mass gatherings, others with small groups of intellectuals or business people; it published newspapers and books; it sought to influence the popular press; it built relationships with organisations which could help, as Alfred put it, 'spread the ideas of tolerance, liberalism and equality of man'; it brought court cases against antisemitism and defended Jews in court; and it lobbied ministers and public officials, providing briefings and assisting legislators willing to defend Jewish rights.

As Alfred later claimed with some justice, the CV understood and fought 'the danger of racism and Nazism not only for world Jewry but the world itself . . . when most others, peoples and individuals, still did not want to see the truth and to recognise the steadily growing danger'.

Alfred was heavily involved with all of these activities. He enjoyed public speaking (one newspaper described him as a 'popular assembly speaker' who 'feared neither hecklers nor rioting Nazis'), but devoted just as much time to journalistic tasks. The CV published a weekly newspaper, the *CV Zeitung*, which in time became the largest Jewish newspaper in Germany, and Alfred served both as its editor-in-chief and a regular contributor. His contributions combined intellectual digression, parish news and accounts of the indignities suffered by Jews at the hands of antisemites.

There is an old Jewish joke, which dates from around this time, about two Jews sitting on a Berlin bench, one reading the Nazi newspaper *Der Stürmer* and the other reading *CV Zeitung*. The *CV Zeitung* reader says to his neighbour, 'How on earth can you read that Nazi filth?' and his friend puts down his copy of *Der Stürmer* and replies, 'It's simple. Your newspaper is full of stories of Jews being assaulted, or their rights being under threat, or their businesses being in danger. Mine says the Jews rule the world.'

The Weimar Republic, formed after the First World War, succeeded sporadically in restoring economic stability. It never succeeded in establishing a democratic culture. And the challenge from insurrectionists continued to grow. At the end of 1923, a new extremist leader emerged, when Adolf Hitler was charged with treason for his failed *coup d'état*, the Beer Hall Putsch. The news coverage provided him with a national platform for the first time. This event made Hitler a household name and marked the beginning of his consolidation of the far right into the Nazi Party.

Despite this, for a period the institutions of government did provide some protection for the Jews. On numerous occasions, the community took to the courts to challenge Nazis and other antisemites, and the CV – and therefore inevitably Alfred – played a central role in some of the most prominent trials of the age.

One of the best publicised was the so-called Talmud Trial, which saw Julius Streicher, the editor of *Der Stürmer* and perhaps Germany's most notorious antisemite, sentenced to two months in jail. Alfred's CV had spent months carefully scanning Streicher's paper for material that broke German law, and eventually they found enough to be able to convince a court. *Der Stürmer* had repeatedly misinterpreted or misapplied quotes from the Talmud, the central text of rabbinic Judaism. It had alleged that Jewish teaching encouraged sexual abuse and ritual murder of non-Jews and that Jews were allowed to commit perjury in gentile courts. Such attacks on any religion were against the law.

Challenging lies in this way, using documents and argument to confront the pernicious lies being directed at Jews, doing it publicly, was very much Alfred's favoured form of anti-Nazi activity. And in spite of their ultimate insufficiency, these efforts were hardly fruitless. Not only were there frequent jail sentences, but the cumulative cost of defending hundreds of cases was a significant burden on the Nazis.

Yet such victories were a mixed blessing, for they could also boost Nazi morale. As Streicher emerged from court, a large and emotional crowd surged forward singing racist songs and shouting 'Heil'. This response wasn't unusual. So alarmed was Alfred at this sort of reaction, that, while he strongly supported the legal strategy, he publicly warned his fellow Jews not to take every opportunity to prosecute antisemites, to avoid making them appear victims of a Jewish conspiracy.

These activities understandably were solidly backed by a large majority of Alfred's fellow Jews. But certainly not all of them.

———

There was a fundamental tension in Alfred's view of the world, one so great that on at least two occasions in his life it drove him to a breakdown.

On the one hand, he was a romantic. His friend Eva Reichmann, who knew him as well as anyone, said that the key to him was his enthusiasm:

Here lay one of the secrets of this active, vital, fulfilled personality, a secret of the magic with which he drew people to himself: he believed he was a cool sceptic, balancing things through a long life of political tactics, but he was an enthusiast. He was an enthusiast in his work, his love for people and books, an enthusiast in life . . . The core of his being was a friendly serenity of such radiance that it shaped the world in his image. He took notice of setbacks only insofar as he had to withstand them. He did not allow himself to be prostrated by them.

Yet this romanticism had to cohabit with his realism, his growing sense of alarm about the charges faced by Jews.

His speeches attempted to expose the contradictions of antisemites who blamed Jews for capitalism while simultaneously characterising them as communists. He used surveys of service records and casualty numbers to rebut the idea that Jews had not played their full part in the German army during the First World War. And he tried to highlight the absurdity of conspiracy theories, such as the ludicrous idea that even the Kaiser was actually a Jew, as a result of an imaginary affair between his grandmother, Queen Victoria, and her Jewish doctor.

All of this was done calmly, logically and with a hint of the humour which usually characterised Alfred's discourse. But it is impossible to avoid noticing the frustration and concern he felt. He worked night and day, ignoring his duties at home, to the point that his CV boss Ludwig Holländer would warn him, 'Don't work so hard or anti-semitism will come to an end prematurely.' This turned out to be one thing he didn't need to worry about.

The contradiction between his optimistic temperament and his appreciation of the danger facing Jews was, however, only one part of the tension he now felt.

The German newspaper *Die Welt* once wrote that Alfred 'devoted his energies to the goal of eliminating the mistrust between Germans and Jews'. This, however, represented a misunderstanding. Because Alfred did not see these two things as separate. He was a German Jew, one indivisible concept. And this was at the heart both of his own campaign against antisemitism, and that of the CV. Alfred fought against extremism and antisemitism not just because it would protect Jews, but because it was essential to protect Germany. He had become famous for his proclamation that 'if there were a Nobel Prize for German sentiments, the German Jews would win it'.

He saw the development of a modern liberal Germany and the development of modern Judaism as dependent on each other, and that an attack on one was an attack on the other. He used to describe fascism as a 'conspiracy against the Ten Commandments'. He was sure that there were enough Germans who agreed with him to enable calamity to be averted, provided they were properly informed by people secure in their facts and arguments.

But not all Jews accepted these ideas, by any means. He and the CV maintained their position against three different sorts of criticism from other Jews, and while the CV's view had the adherence of the majority of German Jews, one can feel in some of Alfred's writing in the 1920s the strain of the disputes within the community.

The least argumentative group of dissenters from the CV view in some ways troubled Alfred the most. Some Jews thought that they could never achieve the full promise of German citizenship if they remained Jews. So they simply gave up their religion quietly and had themselves baptised. It was, at least, understandable. Some antisemites believed you could smell a Jew, and that baptism cleansed them of that smell. But Alfred thought this disastrous and the CV spent a fair amount of its energy trying to make it easier for Jews to maintain their identity and to make Jews conscious of their descent and proud of their past.

Much more vocal critics were the communists. They thought that it was impossible to protect Jews in a capitalist system, and the development of capitalism into fascism they viewed as inevitable. The CV didn't, the communists argued, comprehend what it was facing.

Understandably, this attack annoyed Alfred and his allies, and they responded sharply. The idea that the tiny German Jewish community – one that was, in any case, markedly politically diverse – could have united behind the labour movement and diverted the course of Germany was fanciful.

However, Alfred's most time-consuming internal battle was with the third group of critics. It was with the Zionists.

To those already dreaming of a Jewish state in Palestine, the idea that the marriage of Germanness and Jewishness was a stable or sustainable one seemed a hopeless delusion. Jews who imagined that they would one day be accepted as fully German by their fellow citizens were fooling themselves. The only solution to European antisemitism was to leave Europe. The bourgeois existence of Alfred and Grete, with their children in the local kindergarten, Ruth learning to write with the state-approved right hand, Grete helping local charities, enjoying the cafés and walking among the plane trees on the nearby Kurfürstendamm – well, who were they kidding? This was no future for the Jewish people. The future was in a state of their own.

Alfred rejected this view entirely. He was very sympathetic to Jews who wanted to, and did, go and live in Palestine. His years there as a student and as a soldier left him with a romantic attachment to the land and people, and so he well understood the appeal of a Jewish home there. A home that is, but not a state. And, in particular, not a state for German Jews, who already had a state

– Germany. Support for the Zionist project, in his view, under-
mined the central case of the CV, that the country's Jews were
loyal citizens and as German as anyone else.

His approach to making this argument was characteristic – he
would challenge myths with truths. He thought Zionist claims about
the viability of their proposed state were often mere propaganda.
So, in 1926, he set off on a thirty-five-day tour of Palestine, with
the aim of studying conditions there and reporting back. Grete came
too, as so often his soulmate, his political ally and his secretary.

The result of the trip was a book, published in 1927, *A Critical
Journey through Palestine*. It was Alfred's most successful publication,
reprinted several times and issued in numerous editions, a popu-
larity which indicates that his factual approach was valued, and
his sceptical view of the Zionist project fairly widely shared,
by his fellow German Jews.

During their journey, Alfred and Grete met with the leaders of
the Zionist movement based in Palestine, visited the main settlements, and spoke to as many settlers as they could, with Grete
keeping notes of their exchanges and observations.

Alfred was impressed by how friendly his reception had been,
Grete with the way every Jew they had met seemed to take an
interest in the fortunes of the whole national project and not just
in their particular profession or speciality. Yet one other thing
struck her:

Almost everyone has their own plan for making the country
happy. Far-reaching projects are unrolled the moment the
conversational turn allows. There are the shining eyes of the
dreamer, yet accompanied by a cool matter of factness, as if
the plan were as close to its realisation as today is to tomorrow.

Grete's observation supplied the core of Alfred's critique.
Zionism seemed to him utopian, and the utopians were overlooking obvious practical problems. Just for a start, Palestinian

land, especially cultivatable land, never mind the Jewish share in it, was simply not large enough to absorb the whole of European Jewry. Several pages of *A Critical Journey* are taken up with maps, charts and tables that contrast the size of Palestine and its Jewish settlements with the size of European nations and their population of Jews. Palestine couldn't accommodate the sheer number of even just Polish Jews, for instance. 'The plight of the Jews of the East [of Europe] can essentially only be properly alleviated in the East itself.'

Alfred also wondered if the settlements in Palestine could ever be economically successful. He admits to being uncertain about this. It was obvious to him that the young people were very driven and show a 'splendid will', and it would be rash to predict their failure. But he does note, in some detail, the financial problems of various Zionist institutions and their dependence on money from Jews living abroad. He blames this largely on the socialist idealism of many Zionists, which he decries as 'obstinacy and fanaticism'.

He despairs of their insistence that 'what is impossible to achieve in capitalist Europe and America must be achieved in Palestine, whatever the cost. These efforts have truly eaten up enough money.'

He worried about Zionist chauvinism too. After all, Alfred was an Arabic scholar, with a deep interest in Islam and affection for the Arab world. 'A people with such a rich history, a people whose countries are graced with the most beautiful memorials of unsurpassed architecture, decorated with splendid artefacts . . . such a people should not be ignored or treated with suspicion, rather, one should make every effort to live with them in friendship.' He would repeat this concern throughout the 1920s, fearing there would be violent rejection of Jews, and their home in Palestine would never be secure.

Perhaps the most revealing part of the book is the way it begins. There are pages devoted to denouncing false reports in the Zionist press about his visit and a supposed attempt to use it as 'a battering ram against the Centralverein leadership'. He also writes of repeated attempts by the Zionist movement to ensure he was given the right propaganda. At one point in the trip, waiting for a train to Jerusalem, he noticed a kiosk providing information about Zionism. When he approached it, he was surprised to be addressed by his name, and observed the clerk had a piece of paper in front of him listing all the visitors who might pass through, including 'Dr. Alfred Wiener of the Centralverein, one of the leaders of German antizionism'.

These early pages, almost more eloquently than the rest of the book, speak of the intensity of the Jewish community's internal political argument about Zionism and the alternative of insisting upon their rights as European citizens. Factional fights between people with essentially the same interests can often be the most bitter form of political disagreement. Alfred's concerns about the difficulties the Jews would face implementing the Zionist project in Palestine have been largely vindicated. But reading *A Critical Journey*, it isn't hard to understand how mentally taxing it must have been for Alfred when all his passionate arguments that Germany was the home for German Jews met with the contradiction of Hitler's rise to power.

This was Alfred's tragedy. The greater Jewish tragedy is that, as Jews argued over which solution could long guarantee peace, security and acceptance, history would reveal that none of them could. That none of them can.

———————

Those who remembered Alfred from this period – from the late 1920s and into the next decade – often associated him with a prop. A small suitcase. And inside the suitcase, Nazi literature.

In the summer of 1925, Adolf Hitler published the first part of his autobiographical manifesto, *Mein Kampf*, and was emerging as the leading figure of the German far right, winning the allegiance of the groups Alfred had been warning about since 1919. Alfred began to argue with his colleagues at the CV that the situation on the right was changing, and that the Nazis were now the main threat to Jews in Germany. All the CV's other work should take second place to combating this emerging force.

In 1928, he presented a report to the CV's executive committee which showed evidence of increasing Nazi activity in rural areas, and argued that the voting patterns of the poorer people living there suggested that they were particularly susceptible to Nazi propaganda. He was sharply rebuffed, with the committee telling him that he was reading too much into isolated events. But his arguments, together with a campaign led by Goebbels against Jewish department stores, did make some impact on the CV. Soon agreement was forthcoming for Alfred to start work on a project that, in one form or another, lasted for the rest of his life.

A secret office was established in Berlin, officially not part of the CV but in truth under Alfred's guidance, which would monitor the Nazis' activities. Strategically located between the Reichstag and offices of the President on the one hand and Hitler's Hotel Kaiserhof headquarters on the other, the Büro Wilhelmstrasse would collect Nazi newspapers and leaflets, compile dossiers of reliable information and rumour about them, monitor Nazi speeches, profile Nazi leaders, and provide analysis of the party's policies, attitudes and support.

The Büro's director, Eva Reichmann's husband Hans, and its most senior employee, the archivist and journalist Walter Gyssling, kept records of acts of violence against Jews and their property, the vandalism of Jewish cemeteries and the crimes of individual Nazis. Whenever a Nazi was in court, there would be someone sent by the Büro to take notes. By 1933, the archive contained over half a million items. The volume and scope of the collection was such that in 1932, when the German Foreign Office wanted to know more about the Nazi view of German-Lithuanian relations, it approached the Büro, admitting it had no information of its own. On this arcane topic, the Büro was able to provide it with thirty-five cuttings.

The archive supplied material for CV press releases, essays for distribution to politicians and journalists, and articles in an aggressive and sensationalist CV journal designed to appeal to the same sort of audience the Nazis reached. It also resulted in a publication called the *Anti-Nazi*, which was 180 pages long and was distributed to hundreds of thousands of people. A typical extract presented instances of Hitler's personal cowardice; another detailed how few Nazis had served in the war; still another listed national socialist politicians who had been found guilty of corruption.

As the twenties turned into the thirties, it was selections from this collection – clippings, copies of Nazi newspapers, Büro analysis – that Alfred carried around with him in a little suitcase as he began to tour the country in an increasingly desperate attempt to alert the German middle class to the dangers posed by the Nazis.

He had to be careful with the way he presented the material. Should the archive's secrecy be breached, the mere fact of its existence would pose a danger to him, to everyone else who worked for it, and to anyone who had provided it with information. So, in meetings, he would leave the literature in the case on the floor and then get down on his knees to take out documents whenever he needed them.

Copies of *Der Stürmer* and Nazi anti-Christian literature were particular favourites in his show and tell. In his discussions with civic leaders and business people, he frequently found that Hitler had been there immediately before him, making the Nazi argument. 'Hitler was sitting in that exact chair just yesterday,' he was told as he sat down.

Alfred and his suitcase were met with some sympathy, some hostility, but mostly with incomprehension. He encountered plenty of outright Nazis, but more typical were people who, while not approving of Hitler, weren't especially alarmed by him either. At the Ministry of Defence and the Interior Ministry, he was listened to politely but without much effect. Despite what Alfred was trying to tell them, they didn't seem to appreciate what they were dealing with.

Late one afternoon in July 1932, six months before Hitler took power, Alfred went to see Erwin Planck, Secretary of State in the Reich Chancellery and thus a key aide to Chancellor Franz von Papen, the Catholic conservative politician installed by President Hindenburg. The country was already spiralling towards Nazism as a series of Chancellors, electoral outcomes and political formations spun round in circles, heading towards the drain. Papen was the latest.

Whether Alfred had his little suitcase with him isn't clear, but he certainly had some of its contents. He took Planck through some of the latest violent incidents, read him some quotes from recent Nazi speeches, and showed him the Büro's recently compiled evidence on cemetery desecration. And then he addressed the general question of Hitler and the 'agitation'against the Jews. Could the Secretary of State, perhaps, intercede? 'Planck said that he had, of course, spoken to Hitler many times recently,' Alfred recorded in a contemporary note. 'He (H.) condemned this agitation thoroughly. H. was a decent, idealistic person, if somewhat excitable.' Planck promised to have another word with Hitler and to give him the cemeteries dossier.

On 23 January 1945, Erwin Planck was hanged in Plötzensee prison for his part in the 20 July bomb plot to murder the decent, idealistic, if somewhat excitable Hitler.

─────────

And then it came. All the years of speeches, and articles, and lawsuits, all the truth-telling combating all the lies, and still it came. At the end of January 1933, President Hindenburg brought the curtain down on the Weimar Republic by inviting Adolf Hitler to be Chancellor. A dual life began for Jews in Germany, the home routine and the growing menace outside the front door.

The Wieners were an example. They continued to live quietly and unnoticed in their Berlin apartment. Grete was pregnant again, Eva was growing from a baby into a child, and Ruth was in kindergarten looking forward to graduating to big school. On the first day, she would get a *Schultüte*, a paper trumpet filled with sweets, a rite of passage. There was a year to go and already she was anticipating it. Yet outside the home, Alfred's activities were anything but quiet and unnoticed.

Within a few weeks of Hitler's elevation, there had been the Reichstag fire blamed on the communists, the consequent decrees curtailing civil liberties, and the first waves of political arrests. At the beginning of March, the CV offices were raided and several officials seized. What the Nazis had been looking for wasn't clear at first. It became so within a couple of days.

On 2 March 1933, the CV's chairman, Julius Brodnitz, received a telephone call from Rudolf Diels, aide to the new Interior Minister, Hermann Göring, and soon to become the first chief of the Gestapo. Diels said that his boss had a message for the Jewish community and that he demanded to see Brodnitz. And Alfred too. A meeting was set up for the next day.

A friend who had recently met Göring had told Alfred that 'when he [Göring] spoke he made a very pleasant impression. Nevertheless if one observes more closely, one has the further impression that he doesn't quite have himself under control.' This was also Alfred's experience.

Göring invited Alfred and Brodnitz to take a seat and was polite, affable even. He said he was concerned by the activities of the CV, but as long as the Jews were loyal they really had nothing to worry about. Nobody would touch a hair on their heads. And then, as the hour-long meeting concluded, he added something else. He understood that the CV kept documents to aid campaigning against the Nazi Party. These would have to be destroyed.

This, then, confirmed to Alfred the target of the March CV office raids, and probably of the arrests too – to find evidence of disloyalty and to seize the archive. The Nazis had, of course, raided the wrong building. The secretive Büro was, quite deliberately, housed in Wilhelmstrasse rather than in CV headquarters. Alfred's team now moved the documents out of Berlin and a chase began, with the authorities trying to track them down. It only ended the following year, somewhere in Bavaria, when the archivists concluded that the danger of carrying on was simply too great. They reluctantly destroyed the work of five years.

Meanwhile, Alfred and Brodnitz decided to share the results of their Göring meeting (absent the remarks about the secret archive) with the rest of the German Jewish community. Alfred had an article placed on the front page of the 9 March edition of the *CV Zeitung*, right at the top, as prominent a noticeboard as the community had at its disposal. The article was intended as reassurance for Jews, and probably also to hold Göring to his word. It turned out, however, also to be a provocation.

In a discussion held on 3 March between the Presidential Minister of the Interior, Reichsminister Göring, the Chairman of the CV, Dr Julius Brodnitz, and the Syndikus Dr Alfred Wiener, the Minister stated that there was no evidence that the Central Association of German Citizens of the Jewish Faith was connected with communist and anti-state efforts. Reich Minister Göring also stated that the security of the lives and property of Jewish citizens who are loyal to the government are guaranteed by law.

Immediately, Göring was flooded with protests from Nazi Party members complaining that he'd gone soft. Probably never having intended his genial manner and his reassurances to be taken at face value, and certainly not expecting them to be made public in such a conspicuous way, Göring was furious. He gave a speech directed at Alfred and Brodnitz, which denounced 'the Jews who come whimpering and asking us to soften', before adding:

My police are not a Jewish protection force. They will stand up against anyone who opposes the Nazi state and we will shoot each of them. I will cover for every police officer who shoots and it will be as if I shot them myself.

On 25 March, the Reich Minister called the Jewish community back in, inviting a broader group this time. The tone was entirely different from the previous meeting. Brodnitz noted that it was a 'reception in dictatorial posture, surrounded by a large number of officials'. Göring made his visitors stand as he harangued them for an hour, threatening them with all the things that might happen to the Jews.

Together, these events made Alfred realise he would have to get out of Germany. He couldn't continue his work there, and it wasn't safe for him or the family. Grete agreed. Others may not have appreciated who the Nazis were and what they might do, but they did. And criminal charges were already being laid against some of those who had helped compile the cemeteries dossier. The one that Alfred had arranged to be passed to Hitler. He and Grete would go to Holland with the children, and start again. The decision was rational, but it was not only rational. The whole situation had taken a toll on Alfred emotionally, and he was having a breakdown.

Brodnitz recorded Alfred visiting him one night, 'weeping terribly', with Alfred exclaiming that 'he was physically and mentally incapable of working in Germany'. He was given immediate leave 'as a matter of necessity'. It was suggested Alfred go to Bavaria for a rest and consult a Dr Reinhold there. Before long, the doctor had reported back, confirming that the CV was right to allow him to depart: 'Anyone who means well for Wiener must arrange for him to be placed in a calmer situation, to avoid complete burn out.'

By the end of July 1933, Alfred had departed. Grete would close up the Berlin apartment, settle their affairs, and follow him to Amsterdam by the following Easter.

As his final act on German soil, Alfred wrote a celebrated article – entitled 'Between Heaven and Earth' – which appeared in the *CV Zeitung*. It indicated that although he had to leave, he was not going to give up fighting for the life he valued, and the identity he prized:

According to the ruling of the laws and regulations directed against us, only the 'Aryans' now comprise the German people. What are we, then? Before the law we are non-Germans without equal rights; to ourselves we are Germans with full rights. We reject this . . . We wish to be German subjects with equal rights . . . Thus we are suspended between heaven and earth. We will have to fight with courage and strength in order to get back to earth, in the eyes of state and law too.

And at this terrible juncture in world and family affairs, while the Jews were suspended between heaven and earth, and the Wiener family between Berlin and Amsterdam, Alfred and Grete had a baby. In Charlottenburg, Berlin, on 10 June 1933, Mirjam Emma Wiener, my mother, was born.

DAD

Dolu and Lusia

In 1937, Adolf and Amalia Finkelstein purchased a plot of land at the top of one of Lwów's most prestigious and expensive streets, hired a leading architect, and applied for planning permission for a large villa to house their family and the staff they employed.

Number 12 would be unlike any other house on Herburtów street. Indeed, it would be unlike almost any other house in the rest of this thriving city, the commercial centre of Eastern Poland. Where their neighbours lived in mostly neo-gothic and neoclassical houses, Dolu and Lusia, as everyone called them, commissioned a remarkably stylish modern house.

The award-winning design of the villa would be the pinnacle of architect Artur Stahl's career. The style, which was becoming fashionable in Europe at this time, was known as 'Streamline Moderne', an adaptation of Art Deco. Instead of ornament, Streamline Moderne emphasised clean lines, motion and modernity. Typically, buildings would imitate the shapes of vehicles – cars, say, or aircraft.

Streamline Moderne was often referred to as *le style paquebot*, or 'ocean liner style'. Dolu and Lusia's new villa was a classic example. Stahl took advantage of the plot that my grandparents had bought, which was a wedge situated high above the rest of the steeply inclined Herburtów street. His design resembled a large white cruise ship emerging from the waves and moored to a pier.

A combination of rounded balconies, arcades resembling cruise-ship railings, and a range of porthole windows added to the effect.

Inside, 12 Herburtów was spacious rather than palatial, extremely comfortable but still a family dwelling rather than a stately home. On the ground floor, an open entrance hall connected to a lounge and dining room, which had doors between them that could be folded back to create a large single space for entertaining.

The family rooms were on the first floor, to which you ascended by a carved wooden Deco staircase. As was customary at the time, Dolu had one room and Lusia another, with a connecting door between. And, on the other side of the landing, their only child, my father, Ludwik, had his bedroom and balcony, with his nanny sleeping next door.

Complete with central heating, a garage for the chauffeur-driven car, basement rooms for a caretaker and laundry, and a kitchen where the cook prepared meals for the family, 12 Herburtów was ready for the Finkelsteins to move into by the summer of 1938.

The house was a statement. It spoke, naturally, of the family's wealth. It told of their modernity and progressive spirit. And it announced their solid confidence in the life they were living. Finkelsteins had lived in this region, Galicia, for hundreds of years, and now, optimistic about the future, they had built a home in which it was possible to imagine the family residing for hundreds more.

They would live in it for little more than a year.

———————

Dolu had increased the family fortune, but it was his father, my great-grandfather Maks, who had first created it. Maks, whose father was a cart driver, had made his way to Vienna as a young man to learn the iron and steel business. He had come back to Lwów and, with his partner Gustav Fehl, began a company that was to become a mighty enterprise, the dominant supplier of iron and steel in the region.

In 1911, Maks bought out Fehl, and built a large apartment building and business premises at 47 Słoneczna street, right in the centre of town. Contained in an imposing building with ceramic tiled hallways and company ironwork railings, the flats overlooked a courtyard containing the Finkelstein and Fehl warehouses and offices. Maks took one of the apartments for his own, and lived there with his wife, Charlotte, and their youngest daughter, Lola, now twelve years old. The two older boys, Dolu and Bernard, twenty-one and nineteen respectively, were already beginning to make their way in the world.

The Finkelsteins also retained property – primarily, an upmarket residential address – in Vienna. Before the First World War and the subsequent creation of a Polish state, Lwów had been called Lemberg and was a provincial centre of the vast Austro-Hungarian Empire. Situated at the crossroads between East and West, Lemberg was commercially successful and this success had produced a strong middle class and civic institutions. The emperors allowed it relative autonomy, reflecting the city's pride in its identity and as a way of neutralising the competing nationalist feelings of the city's various ethnic groups. Roughly half of the 200,000 or so citizens were Poles, and the remaining half was split about equally between Jews and Ukrainians. The emperors' policy, very broadly, seemed to work, and relations between the groups were reasonably good.

Dolu and Lusia's correspondence was in Polish, but the Finkelsteins were fluent German speakers, and Maks owned a considerable library of German books and subscribed to the Viennese newspapers. These habits were inherited by Dolu, and the family attachment to German was sufficiently strong that when my father was born in 1929, his parents hired a German-speaking nanny in order to ensure he mastered that language. Speaking German was something that smart, wealthy Jewish families did. It was to show their sophistication, worldliness and attachment to Western culture.

When Maks and Charlotte moved into the new apartment, not only did Dolu not move with them, he wasn't even in Lemberg. He'd completed high school, the IV Gymnasium, in 1909 and gone to study law at the University of Vienna. And when he graduated, he joined the Austrian army as a volunteer and remained in its service, primarily as a quartermaster, for the duration of the First World War. It was only when he was demobilised, as a second lieutenant in 1918, that he returned home to work for his father.

By the time Dolu came back from the war, the uneasy peace between Lemberg's ethnic groups had been shattered. The commencement of the war had revived Polish dreams of establishing a state as in ancient times, while Ukrainian nationalists felt similarly inspired. Then, in September 1914, the city had fallen to the Russians, who had held it for less than a year before the Austrians had returned. A year later, the empire had declared a 'kingdom of Poland', but by the end of the conflict it remained unclear where its borders would be, and whether Lemberg would be part of it.

When Austria was defeated, even this confused proposal collapsed and Ukrainians and Poles ended up making competing claims for sovereignty and, eventually, fighting over it. And when this issue was settled in favour of the Poles, Russia launched an attempt to kill the nascent Polish state and almost succeeded. Its military assault was inspired partly by a desire to settle old territorial disputes, and partly by ideology. The Russians wished to spread the benefits of socialism to their neighbours.

Marshal Józef Piłsudski's leadership of the Polish resistance, and his victory against the odds in 1920, made him a national hero. The Bolsheviks, Stalin in particular, deeply resented it, and the outcome remained controversial with many world powers, who hadn't wanted Poland to expand so far east. It was only in 1923 that the creation of an independent Poland, with Lemberg a part of it, was finally accepted by the international community. Lemberg became Lwów.

The dizzying shifts of power in the city had one constant. Whoever came in blamed the Jews. They blamed them for being too loyal to the outgoing regime, or not being loyal enough to the incoming one, or selling too many goods, or keeping too many goods for themselves.

In 1914, anticipating the arrival of the Russians in the city, large numbers of Jews fled in fear of pogroms. Even before the invaders arrived, a campaign of looting of Jewish shops began, and the Russians joined in when they got there. In the surrounding countryside, there were mass rapes and arson attacks on Jews in revenge for their support for the Austro-Hungarian army. Yet when, the following year, the Austrians returned, the Jews were accused of having welcomed the Russians with flowers and having profited from wartime hoarding and financial speculation. Jewish politicians were hounded out of office and Jewish tradesmen were harassed.

This pattern persisted. As the Austrian grip on the city began to loosen, another round of looting took place and Jews travelling on public transport were beaten up. Rumours spread that food on Market Square, outside the town hall, was being sold to Jews at cheaper prices than to Christians, leading to mob violence against anyone in the market who even looked Jewish.

And the war between Poles and Ukrainians finished with both sides feeling aggrieved towards the Jews. After the Ukrainians left Lwów, there was a pogrom lasting three days in which there were more than seventy deaths and several hundred serious injuries. Many Jews reported Polish soldiers entering their homes and extorting money from them, warning that they would burn down the house, or hanging a noose on a beam and simulating an execution.

This, then, was the city to which Dolu returned in 1918. One which had been not merely bitterly divided, but also ravaged by all the fighting. The city was bankrupt. A quarter of its buildings had been badly damaged or destroyed, its power station was able to produce only a fraction of its prewar electricity, and its water supply had been disrupted by an attack on the pipes. People were walking to work because there weren't enough trams, and hauling their water from public wells.

Yet, for Dolu, there was another side to this. The restoration of Lwów was both a civic challenge for him and his generation and a huge opportunity for a company, like Finkelstein and Fehl, that was in the business of supplying building companies and advertised its provision of 'iron girders, iron plate, gas pipes [and] waterworks'. And, despite everything, Lwów remained a place where Jews could gain and retain standing, could be economically successful, could sustain a community life, and could enjoy a cosmopolitan atmosphere. Besides, it was home. For the Finkelsteins, it had always been home.

So he would stay in Lwów, build the business, and plunge into civic life. But first, he would start a family. Or at least he would try to.

———

On 28 September 1921, the *Chwila* (Moment), a daily Lwów Jewish newspaper, carried an advert in large bold font. 'To our DEAR boss,' it read, 'Mr Adolf Finkelstein, on the day of his wedding with Miss Lusia Diamantstein, heartfelt best wishes from the employees of Finkelstein and Fehl.'

It was a joyous affair, the sort of celebration to be expected upon the union of two wealthy families. Sixty years later, after Lusia's death, one of the guests wrote to my father to tell him that the wedding had been 'for me a truly unforgettable experience. Your mother was so very beautiful, she was a lovely bride and to this very day I remember how beautiful she looked in her gray going-away outfit!!'

Beautiful she may have looked, but that wasn't the only reason that Dolu loved Lusia. She was clever, witty and, most importantly as it turned out, tough. My grandparents had been, as my father delicately put it, 'introduced', but the arrangement had produced a marriage of deep and enduring love.

Born at the end of 1899, the daughter of wealthy landowners in the Lwów region, Lusia was the youngest of seven children. She was closest to her sister Dorotea – the two would cuddle up to each other for comfort at night when they heard exchanges of Polish and Ukrainian gunfire. Her favourite of her four brothers was Wilhelm, because when she was a girl he had indulged her naughtiest pranks, even when they had included cutting off his moustache while he slept. She was almost ten years younger than her new husband, and while she too had been in Vienna during the First World War, it had been to attend school.

Like many other Jews who could afford to, Lusia's family had fled Lemberg to avoid the Russians. She had then enjoyed a notably liberal education, attending the Vienna Free School on Albertgasse, established as part of an effort to reduce Catholic influence in the school system. And then, after receiving her high-school certificate, she returned to Lwów to study history of art at Jan Kazimierz University, and became an accomplished linguist, adding English and French to her German and Polish. Her brothers had received a more orthodox Jewish schooling, but this was considered unnecessary for a girl, while higher education was thought an adornment for someone who would make small talk in society cafés and attend dinner parties.

After their marriage, Dolu and Lusia took an apartment at 28 Akademicka street, a long avenue with a tree-lined promenade down its centre, right in the middle of town, and one of Lwów's two elegant main shopping streets. Dolu's brother Bernard, who after Maks' retirement in 1922 became his partner in the business, working beside him all day, came home at night to his wife Linka in an apartment directly across the road.

Dolu and Lusia's apartment was situated perfectly for a young couple who were part of Lwów's café society. All of the best venues in the city were on their doorstep; there was even a cinema in their building. Next door to Bernard, for instance, was the Scottish Café, where many great mathematicians would gather and collaborate on their hardest problems, eating cake and writing on the napkins. It is probably here that Dolu and Lusia first met Kazimierz Bartel, the maths professor who would be Prime Minister of Poland three times, and who became their friend.

Visits to the homes of others might prompt a trip in advance to the renowned Zalewski confectionery shop a few doors down. Zalewski chocolates were a traditional gift to hosts. The purchase and receipt of such chocolates, the taking of coffee, receiving guests at home, climbing the marble staircase to a box for gala evenings at the beautiful Lwów opera house, holidays in the mountains and spa towns, games of bridge, leaving the house dressed immaculately in white gloves, a beautiful cloth coat and a smart hat – this was Lusia's life.

Yet despite all this, and her love for Dolu, it wasn't entirely a happy life. Because, while their friends all began to have children, it seemed they could not. For eight long years they tried and hoped for a child that didn't come, and then, just as that hope was beginning to fade, Lusia discovered she was pregnant. On 6 December 1929, she gave birth to a son, my father Ludwik. The birth turned out to be difficult and dangerous, requiring a Caesarean section. It was obvious that they wouldn't have a second child.

With the wait his parents had endured, the difficulty of his birth, and the fact that he was and would remain an only child, Ludwik was particularly cherished. He was the centre of everything, he was their future. His destiny, they were sure, was to become a leading citizen of Lwów like his father and grandfather, and to be part of the next generation at the helm of Finkelstein and Fehl.

As he prepared for these inevitabilities, Ludwik enjoyed what he later described as 'a very happy and blissful childhood'. In addition to the attention of his parents, he loved his nanny, Monika Nenza, always known by the Finkelsteins as Teta. And he was fussed over by the rest of the staff too. He was treated indulgently even when he crept into the kitchen and secretly ate all the filling from the pierogi dumplings it had taken the cook ages to prepare.

When he was old enough, Ludwik was sent to a private school. About two fifths of the students were Jewish, but it was a Polish establishment, reflecting Dolu and Lusia's desire that their son grow up a modern Pole. Ludwik was given Hebrew lessons too, but very much as an extracurricular activity.

When my father was asked, late in life, about his schoolfriends, he said they had mostly been Jewish. Then he added: 'I had friends from school. Quite a large number of friends. Few of them, I suppose, survived the war. None that I can trace.'

———————

There was, however, one childhood friend who did survive the war, and remained Ludwik's close friend for the rest of his life, Aldona Paneth. Aldona's mother and father were friends of Dolu and Lusia, and were always in and out of Akademicka street, often bringing Aldona with them. When she was still very young, however, Aldona's parents divorced, and her mother Jadzia married again.

Aldona adored her new stepfather, Major Ignacy Schrage. He treated her with great kindness, and allowed her to ride his horse. Ludwik was also dazzled by him, his gallantry, his decorations for valour, and his uniform. Major Schrage of the Heavy Artillery was an associate of the Polish independence leader Piłsudski, and had fought for Polish independence and been wounded in the cause. All of this added to his glamour.

One of Ludwik's most cherished memories of his childhood was the High Holy Days – the Jewish New Year and Day of Atonement – sitting in the splendid Tempel Synagogue where the progressive Jews of Lwów worshipped under its vast dome. He loved the solemnity of the services and hearing his grandfather's name mentioned in commemoration of special benefactors of the synagogue.

But what impressed the eight-year-old Ludwik most was Ignacy, sitting in front of him, cutting a splendid military figure in full dress uniform, proudly showing both his attachment to his Jewishness and to Poland. And it wasn't just Ludwik. The respect in which all held Major Schrage was obvious.

On 27 May 1934, the Lwów City Council, the centre of power in a region of three million people, held its first proper election since the days of Austrian rule. In the district that encompassed the residents and shops at the heart of the city, the result was a landslide. The candidates of Party List Five received 2,890 votes, with their nearest rivals receiving just 140. And the candidate with the most votes of all was Adolf Finkelstein.

Dolu owed his new position at the apex of Lwów's civic life to four things. The first, undoubtedly, was his wealth.

In the years since he and Bernard had taken over Finkelstein and Fehl, they had managed to grow the business by winning exclusive contracts to supply major building projects on the railways and for waterworks. Bolts, nuts, rivets, hooks, smooth pipes, bandage pipes, axles for trucks, rails for trains, all of them available from Finkelstein and Fehl. The company became the sole representative of a number of ironworks in Galicia, acquiring a sheet-metal mill in Upper Silesia and operating the Malopolska Pipe Centre in Lwów. The expansion had become so great that Dolu had acquired a nickname: 'The Iron King'.

And this was at a time when the city itself was on the rise. In 1921, it had launched the Eastern Fair, held annually in September in Stryiskyi Park on the hill overlooking the town. Each year, about 200,000 people came to town to visit the exposition, bringing their custom to companies like Finkelstein and Fehl from all over Europe.

Yet wealth alone did not account for the high esteem in which Dolu was held. He was also a captivating individual. Handsome, with a full head of red hair and a matching moustache, he was well-read, knowledgeable about art, and engaging to talk to. He was also kind. As one of his employees said of him, having lived in his house for eight years: 'I was treated there as a member of the family . . . He lived a happy family life . . . He always found time not only for his relatives but also for everyone who needed his advice and help.'

And he was energetic. On the Council, he threw himself into creating and supporting schemes to aid the unemployed, and a successful project to build new houses in the Lwów suburbs for homeless people.

He brought the same qualities to the many cultural and humanitarian bodies to which he gave his backing, including the various associations of merchants on whose committees he served. When the university hostel for Jewish students – a centre for their social life and societies as well as for their accommodation – had to be put up for auction, because it could not pay off its massive debt, Dolu stepped in. He ensured that enough money was raised to secure the property, resolved a dispute with the water company which was threatening to cut off the students' water, and arranged for a boiler to be purchased from a factory in Białystok for a very low price. He was a problem solver.

An article published on 9 March 1935 in the independent radical weekly *Krzyk* (The Call) caught this perfectly. It carried a story about a petty disagreement between the President and Vice-President of the Lwów Merchants Association which had become so vicious it threatened to capsize the organisation altogether. A long and complicated tale finished with the news that 'numerous attempts to resolve the dispute had no impact', until

in the last few days Mr Councillor Adolf Finkelstein, one of the most serious members of the committee of the Association got involved. He managed to arrange for both men to apologise to each other, resolving this incident without recourse to courts or further quarrels, enabling the continued and unhindered operation of the Association.

Years later, Dolu would send Lusia a letter telling her about some problem of their living arrangements that he had resolved: 'I managed to find a solution because, as you know, I can conciliate people.' This was Dolu.

The final reason for the size of his Council victory was simpler and less personal. He was a Jew. In addition to Adolf Finkelstein, Lwów's central district elected Leon Rosenkranz, Moses Reich and Jakob Mund. The city's politics was largely ethnic, and Jews predominated in the area where the best retail properties and cafés were situated.

Dolu and Lusia were not religiously observant. They went to synagogue only twice a year, on the High Holy Days, and they did not keep kosher, happily eating anything. But Dolu in particular was proud of being Jewish, and the contemporary Polish Jewish Almanac described him as 'occupying an honoured place in Jewish society'. He ran for the Council as an explicitly Jewish candidate, had election posters printed in Yiddish, and saw himself as a defender of his co-religionists.

My father remembered with great pleasure one of the consequences of this – the free pretzels he would receive when he walked through the market square:

The Polish government, who really intended to suppress or diminish the influence of Jewish business, passed laws that would have meant that lots of pretzel-makers went out of business. My father defended the pretzel-makers of Lwów, the successful Jewish pretzel-makers of Lwów. I remember that I was always offered pretzels because my father was a great hero.

Like the Wieners, Dolu and Lusia weren't Zionists. Indeed, Dolu clashed politically with the Zionists over his housing schemes. They felt that investing so much in Polish infrastructure was a waste of time and money. He responded that, while he regarded it as important that settlements were built in Palestine, there would always be a Jewish community in Poland, and the Zionists were foolish to argue against improving the lot of Poles.

His dream was of a modern, liberal, multi-ethnic Poland, a dream associated with Piłsudski even though the Marshal was no liberal. Dolu joined the Polish army reserve, which turned out to be an immensely consequential decision. In a further demonstration of his commitment to the modern Polish ideal, Finkelstein and Fehl was numbered among the early donors for a 'United Polish Land' monument. Intended to be a little like the Statue of Liberty in the United States, and to celebrate the creation of the Second Polish Republic, it was a symbol of the Poland Dolu hoped for. The project, like his dream, foundered.

In other words, Dolu and Lusia harboured exactly the same hope for their country as Alfred and Grete did for theirs. They believed that the emerging identity of their advancing modern nation was compatible with their identity as Jews, that Jewishness and modern Poland belonged together.

———

Piłsudski had become the effective leader of the country, taking over in 1926 under circumstances Poles still argue about. What is clear, however, is that he saw Poland as a country that wasn't just for the ethnic Poles. His first Prime Minister was Kazimierz Bartel, the mathematician friend of Dolu and Lusia's, who strove, with only limited success, to remove obstacles to full Jewish participation in the life of the nation.

It is for this reason that Jews regarded Piłsudski's death in May 1935 as something of a disaster. In the eighteen months before his death, Poland had agreed a non-aggression pact with Hitler, and there were already fears among Jews about what this might mean. Now the symbol of multi-ethnic Poland had died. Jewish stores and factories closed in mourning, the Jewish community decreed that there were to be no marriages for a month, and candles were lit in every synagogue.

And there is no doubt that, after Piłsudski, civic life for Polish Jews became harder. Attempts to exclude Jews from certain professions; a drive to ban kosher slaughtering; petty legislation which targeted particular types of trading where Jews predominated, such as selling pretzels in the market; and the constant fear that changes to the constitution might remove the protection of minority rights – all these made life worrying and uncomfortable.

When asked as an adult about his experience of antisemitism at school, my father at first said it was merely playground taunts. But when he was pressed, he said, well, yes, there had been one time a boy had 'expressed himself unfavourably about Jews'. Ludwik had followed him all the way home from school. The pursuit was, he said, 'slow but determined', but 'I chased him all the way down, until I managed to catch him round his house and hit him on the nose and it bled'.

Anyone who knew my father would not have been surprised to learn that his chasing had been slow. Nor that it had been determined. The rest of it was unexpected, to say the least.

Possibly the place most hostile to Jews was the universities. Polish students from the large right-wing National Party started declaring certain days to be 'Jew-free', and stood at the entrance gates turning away Jewish students. The Lwów Polytechnic established a quota system restricting the maximum number of Jewish students to 10 per cent of any department. And at Jan Kazimierz University, antisemites pushed successfully for the creation of 'ghetto benches', with Jewish students only permitted to sit in one of the last two rows on the left-hand side of the lecture hall. Many Jewish students attended lectures in groups for safety, and then, as a protest, remained standing.

This ugly atmosphere soon led to deaths, with first one Jewish student and then another being murdered. And then, in the spring of 1939, a Jewish student from the polytechnic, Markus Landesberg, was beaten to death on the university grounds. His funeral turned into a huge political demonstration; 12,000 joined in the procession to the Jewish cemetery. Many were ethnic Poles who wanted to express their solidarity, including Kazimierz Bartel.

The Lwów Jewish student hostel produced a commemorative book which marked both the seventieth anniversary of its foundation and the recent murders of the three students. It included a picture of Landesberg, and an article from Dolu addressing both the material and political challenges faced by the Jewish students. The headline was 'Nil Desperandum'. Never Despair.

Jewish Academic Youth! Don't give up hope for a better future. Our history knows many examples of times like these when we were persecuted and driven from country to country, and yet we survived. Clouds in the sky don't last for ever.

Even at the North Pole, after a six-month night, day comes and the sun shines its rays on the earth and everything that lives on it.

When they throw obstacles at your feet, when you encounter obstacles in the way of achieving your goals, work for yourself and for humanity – do not be discouraged. Increase your efforts and show, as has been your custom so far, that work and creative effort are your motto and you set out with them in your life and into the world.

We, the older Jewish community, promise you, our students, that we will continue to aid you . . . We will work together, fight together for equal rights for the Jewish community and its youth, and for free and unlimited access to sources of knowledge.

And the slogan that enlivens us in our unbending persistence will be: Nil desperandum!

And Dolu and Lusia did not give up hope for a better future. They did not despair. They were committed to their lives in Poland. To look at the home they built in Herburtów street, that sleek white villa, is to wonder about their solid confidence and to ask, did they not have any premonition of what was to come?

Yet this is to arm oneself with all the knowledge we have about the future and assume that, as this future was so disastrous, so overwhelming, surely Dolu and Lusia must have had at least some doubt. And it is to imagine that if they did have doubt, fears, worries, these would have been enough to make them throw up their lives and go. Go where, in any case, and flee from whom? Fleeing would not have been enough; the flight would have needed to be to the right place. And the right place was unknowable, even if the need to find such a place was known.

It is quite possible to be reading this eighty years after it happened and not know the fate that befell the Finkelsteins. It is, therefore, understandable that they did not know before it happened.

So it was that Dolu, Lusia, and Ludwik moved out of Akademicka street into the new house on Herburtów street to begin the next phase of their family life.

Almost every house on the street contained a person heavily involved in the city's public life, particularly those with an intellectual bent. From the balcony outside Ludwik's bedroom could be seen Number 7, the villa of Aleksander Mazzucato, who ran one of Lwów's leading bookshops and publishing houses. Just down the road were the homes of the renowned academic civil engineer Professor Adam Kuryłło and the teacher Mieczysław Kistryn, founder of the Henryk Jordan private school. And at Number 5 lived Kazimierz Bartel, who had returned to academic life after his three spells as Prime Minister, and his wife Maria Bartlowa, who by 1938 had become a member of the Polish Senate.

Herburtów street, in other words, was the home of the Polish financial and intellectual elite that Joseph Stalin and Adolf Hitler would now set out to destroy.

———————

Moscow, 23 August 1939, around midnight. The room hushed as Stalin spoke: 'I know how much the German nation loves its Führer. I should therefore like to drink to his health.'

The negotiations over the 'Treaty of Non-Aggression' that Soviet Foreign Minister Vyacheslav Molotov had been conducting with his Germany counterpart, Joachim von Ribbentrop, had just concluded. The outcome was to the satisfaction of Stalin and of Hitler, who was waiting in Berlin to hear the news. To mark the occasion, the assembled Nazis and communists had been furnished with Crimean champagne. 'Our treat,' recalled Molotov.

Stalin suggested to Hitler's photographer that he not publish the photos he was taking of the Soviet dictator and Ribbentrop raising their glasses. And when Hitler was later shown the pictures of the signing ceremony, he demanded that they be doctored so that smoking, Stalin's smoking in particular, not be visible. Neither side wanted their publics to think the treaty was frivolous. They also wanted them to regard it as essentially a pacific alliance rather than see it for what it really was – an agreement to conquer and kill.

In a secret appendix to the supposed non-aggression treaty, Hitler and Stalin had agreed to divide up Eastern Europe between them. Within a month, both had invaded Poland.

The motives that had led the two parties to this agreement were mixed. Hitler had once hoped to expand the borders of Germany with Polish assent, receiving Danzig in exchange for a twenty-five-year guarantee of the new borders, but he had been rebuffed. Britain had then promised the Poles support in the event of German aggression. At the same time, Stalin had concluded that France and Britain would not be energetic or reliable allies for the Soviet

Union. So the two dictators began to investigate what, despite all their apparent political hostility, Bolsheviks and Nazis might get from each other.

Their relationship was not defensive. As the secret appendix demonstrates, the pact was designed to allow each party to engage in aggressive wars of occupation with the tacit acceptance of the other. The two powers were in alliance to achieve aims that were quite similar – to expand their areas of control and power and to begin these expansions with the destruction of the Polish Republic.

It was not only their military aspirations that were similar but also, despite the superficial differences, their doctrines. As one of the German negotiators in Moscow put it: 'There is one common element in the ideologies of Germany, Italy and the Soviet Union: opposition to the capitalist democracies.'

Fascists and communists both believed that the will of the people was being thwarted by elites, and that the individuals who made up the elites needed to be eliminated by force. They both had their own particular ideas of who these elites were, but they often converged. The Soviets might regard the Jewish owner of a shop as being suspect because he owned a shop while happening to be Jewish, while the Nazis regarded him as suspect because he was Jewish while happening to own a shop.

And, for both of them, the concept of the elites was broad enough to encompass my mother and father, even though at the time the pact was signed they were both under the age of ten.

The agreement allowed Stalin to begin to absorb territory that would include Lwów, and allowed Hitler to invade not only Poland but also, safe from Soviet attack, the Netherlands.

The Molotov-Ribbentrop Pact was the most important political event in the lives of my parents. Nothing that followed would have occurred without it.

MUM

An Amsterdam Childhood

My dear Ruth, my dear Eva, my dear Mirjam,

What a great joy it was last night, when your letter arrived! It was almost as if all three of you came in, bouncing through the door, each of you saying something and wanting something, and Mutti couldn't understand a thing, because of the noise and excitement. But I understood everything, and above all, I am glad that you are healthy and happy and experiencing so many wonderful things. I can imagine, Ruth, how nice it must have been to go to the synagogue with your new prayer book, together with Aunt Nuti. And that you, Ev, are now gluing your puzzle, I think that's great! Surely you will paint it in all sorts of beautiful colours? Mirjam, how good that you crossed out that Betty is 'gek' [crazy]! Otherwise we would have believed it in the end! . . .

Say hello to Aunt Nuti and Uncle Jan. I will write to them soon. In my thoughts I kiss you three just like we always do in the mornings, my beloved doggies!

Your Mutti.

After everything that had happened – the years fighting the Nazi rise, the encounter with Göring, the nervous collapse, the flight from Hitler's Germany to neutral Amsterdam – and everything that was still to come, for the Wieners between 1933 and 1939 there were nevertheless long periods of happiness and routine.

Years when Alfred and Grete would take spa holidays in Switzerland, leaving the girls with their childminder Betty Lewin, and sending back affectionate letters to their young children capturing each of their daughters' characteristic habits and hobbies. The eldest, Ruth, and her scholarly inclination, and attachment to the synagogue and Hebrew studies; their middle daughter, Eva, and her artistic bent, always colouring in and sticking down; and my mother, Mirjam, the baby of the family, a little mischievous but never too much so.

Years when they lived as an extended family. Grete's beloved sister Trude (known by the children as Aunt Nuti) living round the corner with Jan and their young son Fritz and always in and out of the Wiener apartment. Alfred's mother living in the apartment above (until her death of natural causes in 1938), throwing sweets down into the garden for the girls to pick up, much to Grete's dismay. When she wasn't distributing confectionery, Grandma was often praying. Her religiosity, as she paced her apartment in her long black dress, carrying a prayer book, made almost as much of an impression on her grandchildren as the treats.

Years when the family settled in the south of Amsterdam, eschewing the traditional Jewish district in the centre of the city in favour of a more modern area, where other German Jewish refugees were moving, like Otto and Edith Frank and their daughters, Margot and Anne.

The area gradually took on the character of its new occupants, with its main shopping road – Beethovenstraat – being dubbed Brede Jodenstraat, 'Wide Jewish Street'.

The Wieners could join their fellow immigrants on the terrace of the Café de Paris at 9 Beethovenstraat; Alfred bought his cigars from L. de Leeuw at Number 6 (Louis de Leeuw, died in Auschwitz in 1942); Betty and Grete bought vegetables at Number 58 (Samuel Polak, died in Auschwitz in 1942), meat at Popplesdorf-Druijf,

Number 82 (Juda Poppelsdorf and Estherina Druijf, died in Auschwitz in 1944) and poultry from Bamberger's at Number 37 (Hartog Bamberger, died in Auschwitz in 1944); while the whole family enjoyed the lunchroom and pastries, including German specialities like nut and cheese pies, of Delicia at Number 55 (Leo and Lina Pollack, died in Auschwitz in 1943).

The Wiener apartment was in 16 Jan van Eijckstraat, at the end of the road that joined on to Beethovenstraat. A classic Amsterdam house, it was tall, with steep, narrow stairs; the Wieners occupied the ground and first floors. It was relatively newly built, just five years old when Alfred and Grete began renting it in 1934, but inside it didn't feel particularly modern. Alfred's attachment to German culture and his intellectual interest in the Orient were both reflected in somewhat-old fashioned decor. In 1934, Jews could still leave Germany with all their possessions, and the Wieners had done so. As a result, their furniture, as it had been in Charlottenburg, was heavy and continental and too big for the rooms, and it competed for space with Alfred's collection of rugs and antiquities bought on his travels in the Middle East. The girls always remembered their home as overstuffed.

It wasn't just the furniture, of course. It was also, as ever, the books. Wherever Alfred lived or worked, there were always books, and not just in normal, quite-interested-in-reading quantities. Books assembled in row upon row along the walls, books in mountainous piles on tables, books upon the arm of every chair and at the feet of everyone who sat down. 'Books, books and books again,' as Ruth put it.

On the ground floor, aside from a kitchen, there was a nice dining room, big enough for large family meals on festive occasions, and a sizeable living room which doubled as a study for Alfred and Grete. Their desks faced each other, emphasising the role – adviser, secretary, companion – that Grete played in Alfred's work. Upstairs, the three girls shared a large bedroom, with Alfred and Grete's room on one side and that occupied by Betty, their home help, on the other. And there was also a guest room. For there were often guests, even if the girls weren't always quite sure who these guests were.

In later life, talking of these Amsterdam years, the girls would always say how happy they were. They would talk with affection of their grandmother and of Betty, even though she was occasionally strict with them. They adored Alfred and looked up to him. But most of all, they spoke with admiration and love of their mother. Grete, they had all perceived even when very young, was a special person. Soft and caring and warm, but also someone with an acute understanding of other people and of the world. For all of Alfred's ability to make his presence felt wherever he went, it was Grete who set the tone at home.

The nature of that home life, and Grete's sensibility, are well-captured in Ruth's two 'Poesie' books, the autograph albums Dutch and German children used to keep, containing uplifting messages, poems and mottos penned by family and friends.

There are the usual inscriptions from school pals and children living in the street, almost all in Dutch. For instance, ten-year-old Dorothee Miloslawski from up the road at Number 24 wrote: 'Dear Ruth, be a ray of sunshine for everyone, friendly and genuine, life will have nothing but good things to offer you then.' There is also this: 'Dear Ruth, Miles of blessing, Hectometres of joy, Steres of good days, with Hectares of virtue, not a Millimetre of distress, not a Pound of worry, I offer you here, my dear Ruth, your school friend Jacqueline van Maarsen.' Jacqueline later became well known as Anne Frank's 'best friend', and the person to whom Anne addressed a number of farewell letters.

The inscriptions from the adults in Ruth's life are characteristic. Alfred writes in Hebrew before translating it into German. 'To my dear Ruth, as admonition "Who is Might? He that subdues his nature."' The quotation is from Pirkei Avot, the Ethics of the Fathers, a collection of rabbinical teachings which would only be familiar to those who had made a reasonably extensive study of religious literature. It is also quite a solemn invocation, and not an encouragement that the anyway dutiful Ruth really needed.

Grete is gentler but no less intellectual in her choice of message for what is, after all, a ten-year-old child's autograph book.

> Noble be Man,
> Helpful and good!
> For that alone
> Doth distinguish him
> From all the beings
> Which we know . . .

she writes, quoting the opening lines of Goethe's poem 'Das Göttliche' (The Godlike). Underneath, she acknowledges that perhaps her inscription is a little advanced:

My dear child! This is only the beginning of a poem, which you will only be able to understand in a few years time. I'm writing it in your book, because I love it very much, and I hope that the strength, beauty and greatness of these words will give your soul strength, beauty and greatness.

It was Grete whose views held most sway when choosing a school for the girls. The First Montessori School on Corellistraat was, admittedly, less than five minutes' walk from the apartment, and that by itself would have made it attractive. Yet its progressive nature was much more Grete's taste than the more traditional Alfred's. 'Modern, and a trifle anarchic', is how it was once described. The school allowed children to manage their own time, working in their notebooks at their own pace. Every day, they would hand in the book to the teacher, allowing a gentle steer if they were spending all their time on only one subject, or a gentle push if they were lagging behind.

It isn't a style that suits every child, but if it does suit them, it teaches self-reliance along with schoolwork, and there would come a day where the former would prove at least as useful to Ruth, Eva and Mirjam as anything they found in their books. Grete attended the teacher conferences, usually without Alfred, and generally received good reports. All the girls were fairly studious.

There was another advantage to the Montessori system. Whenever the girls needed time off for Jewish holidays, it wasn't a problem, as the school didn't have a timetable nor were there any lessons that needed to be reprised. Possibly for this reason, but probably mostly because the Montessori schools were secular and welcomed Jews, they were a popular choice for the south Amsterdam German refugee community. Margot and Anne Frank were also Montessori educated, in a nearby but different branch.

The famous school photo of Anne Frank at her desk, with her pen in her hand, matches exactly one of my mother. Same backdrop, same pose, same photographer, very similar childhood.

And also same synagogue.

The Wieners belonged – again Grete's choice, to which Alfred acquiesced – to the Liberaal Joodse Gemeente, the synagogue Otto Frank helped to found in Amsterdam after his family fled Frankfurt. German refugees like the Franks and the Wieners strengthened the progressive Jewish movement in Holland and made it somewhat more conservative than in other countries. Grete approved of the liberal spirit; Ruth and her sisters liked the organ music and the young Rabbi, Jacob Mehler; and Alfred found it comforting that it brought German Jews together. That the community didn't have its own building, and camped out in various halls, ending up using one belonging to the Theosophical Society, is another reminder that, solidly middle-class though it was, this was a collection of refugees.

Driven from their homeland, huddling together for warmth with other exiles, the Wieners had their Judaism to provide them with a sense of continuity, community and belonging.

On Friday nights, the dining room of 16 Jan van Eijckstraat would fill with members of the extended Wiener family and the

Sabbath would be ushered in. The candles would be lit, Alfred would make his way round the table and bless each of his children, blessings would be said over wine and over the challah, and then the family would eat. The cooking would be Grete's, occasionally with a little help from Betty, usually chicken soup with matzo balls (to these, she would sometimes add parsley and a little sugar), often with roast chicken to follow, and, for dessert, maybe her almond tart or fruit crumble.

The atmosphere was warm, convivial, comforting. It was almost as if things were completely normal.

——————

For the children, it may all have been schoolfriends and swimming lessons and playing in the garden before running in to get Grete to settle their arguments. For the adults, it was an altogether more worrying time.

The guests who occupied the guest room, or sometimes joined for Friday evening, were part of the growing tide of German Jews leaving a country where repression was rising, to settle in neutral Holland, or to use it as starting point for a longer journey to a safe haven.

Ruth and Mirjam would both later speak of their fondness for the Dutch and say that they did not encounter any prejudice in Amsterdam against Jews, and there is no reason to doubt their recollection. Yet the story of Dutch attitudes to the Jews isn't as simple as that.

After the war, there would be much debate about the complicity of the Dutch. Which was more characteristic – the Dutch people who helped to hide the Jews, or those who reported them to the authorities? The police who joined in search parties and accepted bounties for the Jews they found, or those who did not? The institutions that resisted Nazi lawmaking, or those who simply cooperated?

That, however, is a discussion about what happened after the German occupation began. There is also a debate to be had about the Dutch record before the war, during the halcyon days of my mother's early youth.

Until 1938, visitors from Germany to Holland did not even require a visa, and naturally, due to its proximity and neutrality, the country was a tempting destination for Jews. But the Dutch authorities viewed the new immigrants with increasing alarm. It wasn't just that they were Jewish, it was also the cost. People were arriving with no homes, no jobs and no money. Who was going to pay for the resources that they would need?

The answer was simple. Dutch Jews.

The Nazi-organised economic boycott of Jewish business in April 1933 had galvanised world Jewry, and in Holland it led the Jewish community to start organising itself, and an effort to support the new refugees. The pre-eminent figure in the new committees that were created was David Cohen, a professor of classics at the University of Amsterdam and a leading member of the Jewish establishment.

The historian Bernard Wasserstein describes Cohen as 'cautious, amiable, and hardworking, but also vain and unimaginative'. He provides this assessment – one that few would disagree with – in a biography of Gertrude van Tijn, the other major figure in the Dutch Jewish refugee effort. Of her, he remarks: 'A certain haughtiness of manner towards the refugees in general has been detected in Gertrude . . . the fundamental benevolence of her intentions nevertheless shone through.'

After the war, both Cohen and Van Tijn became controversial personalities, particularly Cohen. How far had it been appropriate for Jews to work with the authorities, first the Dutch and later, far more morally difficult, the Nazis? There were many who felt such cooperation had come close to collaboration. The role Cohen and Van Tijn each played in the lives of the Wieners was significant. And more straightforwardly positive.

The new refugee committee assured the Dutch government that fresh arrivals would not put a strain on the public purse. The Jewish community would support them. Grete joined actively in this effort, working increasingly closely with Van Tijn to create soup kitchens, clothes banks and a food distribution service. They found lodgings for homeless families and paid the rent for those who were destitute. For those who were looking to stay in Holland, the committee arranged vocational training and language instruction. For others – and this later became the subject of recrimination – they acted as a sort of travel agency, encouraging new arrivals to leave again, and organising their departure.

All the Jewish communities in Europe were in a similar position, to a greater or lesser degree. All of them found the financial burden hard to cope with, and felt the same pressure from hostile nations who didn't want their countries to fill up with German Jews. As a result, each Jewish community, the Dutch and British for instance, tried its best to encourage the others to keep the refugees they had. After the Dutch government began imposing restrictions on employment, things got even worse for the committee, and they ended up buying tickets for some refugees and putting them on trains back to Germany.

David Cohen claimed that this was being done only where 'it was possible to do so safely'. By the middle of the 1930s, Alfred was in a position to warn that it already really wasn't.

Because the other way in which life in 16 Jan van Eijckstraat was not completely normal was that if, in these years between the Nazis' rise and the Second World War, you went up the stairs to the third floor of my mother's home and crossed the hallway, you found yourself in the world's most important – the world's only – centre of anti-Nazi propaganda and research.

After the disastrous meetings with Göring, the flight from Berlin and his breakdown, Alfred had found his footing again and resumed his work. He'd kept his little suitcase with him, and one or two boxes more from the old Büro Wilhelmstrasse archive, and at first worked out of a small Amsterdam hotel room. But by the summer of 1934, he had recovered his private library from Charlottenburg, and the family had been reunited. So he'd established an office next door to the family home, and he'd had a wall knocked through so that he could enter Number 14 without having to go outside. Then he had restarted his collection, gradually replacing much of the material that Göring had made him destroy. And adding to it all the time.

The financial backing for this operation – always fairly meagre, but eventually enough for a staff of half a dozen or so, occasionally slightly more – resulted originally from lobbying by David Cohen. At a London meeting in the autumn of 1933, where forty-four Jewish groups from across Europe and the USA gathered to discuss the refugee crisis, Cohen persuaded them to support the creation of a centre to combat Nazi propaganda. He'd made it sound as though the idea of the Jewish Central Information Office had only just struck him, but in fact he'd cooked up the plan with Alfred in advance.

What went on in Jan van Eijckstraat would have to be kept largely secret. The words 'Jewish Central Information Office' didn't appear on a nameplate; editors and staff members weren't identified; nor was the Office address included in its publications, which appeared without an imprint. If the Dutch government found out that they were playing host to one of the centres of resistance to the Nazis, they would certainly try to put a stop to it. They would fear that a Jewish Central Information Office would antagonise their Nazi neighbours and undermine Dutch neutrality.

Even without quite knowing what Alfred and his staff were really up to, the Dutch authorities made themselves enough of a nuisance by harassing the Office's German Jewish staff whose documentation did not let them work in Amsterdam.

As in Berlin, the secrecy was also designed to protect Alfred's sources. He didn't believe that the truth about the Nazis could be obtained merely from the sort of German newspapers that circulated internationally. Instead, he assiduously collected the provincial press, and party publications like the SS newspaper *Das Schwarze Korps* or the weekly *Hitler-Jugend-Zeitung*. And he understood the importance of ephemera. Nazi board games, for instance. Or keeping records of German signs on shops and public facilities which forbad access to Jews.

He collected phone books too, from cities with substantial Jewish populations. After the war, these would sometimes be the only record of a family's existence, and so a vital resource for the mapping and counting of Holocaust victims and for assisting restitution claims. Alfred kept, for instance, the 1938 Vienna phone book, where you could look up the number of Sigmund Freud, which appeared accompanied by a note saying that he was not to be disturbed in the afternoon.

Much of this material had to be acquired by secret agents still living in Nazi Germany. As Alfred explained later: 'Amsterdam, being only five hours from the German frontier, enabled courageous men and women in Germany to dispatch, by devious ways and in adventurous circumstances, such reports and documents as would never have come out of Germany through normal channels.'

Alfred's habit of being secretive, which had begun in Berlin, became an entrenched behaviour during this period in Holland. His colleagues often complained that they didn't know quite what he was up to. He had pulled together a motley bunch of individuals – exiles from the Spanish Civil War mixing with Berlin statisticians, those with the bearing of aristocrats side by side with caricature Prussian civil servants, journalists with language skills and those whose mangled Dutch was hard to comprehend and whose English and French translations were amateurish. All piled into a small space filled with paper and the smoke from heroic quantities of cigars and cigarettes.

The staff found Alfred, as his long-term collaborator and later deputy Caesar Aronsfeld put it, 'driven' and 'unmistakably the boss'. He certainly drove his staff as hard as he drove himself – in other words, very hard – and he could be rather formal. Almost twenty years after they first met, and after sharing many adventures, Alfred was still addressing memos to 'Mr Aronsfeld', and signing them 'Wiener'. Yet they also noted his humour and warmth. And they recognised the urgency and import of the task he had set them and himself.

As did his family. One of the main memories Mirjam and her sisters had of their childhood in Amsterdam was the same that Ruth had of their time in Berlin. A memory of their father being away all the time, working. They minded, but even at a very young age they sensed that what he was doing mattered and they didn't complain too much.

Alfred was a prolific letter-writer, particularly to journalists and to fellow intellectuals and exiles, but his favourite method of communication was to travel to his target and deliver his message in person. Those who received JCIO reports, or one of Alfred's letters, might also expect a visit, and there was scarcely a Jewish organisation in Europe, or a Nazi resistance movement, that missed out on an encounter with Alfred and his suitcase.

By the end of the 1930s, the JCIO had collected about 10,000 books, together with innumerable bound and unbound newspapers and press clippings, information from Nazi meetings all over the world and fascist publications from all continents, everything and anything they could lay their hands on that shed light on the ascent of fascism and the threat it posed to minority groups everywhere it succeeded.

The material the Office collected was not limited to that targeting Jews. Alfred saw his work as combating racism as it affected all oppressed groups, and promoting human rights for everyone.

He would, he said, 'counter the Nazi slanders and Dr. Goebbels' attempt to poison world opinion . . . We were soldiers in the struggle like all the rest, but our weapons were books, newspapers, periodicals, photo-copies, documents revealing Nazidom as a danger not only to Jews but to the cause of democracy all over the world.'

The Office circulated reports to Jewish organisations, human rights pressure groups, journalists and governments worldwide, providing factual information about Nazi activities – speeches by Goebbels, the latest outrageous libel in *Der Stürmer*, the most recent absurd and poisonous piece of Nazi 'scientific research' on the 'alien nature' of Jews, and so on. It did so with a minimum of comment, allowing the material to speak for itself.

And the selection of material was often eloquent. In August 1935, for instance, the Office circulated an article from Amsterdam's *De Telegraaf* which asked: 'What are the non-German countries doing? It is unthinkable that a statesman of a civilised country should not in the long run feel the duty to aid the persecuted.'

David Cohen may have been making promises about the safety of returning German Jews. Alfred was already telling the world the danger that they faced.

And using every weapon he had in a desperate attempt to establish the truth.

The Truth on Trial

One morning in July 1933, Georges Brunschvig embarked on his usual routine. He dropped in on his parents, had a cup of coffee, and agreed to run a couple of errands for them, before starting his working day in his Swiss law office a short distance away.

While waiting at the local pharmacy for his mother's prescription to be filled, he fell into conversation with the owner, a family friend. Did Georges know about the recent Nazi rally in the Bern Casino? Georges did. Well, then he needed to know that the local Jewish community felt something had to be done about it. Georges was a lawyer; perhaps he might be able to help?

The pharmacist explained that, while there was much to bother them about this mass gathering of fascists in the Swiss capital, there was one thing that bothered them in particular, one thing that they thought they might be able to do something about.

The organisers had been selling copies of something called the *Protocols of the Elders of Zion*, and reading out passages from this fraudulent and antisemitic publication over the loudspeakers to whip up the crowd. Bern's Jews had had enough of this document and the lies that it spread. Maybe the publishers were vulnerable to legal action, and maybe Georges was just the man for the job. Was he interested?

The offer wasn't entirely a compliment. Yes, the pharmacist liked the young lawyer, and thought him able, but he also knew the lawsuit was a pretty speculative effort. And he was aware that the twenty-five-year-old Georges might just need the work badly enough to accept.

He was right. Georges was too much of an idealist, and too hungry for the challenge and the work, to say no.

Georges thought too that he had figured out what to do. In 1916, Bern had passed a local law prohibiting the publication of 'obscene literature'. The intention of this law had been to ban pornography, but it provided no clear definition of obscenity. So perhaps a judge could be persuaded to see the *Protocols* as 'politically obscene'. Even if, ultimately, it was determined that the law didn't cover political obscenity, the community would still get the chance to show that the document was a lie, and a consequential lie.

Georges took the job and proposed this approach, filing suit in the Bern District Court against a range of the people who had published the *Protocols* or been responsible for distributing them.

And so began the Bern Trial of the *Protocols*, a case that the distinguished judge and legal scholar Hadassa Ben-Itto has called 'one of the most important of the 20th century', and a British Lord Chief Justice has claimed 'must be one of the most fascinating trials that have ever taken place'.

A week later, Brunschvig was in the boardroom of the Swiss Jewish community meeting the small group behind the effort, 'the inner circle' as they were dubbed by Ben-Itto in *The Lie That Will Not Die*, the main historical account of the trial.

As well as Georges and his partner, the inner circle included the one person with enough knowledge of the *Protocols* to keep the effort on track: Dr Alfred Wiener.

As in his Berlin days, legal action continued to play an important role in Alfred's resistance work. In 1936, for instance, when a young Jew called David Frankfurter murdered the founder of the Swiss Nazi Party, his defence team sought help publicising his cause to sympathetic audiences. As one reporter later noted:

'When the day's proceedings were over, they met in the dark of the winter night in a remote part of Chur in a small office where they helped a man called Alfred Wiener to publish reports and pamphlets about the trial and the Nazi intrigues, and send them out all over the world.'

However, the Bern Trial was by far the most prominent one on which Alfred had worked. And also the most time-consuming. With numerous delays and an appeal, it took years, and when my mother and her sisters wondered where their father was, most often he was in Switzerland, suing the publishers of the *Protocols*.

He thought the time worth it, because he believed that the *Protocols* played a central role in the rise of the Nazis and in their ideology. He had studied the topic carefully, making a point of ensuring that the Office possessed every edition, and carried several of the most interesting with him in his little suitcase. His belief in the power of truth made the trial an ideal forum for him. The Jewish community would prove to the Swiss court that the *Protocols* were a fake, and a dangerous one too. Such a ruling would help Jews everywhere that the *Protocols* were published.

In meetings of the legal team, Alfred would carefully explain to his colleagues what the *Protocols* were and why they mattered, guiding them to cases they should read about, and to things they ought to know about the impact it had made.

In 1905, an antisemitic Russian writer called Sergei Aleksandrovich Nilus had published a book about the coming of the Antichrist, and included within it what he alleged were minutes of a secret meeting of Jewish leaders that had taken place in Basel, at the first congress of the Zionist movement in 1897. In twenty-four chapters, or 'protocols', the so-called minutes describe secret plans to manipulate the economy, control the media, and set religions against each other.

According to the *Protocols*, the Jews planned to weaken governments through liberal reform, thereby creating anarchy; and then, employing above all the 'terrible' Jewish power of the purse, install a dictatorship of Jews. They would use violence, cunning, hypocrisy, bribery, fraud, treason and seizure of property to force states to submit. Financial speculation and constant strikes would combine to destroy industrial prosperity. In detail, much of it absurd, the *Protocols* outlined the tactics that would be employed by the dastardly Jews – assassination, terrorism, execution – to control the senseless and stupid gentiles.

Some readers were able to see at once that the *Protocols* were ridiculous, a conspiracy theory that was unhinged and quite transparently not the minutes of any sort of meeting, Jewish or otherwise. Yet to others it seemed to explain the whole world – the toppling of governments, wars between nations, the rise of liberalism, the questioning of Christianity, turbulent economies, industrial struggles. The *Protocols* made sense of things that didn't make sense.

And so the lie had spread. At a meeting of Brunschvig's inner circle, the lawyer had reported back on publications of the *Protocols* all over Europe and on unsuccessful efforts to take court action. He talked of how they had been carried in the knapsacks of Russian soldiers and used to justify the most grotesque pogroms. The *Protocols* had followers in Britain, where they had been serialised in the *Morning Post*, in France and, of course, in Germany. They had been placed anonymously in front of the chair of every delegate at the Peace Conference in Versailles.

While hearing all this, Alfred had been sitting in the corner of the room, reading the various documents Brunschvig had collected. When the lawyer finished, Alfred looked up with astonishment. What about Henry Ford? he asked quietly. No description of the influence of the *Protocols* was complete, after all, without an account of the role played by the car magnate and industrialist. Fortunately, Alfred had all the relevant information in his archives. A week later, Brunschvig arrived in his office to find Alfred had left on his desk a thick file labelled 'Henry Ford and the *Protocols of the Elders of Zion*'.

In 1918, Ford, multimillionaire, pioneer of mass production, one of the most famous men in America, had become the owner of a local newspaper. He had bought the *Dearborn Independent*, the weekly tabloid paper of his home town, to act as his voice.

Beginning in May 1920, Ford's paper embarked upon a relentless attack on the Jews, citing the *Protocols* as the source of the tabloid's ideas. Jewish Supreme Court judges were using Presidents Taft and Wilson as puppets; the Jews had instigated the First World War; the Jews caused the American Civil War and the assassination of Abraham Lincoln. 'Everything was blamed on the Jewish conspiracy, including jazz, short skirts, rolled-down stockings, rising rents, the Bolshevik revolution, the deterioration of American literature, social conduct, and whatever else came to mind.'

Ford had kept going until, in 1927, his paper had ended up in the American courts. Sued for libel by a Jew, Ford had settled. And that year he gave up his campaign and issued an apology to the Jewish people.

Not that he read the apology before he signed it, or really meant it. In 1938, he accepted the Order of the Grand Cross of the German Eagle from the Nazi government. And in 1940 he told a journalist, 'I still think this is a phony war made by the international Jewish bankers.'

In any case, the damage he had done before his apology, endured. The antisemitic articles were published as a book – *The International Jew* – which, as Alfred told the other members of the inner circle, had been translated into seventeen languages and was for sale in every kiosk in Bern. Actually, he said, that wasn't quite true. Not every kiosk sold it. Some were giving it away free.

Important though Ford had been to spreading the lie in the world's newsagents, that hadn't been his most important contribution to global antisemitism, nor the one most pertinent to the Bern Trial. His most important contribution was twofold.

First, there was the 'Ford Tactic'. In 1921, *The Times* in London had published a series of articles on the *Protocols* by its Constantinople correspondent, Philip Graves. Graves showed clearly that large sections of the *Protocols* had been copied from another book. They had been part of a satirical commentary on the regime of Napoleon III, written in 1864 by a Frenchman called Maurice Joly. The language was identical, the plagiarism obvious and undeniable.

Alfred's dossier explained how Ford responded to this revelation. He said he didn't know about *The Times* or Joly or plagiarism, or anything like that. All Ford knew was that, if you compared the *Protocols* with actual events, you could see that the Jewish plot was unfolding just as the Elders had arranged. The proof of the authenticity of the *Protocols* could be found by reviewing historical events rather than conducting literary analysis. It was this rather brilliant little dodge that was the Ford Tactic, and Alfred expected it to form a large part of the defence's argument in the trial. As indeed it did.

Ford's other important contribution, Alfred had explained to his colleagues, was the influence he had on Adolf Hitler. Hitler kept a framed photograph of him on his desk, and once said, 'I regard Heinrich Ford as my inspiration.' Partly because of Ford, the *Protocols* had a central place in the ideology of the Nazis.

Between 1919 and 1939, the Nazi Party published the *Protocols* in two major editions that were reprinted more than thirty times. And Hitler believed the *Protocols* completely.

———

A long queue formed outside the courtroom on 29 October 1934, the day the Bern Trial opened. As Hadassa Ben-Itto recorded in her account of the proceedings, the city's hotels were filled to capacity with journalists from all over the world and representatives of Jewish communities from across Europe. There were plenty of fascist sympathisers in town too. Restaurants and shops looked forward to doing good business. 'They could not remember when an event had aroused so much interest.'

The inner circle had decided that, before they laid out the story of how the *Protocols* were faked, they needed to call as their first witness a leading Zionist Jew, someone who, with an authority that would impress the court, might dismiss the whole notion of that 1897 Zionist congress in Basel being a secretive conspiracy of Jewish Elders. So the plaintiffs opened their case by asking Chaim Weizmann to take the stand.

Given authority by the prestige he had gained in his career as a scientist and as the Zionist leader who lobbied presidents and kings – a prestige that later made him Israel's first President – Weizmann told the court that the whole premise of the *Protocols* was nonsense. The Basel congress had been a gathering of mostly poor, young Eastern European Jews and intellectuals. The most prominent industrialists and financiers simply hadn't been there.

That having been established, the plaintiffs began to call witnesses who would help to show how and why the *Protocols* had come into existence. The modern court in Bern began listening to an involved tale of Russian court politics in the Tsarist era.

The *Protocols* were a product of a battle for the ears of the inexperienced and easily influenced Tsar Nicholas II and his Empress, with her fondness for mystics and charlatans. The forgery had, the lawyers sought to prove, been commissioned by the head of the foreign department of the Russian imperial secret service, the Okhrana. His aim had been to undermine the liberalisation programme of modernisers who had found favour with the Tsar, by showing that they were pawns of the Jews.

There was another strand to the story, one Alfred had insisted upon adding to the case. The *Protocols* were not only Russian, they were also French, and Alfred had travelled to Paris to consult the leading French expert. While the Russian secret service may have had their uses for the forgery, it was quite clear that there had been heavy French involvement. The employment of Joly's anti-Napoleonic book, for example, showed that, as did the fact that the head of the Okhrana had been serving in Paris at the time the document was produced.

Late into the night, Alfred would talk with Brunschvig about the growth of French antisemitism towards the end of the nineteenth century as Jews fled pogroms in Russia, settling in French cities. This atmosphere had helped to bring about the Dreyfus Affair – the scandalous conviction for espionage in 1894 of an innocent French Jewish army officer – and it surely wasn't a coincidence, Alfred said, that the *Protocols* forgery had happened at around the same time.

And this was important to their case, he thought. The vicious antisemitism of the *Protocols* was not just a part of some incomprehensible squabble in a faraway land, it had been produced in the heart of Western Europe with the involvement of Western Europeans. The judge would be able to see how important a Swiss denunciation might be.

The story told by the plaintiffs in court was highly successful. The defence struggled. Their interventions in court veered all over the place, and were often comical.

For instance, they tried suggesting that Maurice Joly, the French author whose satire had been plagiarised, was in fact a circumcised Jew called Moishe Joel, only for Brunschvig to produce Joly's baptismal certificate. They also tried involving the Freemasons in the Jewish plot, calling as a witness the chocolate manufacturer Theodor Tobler, the inventor of the Toblerone. This ended with the defence team being expensively sued for libel by Tobler.

It proved so hard for the defence to find an expert witness to support their case, that the trial had to be postponed for six months. When they finally settled on one, a man called Ulrich Fleischauer, he proved a disaster. In an academic study of the trial, Michael Hagemeister called Fleischauer's report 'a meandering, long-winded, and unintelligible composition filled with a potpourri of antisemitic stereotypes'.

Alfred was determined that the plaintiffs would win not just the case but the propaganda war as well. There wasn't much he could do about the German newspapers, but the world press was a different matter. So he spent a good deal of his time, as the trial progressed, making contact with news agencies and organising international reporting of the proceedings.

Under his guidance, the Jewish Central Information Office produced a daily digest of proceedings, ensuring they were covered all over the world, even where papers could not afford to send a member of staff. When the court case is referred to as the 'famous Bern Trial', a lot of the credit for its fame belongs to Alfred.

In May 1935, after a final burst of evidence lasting two weeks, came the judgment. The plaintiffs had won on every part of the argument. The judge said that the *Protocols* were clearly a fake, and clearly obscene. Indeed, he found that the Swiss edition of the *Protocols* contained in its epilogue such horrible incitement to violence against Jews that he would have found it obscene even if the minutes of the Elders had been genuine.

But he was clear that they were not genuine. In fact, he said, the adoption of the Ford Tactic – the idea that the *Protocols* possessed an innate truth – was basically an admission that they weren't authentic.

He finished with this:

I hope that a time will come when nobody will understand how, in the year 1935, almost a dozen sane and reasonable men could for fourteen days torment their brains before a Bern court over the authenticity of these so-called Protocols, these Protocols which, despite the harm they have caused and may yet cause, are nothing more than ridiculous nonsense.

The Bern Trial was a success, but not a complete one. In November 1937, the Court of Appeal set aside part of Judge Meyer's ruling. It determined that while he was obviously right to conclude that the *Protocols* were a fake, the obscenity law had clearly been reserved for pornography. While this upheld the central and most important part of the judgment, the defendants were thrilled, and accounts of their 'victory' filled the newspapers of the far right.

Despite this, the plaintiffs had established a clear narrative of how the *Protocols* had been forged. Some academics find the account a little confused, and some of the witnesses unconvincing, but the attempts to suggest the text was authentic had been destroyed.

The trial did not succeed, however, in burying the forgery once and for all. The *Protocols* continued to be printed in Nazi Germany until 1939, when for unexplained reasons publication ceased. And they remain in print even now in large parts of the world, as well as being easily found online. They are extensively distributed and read in the Middle East, for instance.

Equally important, the idea that there is a Zionist plot to dominate world politics, create wars, buy off party leaders and silence critics – all of which comes directly from the *Protocols* – remains part of today's politics on left and right, even among those who would laugh at the document itself. The notion of Zionist Elders secretly manipulating world leaders is a surprisingly common part of political discourse.

Yet the Bern verdict nevertheless had some power. It provided a neutral verdict on the authenticity of the *Protocols* against which publishers would always have to struggle. It meant that Jews could always argue – pointing to Bern – that the *Protocols* were not an ordinary, respectable book, but a proven fraud. It hadn't been a waste of Alfred's time.

There was, however, another reason why he would never regret the months he spent in Switzerland, the years that the case took. Because if Alfred had not participated in the Bern Trial, if he had not spent his days and nights in the company of Georges Brunschvig and his inner circle, my mother wouldn't have survived the war.

Trapped

When my mother Mirjam talked about her childhood, about those early years in Amsterdam, she often spoke about playing in the street with her sisters and friends from the surrounding houses. And with amusement she would relate how, one day, she failed to notice an open drain cover and fell down a hole in the road, hitting her chin on the edge.

Nineteen thirty-eight was the year when the entirety of Western civilisation fell down a hole. It was the year of the Anschluss, of the unavailing Évian Conference, of the Munich Accords and of Kristallnacht. The year when war became inevitable, promising nothing except blood, toil, tears and sweat.

The contrast between the happy life Mirjam and her sisters were living that year, and what that year meant to the world, is heartbreaking.

Since arriving in Holland, Grete had devoted most of her time to looking after the family, largely alone as Alfred was away so much. Ruth later described Grete as a 'stay at home Mom'. But this doesn't tell the whole story. Throughout the Dutch exile, she was giving both counsel and administrative help to Alfred. She could do that from their home because the office was in the same place. She was also helping with the Jewish community's refugee work. And this was initially a fairly light commitment.

The Anschluss changed that. The annexation of Austria in March 1938 brought a new Jewish population under Nazi control, and spread stories of antisemitic violence across the world. The result was an increase in Jews desperate to escape, which in turn produced a reduction in the willingness of countries to accept them. The Dutch government announced that 'a refugee should henceforth be considered as an undesirable element for Dutch society, and therefore as an undesirable alien who must be kept out at the border, or if found within the country, be put over the border'.

This made the work of 'the Committee' – as Grete called the Jewish refugee body headed by David Cohen and guided by Gertrude van Tijn – much harder. Jews kept arriving in Holland, despite the government's policy, yet now it was more difficult to obtain homes for them, or any sort of income. Grete found her commitment to the refugee work growing as the year progressed. At the end of 1938, she received a gift and a letter from the Committee on behalf of the Jewish community, expressing 'great gratitude', and praising the 'great devotion and helpfulness which you have shown to the refugee work'.

Three further events had contributed to the need for this devotion and helpfulness. The first was that President Roosevelt had organised an international conference in Évian in July 1938 to address the issue of Jewish refugees, and it had got nowhere. Britain and the United States achieved their objective of preventing criticism of their own restrictions on entry to Palestine and America, respectively. There were no meaningful offers from any country to accept Jewish refugees. This made Jews even more desperate to come to Holland, and made those who were there even less able to leave it.

The second event, the Munich Agreement in October 1938, had a broadly similar impact. Under the deal agreed between the British Prime Minister Neville Chamberlain and Hitler, Czechoslovakia yielded territory to Germany, and even more Jews came under Nazi control.

The most serious event of all, however, came that November. On the night of the 9th, a massive pogrom, of the sort Alfred had been warning about since 1919, overwhelmed Germany's Jews. It was an officially sponsored, highly targeted, riot. Mobs of Nazi activists overran Jewish property, destroying all they found. Thirty thousand Jews were arrested and hundreds of synagogues were destroyed, many burning down as the fire brigades attended only to neighbouring properties. Thousands of shops owned by Jews were ransacked, and the smashing of Jewish shop windows gave the night its name. The night of broken glass. Kristallnacht.

After it was over, Göring insisted that any insurance payouts be confiscated, so that the Jews had to pay to restore all the damage done to their own property. They were forced to clean the streets the next day, picking up glass with their hands as crowds watched. In addition, a fine of one billion Reichsmarks was levied on the community for, Göring determined, having provoked the whole thing in the first place.

The November pogrom had sent an unmistakable message. As the historian Jay Howard Geller puts it in his study of the German Jewish bourgeoisie in the 1930s: 'After Kristallnacht, it was clear to all Jews that they had to leave Germany.' In the six weeks that followed, the Dutch Committee received over 11,000 letters from German Jews seeking its help to emigrate. The number of refugees arriving in the Netherlands rose to over a thousand a week. Many German Jews who had been arrested simply put their children, unaccompanied, on trains to Holland, and as a result many were found in the woods, penniless and starving. The burden on Grete and her colleagues isn't hard to understand.

The Dutch government panicked. In a meeting with David Cohen, they explained that they were going to tighten restrictions on entry still further, insisting on making a reality of their earlier rhetoric about the border. Anyone who arrived would have to be interned, so that they could be sent back as soon as possible. And the Jewish community would have to find vast sums – the equivalent of more than $10 million in today's money – to establish and run the internment camp.

Within a couple of months, the government had decided that a single large camp should be established in the Netherlands, close to the German border. The government would design it and pay for its construction, but the Jewish community would have to pay them back in instalments and assume responsibility for all the running costs. In return, illegal refugees would be allowed to stay in the camp legally until they found somewhere to emigrate to.

By the summer, work had begun in the village of Westerbork. The Jews of Holland were building and paying for what was to become their prison camp.

———

There was another consequence of Kristallnacht that had at least as much impact on the Wieners as the building of Westerbork.

When the Nazis did anything, however small, Alfred and his team would collect the evidence. So naturally an incident the size of the November pogrom spurred them to make great efforts. The Jewish Central Information Office collected many testimonies, which today constitute one of the earliest collections of eyewitness accounts of Nazi crimes. They also made themselves busy sending to the world's press information on what had happened. This high-profile work made the Dutch government very nervous.

Soon David Cohen – who remained Alfred's close associate and champion – found himself summoned by Hendrikus Colijn, the Dutch Prime Minister. A book about Kristallnacht, which Cohen admitted had been written in Jan van Eijckstraat, contained passages which, the Prime Minister said, might endanger Dutch neutrality. It would have to be withdrawn.

Cohen knew what this meant. The game was up, he told Alfred immediately. It wasn't only that they would have to comply, undermining the whole point of the Office. It was also this: if one book could cause this sort of diplomatic and political problem, imagine what might happen if the Dutch – or the Germans – found out about the whole archive. Imagine if they properly understood what Alfred and his team were really up to. Holland wasn't safe for them any more. The Office would have to move. The same thought had struck Alfred, and he readily agreed.

He would have to go to London and take the archive with him, and those of his staff who were willing to come.

Alfred had already spent time in Britain, and had a number of useful contacts. He brought with him from Amsterdam a young man called Louis Bondy, whom he had originally recruited in London, and who could compensate for what was, at this point, Alfred's relatively poor English.

Bondy's account of meeting my grandfather for the first time captures Alfred particularly vividly. 'My first contact with him,' remembered Bondy, 'was when he phoned me in London during the winter of 1937/8 in reply to my application for a job at the Jewish Central Information Office in Amsterdam. Half an hour later I arrived at Ford's Hotel, Manchester Street where Dr Wiener usually stayed.'

Bondy continued:

We shook hands and exchanged a few words. Then, quite abruptly, Dr Wiener bent down, lifted a huge parcel which had stood on a pile near him, asked me to hold it, heaped a second parcel of considerable weight on top of it, took a third one into his own hands and propelled me out into the street. He hailed a taxi, bundled me into it, followed, slammed the door and off we went on the way to the General Post Office. Only then did he explain to me that he had to post these packets urgently, was none too familiar with the required procedure and asked me – nay ordered me – to look after the dispatch. What characterises the unique qualities of Dr Wiener more than anything was the fact that I did not for one single moment resent being thus made use of by a complete stranger; on the contrary, I felt delighted at having been drawn so quickly into the orbit of that delightful personality.

While, for the moment, some staff stayed behind in Jan van Eijckstraat, the bulk of the archives were boxed up, shipped out, and arrived in the London docks somewhere between Tower Bridge and London Bridge. Bondy's job was somehow to collect them from a huge warehouse and transfer them to the office that had been rented on the first floor of 19 Manchester Square, right in the centre of town, just north of Oxford Street.

On Friday, 1 September 1939, the Jewish Central Information Office opened in London. That Sunday, Neville Chamberlain declared that Britain was at war with Germany.

———

In their struggle to keep their family safe, and to save others, indeed to help save their conception of civilisation itself, Alfred and Grete had always been one step ahead. Often more than one. They had seen what was coming before it arrived, and they had understood what they were seeing. Now, however, they had made a terrible, fateful, mistake.

Why didn't Alfred bring Grete and their daughters with him when he went to London at the beginning of 1939? It was a decision with awful consequences, and a mystery our family has puzzled over for years.

But once Alfred had settled in Ford's Hotel, Grete and he engaged in a correspondence. Alfred's letters haven't survived, but several of the ones Grete wrote have. And the letters make their thinking quite clear. Grete stayed for the children.

The letters are a mixture of loving messages (complete with pet names; she calls him 'Muli' and signs herself 'Munz'), bits of news about the girls, anxious commentary on their situation, administration of office matters and domestic finance, and consideration of the choices they face. Once the war between Germany and Britain started, Grete tried writing in English, but she found it an effort. In any case, as Alfred's English still required improvement, she often felt that he wasn't answering her questions precisely enough. 'I ask you emphatically,' she wrote impatiently on one occasion, to answer 'in German because . . . I fear that we are talking past each other in English'.

Their letters may have been in German but they were not being exchanged between two German citizens. In August 1939, the *German Reich & Prussian State Gazette* contained a list of people who had been stripped of citizenship under a law passed on 14 July 1933. The legislation allowed for the removal of citizenship from those living abroad 'who have damaged German interests through behaviour that violates the duty of loyalty to the Reich and the people'. The entire Wiener family was on the list.

The notice, said Grete, 'startled me a little at first and touched me in a strange way, but now it's like a liberation, especially in view of today's situation. We are now completely free!' This letter was written on 3 September, so 'today's situation' refers to the declaration by Britain of war on Germany. 'When I came to the Committee this morning,' she wrote, 'the news of Chamberlain's speech had just come out.' She added: 'It's almost impossible to grasp the full extent of it. I'm under the impression that everything is still in a daze and it's not yet possible to understand what has come over us today.'

Despite all Grete's talk of liberation, the loss of citizenship was a grievous blow. For Alfred it was a disaster emotionally to have his status as a German revoked, an emphatic denial of what he had fought to maintain. For the rest of the family – Grete, Ruth, Eva and Mirjam – it proved of profound practical importance.

Robbing people of their citizenship was one of the most powerful and most frequently employed Nazi techniques for making their targets vulnerable. People without a state found that there was nobody with a duty to protect them or take them in, no state authority who would object if they were imprisoned or killed. Grete was liberated from responsibility for Germany, but Germany was also liberated from responsibility for her. And no other country had that responsibility. From the moment that the Wieners lost their citizenship, they were, effectively, on their own. The search to find somebody to provide papers and protection steadily became more desperate over the coming years.

Before their lack of citizenship became a crisis, however, it was more like a nuisance. How could Alfred come back to visit if he didn't have the right sort of passport? If he didn't come back soon, what should Grete do about getting him his winter socks, since she 'could no longer take responsibility for you walking around without a winter coat and in cotton socks'? Should Grete try to get some sort of temporary Dutch papers for all the family to use, and, if so, could Alfred send her the documents she needed to submit? And could he please answer plainly, since the vagueness of his responses in English was irritating?

On top of all this to and fro, the couple were clearly worried about money and the future of the Office in Amsterdam.

Grete still continued her work as Alfred's aide, sending him quotes from books that he wanted to consult, or messages from people who called round to Jan van Eijckstraat. And acting as his representative in meetings with David Cohen and the Jewish Central Information Office staff about what to do next.

Cohen was arguing, and Alfred agreed, that the Amsterdam Office would have to close, but some staff were resisting. The argument primarily concerned the political value of continuing. Grete's main concern, however, was how to pay for everything.

Alfred was living in a hotel in London, with all the bills that involved. As yet, he hadn't raised much money for the British operation, and so he and Grete were effectively financing the archive and its resistance work out of their savings. When Alfred tried sending a letter to Grete of reassurance, she found the content 'distressing', adding that 'sliding downhill on a sleigh in the beautiful snowy weather we had here since yesterday is quite a pleasant feeling, but not sliding downhill in financial terms. That is much too steep and it's not easy to get up again.' Or, in a different letter: 'Sometimes I toss and turn during sleepless nights, thinking about the problem of how your private expenses from your stay in England will ever be settled.' With the funds to pay his salary in Holland but his work in London, what should they do?

The exchanges are a reminder that, in addition to the threat posed by the Nazis to the lives and freedom of their victims, more mundane things mattered too, and produced great strain. The administrative requirements and the financial obligations of being a refugee were a constant and significant burden.

Beyond the uncertainty, the correspondence shows how difficult Grete was finding life even before disaster completely engulfed them. She says in one letter that 'I'm not prone to anxiety and nervousness', and by all accounts she was a very balanced, resilient person, but the letters speak often of being exhausted. 'I think the constant tension makes me tired.'

It wasn't just the tension, of course. As well as 'helping at the Committee for some hours a day', she was looking after the family as a single parent. There were three young girls, the constant presence of cousin Fritz, and all the domestic duties including nursing them all through sore throats and getting them to school on time. Notwithstanding Betty's help and that of Grete's sister, it was naturally quite an effort.

But it was also a great joy. The letters are full of parties the girls have gone to, of Ruth coming home late from a swimming gala, of them all being in school plays, of Eva passing her bicycle proficiency test, of Trude taking Mirjam and Fritz to the circus, of Chanukah presents and Friday-night meals. And – for all the delays and difficulties imposed by their administrative and financial position – the stability and happiness of their children's lives is the major reason for the choice, the error, that Alfred and Grete made.

Alfred had gone to London because he could no longer work in Amsterdam without threatening Dutch neutrality. But that very neutrality was widely believed to protect the people who lived in the Netherlands. It was, for instance, a major reason why so many migrants were coming to Amsterdam.

In the autumn of 1939, after the war had begun but before it had reached the Netherlands, Gertrude van Tijn told the Zionist leader Chaim Weizmann that 'the Dutch at least [do] not expect a German invasion'. The country had been safe and neutral in the First World War, now it would be again. Given that Gertrude worked with Grete and had only just returned from a visit to Alfred in London when she said these words to Weizmann, it is quite likely that the Wieners shared her analysis.

In any case, such confidence was widespread. To many people Holland seemed to be just another Switzerland. Knowing what was to come makes it seem entirely obvious that Jews would be safer in Britain than in Holland, but in 1939, when the decision had to be made, that wasn't certain at all. Indeed, the idea that anybody would definitely be safe in Britain would have appeared quite eccentric.

It would be hard to find three people with a greater appreciation of what the Nazis might do to the Jews, a better understanding of the importance of evading their grasp, than Alfred, Grete and Gertrude van Tijn. But by itself that knowledge wasn't enough. To see people whom the Nazis captured as somehow complacent or naive is to misunderstand the judgements that were involved.

In November 1939, Grete told Alfred that she had been discussing the whole situation with David Cohen, regarding him as level-headed whereas 'most people outdo themselves in their fantastical reports'. The professor had agreed with her that they should try to get permits for the family to go to Britain, with Betty if possible.

I don't know if there is any chance at all, but you will be able to assess this better. In case the situation is changing here, I would then have the possibility to come to you. Even though I'm not really afraid, as I want to stress again, it would be very good to have the opportunity.

My mother used to say that she thought Grete had decided to stay in Amsterdam because she didn't want to be separated from her sister. Grete knew that the Abrahams – Trude, Jan and Fritz – wouldn't be able to come with them. This is certainly plausible, given how close the sisters were, but there is no mention of this consideration in the correspondence. Instead, after stating that she wanted the opportunity, Grete added: 'However, if the situation here remains unchanged, I'm of the opinion . . . that it's better to stay here for the sake of the children.'

In other words, she didn't want to disrupt their happy and stable lives and the children's education to join up with Alfred just because he was working abroad. And she didn't, for the moment, think Holland was about to be invaded. Possibly Grete let Mirjam believe she had stayed for Trude, in order to relieve her children of any feelings of guilt or responsibility if they learned the truth.

Alfred made a final visit to Amsterdam in February 1940, flying in by plane, an exotic thing to do. The trip was all too brief. A few days later, Grete and the girls saw him off at the airport. My mother wouldn't see her father again for five years.

After the flying visit, there are no more letters that survive, but by this point Alfred had definitely begun efforts to secure visas for them to come to Britain. This didn't prove easy, however, and it wasn't until almost the end of April 1940 that the breakthrough came. The family were informed that the visas would shortly be available.

At around this time, Alfred received a visit in his office in Manchester Square from a man he later described as 'an Englishman known to us who had the relevant connections and who had worked with us in London from the beginning'. Almost certainly he meant someone in military intelligence. The Englishman confirmed that the Wieners' visas would be arriving soon, and that 'he would like to recommend that they all come to London. That was a warning from a significant quarter.'

Alfred realised they were in a race against time. The family needed to travel right away. He tried all of his connections, but wartime communications were his enemy. His attempt to enlist the help of the British Embassy in the Hague by sending a telegram to his friend, the press attaché Lord Chichester, failed.

Among my mother's papers, there is a letter dated 6 May 1940, from the British Passport Control Office in the Hague, begging to inform Grete that it was authorised to grant visas to her and the girls. The day it arrived in Jan van Eijckstraat was the day that the Germans invaded Holland. It had all happened too late.

My mother, my grandmother and my aunts were trapped.

PART TWO

DURING

DAD

A Knife in the Back

It was the summer, 1 September 1939. I remember it, a beautiful day. I played in the garden of the neighbours . . . And, suddenly, I saw three planes flying overhead. I was aware of political tensions or whatever, because I was aware they were being discussed. But, suddenly, there were three planes and like a normal boy of that sort of age, I said: 'Oh, they're German planes.' And everybody said: 'Nonsense.' And then the bombs dropped on Lwów and that's when life changed entirely.

It was just before Ludwik's tenth birthday that the German warplanes arrived, and it began. For that is how the communist terror started. With Nazi bombing.

My father was about to become a victim of one of the war's greatest crimes: Stalin's attempt to eradicate the Polish nation by murdering its elite and scattering its entire leadership. It was a crime that saw the expulsion from their homes of hundreds of thousands of people, deported to become slave labourers, and saw hundreds of thousands more imprisoned in terrible conditions. It's a story little told, often denied, and even now, to most people, entirely unknown. Ludwik's story is one that history has half hidden.

To a child, it may have seemed that the planes had come out of a clear blue sky, but the adults of Lwów had realised for some time that war was likely, and had become increasingly tense.

A week earlier, Dolu had written to Lusia and his precious son, his 'Ludwis', from a solo holiday that he had apparently taken in order to calm his nerves. The family often stayed together at the Patria hotel in Krynica Górska in Southern Poland, a spa town famous for the supposed healing qualities of its waters. This time, unusually, Dolu had gone on his own. He lay on a deckchair on his terrace in the mornings, took a bath and mountain air in the afternoons, and danced after dinner. He looked forward, he told his family, to returning to them rested and less on edge than he had been when he left.

He finished his letter with what amounted to a prayer. 'God willing that we will continue to live in harmony and love for long, long years as we have so far been able to do in our beautiful home, and that the events of the time will end with a small rain from a large cloud.' His prayer was to go unfulfilled.

Dolu wrote this to his family on the very day that Molotov and Ribbentrop were meeting, and before they had signed their pact. Until they did so, Poles felt that war would come, but it wasn't going to come to Poland right now; they were safe for the moment. The whole world was against Germany, they reasoned, and surely Hitler wouldn't be reckless enough to try to fight everyone at the same time? Stalin changed all that. It was he who gave the Germans permission for their war of occupation.

Once the cigarettes had been lit and the champagne drunk in Moscow, and the Russians and Germans had announced what the historian Roger Moorhouse has called their 'Devils' Alliance', the threat to Poland became immediate. Dolu returned from his holiday to the family in Herburtów street, and, as an army reservist, on 31 August 1939 he was called up to serve once again as a second lieutenant and join in the desperate, doomed fight to save Poland.

There were moments of optimism. The first came on 3 September, when Britain and France declared war on Germany. 'I remember standing by the radio when the news came,' recalled my father, 'and we said: "Oh well, the war is won now. It's okay now."' It didn't take long to appreciate that this was wrong. The Germans were getting closer and closer. And meanwhile the bombing continued.

Just as she had when she was a young girl, Lusia looked to her sister Dorotea for solace. Lying together in bed, hugging each other, is what, after all, they had done in their youth when there had been battles for the city. So, taking Ludwik with her, Lusia headed to the home which her sister shared with her husband, the lawyer Szymon Grüner, and their daughter Halina. The Grüners lived nearer to the centre of Lwów and, more importantly, they had a large cellar. Here they all stayed until the shelling had abated.

Before it did, however, it brought calamity for another member of the Finkelstein family. Having fled to Vienna during the First World War as a teenager, Dolu's younger sister Lola had fallen in love with it. As an adult, she had returned to the Finkelstein apartment in the centre of that city, and there she had married and had a daughter. She was still there when the Anschluss happened in 1938 and, once the Nazis had taken over in Austria, she had fled to Italy with just a suitcase or two.

While she waited to emigrate to New York, Dolu and her other brother, Bernard, had arranged for all of her possessions to be shipped to Lwów and stored in a warehouse. When the first German bombs fell on Poland, they fell on the warehouse. Lola, her husband Robert and their daughter Renate were left with nothing. It was the first part of the Finkelstein family fortune to be destroyed. Within a few years, there would be nothing left.

––––––––––––

As the Nazis made their way through Poland, people began to flee before them, some trying to leave the country, others just trying to stay ahead of the approaching invaders. There was chaos, every road crowded, every car running out of petrol, every train cancelled, horses everywhere pulling carts full of belongings that had seen better days. Low-flying German aeroplanes strafed the roads, and the blood of civilians who had been attempting to escape flowed freely in the streets.

Lusia and Dolu had been talking about leaving Poland for weeks, but now they found it was too late. The advancing German army and the danger on the roads meant that their chosen route to Italy via Hungary or Romania was no longer viable. Dolu couldn't even reach his regiment to join it. Giving up the idea, Lusia and Ludwik returned to Herburtów street. Dolu made himself busy at army headquarters in Lwów.

Soon the battle for Poland had become the battle of Lwów. The city hurriedly began to arrange its defences against aircraft and tanks. Dolu, always a quartermaster when in the army, was involved in the central task of ensuring supply, both of equipment for Lwów's forces and food for its civilian population. This latter undertaking was given added urgency by the influx of refugees from Western Poland, doubling the number of inhabitants. And on 12 September 1939, German armoured cars appeared on the city's western edge, cutting off all but the eastern and northern supply routes.

Since 1936, Lwów's mayor had been Dolu's school classmate and friend Stanisław Ostrowski. He now set about organising the City Council and rallying the civilian population. As the German artillery shells fell in greater and greater number, Ostrowski gave a radio address appealing for calm and promising, 'I will stay with you through good and bad.' He showed great courage himself, and would later say how much he had valued 'reliable' and 'loyal' Dolu.

Then came a second moment of hope, extinguished even more quickly than the first. On 17 September 1939, the Soviets entered Poland from the east. Ludwik recalled later that when they first heard this news they were encouraged. 'We believed that they were possibly coming to help the Poles defend themselves.' This was not just the naivety of a nine-year-old. In many places, the Soviet troops were greeted with flowers and kisses as they made their way through the countryside.

What was really happening soon became apparent. The Soviets were invading. And they were doing so in partnership with the Germans, as a result of their secret agreement.

Moments before the Soviet operation began, the Polish ambassador in Moscow had been summoned to the Kremlin to meet the Soviet Deputy Foreign Minister. The ambassador was informed that as 'the Polish government has disintegrated', all Soviet agreements with it 'ceased to be in effect'. The Soviets had decided that they would have to enter Poland to 'take under their protection the lives and property of western Ukraine and western Byelorussia'. In other words, take under their 'protection' land that currently comprised Eastern Poland.

What the Polish ambassador was not told is that, before he had been summoned, the German ambassador had been called in. Stalin himself took that meeting. He wished to let his new allies know personally that the Red Army would cross the Polish frontier at dawn.

There was no declaration of war, and indeed the Soviets would claim for decades that their actions did not, in fact, constitute an invasion. Until 1989, the Soviet government denied the existence of the appendix to the Molotov-Ribbentrop Pact which divided Poland between the Nazis and the communists. Even then, they would only acknowledge that its existence was 'probable'.

When Ostrowski heard news of the Soviet advance, it did not take him long to absorb the true implications for Lwów. It was, as he observed in his memoirs, 'a knife inflicting a death blow in the back of the Polish army'. With the Lwów corps commander, he began to discuss the choice that the city might soon face – surrendering to the Russians or surrendering to the Germans. The commander said that at least the Soviet army was Slavic. Neither of them fully appreciated that the decision wasn't one the city would get to make. The Soviets and the Germans had already decided Lwów's fate between them.

Despite a blizzard of German and Soviet propaganda leaflets urging surrender first to one side and then the other, and despite German threats to raze the city to the ground if the Polish authorities did not comply, by 19 September 1939 the Nazis were already organising their withdrawal in accordance with the provisions of the secret agreement. Lwów was to be Soviet territory.

Later that year, Hitler sent Stalin birthday greetings, wishing him and the Soviet Union a 'happy future'. Stalin responded that the friendship they had embarked upon would be solid and lasting because it had been 'cemented in blood'. In all the discussions over which of these dictators was worse, it should never be forgotten that they were conspirators in many of the same murders and partners in many of the same crimes, that each must take some responsibility for the offences of the other along with the offences they committed by themselves.

A series of meetings of Lwówians began in the town hall and army headquarters, as Ostrowski carried the messages between the two that all hope was lost and capitulation to the Soviets was the only option. Coming out of his last meeting with the military command and heading back to the town hall, Ostrowski encountered a large group of officers, perhaps 2,000 or more, gathered together, ready to take action if someone told them what to do. When he met some who were 'friends from the school benches' and some who were fellow doctors, he was quite frank that the game was up. If they really wanted to know what to do, his advice was to leave straight away.

Many ignored the warning, and soon joined the thousands of Polish officers taken as prisoners of war as part of Stalin's invasion. Among these prisoners was Major Ignacy Schrage, the man whose presence in uniform had so dazzled my father in synagogue. The cream of the Polish army, its most gallant officers, became Stalin's captives.

But at least one 'friend from the school benches' did as Ostrowski advised. Dolu had been dashing between the town hall and military headquarters just as the mayor had been, alternating between his dual functions as soldier and councillor. He went home to Herburtów street and buried his service revolver in the garden.

He departed just in time. Soon large numbers of Soviet tanks appeared on the city streets, and the infantry seized the town hall. An officer of the NKVD, the Soviet secret police, followed Ostrowski everywhere with a revolver until the formalities had been completed and the city was fully under Soviet control. Then the mayor was arrested and sent to prison in Moscow.

Meanwhile, Lwów's population confronted the calamity that had befallen them. The first Soviet soldiers that the Poles encountered boasted of the abundance in Russia, and how much money they earned. They would ask civilians what they had, and then say they had more and better. 'We have everything,' they claimed. Their carefully rehearsed propaganda didn't convince. The Poles soon cottoned on, posing questions like, 'And do you have Copenhagen?' and receiving the reply: 'Of course, there is Copenhagen too, as much as you want!'

The Soviet soldiers' claims of wealth were hard to reconcile with how they looked. They had 'torn uniforms, dirty coats, hands and faces, they washed their boots in puddles, they picked papers off the streets and rolled cigarettes, they were pitiful', observed one of Ludwik's contemporaries, a Lwówian ten-year-old. Another clue was the way that they ran into every shop, buying up all they could: rolls, sausages, dress fabrics, bicycles. Poland's own communists found the whole thing very disillusioning. 'We waited for them to ask how was life under capitalism,' said one, 'and to tell us what it was like in Russia. But all they wanted was to buy a watch. I noticed that they were preoccupied with worldly goods, and we were waiting for ideals.'

Lusia and Dolu's beautiful city, their city of boulevards and café society, of bridge nights and parties, the city they had rebuilt after the First World War, quickly became, as one visitor remarked, 'a temporary camp, a spectacle of confusion and unrest'. Military communiqués, interspersed with Chopin, bellowed from loudspeakers, and portraits of Soviet leaders appeared everywhere. On every street corner, queues formed outside empty shops, people trying to buy bread, or vodka, or basically anything.

Disorder was partly the accidental result of war and partly a deliberate Soviet policy. For, as they made their way westwards, the Russians set criminals free and made it clear to every aggrieved worker or customer or debtor that they were at liberty to take vengeance against anyone that they resented. It was the Soviet way of overturning the social order and of creating an atmosphere of fear which made their own authority seem preferable. Ludwik always associated the marching in of the Soviets with newly released criminals terrorising the local population, shooting at will.

This being Lwów, there was, naturally enough, an ethnic dimension. Many Ukrainians would have preferred the Germans as invaders to the Russian ones, but they preferred both to the Poles and the Jews. While, in theory, the Soviets were neutral between the ethnic groupings, when they talked about revolutionising the masses and decapitating the boss class they were quite well aware that by masses they meant Ukrainians, and by bosses they meant Poles and Jews. They were quite well aware that they were revolutionising and decapitating different sides in an ethnic war.

Those who failed to show deference to the new masters were particularly vulnerable. When the order came for every house to put up a red flag, Dolu and Lusia wrestled with what to do. Naturally, Dolu didn't have a red flag, only the Polish red and white one, and the city emblem of Lwów. But he could obtain one. The question was whether to do so. It would enhance the family's safety, but would it be a betrayal of his homeland and his ideals? He crossed the road to 5 Herburtów street, and went to consult Kazimierz Bartel. The professor, with his great political experience as Polish Prime Minister and the logical mind of a mathematician, would surely be able to advise. He obliged. The town hall had a red flag, the buildings had red paint, the communists were wearing red armbands. Resistance was impossible, he said. 'Put out the flag.' And Dolu did.

Within days, the Soviet political command arrived in Lwów, ready to implement their plans for dismembering Poland, for arrests and deportations, and for the absorption of Lwów into Soviet Ukraine. The publisher Aleksander Mazzucato had fled from 7 Herburtów street, eventually to end up in Britain. Now into his empty house, the one across the road which you could see from Ludwik's bedroom balcony, moved the First Secretary of the Communist Party of Ukraine. The First Secretary had other houses in other Ukrainian cities, but he liked to be on the spot when there was important work to be done. And Lwów was where the important work was right now.

And so it was that, in September 1939, Dolu, Lusia and Ludwik became the neighbours of Nikita Khrushchev.

After the death of Stalin, Khrushchev made a famous speech denouncing his former leader, and enumerating those of Stalin's crimes with which he wasn't personally involved. It is this address, made in 1956 once he had assumed leadership of the Soviet Union, for which Khrushchev is now best remembered. But this list of Stalinist offences had to be carefully edited because Khrushchev had so often been present when such offences had been committed.

Indeed, his strategy had been to work out where Stalin was going and try to get there first. It had been immensely successful and his rise had been unstoppable. But the moral cost was great. As his biographer Edward Crankshaw put it, my father's neighbour 'achieved his eminence at a time when it was a disgrace for any Russian to succeed, and when success could only be obtained by atrocious methods and over the dead or broken bodies of innumerable comrades'.

And high among these crimes is what he now did to the people of Eastern Poland, to the people of Lwów, to my father. To the 'Trotskyite-Bukharinite-Fascist-Spying Filth' and bourgeois nationalists, as he believed they were. Or at least as he chose to term them, since it isn't obvious Khrushchev really believed in anything except his own power and the might of Soviet Russia. There were many criminals who acted with him in the theft and imprisonment and murder that were visited upon the people of Lwów, many soldiers and policemen and administrators, but they all worked for the man the party organ called that 'unswerving Bolshevik and Stalinist, Nikita Sergeievich Khrushchev'.

The Red Army may have entered as liberators and protectors, Khrushchev instructed its soldiers, but they were to 'wipe from the surface of the earth anyone and everyone who seeks to obstruct the realisation of this great historical cause of the emancipation of our brothers'. Given that Dolu was to live opposite such a man, Bartel's advice to put up the red flag seems wise counsel.

Settling in to 7 Herburtów street, Khrushchev began to consolidate the Soviet position. Elections would be held in Lwów and throughout the region on 22 October 1939, to create a National People's Assembly of Western Ukraine. This Assembly could then – in the happy circumstance that its newly elected members wished it – apply to Kiev and Moscow for Lwów's incorporation into both Soviet Ukraine and the Soviet Union. A tactic common to both Nazi and communist dictatorships was dressing up their authoritarian thuggery in the clothes of democracy. The elections were a classic manoeuvre, allowing the policy of arbitrary confiscation, arrest and deportation to be presented as the lawful operation of freely chosen institutions and allegiances.

The elections were, of course, a farce. Attendance at rallies was compulsory, the candidates were all picked by the Soviets to be compliant, and voters were intimidated or assaulted if they showed signs of hesitation before doing what they were told. Khrushchev and his aides provided their captive rally audiences with the comical assurance that if they wished to join the Soviet Union, the Soviet Union wouldn't stand in their way. NKVD operatives marched the inhabitants of entire streets to the ballot box, and anyone who still resisted was arrested within a few days of the election. Even then, the authorities falsified the results to inflate the size of their victory.

Four days after the vote, the Assembly met. A band played the Soviet anthem, the 'Internationale', repeatedly, and every third seat was occupied by an NKVD agent in order to ensure that there was no backsliding by the delegates. Only one, a Lwów lawyer called Vinnickenko, opposed the resolution, and he was arrested within a few days and sentenced to eight years in a prison camp. The motions applying to join the Soviet system were duly passed, and a commission sent to Moscow and Kiev to make it all official. Dolu, Lusia and Ludwik had become Soviet citizens, subject to Soviet law.

The motions passed by the Assembly weren't limited to Lwów's incorporation. Two other major policies were adopted – the confiscation of large private landholdings, and the nationalisation of banks and large industry. Within a few weeks, all the Finkelsteins' property had been confiscated. At the end of the year, Finkelstein and Fehl was listed as having been nationalised. Dolu was made to continue for a period as the head of the business, but eventually was put to work in a junior role in the company pipe centre.

The small salary he earned from this new position, he was now completely reliant upon. In mid-December, Lwów having become part of Soviet Ukraine, the Polish złoty was withdrawn from circulation there. People were allowed to convert only a tiny amount of their złoty into Soviet rubles, wiping out everyone's savings. Dolu and Lusia's remaining wealth consisted of their furniture and other belongings, their flat in Vienna, and a little money they had loaned to friends, or sent abroad. These included loans to the Bartels and also money deposited in London under the management of Dolu's cousin Jules Thorn, who had moved to Britain in the 1920s and established what was to become the giant Thorn Electrical Industries.

Even the money they still had in hand couldn't buy them much.

The queues that had started in mid-September now got longer. The normal waiting time for a loaf of bread was two or three hours, and it might take four or five to buy some sugar. Clothing and shoes, you couldn't get at all. If you really wanted to buy something, it was best to start queueing the night before.

Dolu, and his fellow Poles, didn't have a problem understanding why this was. Since your choice of occupation wasn't voluntary and you couldn't leave, nobody much cared what they produced or whether they produced it. Money was saved by paying starvation wages and spent instead on supervisors, and supervisors over the supervisors, to try to force production out of uninterested workers. There was always the threat of imprisonment, but while it could induce effort, they couldn't produce creativity or willingness. The hairdresser was surly, the café was dirty, and services were bound by impenetrable rules and obstructive bureaucracy.

When the communists came to town, they had brought their economic system with them.

As all this unfolded, the Finkelsteins continued to live in 12 Herburtów street, but only in part of the house. As became routine in Lwów, they had to share their home with Russian soldiers. The camp bed in the front room and the sheet partition is a common Polish memory from these days.

At first the relationship with the junior officers billeted with them was fairly civilised, even as their numbers rose. Dolu, Lusia and Ludwik were still allowed their own part of the house. Then the NKVD allocated the home to one of its colonels, and things quickly became highly unpleasant. The colonel wasn't keen on having to share and began to make this very plain. In the evenings, he would entertain Dolu and Lusia with stories of executions that had been performed that day. The intimidation was obvious.

Dolu sought reassurance from the colonel's commanding officer and got it. He couldn't rent out property, but he could live in his own house, he was told. That was Soviet law. It didn't, however, provide much protection. One day, in February 1940, the family were told that they would have to move out anyway. Dolu protested that they had the commander's permission to remain, and went into town to find him. He located the commander, but it did no good, as he promptly came to Herburtów street and expelled the Finkelsteins in person.

Ludwik's grandmother Charlotte still lived in the centre of town, in the apartment building at 47 Słoneczna street that her late husband Maks had built as part of the business premises. Now her son, daughter-in-law and grandson moved in with her.

They were not there for long, however, for Dolu was already a marked man. Even before arriving in Lwów, the Soviets had begun to collect the names of those people they regarded as socially undesirable. An equivalent list survives from the 1940 annexation of Lithuania; but, as the historian Tadeusz Piotrowski asserts, 'no doubt this list of "anti-Soviet elements" applied to all Soviet-occupied territories, including Eastern Poland'.

'Accounting must embrace all persons,' the People's Commissar for Internal Affairs instructed his agents,

> who, by reason of their social and political background, national-chauvinistic and religious convictions, and moral and political instability, are opposed to the socialist order and thus might be used for anti-Soviet purposes by the intelligence services of foreign countries and by counter-revolutionary centers.
>
> These elements include:
>
> a) All former members of anti-Soviet political parties, organizations and groups: Trotskyists, Rightists, Socialist Revolutionaries, Mensheviks, Social Democrats, Anarchists, and such like;
>
> b) All former members of national-chauvinistic anti-Soviet parties, organizations and groups: Nationalists, Young

Lithuanians, Voldemarists, Populists, Christian Democrats, members of Nationalist terrorist organizations ('The Iron Wolf'), active members of student fraternities, active members of the Riflemen's Association (the National Guard), and the Catholic terrorist organization 'The White Steed';

c) Former military police, policemen, former employees of the political and criminal police and of the prisons;

d) Former officers of the Tsarist, Petlyura, and other armies;

e) Former officers and members of the military courts of the armies of Lithuania and Poland;

f) Former political bandits and volunteers of the White and other armies;

g) Persons expelled from the Communist Party and Comm-Youth for anti-Party offenses;

h) All deserters, political emigrés, re-emigrants, repatriates, and contrabandists;

i) All citizens of foreign countries, representatives of foreign firms, employees of offices of foreign countries, former citizens of foreign countries, former employees of legations, concerns, concessions and stock companies of foreign countries.

To this was added:

j) Persons maintaining personal contacts and correspond-ence abroad, with foreign legations and consulates, Esperantists and Philatelists;

k) Former employees of the departments of ministries (from Referents upwards);

l) Former workers of the Red Cross and Polish refugees;

m) Religionists (priests, pastors), sectarians and the active worshipers of religious congregations;

n) Former noblemen, estate owners, merchants, bankers, businessmen (who availed themselves of hired labor), shop owners, proprietors of hotels and restaurants.

In Lwów there were also included 'university professors, teachers, doctors, engineers, the forestry service, well-to-do peasants and even poor peasants and certain categories of workmen, the families of soldiers of all ranks who went abroad, refugees from other parts of Poland and "speculators," which was a term applied to small traders and merchants'.

In other words, almost every person of standing in Eastern Poland, even standing of the most minor kind, faced the prospect of imprisonment or deportation. And Dolu qualified for this distinction in a number of ways. He hadn't been in correspondence with any stamp collectors, and he didn't speak Esperanto. But he was a businessman, a councillor, he had opinions which might convict him of 'moral and political instability', he attended a synagogue, he had been an army officer.

Qualifying, however, really wasn't necessary. You could be added to the list at any moment just because you were denounced by someone who resented you, or because a moment's carelessness or a minor error brought you to the attention of the authorities. Or you might have the bad luck to be staying with a relative when they were arrested. There was a Soviet maxim that now applied to Soviet Lwów: 'In the Soviet Union there are only three categories of people – those who were in prison, those who are in prison, and those who will be in prison.'

One of the first measures taken by the Soviets upon arrival had been the arrest of Lwów's most senior political leaders, people like Ostrowski. And at the same time they had swept up anybody who claimed to be a socialist but whose vision departed, or might in future possibly depart, from that of Stalin. After all, who would be more opposed to the 'socialist order' than other socialists?

In February 1940, there had been the first mass deportation to the frozen wastelands from what had once been Eastern Poland. The target on this occasion was anyone who had ever been an official in the state administration of a town or a village, as well as farmers and forestry workers. The nature of the policy immediately became apparent. It was whole families that were seized and dispatched into the unknown. Not just farmers, or former town clerks, but also their wives, their children, maybe their parents too. Old people who were already dying, pregnant women, young children in bed with measles: it didn't matter how unfit they were or what they had done, if the head of the family was arrested, they were coming with them. Caught entirely unprepared, they were expelled from their homes and transported into the ferocious Russian winter.

There was no formal count and there are wildly different numbers, with many estimating that more than a million people, out of a population of 13.5 million in the areas annexed by the Soviets, were eventually victims of this policy. But even the most conservative calculations suggest that the number was more than 400,000.

In April 1940 came the turn of the Finkelsteins. On the night of the 10th, Ludwik woke up to find his grandmother's flat full of soldiers and militiamen. They had come, they said, to search the flat for firearms. The usual practice was to gather all the members of the household in one room, get the head of the household to face the wall, and then go through the property, stealing whatever they fancied while they were at it. Dolu didn't have any arms, having buried his service revolver in the garden at Herburtów street, and once their search was complete, the military were ready to leave.

As they were heading out of the door, they turned. 'Just one more thing, Mr Finkelstein. We are happy that you don't have any arms, of course. But could you please come with us to the Commissariat of the Militia to sign that we left the apartment in good order?'

Then Ludwik watched as they led Dolu out of the flat, and his father simply disappeared.

By the next morning, Dolu had not returned, and Lusia began to appreciate that he hadn't been the only person picked up the night before. Dolu's brother Bernard had been too; thousands were, perhaps 5,000 in all. The militia hadn't had any papers for Dolu to sign. Her husband had been arrested.

Leaving Ludwik in the flat, Lusia headed over to the Lwów prosecutor's office to see what she could find out. A large crowd of women were already gathered outside, all seeking news. The message from the officials inside was one of reassurance. There wasn't a major problem, Lusia was told. They were just interrogating a whole range of people. 'You come back on the morning of the 14th, and we will give you exact details of where your husband is.' For now, she should return to Słoneczna street. So she did. What else could she do?

On the night of the 13th, the NKVD came for the rest of the family.

MUM

Overrun

'Attention! Attention! One hundred planes over Rotterdam.' 'Attention! Attention! One hundred planes over Rotterdam.' The radio kept repeating itself. It was Friday, 10 May 1940, and Holland had been invaded.

Mirjam remembered standing in the street, little groups of neighbours talking anxiously. Ruth remembered sirens blaring, 'every hour, day and night'. But the middle sister, Eva, has a different memory.

She recalled that the first thing Grete did when a neighbour informed her of the invasion of Holland was to fetch a screwdriver. Then Eva helped her remove the nameplate on the front door which identified their home as the place where Alfred Wiener and his family lived.

Grete shared the general Dutch concern about the invasion, and, of course, she knew what Nazi rule might mean for the Jews in general. But she was also worried about something more specific, something closer to home. She worried that the moment the Germans took control of Amsterdam they would come looking for Alfred and his archive. She was worried that Jan van Eijckstraat and the home of the Wiener family would be among their earliest targets.

Alfred, of course, was in London, and he'd taken most of the

Jewish Central Information Office documents with him. At the end of April 1940, David Cohen had informed the remaining Dutch staff that the Office in Holland would be closing. But there was still plenty of incriminating material in both the Wiener house and in the Office next door, should anyone be minded to look for it.

So Grete started a fire in the big open fireplace in Number 16, one they rarely used, and she and her daughters began to shred everything they could find, and then burn it. They had to do most of the work themselves. One member of the Office's staff, Josef Bettelheim, lived on the premises, and two others had arrived very early. But further assistance was cut off by the imposition of a curfew. Fearful of spies and their sabotage, the Dutch government confined all Germans and German speakers to their homes.

The work was also disrupted by a fearful row. Alfred's deputy, Kurt Zielenziger, had been firmly opposed to the plan to close the Amsterdam Office, despite the fact that keeping it open was both unsafe and financially impossible. Alfred and Grete had both been drawn into endless meetings and correspondence about this, even though the outcome was completely inevitable. Zielenziger's opposition had been passive-aggressive: 'mute but defiant' is how Alfred described him. Now, at this inopportune moment, the aggression remained, but the passivity had gone.

Bettelheim, a former waiter and a rather brave trade unionist often sent to retrieve information from Alfred's agents in Germany, and Zielenziger, once the press secretary to the mayor of Berlin and a more deskbound type, were opposites; and in this case opposites did not attract. In Bettelheim's view, Zielenziger had totally lost his composure, and he was hindering the destruction of the confidential material, rather than helping. It would be better, Bettelheim said, if he went home. Not that this was very practical advice, given the curfew.

All this was bad enough, but then things got worse. Among the papers on Zielenziger's desk were found visa documents that Alfred had arranged for the staff to receive. It seemed as if

Zielenziger had kept them there for weeks, not telling the others, in order to avoid the Amsterdam Office closing down. 'A bitter argument ensued in the course of which Dr Z declared that he had had no interest in going to London.' This, at least, was Bettelheim's account, but its accuracy was still being disputed decades later. Zielenziger's son would always maintain that the story of the travel documents was 'totally absurd'.

The bickering was a burden Grete could have done without, at this moment of great peril, with three young girls and a fire to tend. But its importance lies elsewhere. The visa controversy is a very typical Holocaust story, a classic of its kind. Kurt Zielenziger died in Belsen in 1944, and there were other members of the Office's staff that did not survive the war. Did he make mistakes? Did his mistakes contribute to his own death? To that of others? If he did, were they his fault? There are so many tales like this, attached to so many similar questions. And my mother never had much time for any of them.

When you look back at what happened to my family, to their friends, to millions of others, there are so many things that could have been done differently, given perfect knowledge, given perfect people. There are so many deaths, so many ruined lives, where one can go back and ask whether greater decisiveness might have helped, or more imagination, or less complacency. Sometimes these failings are attributed to an individual, sometimes to a community's leadership, sometimes to the Allies.

But my mother would always listen politely to such talk and then quietly reply: 'It was the Nazis who were responsible.'

It wasn't just that she was very understanding of people's foibles and mistakes, although being gently amused by our eccentricities was a central part of her character. It was that she felt that seeking to attach responsibility for the Nazis' crimes to anyone other than the Nazis was, at best, diminishing their guilt, and at worst, blaming the victim.

Eventually, the row in Jan van Eijckstraat came to a temporary stop, the burning reached a natural conclusion, and Grete had to consider what to do next. For several days, there wasn't much choice, since the curfew meant they had to stay indoors, relying on Dutch friends to bring food or other necessities. The girls spent the time looking out of the windows. Eva in particular, with her natural artistic bent, found the sights fascinating. When the Germans finally occupied the city and she saw their forces pass the apartment, she visualised their ranks as 'a big caterpillar crawling along the ground'. But by the time the curfew ended, Grete had a plan. They would have to leave their apartment and go into hiding.

The Wieners had various relatives – second cousins, distant uncles – who just about had room for them. None, however, had a perfect hiding place. The extraordinary story of Anne Frank, who hid in an attic for two years, was made possible by the existence of something rare – a living space for two entire families, sufficiently distanced from other homes to be relatively secure, and supported by non-Jews. Even then, they were eventually caught.

Grete took the children to some cousins. They were Jews themselves and didn't have anywhere special to hide, just a large house. And Mirjam and her sisters found it frightening, waking up somewhere strange and getting lost on the way to the toilet. The two younger girls remember crying a lot. It clearly wasn't a long-term solution, and after friends reassured Grete that the German occupiers had not been to Jan van Eijckstraat, and Bettelheim reported that he remained at liberty despite his many mentions in the SS magazine *Das Schwarze Korps*, she decided the best bet was to return home.

———

While safety had been Grete's first concern upon hearing of the invasion, a second one soon began to press upon her. The family didn't have any money. The problem dwarfed their earlier financial difficulties.

Alfred was cut off from Holland entirely, and there could be no question of receiving any of his income. If there was any. During the previous year, the flow of money had been from Amsterdam to London, and the couple ran down their savings supporting the new office and Alfred's stay in Ford's Hotel. So now there was no income and little else to fall back on.

There were a lot of hushed conversations about this problem between Grete and Betty, the home help having become something of a confidante in Alfred's absence. The immediate solution was to sell a few items, just a handful of what Ruth called 'family heirlooms', some silver, which fetched a little cash. A distant cousin lent some money and was given a silver fruit bowl as collateral. It was, as it turned out, a good idea to dispose of this stuff now, since the Germans later confiscated what remained. Grete also decided to sell Alfred's large stamp collection, a decision she had to make without being able to consult him about it.

The money from these few bits and pieces wouldn't last long, and Grete realised that she would have to get a job. The obvious thing to do was to approach Gertrude van Tijn and see if Grete could turn into paid employment the voluntary work she had been doing helping refugees. In January 1941, she began the first of a series of jobs for Van Tijn, initially helping her with her training centre for young adults.

Even though Grete had a PhD, and had spent years as counsel to Alfred, the work she was given was secretarial. Eventually, she would become Van Tijn's most senior administrative assistant, but never had a place in decision making. Being a woman excluded even Van Tijn herself from the highest community roles. However unjust this was, in many ways it was fortunate for Grete, since the moral choices the Jewish leadership now had to make were almost intolerably difficult. They remain controversial even today.

On 12 February 1941, the German occupiers mandated the creation of a Jewish Council, which would have responsibility for maintaining order in the community. David Cohen was designated as co-chairman, along with the diamond trader Abraham Asscher. Gertrude van Tijn and her previously independent refugee committee were now answerable to the Council. Given that only men sat on the Council, she ended up sharing responsibility for its decisions without even being able to attend its meetings. Sometimes she found this acutely uncomfortable, and Grete, from her far more junior position, almost certainly felt the same.

The Dutch Jewish community faced an immediate moral dilemma in the first days of the Council's establishment, a dilemma that wouldn't go away. In mid-February, there was a series of skirmishes between Dutch Nazi thugs and young Jews determined to resist them. The fighting led to the death of one Dutch Nazi and the arrest by the Germans of 425 young Jewish men. Most of these were sent to the Mauthausen concentration camp in Austria. A few weeks later, their relatives received small cardboard boxes with their ashes in them.

Then, towards the end of the month, came a much bigger act of resistance – a communist-inspired strike of non-Jews in the ports, factories and Amsterdam's public services. The Germans fought the strikers, killed nine of them, and then warned the Jewish Council that another 500 Jews would be arrested if the strikers did not go back to work. The Council pleaded with the strikers to call off their action, and the next day, mainly as a result of violent police repression, they did.

This was only the first of dozens of similar positions the Council was to take, and which critics, particularly communist critics, thought were both morally and strategically flawed.

For Grete in 1941, most of these issues were theoretical. As they were for almost all the approximately 17,500 other people ultimately employed by the Council in more or less junior roles. They didn't have the option to leave Holland, and they needed money to support themselves at a time when Jews were barred from most other kinds of work.

With the stamp collection and the cutlery gone, Grete's job paid a small but vital wage to support her three daughters. Life would have been almost impossible without it.

Joy and Glee

After the frenzied days of shredding and burning and hiding came a lull. Certainly as far as the girls were concerned.

Life, of course, wasn't quite the same as before for anyone in Holland. There was rationing, for instance. And blackouts. 'Blackouts impressed us,' recalled Eva:

All the lights went out, and the city looked black and sinister. The canals in Amsterdam had no rails, and people would sometimes walk into the water. They would have to swim. Some lives were taken, and others were seriously injured. One of our friends walked into a canal and had to climb out of it. Amsterdam was difficult to black out because of the reflection from the water. We, the children, thought blackout was an adventure and a novelty. But we were also afraid that people would knock on our door to warn us that lights could be seen.

Jews feared this knock more than their neighbours did. The blackouts were designed to prevent the bombers of the Allies from finding their way over the Low Countries, and there was a danger that any breach would be seen by the Germans as a deliberate act of sabotage. Jews were particularly vulnerable to this suspicion.

Indeed, one of the first specifically anti-Jewish measures introduced by the Nazis after their occupation of the Netherlands was to exclude Jews from working in air-raid protection.

Such a policy needed the registration of Jews, and in their first year of occupation the Germans gradually increased the requirement of Jews to register themselves. It started with requiring all those employed in the civil service, or in education, to fill in one of two different forms – Form A for 'Aryans', or Form B for 'non-Aryans'. Later, some signatories regretted it, with 'Aryans' feeling that signing had been a terrible betrayal of their principles. But 'non-Aryans' would have cause to regret it more. As one friend of Alfred's put it: 'Each signed his own death warrant, though few appreciated this at the time.'

For now, what the Jews were signing was their own employment termination. The form-filling was followed by policies that forbad Jews from being appointed to public office or jobs in education, and fired those already working in these areas. There was some protest by Dutch officials and citizens at this, partly in defence of the Jews and partly in defence of their own autonomy. A few professors refused to fill in the form, a few more signed a petition. But the protest didn't amount to much, and certainly didn't prevent the exclusion going ahead.

There were also the first signs of the restrictions that would eventually cut Jews off entirely from mainstream social and economic life. In September 1940, for instance, it was decreed that Jews were excluded from Amsterdam's markets. And at the beginning of 1941, the Dutch Cinema Association announced that Jews were no longer allowed to enter cinemas. Ruth, in particular, was upset about this, as she was looking forward to being fourteen and going to the pictures with her friends, a coming-of-age ritual.

In other words, 1940 and early 1941 saw the beginning of what would eventually become a catastrophe for Jews. Yet it was still possible to live a fairly unremarkable family life. The girls were aware that they were separated from their father and that this was more than his usual absences, they realised Grete was struggling financially, and they sensed that the adults were afraid. They became used to the little huddles – Grete and Betty, Grete and her sister Trude – where the talk was secretive but anxious. Mirjam once came upon some coupons in the street, and Grete's pleasure spoke of how hard she was finding it scraping by.

But despite all this, they weren't really afraid themselves. Despite all this, the normal pleasures and dreads of school and friends, and playing in the street, and hobbies and sports, were still more potent to them than world affairs.

Partly this was because nobody – even the Germans themselves – yet realised how far the Nazis would go. But it was also because when you are young you trust your parents. It was hard for them to imagine that there were things that could happen to them that even their mother couldn't control.

And they were, after all, still very young. In the summer of 1940, Mirjam turned seven, Eva had her tenth birthday, and Ruth became thirteen. The two younger girls were still attending the First Montessori School, only Ruth had moved on to the Municipal Lyceum senior school.

They all made plenty of friends in class, augmenting them with pals at the swimming pool. All three girls were part of the Amsterdam Women's Swimming Club, and by April 1941 had practised enough to take part in the national swimming competitions. Mirjam and Eva swam the twenty-five metres breaststroke, and Ruth won her fifty metres backstroke heat with a time of fifty-four and nine tenths of a second, more than a second faster than the next girl.

The pool was about a twenty-minute walk from Jan van Eijckstraat, but it was only six minutes by bike. And that first year they were still able to ride their bikes pretty much anywhere. Ruth even went on a summer camping trip with her friends, cycling off into the woods and putting up tents.

They also continued to enjoy a Jewish family life, gathering for the Sabbath, lighting the candles, going to religion school. In Alfred's absence, they were invited to celebrate Passover at the house of Ruth's Hebrew teacher, Elfriede Cohn Strauss, which they did before the Cohns went into hiding in 1942. The girls had a strong memory of Mrs Cohn Strauss serving them beetroot salad, and their having to eat it under the watchful eye of Grete, who thought it would be rude to leave it on the plate. Ruth would laugh later at remembering such a banal thing. An ordinary childhood memory among all the extraordinary events.

In other words, life was as normal as it could be during that first year of occupation. And what they enjoyed most was the normal Dutch childhood pleasure of playing in the street outside the front door of their apartment.

MEMBERSHIP CARD Jopie Cohen Jan v Eijckstraat 30 Amsterdam South wishes to become a member of the Joy and Glee Club. [Signed for] The Board: E Blüth, R Wiener.

Nineteen forty-one saw the formation of the Jewish Council, the consolidation of Nazi rule, the institution of the Aryan Attestation. And the creation of the Joy and Glee Club, headquarters 16 Jan van Eijckstraat, board members Ellen Blüth, Ralph Prins and Ruth Wiener.

Like most Dutch children, the Wiener sisters liked to play on the pavement with the kids from the neighbouring houses. Marbles, hopscotch, hula hoops, ball games, and most of all biking, loads of biking. In 1941, the girls decided to put all this playing on a more formal basis and create a club, with a list of members, membership cards and a newsletter. It was all very earnest, and it is hard not to notice how very 'Alfred' all the organising was.

Of the twenty members, fourteen lived on Jan van Eijckstraat itself. Apart from Marianne Knapper, the thirteen-year-old girl living at Number 43, they were all Jewish, and mostly German refugees.

As well as the sisters and Ellen Blüth (Number 12), there were the ten-year-old Duizend twins Harold and Paul at Number 22; Dorothee Miloslawski, the eleven-year-old girl at Number 24, who signed Ruth's Poesie book; Evelyne Frank (Number 25), twelve years old and not related to Anne and Margot; twelve-year-old Rini Soep (Number 32); and seven-year-old Harald Hahn (on another floor of Number 22). Marion Amster, the thirteen-year-old Joy and Glee member living at Number 39, shared this address with the Cohen brothers, nine-year-old Sammy and his younger brother, seven-year-old Jopie.

From the surrounding streets there was, naturally, Trude's son Fritz, the girls' only first cousin, who was now twelve. And from the same street (Corellistraat), Ralph Prins. As Ralph was fifteen, and significantly older than the others, his membership is a little bit of an anomaly. He may have been a cousin to the Duizend twins (their mother was a Prins), or he may just have been admired by one of the girls. Nine-year-old Ursula Klau (known as Uschi by her family) was the furthest away, and even she only had a five-minute walk from her home at 56 Minervalaan to the club's epicentre.

The club had its own newsletter and a subscription of one cent a month, with the board announcing in June that this would be more than doubled to one cent every two weeks. There was further bad news – 'a collection of funds for a new notebook' would soon take place. The money helped to fund prizes, with Harald winning a propelling pencil for his solution to one of the fortnightly puzzles, and Dorothee winning some marbles for another.

The Joy and Glee newsletter, neatly typed by Ruth on Grete's typewriter before being copied, contained several short stories, some riddles, colouring competitions, and drawings by Ralph. Ursula also contributed a Sinterklaas poem, which was printed in the 1 June edition, even though the Sinterklaas festival takes place on 5 December.

There was a pleasing seriousness, even pomposity, to the announcements.

We hereby announce that Ralph Prins has joined the team of editors. He will start a new column, which will be a Q&A column. You can submit any questions to him. Scribble your question on a piece of paper and drop it in the mailbox at 5 Corellistraat. Make sure to include your question and your name and age. Do not approach him on the street. If so, your response will not be included in the next edition!!!

And there were also outings. A trip to the beach. Bring sandwiches and some sweets. Don't forget to bring your membership card. If it rains, there will be games at Ellen Blüth's.

In mid-July 1941, the Wieners moved from Jan van Eijckstraat, and the Joy and Glee Club came to an end. The 15 June newsletter announced Jopie Cohen as a new member, but he never received his card, which was still among Ruth's papers when she died, decades later.

_____

Here is what happened to the members of the Joy and Glee Club.

On 20 June 1943, a boy called Eddy Posthuma de Boer (later to become a celebrated photographer) was walking through Amsterdam towards the centre of the city, when he came across a sight that shocked him. A confusion of trams and armed guards and suitcases and signs and hundreds of Jews, the latter clearly under arrest. And then he noticed something that shocked him even more – one of the Jews was the boy who used to sit next to him in class, at the Cornelis Kruseman School. It was Paul Duizend. And his brother Harold was there too. Eddy waved to the twins, and the twins waved back.

'Of course,' said Eddy,

I didn't know what was going to happen to them, but there was that feeling of doom. The feeling that this is no good. My father did not know what would happen to them either. At the time, he mainly wondered how he could protect his own children. We reacted like all families at the time, we cocooned ourselves . . . And no, Paul and Harold Duizend did not come back.

On 2 July that year, Paul and Harold Duizend were murdered in the gas chambers at Sobibor, along with their mother Erica and their father Bernard. The twins were twelve years old.

Dorothee Miloslawski, who wrote in the Poesie book and won the marbles, was thirteen years old when she was murdered with her mother in the gas chambers at Auschwitz, on 10 September 1943. Her father Max, an accountant who had understood the Nazi threat well enough to leave Germany in 1934, died in Auschwitz the following March.

On 7 May 1945, the Germans signed an unconditional surrender at the Allied headquarters in France. The same day, Resa Klau died in the arms of her thirteen-year-old daughter Ursula. The girl who had once filled the front page of the Joy and Glee newsletter with her poem, was now an orphan.

Like the Miloslawskis and the Wieners, the Klaus were originally German Jews. Oscar Klau, a highly successful Frankfurt lawyer, had liquidated his business and brought the family to Amsterdam in 1936. They had all been arrested in 1943, and the first to die had been Ursula's grandmother Bella, gassed in Auschwitz. Oscar had died later in Belsen, but Ursula and her mother had survived until the last days of the war.

And then, as the liberation approached, Himmler evacuated them by train, destined for another camp. Two weeks later, the train and everyone in it were abandoned by the guards and driver at Tröbitz. The passengers on what became known as 'the Lost Train' were disease-ridden, had no toilets, no food and nothing to drink. Even once the Soviets found the train and liberated them, hundreds still died. And Ursula's mother was one of them.

Ursula herself almost succumbed to tuberculosis. But in the end she recovered. She made it to the United States, where she had some surviving relatives, and lived in Baltimore until she died in 2007 at the age of seventy-five.

Evelyne Frank was born to American parents and was eventually able to return there; Rini Soep survived Belsen; and Ellen Blüth survived Westerbork.

The other club member to survive was Ralph Prins. Ralph was transported to Westerbork in 1943, but lived through both that and Theresienstadt, making it to Switzerland in 1945. In both camps, he drew portraits of those who asked.

The illustrator of the Joy and Glee newsletter became a celebrated artist, designing logos, posters and book covers. He won international prizes for his photography, and became chairman of the Dutch professional photographers association. And he was asked to design the national monument for Westerbork. In 1970, Queen Juliana of the Netherlands unveiled what he had designed, a striking combination of railway sleepers, buffers and boulders.

There is one more story from the Joy and Glee Club. Or rather, two connected ones. In the spring of 2016, the *Israel Philatelist* – the journal of Israeli stamp collectors, 'devoted to the philately of the Holy Land' – published an article relating the history of the Amster family during the Holocaust. It used first-day covers and stamped envelopes provided to the magazine by Jack Klugerman, who had been married to Marion Amster, the Joy and Glee member who lived with the Cohens – with Sammy and Jopie – at 39 Jan van Eijckstraat.

Marion, it turned out, had been one of those German Jewish children who had been sent off to Holland on a train when her father had been arrested after Kristallnacht and imprisoned in Buchenwald. She had been one of the unaccompanied minors that Gertrude van Tijn and Grete had scooped up and looked after, placing her in an orphanage while they looked for somewhere better.

Before long, Abraham Cohen and his family had taken Marion in; which is how, by 1941, she came to be playing with Mirjam, Ruth, and Eva on Jan van Eijckstraat. The journal then relates what happened next. 'One day when Marion returned from school, the Cohen family had left and gone into hiding.' The little girl was taken in by one of Grete's friends, another secretary to Gertrude van Tijn.

Marion ended up in Belsen and, like Ursula Klau, was on the 'Lost Train'. Unlike Resa Klau, she somehow survived the ordeal. Her own mother had died in the Stutthof concentration camp near Danzig in March 1945, but her father had made it to the United States. Marion was reunited with him there, married Jack Klugerman and lived until 2012, when she was eighty-two.

This was how she and her family understood her story, or at least how it was told to the journal. But, as it turns out, this understanding wasn't quite right.

The one non-Jewish member of the Joy and Glee Club, Marianne Knapper, had a brother called Nico, who grew up to become a successful singer and TV director. And in 2012, when Nico was telling his fans about his upbringing, he talked about his best friend. Sammy Cohen. Jopie's brother. Abraham's son. Of how he lived two houses away on Jan van Eijckstraat. Of how he and his friend would walk across the roof to each other's rooms.

And of how Sammy and Jopie died.

While Marion Amster may have thought – perhaps may have been reassured by her new foster parents – that the Cohens had gone into hiding, Nico knew better. His friend's family hadn't simply gone off without warning, leaving a little girl homeless and without protection. The Germans had arrested them and sent them to Westerbork. After the war, the Cohens' one surviving relative had called the Knappers to let them know what had happened. Sammy and Jopie Cohen had been murdered in the gas chambers of Sobibor on 4 June 1943, along with their father and their mother Henriette.

Nico had a final memory of how his friendship with Sammy had ended:

> When the whole family was taken away, we heard that the house would soon be occupied by a family of Germans. I went over the roof to Sammy's room one last time. I saw all his things and the tin soldiers, which I had always envied very much. I toyed with the idea of taking them with me, but I couldn't. I would rather have some German-minded boy play with them than having to think about the fate of Sammy and his family, every time I saw those soldiers . . . I didn't want to take advantage of the injustice that had befallen them.

Nico later reflected that leaving the tin soldiers was one of the most important decisions of his childhood.

Almost every member of the Joy and Glee Club was imprisoned, except its one non-Jew. Almost everyone who wasn't killed outright, faced starvation and disease and was taken to the brink of death. Yet even so, the club's survival rate was higher than that of Jan van Eijckstraat in general.

The inhabitants of 1 Jan van Eijckstraat were murdered by gas in Sobibor; Number 3, killed in Amsterdam; Number 5, murdered by gas in Sobibor; Number 8, murdered by gas in Auschwitz; Number 9, murdered by gas in Sobibor; Number 11, starved to death in Belsen; Number 12, murdered by gas in Sobibor; Number 13, starved to death in Belsen; Number 14, murdered by gas in Auschwitz; Number 15, murdered by gas in Auschwitz; Number 17, murdered by gas in Auschwitz; Number 19, murdered by gas in Auschwitz; Number 22, murdered by gas in Sobibor; Number 22 (ii), murdered by gas in Sobibor; Number 23, starved to death in Belsen;

Number 24, murdered by gas in Sobibor; Number 25, murdered by gas in Sobibor; Number 26, murdered by gas in Auschwitz; Number 28, killed in Mauthausen; Number 29, murdered by gas in Sobibor; Number 30, murdered by gas in Auschwitz; Number 32, starved to death in Belsen; Number 34, murdered by gas in Auschwitz; Number 37, starved to death in Belsen; and Number 39, murdered by gas in Sobibor.

It would be easier to identify houses that the killers didn't visit. Ninety people murdered in a single short street.

The Departing

Towards the end of November 1941, an invitation went out to representatives of the major government departments of the Third Reich. There was to be a meeting in a grand Berlin villa by a lake. There would be representation too from the Nazi Party organisation and the SS. And afterwards, there would be a buffet.

Two months later, the meeting took place. On a snowy Tuesday morning in January, fifteen people gathered around a table under the chairmanship of Reinhard Heydrich, the chief of the German security police. They were an educated, cultivated group, and also young, many under the age of forty, with higher degrees. The formal proceedings lasted an hour and a half, during which the group agreed to murder all the Jews of Europe. Then they had lunch.

Heydrich regarded the whole thing as most satisfactory. Once his guests had gone, he sat by the fireplace and smoked a cigar. Adolf Eichmann, his assistant and the man in charge of conference administration, sat with him. They drank cognac – 'a glass or two or three' – which Eichmann said he had not seen Heydrich do in years.

The cause of the satisfaction was that now, at last, they felt they had a plan. The Wannsee Conference, as it became known, did not initiate the policy of killing Jews. But it did bring coherence to what had been quite a chaotic policy.

The core of the policy had always been consistent and clear – a hatred of Jews and a determination to end their influence. But around it there had been a muddle of ideas, of people, of politics, of vested interests and of practical imperatives. Individuals competed for control, and to show that they alone best understood the will of Adolf Hitler.

Alfred had long ago identified a central cause of the confusion. The Nazis believed Jews to be a race that was simultaneously inferior and superior. They thought that Jews were the scum of the earth and the rulers of the world. They wanted to rid Germany, and German-occupied territory, of the pernicious influence of the Jews, who were weighing society down. Yet they thought Jews were showing guile so great it was beyond German wit to detect.

Hitler supported a policy of compulsory emigration, yet he also feared its consequences. As Alfred had once explained to a stunned inner circle during the Bern Trial, Hitler believed the *Protocols of the Elders of Zion* revealed the real plans of the Jews. So if you expelled them from German territory, you would be setting them free to implement their schemes elsewhere. Hitler had long thought he detected the influence of world Jewry in the antagonism of the United States towards Nazi Germany. A successful policy of expulsion might just speed up Jewish world domination.

By the beginning of 1942, this fear was not the only problem with the policy of emigration. There were real, practical questions. Most importantly – where would the Jews go? The Germans could try to create an enclave, and make the enclave as unpleasant as possible, but no Nazi governors wanted that enclave on their territory. How would the Jews get there? Who would feed them? And whatever the answer to these questions, given both the inferiority and superiority of the Jews, an enclave would really be only a temporary solution. No, what was needed was a final solution.

That was the job with which Göring had tasked Heydrich. And which Heydrich now sought to advance by codifying the policy and getting agreement of all the parts of the Nazi apparatus that would need to be involved.

Every department had its speciality – governing people, categorising people, transporting people, killing people – and wished its own expertise and personnel to have the upper hand, bringing with it power and prestige. Heydrich's main aim at Wannsee was to create collective responsibility for a single policy, and, along the way, to establish his own primacy. He only partially succeeded. Factions continued to jostle for power. And Heydrich himself died that June, after an assassination attempt, with Heinrich Himmler accumulating power. Yet Wannsee nevertheless was a landmark.

In the minutes of the meeting, circulated afterwards as a way of ensuring that everyone else was signed up to Heydrich's version of the discussion, there is a succinct description of current policy: 'a) the expulsion of the Jews from every sphere of life of the German people; b) the expulsion of the Jews from the living space of the German people.' And this is followed by an equally succinct description of the policy that would be followed from now on: 'Instead of emigration, the new solution has emerged, after prior approval by the Führer, of evacuating Jews to the east.'

The use of this euphemism for mass murder – 'evacuation to the East' – was doubtless designed to make their guilt deniable. Yet could anything more revealing ever have been committed to paper than this? They knew sufficiently well how appalling their policy was that they did not dare to make explicit what it really involved.

In the Netherlands, once the lull was over, my mother and her sisters became subject to both these policies – the 'new' and the 'old'. First the Germans began to expel Jews from every aspect of mainstream social and economic life. Then they started to collect them together, and kill them.

The reason Grete moved the family from Jan van Eijckstraat in the summer of 1941 was simple. She could no longer afford their old apartment. And she no longer needed to live there now that the archive had moved and the Amsterdam Office had closed down.

So she rented an apartment at 25 Westerscheldeplein, about a twenty-minute walk away, to the south and east. The new place was in a perfectly nice area, though definitely a less expensive part of town. And they still lived in a heavily Jewish district. They had moved quite a bit nearer to Margot and Anne Frank, for instance. But it was smaller than they had been used to, and on the second and third floors, rather than the ground and first.

Trude and Jan didn't move with them, for once. The Abrahams stayed in Corellistraat. Now that Jan could no longer get work in his chosen profession as an architect, they had been forced to turn their house into a care home. Jan's sister, Else Lazarus, had come to stay there as well, to share the work and the rent. The home was called the House Marion, after the Lazaruses' daughter.

The Wieners' move only relieved the financial pressure a little. Grete was earning what would today be about £850 a month, and spending about £350 of it on rent. As legal restrictions on Jews increased, it became harder to buy goods in ordinary places at market prices, greatly increasing the cost of living. And there were all sorts of financial obligations placed on Jews – forced to pay the costs of their own oppression – which became harder and harder to meet.

In February 1942, the Jewish Council sought payment of a levy amounting to what would today be £1,300. In other words, far greater than Grete's monthly income. She couldn't pay it. The Council agreed to accept an undertaking that the 'amount will be paid as soon as you regain free disposal of your capital invested abroad, or leave the Netherlands'.

Eventually, the Germans confiscated all possessions of Jews – not just savings, but household items – above a total of about £2,000 in today's money. The radio was taken, leaving them a dial on the wall that only broadcast Nazi propaganda. They could keep their furniture, and the piano that Grete played daily, but anything of any value which was portable had to be handed in.

This blow didn't fall until May 1942 and, by then, the Wieners anyway had almost nothing left. There was, however, Alfred's collection of Oriental antiquities. Its emotional value far outweighed its financial one, but it would certainly have been taken away if it had been seen. Using cloth and oilpaper, Grete wrapped up all the items carefully, together with some books on Palestine and the Orient, and took them to De Boekenbron, bookseller and antique dealer, who agreed to hide them and return them all when the war was over. The bookseller kept his promise.

By the time of the confiscation, life had become very difficult for everyone in the family. Jews couldn't enter cafés, or libraries, or zoos, or museums, or galleries, or parks, or pretty much any public facilities. The girls felt particularly keenly that they were no longer allowed into swimming pools, which until then had been such a big part of their lives. Ruth was given a new tennis racket as a birthday present, and the promise of tennis lessons, but before she could use it, Jews were forbidden to play on the courts. There were signs up all over Amsterdam reading 'Forbidden for Jews'.

These signs couldn't be ignored, because Jews were now forced to wear a yellow six-pointed star with the word 'Jood' (Jew) on any visible item of clothing. If it was on a coat, and you took your coat off, there had to be a yellow star on the clothes underneath.

The introduction of the star provided a perfect example of the dilemma faced by the Jewish Council. When called in by the senior SS officer Ferdinand aus der Fünten and informed that the star was to be introduced, David Cohen had protested vigorously. Even the choice of yellow as a colour, he said, was a humiliation. He protested further when told that the Council would have to distribute the stars. They would be given just three days to do it, one of which would be the Sabbath. It was, he said, totally impractical. And totally unfair that any Jew not wearing the star at the end of that period would be subject to a vast fine or imprisonment. Cohen's objections were ignored, so what was he to do?

The Council staff, including Gertrude van Tijn and her team, worked through the night to distribute the stars, and while they worked, they argued. If they were not passing the stars around, said some, it would take the Germans weeks and weeks to do it themselves and would divert their resources. Yet during this period, responded others, many Jews would not have the stars and would not be able to leave the house – to work or to shop or to go to school – without risking severe punishment. No doubt it was a mistake for the Council to distribute the stars; it would also have been a mistake not to. The Nazis had, quite deliberately, left no good alternative.

Jews received sheets of stars, and then had to cut them out and sew them onto their clothing themselves. My mother was struck by another feature of the policy: 'I've always thought it very strange. You had to actually buy those stars . . . only the Germans could think of this.'

The stars meant Jews would be instantly spotted. When, after the war, the Wiener girls talked with fondness of the Dutch people, it was partly because of what happened when they went out wearing their 'brand'. 'On the way to school,' recalled Eva, 'people would stop and talk to me. They abused the Germans and showed sympathy in various ways. Once they slipped us some candy, and we felt pretty wonderful.'

But the practical consequences remained. In addition to barring them from public recreational facilities, the stars, along with identity cards with a large 'J' stamped on them, also meant that Jews were not able to travel on public transport. They were not permitted to drive, either, and had to hand in their bicycles, so they all did a lot of walking. Since Jews weren't allowed to shop in ordinary stores and needed to go to special Jewish markets, the distances could be quite long, especially with food to carry. There was, however, one alternative to going on foot. My mother's scooter, child-size but with big, thick tyres, was her pride and joy. It escaped the bicycle ban and became, as Mirjam called it, 'the family Rolls-Royce'.

So Betty or Grete would hop on it and set off to hunt down

fruit and vegetables or even, on rare occasions, meat for dinner. And Ruth would often be allowed to borrow the Rolls-Royce to go to school. For she was now attending a new school, and it was quite a journey from the apartment.

———————

On the wall of the Anne Frank House in Amsterdam, as visitors walk into the secret attic where the family hid, they see a letter from Margrita Freie, the headteacher of the Municipal Gymnasium senior school, dated 16 July 1941. It is addressed to the Government Commissioner for Amsterdam and begins: 'In reply to your letter of 9 July 1941 No. 2802 dept.0, I have the honour to forward to you the following list of pupils "of Jewish blood".'

Below this introduction is a list of the names and addresses of forty-nine children. One of them is Margot Frank ('Frank M.B. Merwedeplein 37 II'); and, a little lower down the list, is Ruth ('Wiener R.H. Jan van Eijckstraat 16'). The segregation of Jewish school students in Amsterdam had begun.

As part of the 'expulsion of the Jews from the living space of the German people', it had been decided that 'persons of Jewish blood' should be concentrated in their own schools. Within the German government there was a vigorous debate, simultaneously revolting and preposterous, about what having 'Jewish blood' meant. For the purposes of the schools policy, children were considered Jewish if they had at least two Jewish grandparents, or if they or their parents were members of a Jewish congregation, or if they were being raised in an observant Jewish home. This led to a scramble to find documents which might prove that, for instance, a Jewish grandparent had in fact converted to Christianity. Such a document might be life-saving.

A few Protestant schools refused to provide the lists, and a few Catholic schools protested. But most headteachers, and certainly Margrita Freie, were prompt and helpful in their replies to the authorities. The Dutch authorities did not require any intervention from the Germans in order to implement the policy. The identification, extraction and segregation of Jewish students proceeded smoothly, and the new Jewish schools, twenty-five in Amsterdam alone, were opened on 1 September 1941.

All the Wiener girls found being expelled from their existing schools traumatic. For Eva, taking leave of First Montessori was 'terribly upsetting'. Together with Mirjam, she had been 'sent to the principal's office where Mother was. Everyone said goodbye, and tears dwelled in many an eye.' Many of their friends they would rarely, if ever, see again, because Jews were no longer allowed to visit the homes of non-Jews.

Conveniently, Mirjam and Eva's new school was just round the corner from their new apartment. But that was pretty much its only advantage. The school building was a converted bicycle garage and there were, at least at the beginning, neither enough rooms or enough teachers. Age groups therefore had to double up, and the teaching, naturally, suffered. The war made a bigger impression on my mother and my aunt than anything that they were taught. They both had more vivid memories of fighter planes overhead than they did of their lessons. They remembered one girl being struck in the leg by the ricochet of a bullet, as ground forces fired into the sky.

Ruth, because she was already in secondary school, did not attend the converted bicycle garage. She was sent to the Joods Lyceum (the Jewish High School), housed in a building on a small street in the centre of Amsterdam, a forty-minute walk from the apartment, or slightly quicker when she was able to take the scooter. The Lyceum was also the school Anne and Margot Frank attended, and whose pupils were immortalised in Anne's diary, often not very flatteringly.

Unlike with my mother's school, many pupils who survived the Holocaust had warm memories of the Lyceum itself, even though these were mixed with much darker memories of war and oppression. The school premises may have been shabby, but in historical accounts the pupils remember the teachers as particularly good, and the teachers remember the pupils as particularly bright. Dienke Hondius, who wrote a history of the school and has studied its records, thinks that these accounts are somewhat 'polished' ones.

The reality is that the teachers, in meetings, talked of pupils just as they did in any other school. Some children were completely hopeless, some weren't worth teaching any more, some were lazy, some had a bit of promise. The teachers were still saying these things to each other in April 1943, when more than half the pupils were dead or in prison or in hiding. These were children just like any other children.

Hondius suggests that 'survivors hang on to [the] positive memory of togetherness in 1941–42 as a protective shield against their simultaneous naked, direct memories of fear, loss and death'. Ruth's comments about the school certainly reflect this. She said that the teachers were wonderful, she recalled singing groups and volleyball and an atmosphere of great solidarity.

Although this was a very difficult period with the war and things happening and students disappearing, and we didn't know where they were off to, it was one of the happiest in many ways, or closest, perhaps, relationships I had with my friends. And those that survive I am still in touch with.

'And those that survive.' A total of 489 students attended the Lyceum; 222 were murdered. And even this was a relatively high survival rate, since more than 75 per cent of all the Jews in the Netherlands died in concentration camps.

Although full at the beginning, attendance at both Mirjam and Eva's school and Ruth's began to decline once the policy of 'evacuation to the East' was instituted in 1942. Pupils would arrive one morning to find that a favourite teacher had disappeared and there wasn't an obvious replacement. Or a friend who had been there one day didn't turn up the next, and never showed up again. Had they been arrested? Or had they gone into hiding? No one in school knew, although they could sometimes guess.

On her way to school, Eva would routinely stop by her friend Magda's house to pick her up. 'One day, her mother told me that she was ill. Various excuses came day after day, and finally I realised what had happened. Her parents, being very brave, [had] put her into hiding with another family.'

Jacob Presser, later the author of the definitive account of the Dutch Holocaust, was a teacher at the Lyceum. His class began with twenty-eight children; by May 1943, when he went into hiding himself, there were only four left. Even those didn't turn up every day, because they feared being arrested in a city-centre round-up.

When Ruth arrived for school on Monday, 3 July 1942, having made her way through the rain, among the children who failed to appear were Margot and Anne Frank.

After the war, when Ruth first read the diary of Anne Frank, she was amazed. 'I was totally flabbergasted,' she said. 'I had no idea what was behind this particular girl.' People would often ask her what Anne was like: 'I always hate to disappoint [them] and tell them that, to me, she was just a kid in the class, a kid in the school, a kid I knew, and she never had – to me – anything too special.'

Some of this was age. Anne was younger than Ruth, and so there was a degree of condescension. But Mirjam, who was younger still, felt the same about Anne. In 2013, the pop star Justin Bieber went to the Anne Frank House and wrote in the visitors' book: 'Truly inspiring to be able to come here. Anne was a great girl. Hopefully she would have been a belieber.' His employment of the term used for his fans was thought hopelessly crass, and he was almost universally criticised. But my mother defended him.

What made Anne Frank important, Mum felt, was not really her precocity or the way that her writing sparkled. It was her ordinariness. The diary is affecting because it portrays a young girl who was just like thousands of others. Someone with the same teen passions. Someone who covered their wall with the pictures of film stars. Someone who absolutely could have been a belieber. Justin Bieber had visited the Anne Frank House and from it grasped better than most who Anne Frank really was.

Ruth had a more positive view of Anne's older sister than she did of Anne. 'Margot, who was a little older than I was, was very bright. Very, very, smart. A little serious as well. And I always looked up to her, as a matter of fact.' Ruth shared this seriousness, and the girls got to know each other as members of the same synagogue community, with similar attitudes to Jewish learning.

Typically, Alfred hadn't thought that the religious education classes offered by the liberal synagogue were good enough for Ruth, and he'd arranged for her to have tuition from an orthodox teacher. Ruth went to Mrs Cohn Strauss's home a couple of times a week, mastered the prayer book and became pretty proficient in Hebrew. By the time that Ruth was in her mid-teens, she had become committed to the synagogue, its services and its youth clubs. As had Margot.

In late 1941, the two girls were studying together when the Rabbi asked them to do him a favour. A young couple wanted to get married, and the ceremony would have to be done in secret. Would Margot and Ruth agree to act as bridesmaids and witness the marriage? The two girls went alone to the empty synagogue to help the Rabbi. Ruth would always wonder what happened to the young couple whose wedding they facilitated that day.

A few months later, Margot disappeared from school and went into hiding. She vanished from the lives of almost all her friends. But it wasn't, quite, the last time Ruth or my mother saw her.

What had sent the Franks into hiding was the receipt of a letter. Margot was being called up to 'a labour camp in Germany'. The Franks knew what that might mean, what it probably meant, and they weren't going to wait about to find out for certain. What it might mean, what in most cases it did mean, was death. For the second part of the German policy, the part that involved the elimination of the Jews, had begun.

Over the previous year, Jews in the Netherlands – the Wieners and Franks included – had been required repeatedly to fill out lengthy forms, with the latest fairly obviously designed to allow the Germans to acquire their assets when they were 'deported'. The Jewish Council would protest, but always concluded that things would be worse if they didn't cooperate.

The forms allowed the Germans to create a card index which, from the end of June 1942, they used to select Jews to be 'called up' for the so-called 'labour service'. Initially these call-ups were delivered by registered mail, and it was one of these letters that Margot Frank received in early July. Margot had already turned sixteen, and could therefore be sent away on her own.

Otto Frank had been prepared. He had arranged a hiding place. But those that hadn't or couldn't, those who responded to the call-up, were not sent to Germany. They were sent to the camp that the Jews had paid for, were still paying for, and had helped build in order to house refugees. They were sent to Westerbork. And from there they would be, to use the language of Wannsee, 'evacuated to the East'. In other words, murdered.

Because Grete was working for the Jewish Council, her family was, for now, exempt. The Germans would cross-check their call-up lists with lists of people they accepted were doing essential work, scoring out those names. Van Tijn had deliberately inflated the number of workers assisting her, in order to protect as many people as possible for as long as she could. The emigration department she ran, and Grete worked for, had less and less to do, as few people were allowed either in or out of the country. But it still retained a large staff, many unpaid.

As the numbers of deportations grew – and were less often by letter and more often the result of police raids and round-ups – Van Tijn's team took on the additional task of providing 'Help for the Departing'. They sourced and distributed blankets, coats, sanitary towels, nappies and toothpaste to those who were called up or arrested. And they organised the dispatch of food parcels to Westerbork. Should they have done this? Was it helping the Germans deport people? Yet if they had not, people would still have been picked up and taken away. Just without a coat.

Grete was aware that the exemption for her work would eventually come to an end. She could see that the Germans would come for all of them in time, and then they wouldn't need a Jewish Council any more. And her time would be up long before that, because she was only part of the administrative staff. So she took it seriously when a friend and her husband made a very generous offer. They were willing to hide Mirjam.

The friend had worked for Alfred and was Jewish, but her husband was not. They were, therefore, at least for now, relatively safe (though many mixed couples would later be forced to choose between deportation and sterilisation). They lived an unobtrusive life in a modest house in the Amsterdam suburbs, and they had room for one small child – my mother was nine by this point – whom they could pass off as their own, or as a niece. But there was no question of taking the rest of the family. There simply wasn't space. They would all be caught almost immediately.

Grete agonised over the decision. It was at times like this that she found making all the decisions alone, without Alfred, particularly burdensome. It was up to her now to keep the girls safe, to somehow ensure their survival. She told Ruth how she had gone back and forth over it. There wasn't an obvious place for them all to hide, nor an easy cover story. So she could see what might happen if they stuck together. That they would all be seized, that they might all be murdered. Hiding Mirjam *could* save her from that fate. But to break the family up? And expose Mirjam to an alternative danger, and the rest of them, if she was discovered?

There were stories of Jews being sent to the worst camps if they were caught hiding, or even being shot, having first been made to dig their own graves. Her friends who had made such a generous offer were risking their own lives as well. And Grete would have to part with her youngest. She decided not to. Given all that followed, it's impossible to say whether she was right.

The choice made, the family began to prepare for what they knew would soon be their own arrest. Ruth, for instance, asked a non-Jewish friend, Tina van den Bijllaardt, if she would look after a few of her childhood 'treasures' – her Poesie books, the records of the Joy and Glee Club, a few photos, a few postcards. And Tina agreed, even though it was dangerous. In fact, even having Ruth in the house was dangerous. Tina's parents knew what their daughter was doing, and Ruth thinks that they would have hidden her as well as her treasures, if they could have. But they were a working-class couple with only a small two-bedroom apartment, so it just wasn't possible.

Meanwhile, Grete packed. Jews had to have their luggage ready, because arrest could come at any moment. The 'Help for the Departing' team was giving advice to deportees on what to include, and naturally she followed it. To start with, that meant packing rucksacks rather than suitcases, because anything they took they were going to have to carry themselves. And that included the children carrying their own bags. There was an endless list of items that might be useful, but it wouldn't do to make the rucksacks too heavy.

So part of Grete's plan was for them all to wear several layers of winter clothes, together with sturdy shoes and a thick overcoat. This saved room in the rucksacks for toiletry essentials – soap, toilet paper, a toothbrush, a wash cloth, insect repellent, aspirin and diarrhoea tablets – along with two blankets each, and pillows, plus a penknife, writing materials and a cheap watch for the family.

The advice for the departing was also to place a bread bag and water bottle in the middle of each rucksack, and 'to bring food for three days (rye bread in cellophane wrap without butter or jam, a terrine of butter, a piece of cheese, tea, chocolate, chewing gum, condensed milk or milk powder)'. A little German money and a diversion, such as a favourite book, were also suggested.

The Wieners' packed bags, and Betty's too, waited by the door for the Germans to come.

The tension was almost unbearable, as news came of one police raid after another, of one friend after another rounded up. When arrest came, it was experienced by many families almost as a relief.

Towards the end of May 1943, David Cohen and the Jewish Council leadership were told by Aus der Fünten of the SS that they would have to provide the names of 7,000 Council employees for deportation. If they did not, they would 'face such measures as the Jews of the Netherlands had never even imagined'. After registering futile protests, Cohen and his co-chairman agreed. This surely was a great error of both practical and moral judgement.

Practically, the argument for carrying out the order was that not to do so would be worse. But how, really, could it be much worse? And by May 1943 they realised this, they understood that death awaited many of the 7,000 they listed. Or at least they should have, notwithstanding that Cohen was still astonishingly naive about the Germans even at this late point.

The Council leaders reasoned that if the Germans chose the deportees at random, not only might they arrest more people, they might also choose people who were vital to the Council's continued efforts, efforts they believed were still serving the Jews. Yet this reasoning, inevitably, pulled them all into subjective judgements about the value of individuals. It left room for favouritism and nepotism. It was a grotesque calculation to make, even at the point of a gun.

There were chaotic scenes at the Council offices as staff carried index cards back and forth, some of them spotting their own names on the deportation list. Van Tijn handed in her resignation, which was refused, and engaged in a furious row with Cohen which broke their relationship, leaving a bitterness they both took with them to the grave. By the time the terrible task had been completed, Grete knew her stamp of exemption, the one keeping the family off the list, would not be valid for long. It would not be long before the Nazis knocked on her door and she and the girls would have to go with them. Evacuated to the East.

On 10 June 1943, my mother celebrated her tenth birthday, and Grete gave her a large book, a rich treasury of facts for young people, full of black and white pictures. *De Vaderlandse Geschiedenis in een Notedop.* Dutch History in a Nutshell. Mirjam didn't get time to read much of it. It was too big for the rucksacks. And on Sunday, 20 June 1943, the time for the rucksacks finally arrived.

The first warning came early in the morning, as early as 3.30 a.m. There were sounds in the street. Muffled ones, but enough to wake up Grete, enough to wake up Ruth. The soft but unmistakable sound of footsteps, bootsteps actually, on the pavement. A car stopping, muted voices, then silence. Grete and Ruth went to the window and, seeing nothing untoward, tried to calm each other down. A half-hour went by and the noises began again, a little louder now. And, returning to the window, it was no longer possible to mistake what was going on. There were soldiers everywhere.

A pause, and then, in the distance, a broadcast of some kind, coming nearer, getting louder. 'Achtung! Achtung! All Jews need to get ready with their hand luggage! The Aryan population is not allowed to leave their homes! Police orders are to be obeyed!' This message, over and over again.

Inside the apartment, Ruth woke her sisters and Betty, while Grete completed the packing, adding the food they would take, filling the water bottles. Eva asked to bring a sketchbook, along with colouring pencils; Ruth took a 1943 pocket diary she had won in a magazine competition but hadn't used. Everyone got dressed in the three layers of clothes that had been left out for them. Eva recalled being 'panic stricken and terribly afraid', but Ruth thought they were more 'dazed'. And while 'relief' wasn't quite the right word, there was a feeling that at least the waiting in trepidation had come to an end. That this was it.

My mother remembered eating a rather odd breakfast, 'with all sorts of unusual things because we thought we might as well. The things one keeps for special occasions, one might as well eat them.' Betty later recounted that for at least one of the delicacies there was a different explanation. It was her ninth anniversary of working for the Wiener family and she had asked an Aryan woman to buy the household some strawberries, as a treat, so that they could all celebrate. But Jews weren't allowed such things. They were prohibited from shopping in the markets that sold strawberries. Betty realised that, along with all their other troubles, there might be further punishment if they were caught with the forbidden fruit.

That is why, as the soldiers outside divided up their lists and split into pairs, and two of them made their jackbooted way up the stairs to the apartment, the Wieners were sitting at the breakfast table in three layers of clothes, eating strawberries.

At the door, the soldiers read the list – Margarete Wiener, Ruth Wiener, Eva Wiener, Mirjam Wiener, Betty Lewin – and demanded to see everyone's papers. One of them asked Betty if she was an Aryan, but then saw the 'J' stamped on her ID card. Grete tried showing Alfred's war medals, but the soldiers were unimpressed. They counted the family members. One, two, three, four, five. The family must close the windows, bring the front-door key with them, and be downstairs in ten minutes.

At that tense moment, an air-raid siren sounded. Betty asked if perhaps they ought to wait until the air raid was over. To this one of the soldiers responded by shouting: 'Enough with your Jewish excuses! Stop them or I will make you get a move on.'

Then the officers left in order to go and collect the other Jewish tenants in the building.

Ten minutes later, there they were, the family, one, two, three, four, outside the apartment with their rucksacks, ready to be taken. Ruth found it odd just to shut the front door and leave behind everything they still possessed, not even being able to give it away.

After all the hurrying, they were now left waiting on the pavement for what seemed an age. A small crowd of neighbours gathered, and my mother spotted a young friend among them. And as the soldiers finally began to herd the arrested families together and move them along, she had the presence of mind to tell her friend where her scooter was, and to take it.

Fortunately, she also had the presence of mind not to ask: 'Where's Betty?'

Betty from Nottingham

When I was a young boy, we'd often take holidays that involved long car journeys. We visited the Lowlands of Scotland three times, for instance. Since my father didn't drive – he would have been a terrible driver, daydreaming about Wittgenstein as the traffic lights changed – we needed places for my Mum to stop on the way. Somewhere in the Midlands, preferably.

So, more than once, we stayed with someone we always knew as 'Betty from Nottingham', and her sister Kathy. They were kindly, seemingly perfectly ordinary, people. Betty was a state-registered mental-health nurse, and I'd get her to talk about her work. Mostly I was interested in the fact that Britain's leading pharmacy chain, Boots the Chemists, and the legendary outlaw Robin Hood came from Nottingham, and so did Kathy and Betty. As it turned out, the link between Robin Hood and Betty was stronger than I appreciated.

As was the link between Betty and my Mum. In addition to our holiday visits, Betty would sometimes come to stay with us in Hendon, and on birthdays there would always be a card, and occasionally also a present from Nottingham. I slowly began to appreciate that Betty thought of herself as part of our family, that she referred to my grandfather as Papa Wiener, and that my mother thought of her in that way too.

Exactly who she was, though, remained hazy to me. But now I have the full story, I realise that even my mother's understanding of who Betty Lewin really was wasn't complete. For the person I knew as Betty from Nottingham, and my mother thought of as Betty from Amsterdam, was also secretly someone called Jo Bosch.

Betty had joined the Wiener family in 1934, almost as soon as Alfred and Grete had set up home in Jan van Eijckstraat. Brought up in Germany, living in Berlin, she had understood immediately what the rise of Hitler meant for Jews like her, and, in 1933, decided that she had to leave.

She hadn't had an easy time of it. She was twenty-one years old and a refugee without money, contacts or protection, hers a common Nazi-era story alongside those of murder and imprisonment. She had replied to a newspaper advert looking for a domestic servant to work in France, and had ended up in a series of jobs that had gone wrong. One employer suddenly announced that they were going away and dismissed her without warning; another had an elegant flat but, as Betty put it, also 'a pet dog that had more rights than I did'. The dog had a daily bath, while Betty could only wash in the kitchen sink.

Deliverance appeared to arrive in the form of an invitation, eagerly accepted, to go to Eindhoven in the Netherlands, to rejoin the family Betty had been employed by in Berlin. They too had fled, but to Holland rather than France. Unfortunately they were struggling as badly as Betty. It became difficult for them even to pay for food, and the local shops wouldn't extend credit to refugees. Before too long, the family had given up the fight and decided to return to Germany. The risks posed by the Nazis seemed preferable to their immediate, and increasingly desperate, poverty.

But Betty didn't agree with this calculation, and she wasn't going to go back. Instead, she availed herself of the temporary accommodation being provided for refugees by the Jewish community in Amsterdam. Twice a week, she was given a list of job vacancies, and one of these lists said that a Dr Wiener was seeking a home help. On 20 June 1934, she moved in with Alfred, Grete, Ruth, Eva and one-year-old Mirjam.

And, just as it was for the girls, the next six years were happy, safe and content. With Alfred so often away, and Grete engaged in both her husband's professional life and her own refugee work, Betty was a big presence in the life of the three Wiener sisters. She was, by all accounts, pretty strict, but also well-loved. In addition to childcare, Betty helped Grete with the shopping, cleaning and cooking.

Her importance to the family was only to increase. When the Germans invaded in May 1940 and Alfred was cut off in Britain, Grete relied upon Betty more and more for adult company and advice. And the girls needed her even more, because Grete now had a paid job. As restrictions on Jews increased, ordinary tasks – cooking with fewer available ingredients and less money, shopping when markets were closed to Jews, keeping the children occupied with no parks or pools – became harder.

Like the rest of the family, Betty had to fill in the questionnaires, and have her photograph taken for ID, showing her ear to the camera, having a 'J' stamped on the resulting card. But, unlike the rest of the family, she didn't have a stamp of exemption. And when the first call-ups to 'work in Germany' were issued – call-ups that were in fact a summons to Westerbork, and a prelude to death – Betty was one of the earliest recipients. She went to the Jewish Council offices and asked what to do about it, and was told, 'You will have to go.' This sort of advice is what critics most hold against the Council.

Grete had a different plan. She found Betty unpaid work with the Council, one of the hundreds of jobs Van Tijn had created in order to protect as many Jews as possible, for as long as possible. Betty would use her sewing skills to 'help the departing', and those in camps. All day, for no money, she mended clothes and linen that had been donated, and which the Council then passed on to Westerbork and to those in need who were destined for Westerbork.

The strain was terrible. The job was six days a week, Sundays as well as weekdays, and it started with a long journey for which Betty was only sometimes able to use Mirjam's scooter. Even when the 'family Rolls-Royce' was at her disposal rather than Ruth's, the travelling was sufficiently tiring that she would get help from passing cyclists who would push her along. She always feared that even the scooter would one day be confiscated. After coming home from a full day of work, Grete and Betty then had the housework and the cooking to do. Ruth tended her younger sisters while the adults were out, but they still needed attention when the adults came home.

In addition to the physical burden, there was also the guilt. Betty felt, she said, 'deeply ashamed' that she now had an exemption that her friends did not have, and that she wasn't able to do anything to help them. 'Never again have I heard from them,' Betty lamented after the war; 'they shared the fate of the six million people who were killed.'

Perhaps it was because of this that, despite the weight of her two jobs, Betty now took on another. And a second identity which my mother, to her dying day, never knew about. She started to raise money for the Dutch resistance. To support her work, she was supplied, through a friend, with secret lodgings and with a fake ID card.

During the day, she was Betty Lewin, a Jewish woman who wore a yellow star, shopped in the few stores available to Jews, and sewed for Jewish prisoners. At night, she was Jo Bosch, Aryan woman and resistance fundraiser. All the activists who had gone underground required identity and ration cards and somewhere to stay, and it was all very expensive. Jo Bosch's job was to find donations. Meanwhile, she was herself encouraged by 'the organisation' to stay 'legal', to remain Betty Lewin, for as long as possible.

This double life was very risky. The risk wasn't just being caught as 'Jo', but also remaining as 'Betty'. In the spring of 1943, for instance, the lists of Council staff were constantly being reviewed, at German insistence, in order to reduce numbers. During one of these reductions, Betty lost her exemption, and only got it back at the last moment. Then there was a round-up in the city centre, with the bridges over the canals hauled up so that no one could escape. Betty managed to retreat to Jo Bosch's lodgings for a few days, and camped out until she felt that it was safe to return to her Council work.

And then finally, on 20 June 1943, nine years to the day after Betty's arrival in the Wiener household, the soldiers came to the door at 25 Westerscheldeplein with their list. There was no easy way out. Betty realised that if she presented her Jo Bosch ID, she might not be believed. Her real name, Betty Lewin, was on the German list, after all, so they would be suspicious if Jo appeared and Betty did not. Her punishment would surely be much worse. Yet if she was believed, things wouldn't be much better. Then she would be an Aryan who had stayed overnight in the home of a Jew. Again, the punishment might be worse. Or at least more immediate.

So Betty experienced the supreme irony of being asked by the soldier at the door whether she was an Aryan, and disabusing him of this idea by showing him her Lewin ID card, with the 'J' stamped on it. 'We were like mice caught in a trap,' she said later.

When the soldiers had left, and the ten-minute warning period was almost up, Betty took the three girls downstairs with their blankets and went back inside to collect her own rucksack, water bottle and bread bag. And as she did so, she said, 'there seemed to be an inner voice saying to me: "Don't go".' She listened to it.

With her coat on, her bread bag hanging from her shoulders and a handbag under her arm, she left the apartment and crept up to the attic that belonged to the downstairs tenants. The attic had a toilet and she hid in that, careful not to make a sound. She could hear commotion in the hallway downstairs, with the Germans cursing and shouting at the Wieners and the other Jewish occupants that they weren't moving quickly enough. She readied herself for discovery at any moment. She knew there would be terrible consequences. Yet, extraordinarily, she heard the front door close with a bang, and there was silence.

The Germans were famously thorough, and it seems almost unbelievable that they should have departed without all the Jews on their list. They were, however, also used to being obeyed without question. They had said 'raus', and they assumed everybody would, as it were, 'raus'. It was the one chink in their armour. And Betty had found it.

Betty sat on the toilet in the attic for what seemed like an age, and then went back down the stairs to the flat, crawling on her hands and knees to avoid being seen at the window by any patrols outside. Fortunately, she had left the flat door ajar – the Germans now had the keys: if it had been closed, she would have been locked out – so she was able to get back in, and there she waited until the guards outside left.

At about six in the evening, just carrying her handbag, just Amsterdam's Jo Bosch returning from the office after work, she headed to Jo Bosch's lodgings for her first night underground. Betty Lewin's first escape from the Nazis had been successful.

———

Betty had received from the resistance what amounted to about £2,000 in today's money, but this wouldn't last all that long. She would need to find a job. The first one she obtained – as a charlady going twice a week to the premises of a tailor in west Amsterdam – didn't last because her employer became suspicious. But then she got a job working from 9 a.m. to 2 p.m. with a German couple living in south Amsterdam, one of whom was Jewish but the other not. Since Jo Bosch was an Aryan Dutchwoman, she had to pretend that she hardly understood a word the German couple spoke to her, a deception she rather enjoyed.

She also enjoyed her journeys to and from work, since she walked through the Vondelpark, the city's beautiful urban park with its rose garden and teahouse, which Jews were forbidden from entering. She liked the park itself, of course, but the 'daily walk meant double pleasure and satisfaction for me since I was misleading the Master Race'.

Then something happened to Betty, an ordinarily unthreatening thing that in her position was very dangerous indeed. She fell ill. Like many people in hiding, she wasn't quite sure what to do about it. Seeking medical help involved interaction with authority and with strangers, both of which were risky. But her sore throat and inflammation of the gums steadily got worse. Her mouth became so painful she couldn't eat anything, and eventually couldn't swallow either. Her friends thought she might have diphtheria. She would have to consult a doctor.

Eventually, her resistance colleagues found someone who was reliable and his advice was reassuring. It was hand, foot and mouth disease, a virus, and it would pass by itself. In the meantime, he said, she should eat grapes. Relieved as she then was, Betty was still complaining about the price of Dutch wartime grapes years later.

No sooner was she well, than a new challenge faced her. In October 1943, her landlady needed the room at her lodgings back, and Betty had to find somewhere else to live. Fortunately, a woman she had met through work was willing to offer accommodation. She was financially well off and the attic room she provided was very comfortable, but there was a wrinkle in the arrangement. The woman's husband was a German soldier, and his daughter worked for the Wehrmacht. The house was full of German officers.

By this point, Betty was so accustomed to being Jo Bosch that, she said, 'I would have been able to reel off all the details about my identity if I had been woken up from sleep.' She didn't feel afraid of meeting all these Germans; indeed, she sometimes felt the whole situation quite natural, almost forgetting that she was living there illegally, that she was underground.

The feeling, however, was illusory. And it would disappear when she was doing her latest resistance work, distributing illegal newspapers. Then the sense of danger would be very sharp, and that sense was well-founded.

On Thursday, 13 January 1944, Betty went to her domestic work as usual and then, at 2 p.m., she headed off, as she had often before, to meet her resistance contact and collect her newspapers. Out of the blue, two men in civilian clothes appeared. Gestapo. They demanded identity cards. And then: 'You will follow us to Gestapo headquarters.'

Arriving at the building in south Amsterdam, two minutes' walk from 16 Jan van Eijckstraat, Betty and her contact were taken to the top floor and locked in separate rooms.

The moment she was alone, Betty opened her handbag and looked for anything that might incriminate her. The only possession she worried about was her front-door key, which might lead them to her home and enable them to search her flat. She hid the key behind a big set of shelves. Then she started looking around for a means of escape.

There was a door onto the roof, but that was locked. It did, however, feature a small, high, sliding window. Betty thought, as she was small herself, she might just about fit through it. If she did, she would be out on the roof, and free. After all, in neighbouring Jan van Eijckstraat, as in most Amsterdam streets, you could go from one house to another across the roofs. Just as Nico Knapper did, when he used to visit Sammy Cohen of the Joy and Glee Club. Betty decided to give it a go.

Summoning all her strength, she swung herself up and forced herself through the opening. Then she jumped down onto the flat roof. Frightened and excited, she hadn't considered that the Gestapo building's roof wouldn't be like neighbouring ones. It was cut off from the others. It did not offer an escape route. 'I was now standing on the roof, cold and trembling, my stockings and my coat were torn, and try as I might I could not climb back in.'

Just then, she heard the key in the door. An officer had come to fetch her for interrogation. When he saw that the room was empty and spotted Betty outside the window, he delivered himself of a line that will reassure the writers of both sitcoms and Hollywood movies about the authenticity of their dialogue. With a sneer, the Nazi officer declared: 'You thought you could escape. But that does not happen with the Gestapo.'

Refusing to unlock the door, he took Betty's hands and dragged her back through the window. When she dropped onto the floor, head first, he pulled her up and took her off to be questioned.

Her interrogators were two members of the NSB, the Dutch Nazis. In Betty's view, their hatred for Jews and the resistance was even more intense than that of the Germans. She told them that her name was Jo Bosch and gave as her address the one on her identity card – the original Jo Bosch lodgings. They immediately replied that she was 'a damned Jewish liar'. They told her that they knew her name. Her initials were 'B. L.'

It was, said Betty, 'a slap in the face'. The Gestapo hadn't happened upon her by accident, nor did they catch her in their net while fishing for her contact. It was her that they had been looking for, and she had been betrayed by someone with enough inside knowledge to provide her real name.

With all such betrayals there were many individuals who might be responsible. A double agent, someone themselves threatened with torture or death and forced to give up information, someone with both a grudge and a hunch. It was what made the whole thing so dangerous. Betty never did find out who was to blame.

The interrogation over for now, the two men searched her handbag, took all her money (a fair bit of cash), and sent her off to spend the night in the Marnixstraat prison, a ten-minute lorry ride away. She was placed in a cell with a plank bed, a chair, a washbowl, a toilet, and walls covered with names, threats and farewell messages. A woman came in, searched Betty, and took away her scarf, gloves and shoes to prevent her from trying to kill herself. But Betty wasn't so easily defeated. She somehow managed to keep concealed twenty aspirins that she had smuggled in.

After a broken night, woken repeatedly by banging cell doors, Betty was roused early and given a small piece of soap, a towel, an iron comb, and a little water for her washbowl. Later, an officer came in with a mug of coffee and the day's rations – four slices of bread. But Betty's thoughts weren't of food. They were of escape. She tried persuading the prison officer to let her out of her cell, so that she might help him with his rounds, an astonishing thing to have attempted. It didn't work. Whether or not the officer perceived her real intent, he told her that she would soon be returned to the Gestapo, so she wouldn't have time.

Back in Gestapo HQ, Betty was first taken to the cellar, joining there a dozen other Jews, and then hauled upstairs for further interrogation. Again came the same questions. Who was she really? Where did she really live? Who were her contacts? And a new one – who had provided her with the ration cards she had been using? Betty said it had been a man called Piet. That was all she knew about him. The interrogators shouted a bit, threatened a bit, insulted her a bit, but Jo Bosch stuck to her story.

This time, she was taken to nearby Weteringschans, the notorious Nazi prison for political offenders, where the Frank family would later be brought after their hiding place was discovered. There she managed to hold on to her aspirins through a second search.

The conditions in this prison were even worse than the last one. But there was, at least, company. Fifteen other Jews, who had been arrested in recent days; and between them, one bucket for drinking water, one for washing, and one to use as a toilet. The last was only emptied once a day, by which time the smell was awful. There was food to match – a few slices of bread and two bowls of what

Dolu in the early 1920s with his 'best friend', business partner and brother Bernard

Dolu and Lusia promenading before the war

Lusia with Ludwik and the family's
chauffeur-driven car, 1932

Major Ignacy Schrage and Jadzia,
Lwów, in the late 1930s

The villa on the hill,
12 Herburtów street

Ludwik and Dolu
at the family's
favourite holiday hotel,
Patria, in 1939

General Władysław Anders
who led the family to freedom

Dolu's commission to go to
Yangiyul, signed by General
Anders, 1943

DOWÓDZTWO POLSKICH SIŁ ZBROJNYCH
w Z.S.S.R.

L.dz. 52.0.35......
Buzułuk 7.1.1942...

                    Z a ś w i a d c z e n i e

          Niniejszym stwierdzam,że okaziciel niniejszego podpo-
rucznik int. FINKELSTEIN Adolf udaje się do m. Jangi - Jul jako
kwatermistrz i upełnomocniony do załatwiania wszelkich spraw
intendenckich,związanych z organizacją i dyslokacją polskich jed-
nostek wojskowych na terytorium SAWO.

          Władze wojskowe, N.K.W.D., administracyjne i kolejowe
proszę o okazanie podporucznikowi int.FINKELSTEINOWI Adolfowi
wszelkiej pomocy.-

                              DOWÓDCA POLSKICH SIŁ ZBROJNYCH
                                      w Z. S. S. R.

                                    / A n d e r s /
                                      Generał dywizji

Dolu, Lusia and
Ludwik in Tel Aviv,
2 April 1945

Ludwik and Lusia
in Hendon in the
early 1950s

Ludwik on Friday evening with (left to right) me, Anthony and Tamara, 1970

Lusia outside our family home in the early 1970s and about to go shopping

Mirjam and Ludwik
on their wedding day

Mirjam with Ludwik. Dad is wearing a jacket and tie on the beach

Mirjam and Ludwik out to an engineering profession dinner in the early 2000s

was effectively hot water, though one was designated coffee, and the other, soup.

After two days in the cell – with a daily half-hour of fresh air in the courtyard, walking in a circle, threatened with a beating if anyone spoke – Betty was called for her third interrogation.

Almost from the beginning, the interrogators – a German now with the two Dutch Nazis – were shouting at her. She was a damned liar. They knew the road she was living on. What was the number? What was the number? What was the number? She didn't break, but it made no difference. Betty heard later that they searched every house in the street until they found the family she was staying with. They had pulled them in to Gestapo headquarters too. But all the couple said was that they thought she was a Dutch Aryan called Jo Bosch.

Furious at her refusal to crack, the German officer dragged Betty down to the basement and opened the door of a tiny room. It was pitch-dark. It was ice-cold. It stank. 'We will cure you of lying,' he said. 'Twenty-four hours here and you will not be going back to work for your Germans any more.'

Betty was near breaking point now. Spare me the torture and just shoot me, she said. 'My only crime is that I was born a Jewess. Do you not have a mother? Do you not have a sister? Do they not raise some pity in you?' The officer looked at her. The Führer, he said stiffly, had not ordered or entitled him to shoot her. He took her back to her cell with the other women.

When the door slammed behind her, Betty collapsed. She couldn't face another interrogation like that, and that night she couldn't sleep. She decided to take the aspirin tablets. Perhaps they would kill her, perhaps they would simply render her too ill to answer any more questions. The pills did the trick. At first she was very sick. A doctor came and, pointlessly, a monk too. But slowly she recovered, and by the time she was well enough to sit up, it was to receive the news that all the women in the cell, her included, would be sent to Westerbork.

Never mind the monk – what, really, was the point of the doctor? For a woman they were now going to send to a camp, which was just a stop on the way to the gas chambers? Everything the Nazis did had to be done in an orderly fashion and to the book. Except when it didn't have to be done in an orderly fashion and to the book, which was a lot of the time. It was as puzzling as it was obscene.

At 9.30 on the Thursday morning, a week after she had been arrested, Betty stood in the prison courtyard together with eighty other prisoners, assembled in rows of four, carefully watched and counted over and over again by armed SS officers. It rained non-stop. It was miserable.

Then they were led under guard to two waiting trams, and set off for the railway station. Betty looked out of the window as she passed through Amsterdam, 'the beautiful city, which I would never see again'. She felt entirely without hope.

———

At the station, the prisoners were counted again, before being led to special train compartments that had been reserved for them. Each compartment was watched by four armed SS men. The ones watching Betty's seemed extremely friendly. They were young and personable, and sought to engage the prisoners in conversation. They listened intently as some of their captives talked about how and where they had gone underground, and how they had been betrayed. They offered to post any messages to friends and relatives. It felt comforting and seemed human, but it was a classic espionage technique. It's very possible that Betty's own arrest had been enabled by this sort of approach to some earlier prisoner.

But then came a stroke of luck. After about two hours, at around 3.30 p.m., the train came to a stop in Assen, rather than arriving in Westerbork as had been planned. The passengers were told that they would have to alight. Lorries would now take them on a final twenty-minute journey to the camp.

Again the prisoners were lined up in rows and counted. As was quite common, a group of spectators gathered in the square to watch the show. This time, as it happens, most of them were schoolchildren on their way back from class, satchels on shoulders, either strolling home or standing, gawping. There was also a parked bus, with passengers waiting to be taken to the next village. The square wasn't packed, but there was a confusion of people. Minor, but sufficient for what Betty did next.

The prisoners were ordered to approach the lorries and get in. As Betty was doing so, an SS officer screamed at her. 'Old people first!' Betty climbed down, and found herself last in line. Then she realised that she was still holding the luggage of one of the older people – she had taken it in order to help out – and was in danger of being separated from the lady it belonged to. She started walking back down the line to reunite luggage and owner. And suddenly she noticed that she was no longer surrounded by other prisoners. She was surrounded by the onlookers. She was surrounded by the schoolchildren.

Betty's tiny physique came in handy again, as it had when she climbed out of the Gestapo window. She hid behind a tall man. Then, hurriedly, she tore off her headscarf, took off her glasses, rolled her stockings down to her knees, and put her handbag under her arm like a school bag. Without thinking, for delay would have been fatal, she started walking off down the street with the children.

She didn't turn round. At any moment she expected to hear a shout, or the sound of a gun being fired. But Betty reasoned that she had nothing to lose. The lorry would have taken her to the site of her murder and, she said, 'I preferred a quick end to a slow death.' She kept going. She walked 'some kilometres', expecting death with every step. And then she began to realise death wasn't coming. She began to appreciate that the guards weren't following.

It was Betty's third escape attempt from the fascists and, for the second time, she had been successful.

———————

Even years after the war, Betty didn't say who helped her now, but by the evening she had enough money for a train ticket and was heading back to Amsterdam. There she received new identity papers and ration cards, and advice to leave the capital. She hid with a Dutch family, did some housework in return, and in the evenings wrote an account in shorthand of all her experiences.

In the last, hard days of the war – as the Dutch struggled for lack of food in what was known as the 'hunger winter' – she returned to Amsterdam, working as a seamstress in a clothes factory, and living in an attic with four others who had also gone underground. It was here that victory found Betty Lewin, home help and resistance hero.

And in 1947, with Alfred's assistance and a British passport, Betty from Berlin, Betty from Amsterdam, Jo Bosch, acquired her final identity as Betty from Nottingham.

DAD

Into Exile

There were standing orders on how Soviet troops – members of the People's Commissariat for Public Security – should execute deportations, and the NKVD officers and militiamen who knocked on my father's door in Lwów on 13 April 1940 followed their instructions conscientiously.

Ludwik, his mother Lusia and his grandmother, Dolu's mother Charlotte, were all asleep in the family apartment when the soldiers arrived. It had been an anxious couple of days as they waited for the news of Dolu that they had been promised. But, despite what had happened in February to some other families, they hadn't been given any reason to expect arrest themselves. The knock had come as a surprise.

The soldiers were ordered to break the door down if they met resistance, but Lusia opened it and let them in. They assembled the family in one room and, as instructed, searched Lusia, Ludwik and Charlotte individually to ensure none of them were carrying hidden weapons. After that, one NKVD officer kept them under guard while the others searched the apartment for guns, foreign currency and 'counter-revolutionary literature'.

Having checked that the people on their list were all present, the next part of the protocol was to inform them of the deportation order. They would be taken, the officers told Lusia, 'to meet your husband in another part of the Soviet Union'. This, she was assured, would be somewhere close to Lwów. The purpose of this lie (for it was a lie) was so that the officers could enforce the deportation as they had been commanded. 'Throughout the operations, firm and decisive action shall be taken, without the slightest excitement, noise and panic.'

My father remembered that while his grandmother Charlotte was by this point 'somewhat hysterical', he had been 'rather calm'. For a boy, 'it seemed like an adventure'. He helped Lusia pack. Each family was allowed to take with them a trunk, 'not exceeding 100 kilograms in weight', filled with clothes, bedding, dishes, kitchen utensils and enough food for a month. Ludwik reminded Lusia that Dolu would need an extra suit, because he had left just with the clothes he was wearing. And to the collection of food Lusia had put in the trunk, he added a tin of sardines. Dolu liked sardines.

Before deportees left their homes, they were always given an inventory of the contents of the property, often presented later as if it constituted consent to be exiled. The list handed to Finkelstein Amalia Isaacovna (as the document called Lusia) was scribbled in Russian, full of misspellings, rough and incomplete. A writing desk, two dining tables, a glass cupboard, a couch (soft), a crockery cupboard, four wardrobes, three beds, two mirrors, eight Viennese chairs, six other chairs, one radio, two wall clocks and a kitchen table. All this signed for by the 'Head of the Passport Office', and countersigned by two neighbours who had been called in as witnesses. It was an entirely useless piece of paper.

And then it was time to go. It hadn't taken long, the whole thing. Within what seemed to Ludwik no time, the three of them were ushered out of the apartment, the door shut behind them, and they were on their way to another life. Or, to put it more truthfully, on their way to no sort of life at all.

———

The moment Lusia, Ludwik and Charlotte reached the bottom of the stairs and came out onto Słoneczna street, they realised that the whole town was on the move. Tens of thousands of people had been woken in the night, tens of thousands had packed trunks, tens of thousands were being expelled from their homes and sent to 'another part of the Soviet Union'.

And now the Finkelsteins were loaded onto the back of an open-topped lorry, which set off very slowly towards Lwów goods station. The speed was determined by the fact that the city, especially the narrow roads leading to the station, had become a gigantic traffic jam.

Among those caught in this jam were dozens of their friends and relatives. Linka (the wife of Dolu's brother Bernard) and her two children, Marta and Irena, for instance. And Ludwik's friend Aldona, with her mother Jadzia Schrage. The April deportation took the families of everyone who, like Dolu, had already been arrested for political 'crimes', or, like Ignacy Schrage, that dashing major, had been captured in battle. Other deportees had been swept up because their relatives had fled abroad.

As a result, unlike other waves of deportation, there were few able-bodied men in the group. Women and children predominated. And there were many old and sick people – paralysed, say, or otherwise disabled. Ludwik's grandmother Charlotte was seventy-eight years old and a diabetic, and it didn't matter to the Soviets in the slightest.

Sitting on the back of the lorry, Lusia and Ludwik had already begun to sense that they weren't being taken to meet Dolu, certainly not anywhere nearby. They did not yet know for sure where exactly they were going. But they could begin to guess from what they knew about other people's experience that 'another part of the Soviet Union' meant Siberia. In fact, they were to be sent 5,000 kilometres to the east, to work the land.

They received no penal sentence, were charged with no crime. Their destination was not a prison. However, the difference between exile and imprisonment would prove hard to detect. They were being sent somewhere that they didn't wish to go, would not be allowed to leave, and couldn't escape. And there they would be assigned work they would be forced to do and would not be rewarded for. They would be free people, just without any freedom.

Ordinarily, the Soviets were good at dreaming up crimes for which to convict people who had done nothing wrong. They were experts at judicial processes that involved no judging and no process. Sentencing was a Soviet art form, with the length selected almost at random and detached from any reasoning at all. Yet in the cases of Lusia, Ludwik and Charlotte, in the cases of the tens of thousands exiled from Lwów on that April night, in the cases of hundreds of thousands of Polish deportees, even this pretence of justice was dispensed with.

The exile into which the Finkelsteins were being sent was a permanent one, and it was not accompanied by any explanation, deliberation, or appeal.

There are two ways of understanding the policy to which my family had now fallen victim. The first is that it was the latest example of a form of oppression that has happened to many peoples throughout history. They were displaced to allow others to consolidate their power and engage in economic exploitation.

Nikita Khrushchev – the man directing my father's deportation – was not naive or an idealist. Nor was his boss, Joseph Stalin. They wished to destroy the Polish nation, and to scatter its people. For all their rhetoric, they understood that the annexation of Eastern Poland had been achieved through force and that the elections which had validated it had been rigged. They knew the population would be resentful. Deportation ensured that people feeling this resentment would struggle to find leadership. Nor would there easily be a resurgence of nationalist feelings or independent-mindedness. That was why whole families were deported, and not just the heads of families. Ludwik might have been ten in 1940, but he would not always be ten.

As Khrushchev's officers told the people of Lwów in communal meetings after the deportations:

> This is how we annihilate the enemies of Soviet power. We will use the sieve until we retrieve all bourgeois and kulaks, not only here, but in the entire world. You will never see again those that we have taken away from you. They will disappear over there, as a field mouse.

In many cases, the exiles would die very quickly. They would die on the way to their place of labour, or they would die soon afterwards of exhaustion and disease. That would be fine from a political point of view. It would be positively advantageous. Fewer dissidents and nationalists to worry about.

But while the exiles lived, they would populate the interior of the Soviet Union, furthering the development of areas that were otherwise isolated and poor. They would advance the economic objectives of the state by working the land and feeding its cities with their slave labour.

Yet there is a second way of understanding the deportations. They were an implicit acknowledgement of the flaws of communist ideology. People did not abandon their ambitions, or their middle-class lives, or their nationalist attachments, as the result of some semi-mystical process of enlightenment. Wants, needs and desires didn't miraculously disappear upon the arrival of communism. Humans didn't suddenly take it into their heads to move to deserted villages in order to help the common good. All these good things would have to be forced upon them. Starting by knocking on their front door in the night, carrying a gun.

———

Eventually, the lorry reached the station, the terminal usually used for freight rather than people. The passengers tumbled out and, under guard, were herded into the station and towards the train. As they headed towards the tracks, Ludwik was prodded in the back with a bayonet, fell, and rolled down an embankment. He picked himself up and, with Lusia and his grandmother, climbed in.

They were in a cattle truck. Inside, there was nothing, save for two long wooden shelves to sit or lie on, and a sort of vertical pipe that looked like a very low seat but was actually a hole in the floor to be used as a toilet. The door was shut behind them and, with only the one high, barred window, the wagon was dark. They sat down where they could, and tried to settle.

As their eyes adjusted, Charlotte realised where she was sitting. She had perched herself on what she now could see was the waste pipe. The fur coat that she was wearing was covered in excrement. She stood up. 'Lusia,' she said, 'I don't like it here.' Ludwik and his mother exchanged glances. Of course she didn't like it here. Who liked it here? But what was anyone supposed to do about it? To the amazement of Lusia and my father, Charlotte had an answer to that question.

Though loved by her relatives, Charlotte was considered by them to be, as my father put it, 'spoiled by luxurious living', and a person 'so indecisive' that he remembered Lusia receiving a call from a retailer saying that 'Mrs Finkelstein senior is in the shop trying to find a colour of stockings. Could Mrs Finkelstein junior come and help her choose?' Yet now she knew exactly what she wanted to do, and how she was going to do it.

Lwów goods station was in chaos, the train nowhere near ready to depart, and the prisoners only lightly guarded. The militia were allowing people out of the trucks to use the public latrines. Charlotte started banging on the side of the wagon, demanding to be allowed to go and relieve herself. Eventually, one of the guards responded, and opened the door to let her out.

Despite her age, her infirmity and what everyone in the family thought they knew about her character, Charlotte went to the station toilet, dropped her soiled coat onto the floor, gave the remaining guard her gold watch, and simply walked off.

A couple of hours later, when the guards returned to the truck and started counting, they noticed that the numbers didn't tally. 'Charlotte Finkelstein? Where is Charlotte Finkelstein?' Lusia stepped forward and confidently responded: 'You've miscounted. My name is Amalia Charlotte Finkelstein. You've got me down twice.'

The miserable truth about the Soviet guards became an advantage at this moment. Just as they hadn't cared that Charlotte was seventy-eight and a diabetic, they didn't care that she was missing either. Sounding the alarm, questioning the guard who had let her out, apprehending the officer who had accepted a bribe, it was all too much trouble. They adjusted their list and moved on.

Charlotte's story does not have an entirely happy conclusion. She could not, of course, go home to Słoneczna street. Nor could she go to her brother in the Lwów suburbs, because if the Soviets noticed that she had absconded, Nasio Landes' house was the first place they would look. So she went to live in the country, in the home of her cook Maria Polanska, where Nasio paid her bills and walked the one and a half hours each way to give her a daily insulin shot. What few belongings she had, she had left on the train, and in Soviet Lwów there was no way of replacing any of it. And she felt lonely and worried about the fate of her family.

Yet for all this, when she died in 1942 at the age of eighty, it was of natural causes, in a bed and in relatively civilised surroundings. And that, however modest, was some sort of triumph, at least.

———

Now there were just two of the family in the wagon. Lusia sat on one of the shelves, while Ludwik climbed up to the high, barred opening and stared out at the milling crowds on the platform.

He noticed a girl with a rope, rather incongruously skipping along, dodging prisoners and weeping families. He wondered what she was doing. And then he noticed that with every skip she was chanting. 'I' (skip) 'am' (skip) 'a' (skip) 'scout' (skip) 'and' (skip) 'I' (skip) 'carry' (skip) 'messages'. Ludwik told Lusia, and the two of them managed to get the girl's attention. Could she fetch Lusia's sister, Dorotea? The scout went away to find her.

Another family took advantage of the chaos on the station to pass their baby through the bars. A brave act, as they were unlikely to see their child again. But also a sensible one, since the baby would have been unlikely to survive what was to come. When Dorotea arrived, there could be no question of doing the same with Ludwik. He was too big, it would have been too conspicuous, and with two family members missing, even the Soviets might have started asking questions.

Dorotea was, however, able to pass them some money, having stuffed the rubles into a loaf of bread she had bought from a bystander. They discussed what to do with the few goods and little money that Lusia had left behind. And then they just talked, saying their goodbyes, everyone distraught, even Ludwik's calm now gone, until eventually Lusia said: 'Enough – it's becoming dark. Come tomorrow morning.'

That night, the train left the station. Lusia never saw her sister again.

The moment the train pulled out of Lwów was a terrible one. There were tears, a chilling fear, bewilderment, despair. There were around eleven hundred people spread among sixteen wagons, and the wailing of children and lamentations of old people could be heard from every carriage.

In one respect, Lusia and Ludwik had been fortunate. The waves of deportations were spaced about two months apart, allowing the trains to take a month for the outward journey and at least a month back. The February trains had left in freezing weather, and the biting cold had killed thousands before they reached their destination. The June transport was intolerably hot and many died from the other extreme, stifled to death.

So it was better to be deported in April, although the conditions were miserable enough. There were approximately seventy people in each truck, many sickening, all suffering. There was almost no light, almost no air, barely enough space to lie down. There were lice everywhere. People relieved themselves in the hole in the middle of the truck near where others were sleeping. Some didn't make it all the way to the hole before relieving themselves.

Occasionally the train would stop, and a meagre bread ration would be distributed. But most of the families had packed at least some food, so the bigger problem was a lack of water. Everyone was suffering from terrible thirst, and many were dying. At stops in larger towns, families might pass the body of a mother, or of a child out of a wagon, and then the train would move on, leaving the corpse by the tracks.

Initially the captives hoped that, when the trains halted at stations, they might be able to swap some clothing for a little milk, say, or something else that was fresh. To their horror, they found that the locals were instead begging from them, begging from prisoners, desperate for their bread. It increased the anxiety of the deportees about where they were being taken.

The worst thing about the stops was that it meant there would be starts, for these often jolted the train, throwing passengers from one end of the truck to the other, falling over each other in the dark. And as they travelled like this, the prisoners cursed their fate and speculated about their future. Lusia was 'extremely agitated', talking often of the family's aborted attempt to escape Lwów before the Soviets had come.

So it went on. Stops and starts. Darkness and despair. Hurtling towards who knew where. For three long weeks, transported like animals.

And then, at long last, the train came to a final halt. The passengers climbed out, blinking, into the light. They were in a place called Zhangiztobe. It was in eastern Kazakhstan, the Siberian borderlands. And before they were moved on, they were treated to a little speech about their newly acquired status and how they must leave behind middle-class pretension. 'You are now the new workers and your job is to accommodate yourself to the old workers.'

Then the group was divided into sections to be taken up country. The first leg took a day by lorry, travelling to Vorontsovka, a further 700 kilometres to the north. There they were divided again as they were allocated places to work in the area. Lusia and Ludwik were left as the only two Jews, and Ludwik the only child, among ninety Poles, and spent a further day – now in the heat of May, thirsty, hungry, scared – travelling in ox wagons to their new home. The place where the group was told they would now live. The place where many of them would now die.

Lusia looked out upon the steppes. She could see there was no escape. There was nowhere to go, and no way of going there. She knew that whatever the Soviets were about to force her to do, she had only one real job. She had seen the children fall ill in the cattle truck, seen their bodies left behind as the train trundled on. She would not let that happen to Ludwik. She would struggle and fight and never give in. She would deliver their precious boy, the boy it had been so hard for them to have, back to her Dolu. One day, she would.

The Island of Hunger and Death

'You are an educated woman. We will allocate you to cow milking.' Lusia and Ludwik had arrived at a *sovkhoz*. A Soviet state farm. The highest form of socialist agriculture. And now Lusia would be put to work.

When Stalin had collectivised agriculture, two sorts of farm had emerged. One was the famous *kolkhozy*, the collective farms, groups of smallholdings which, according to the officially approved story, had come together voluntarily and ran as cooperatives. The other form, regarded by the regime as more authentically socialist, was the state farm, managed by government officials. These farms proceeded from the expropriation of large estates.

In practice, there wasn't much difference between them. They were both the result of coercion and had both been an economic disaster. Farmers believed – correctly – that there wouldn't be much of a relationship between the effort they put in and what they received. They also knew that they wouldn't have much control. During the process of collectivisation, food production had collapsed as farmers stopped working. And if they did grow anything, they hid their produce. In both kinds of Soviet farm, workers were sullen and inefficient. In neither the *kolkhoz*, where wages were supposed to vary with production, or the *sovkhoz*, where wages were supposed to be guaranteed, did anyone receive much of anything at all.

The highest form of Soviet agriculture involved freezing and starving and, for the deportees, reluctantly doing what one was told so as to survive for as long as possible. Lusia would later call the Baskermelte ranch to which they had been sent 'an island of hunger and death'.

When the jobs were first handed out to the Poles, Lusia was assigned the milking of cows. This was regarded as one of the more sophisticated tasks, utilising her education. But it was quickly clear that she was hopeless at it. Ludwik tried to help her, holding the tail of the cow, but he had no more clue what he was doing than she did. So, after a couple of days of flailing, she was told that she would be demoted to the lowest category of unskilled labourers.

Her job now was to make adobe bricks out of cow dung. This involved the collection of the dung, the mixing of the dung with water and clay, its formation into bricks for building or heating, then drying and storing the dung bricks they had made. This task, hour after hour, day after day.

The reward was to be hungry and homeless. In these early days, they were almost entirely dependent on a small ration of unsieved flour which they were given as wages. From the flour, under the tutelage of the locals, they could make a sort of unleavened pitta bread. Whether it was the dung or the flour, Ludwik soon developed bad mouth ulcers.

At night, they retreated to the cowshed. The village in which the farm was situated was home to 120 Kazakhs, and the farm had only five buildings. Now there were ninety Poles to accommodate, and nowhere to put them. Since at that time of year the cows were out to pasture, the obvious place for Lusia and Ludwik to live was in their shed.

They soon began to see this as comparative luxury. After a few weeks of dung brick-forming, the hay needed to be made, and the exiled women were sent out onto the steppes to mow and bale. Lusia kept Ludwik with her, of course. She tried never to let him out of her sight. His job was to walk behind the working party and carry their drinking water. And then, at night, they all slept out under the open skies. The experience sounds romantic. In fact, my father said, it was dismal.

For the rest of her life, Lusia kept the secret of her survival in Siberia, and that of my father, in a small plastic bag. I found it only many years after her death. The bag contained a collection of tattered pieces of paper, filled to the edges with scribbled messages in Polish. Every one of them, a letter.

Perhaps the only important difference between Lusia's deportation and a prison sentence was that the Finkelsteins, as free Soviet citizens, could send and receive letters and parcels more freely. And this freedom saved their lives.

Not every member of the family had been arrested, at least for now. Soviet policy was enforced quite inconsistently, and there were still quite a few of Lusia's relatives in Lwów and surrounding villages. Shortly after arriving at the state farm, Lusia wrote to her sister Dorotea, to her favourite brother, Wilhelm, and to her Uncle Nasio, who was looking after both his sister Charlotte and the remaining family resources. It was the end of May before any of them received her letters. They replied immediately. Over the coming year, between them they would send more than ninety letters to Lusia and Ludwik. Dorotea and her husband Szymon (or Szymek as he was commonly known) were particularly assiduous correspondents, sometimes sending several missives in a week.

Dorotea's letter-writing was fuelled by the desperation she felt at her sister's arrest. She describes herself as being like a 'lunatic', unable to sleep, getting up early in the morning and feeling almost immediately the 'first sharp pain of misery'. She understands that her anguish is a burden to her husband and her child, before adding the striking words 'but my love was always greater for you, my sister'.

Together with Wilhelm and Nasio, she began to send parcels of food. These might take a month, or even three months, to arrive, and many never arrived at all. Those that did were vital. In summer, there was little food on the farm; in winter, almost none. Lusia would later say that Dorotea's ability to send the parcels were her and Ludwik's 'great luck, otherwise we would have died of hunger'.

As many as nine parcels at a time might be on their way to Siberia, because, in addition to the inevitable theft and loss, the post office often imposed weight limits. The letters typically ask anxiously whether previous packages have been received, while listing the contents of the ones that had just been posted.

> I just sent you a 3rd parcel since the beginning of March. It consists of 1kg of dried biscuits, 1kg of chocolates, 1kg of sausages, 2kg of sugar, 1kg of cornmeal, white pants and a shirt for Lulu, a kerchief for you and some little things. Today I will make lard; I bought 3kg of pork belly paying 18 rubles per kg. I will enclose the leftover solids in a different can so that it won't spoil the taste of other items. I bought 1kg of excellent plum jam; it will be mailed out with lard in a fourth parcel in March.

If only all the food had arrived, and was in reasonable condition when it did so.

Reasonable, rather than good, condition. Given Lusia and Ludwik's dire circumstances, no one was being fussy. 'Lusia, what condition is the sausage in when you get it? If it is mouldy, take a wet cloth and wipe the mould off. It is still fine to eat.'

The bigger problem was that the mould and the sausage often didn't arrive at all. Dorotea often tells of her dismay upon learning from Lusia that her most recent efforts had come to nothing. 'It caused me heartbreak that you still have not received any parcels,' she wrote in May 1941.

> I met the postman in front of our house and I burst into tears.

Hala [Dorotea's daughter Halina] only just dragged me home. Every parcel I pack with such care, I put so much heart into it and you get nothing. Since January 1st I have 18 receipts, and you only received two of them. A person could go crazy because of this. So many things I sold, so much money I spent, and there is no relief for you. My dear, wonderful sister, God must have mercy for this is our only hope.

When news came later that month from Lusia of the arrival of nine packages, Wilhelm declared that 'today is a joyful day'.

Dorotea's reference to the money she had spent tells its own story. Creating these packages was hard for Lusia's family. Wilhelm, a country landowner but often a city dweller, had only narrowly avoided Dolu's fate of arrest followed by disappearance. The Soviet authorities did not allow him to enter Lwów, and it was often difficult to obtain goods in the surrounding villages. In Lwów itself, supply varied. But even when there were goods in the shops, Dorotea had to pay for the food and clothes they sent. And with what? Her husband had been an attorney. Now he was employed catching rodents for what passed as a living.

Everyone sold what possessions they could in order to buy food for themselves and for Lusia and Ludwik. But the cost of sending the parcels caused a nasty family row. Nasio Landes had control of what remained of Dolu and Lusia's property, partly because he was looking after Charlotte. And Dorotea and Wilhelm believed he wasn't using enough of it to send packages to Siberia. Nasio, meanwhile, was seized of the idea that the war would soon end, and that Lusia and Dolu wouldn't want him to sell all their property. To stave off Lusia's siblings, he pretended that there was an official limit on how many parcels he could send. Predictably, they soon found out this was untrue.

The whole thing had come to a head in early September 1940, when Wilhelm and Dorotea stormed into Nasio's house in Lwów and physically assaulted him. In response, he threatened to report

Wilhelm to the authorities for being in the city illegally. Before it all ended in catastrophe, Dorotea and Wilhelm decided that it wasn't worth it. They reached the conclusion that Nasio was well-meaning but more than a bit of a fool. 'You have no idea what kind of simpleton, dimwit and boor he is,' Szymek wrote. Lusia agreed. 'A moron, that is all,' she declared after it was all over.

———

On the farm, Lusia, always mentally tough, became a warrior. Her spirit was incredible. A certain imperiousness, always present in her personality, gave her a natural authority which even the Soviet administrators might bend to.

The bread store didn't open and Lusia threatened the storekeeper with a weight from the scales until he relented. Lusia fell ill and a supervisor rode a horse right into the shed where she was resting. He demanded she come to work, and her tirade drove him out. She became seen as something of a leader by the other deportees. In their letters home, the other exiles would write of her to their relatives, and they remarked upon it to Dorotea.

Yet Lusia and Ludwik were desperate and miserable. Even with the packages, the hunger, the starvation, was dreadful. When Dorotea did not hear from Lusia, she was sick with worry, fearing that silence meant the worst. At times there might be a gap of two months or more when she heard nothing. But when she did hear, she found the content hard to read. 'Your letter from December 7th completely beat me down. I see there is no end to your suffering.' She frequently told Lusia not to lose heart, that one day all this will be over and she and Dolu will be reunited.

However bad it had been living in the cowsheds and under the open skies, what came next was worse. When the working parties came back from the haymaking, they found themselves once again homeless. The cows had now returned from the fields and reclaimed their lodgings. Lusia was told that she would have to build somewhere to live, using the cow-dung bricks that, earlier in the summer, she had been helping to create.

Together with Ludwik and a group of four or five other women, Lusia set to work building an adobe hut. It wasn't, naturally enough, a skilful piece of work. They created a lean-to against another building, with a sort of wicker entrance porch at the front, and tried to shape a chimney and a window. Both of these were a bit of a disaster. The chimney didn't work properly, and the opening for the window was too big for the tiny amount of glass that was available. This was bad enough in late summer, when they first moved in, but became a serious torment in November, when it started to become colder.

Lusia and Ludwik shared one small room of the shack with four other people. Two were the Pirgo sisters, Dorota and Ewa, their brother Marian Helm-Pirgo having been a municipal architect in Lwów, and an associate of Dolu's when he was on the City Council. The other two were from one of Poland's most famous families. The Finkelsteins lived in their ramshackle home with Countess Potocka and her daughter, Zosia. Each pair possessed a wicker basket in which they tried to sleep.

Winter came. And terrible it was. It began with a calamity. Zosia Potocka fell ill, developing diarrhoea and severe stomach pains. The weather was worsening, but it was still just about possible to move around the village, and Lusia went to see the Soviet farm administration. They needed a doctor, she explained. That would not be possible, the farm manager replied impassively. The nearest doctor would have to come by ox wagon, and it would take a day to send for him, and a day for him to come. He wasn't willing to call him out. Lusia said she feared that, without medical attention, Zosia would die. The manager shrugged. 'Everyone dies. Even great doctors die,' he said.

With nothing to relieve her symptoms or treat her condition, Zosia declined. Soon she began screaming with pain. Lusia saw to it that Ludwik was moved into the small adjacent room inside the shack, with the neighbouring family. But still he could hear everything through the thin wall of dung and clay. Zosia screamed and screamed until eventually, around New Year, she stopped screaming. It took a party of strong men to dig a hole in the hard ground big enough to bury her. She was just twenty-nine years old.

It had already begun to snow, and soon the snow was so deep it was virtually impossible to go outside, even if it was daylight. And it wasn't daylight for long, as it became dark at three in the afternoon. The weight of the snow was so great that the entrance porch to Ludwik and Lusia's hut collapsed, and some men from the farm battled their way to the door to create some sort of opening, a tiny shaft to crawl through. This was needed because once a day someone had to leave the shack to get water.

This job fell to Lusia. She was the only one remotely strong enough to be able to take it on. She had to wear every item of clothing they had in order to be able to withstand the cold. Ludwik would always remember her wearing his coat on her head, as a form of hat. It was, he said, 'a terrible expedition'. The snow on the ground was bad enough, but then there were gale-force winds. You were taking one uncertain step in deep snow after another, all the time facing a blizzard. Some men had made a hole in the ice of the frozen river, and Lusia would have to make her way there, and then, far worse, travel back the considerable distance, carrying the water.

When Lusia told Dorotea of these journeys, her sister pleaded with her to stop. She should melt some snow instead. But Dorotea did not realise that – quite apart from the fear that the snow might not be clean – they couldn't melt snow, because they had nothing to melt it with.

While it had still been possible to move around the farm, Lusia had obtained fuel by leading a couple of raids on the government stock of cow dung. Even then, she had to be careful not to take too much. But once deep winter arrived, such theft went from being imprudent to being impossible. As a result, they couldn't light a fire. The room in which they were living was below freezing almost all the time. And even if they had flour, they couldn't cook it. They were entirely dependent on the parcels Lusia and Ludwik had received in the autumn, shared between the five of them.

The other consequence of their limited water supply and lack of fuel was that it was almost impossible to keep clean. There could be no question of a bath or a shower, obviously, and both Lusia and the Countess felt keenly that they were constantly dirty. Ludwik remembered only washing twice in the entire winter. All five of them were soon covered in lice.

There were no toilets on the farm, even in summer. You had to go in the fields. In winter, they relieved themselves into a tin, since they didn't have a pot of any kind. Then they would crawl to the hut's entrance to dispose of it, somehow, in the snow. It was another reason why Lusia wasn't keen on Dorotea's snow-melting idea.

Ludwik soon became too weak to stand, malnourished and freezing cold as he was. He lay all day in the wicker basket, covered with whatever clothes they still had, except when Lusia needed the clothes for her water-collecting forays. Yet despite this, his mother was determined that she would educate him, and not let his mind waste away along with his body.

She lay by him and taught him the *Iliad* and the *Odyssey* from memory. She instructed him in the plays of Friedrich Schiller, and sang songs to him. He was to become an exceptional linguist, and Lusia laid the foundations for this in Siberia, in the depths of winter, reinforcing the German he had learned when still a toddler, adding a little English into the mix. Ludwik, always a solemn and diligent child, absorbed what he was taught and would never forget it. Neither would the tight bond he formed in these days with his Mamusia, his Mummy, ever loosen.

When Lusia wasn't teaching him, he would read and think. Before they were all snowed in, the Poles had swapped with each other the books that some had brought. The two or three Lusia and Ludwik had ended up with when they could no longer go out, were books of poems. For the rest of his life, my father could recite by heart seemingly endless verses of Polish poetry.

He would also lie in the basket reflecting upon the world and how it worked, and asking questions about it. Lusia would long remind him of the time that she struggled back into the shack with the water, barely alive after making her way through the blizzard, only for Ludwik to greet her with: 'Mamusia, what is the difference between an anode and a cathode?'

Just when it felt as if any more winter would be unendurable, the first signs of spring appeared, and the snow began to recede.

Ludwik rose from his bed, crawled out of the entrance to the shack, and promptly collapsed. He was revived with alcohol. He was suffering from vitamin deficiency and was covered in ulcers and boils. These were quite common among the deportees. They were known as 'Soviet visas', and they stayed on Ludwik's body for years.

My father had barely survived his first winter in Siberia. Many of the others were not so fortunate. Zosia Potocka had been just the first to die. When the thaw began, they buried twelve of the ninety Poles. Lusia realised that another winter like the one just past and they would surely perish too. At around this time, my father recalls encountering a villager who looked surprised to see him. 'Oh, Finkelstein,' he said, 'I thought you had died.' When Ludwik observed that he had, in fact, not died, the man said: 'Oh, never mind. Maybe next year.' My father was eleven years old. That was the carelessness with which human life was regarded.

Why did the Poles keep dying, while the Kazakhs seemed to survive? The question began to obsess Ludwik. While lying in bed thinking, he had put the Finkelsteins' survival down to their defiance, to their spirit of resistance. Now he began to work out that these wouldn't see them through another winter. 'I came to realise that survival very much depended upon the practical things. All the other things were not that significant; it's the practical things – the water, the shelter, the food and so on.'

And at the top of the list was fuel. Lack of fuel meant they had endured bitter cold, and had been unable to cook what little food they had. The Kazakhs had built up reserves of fuel for the winter, while the uninitiated Poles hadn't been aware of the need. So Ludwik applied himself to putting this right. Morning, noon and evening, he collected cow dung. He established, as he later put it, 'one of the best cow dung piles in the village. It was admired! It was beautifully done!' And it set the course of his life. When he later became an engineer, it was because of what he had learned about the importance of the practical.

Now winter was behind them, there was a little more food. Not much, even then, but a little. The Kazakh families were each allowed by the Soviets to possess one cow. Because it was the one part of the farm they owned themselves, it was the one thing they tended with any care. They milked it, made cheese, dried the cheese on the roof, and it could then be eaten with salt. They were willing to swap this for goods that the Poles had brought with them. An item of Lusia's luggage, for example, provided leather for them to make boots. In return, the Finkelsteins got a few tiny pieces of cheese.

During the spring and summer, Ludwik and Lusia twice had meat from the cows. Their neighbours' ox was close to death and they decided to slaughter it. Ludwik watched them do it, and received a piece of it to eat. On another occasion, an ox drowned in the river and, said Ludwik, 'we were lucky enough to get some of the fat from that'.

Besides the cheese and these two pieces of luck, there was the occasional ration of flour that could be used to make what my father always called 'glue', a sort of gruel. It was just about edible with a pinch of the sugar that had been sent from Lwów. Making it required surmounting two obstacles. While Ludwik's cow-dung pile dried, there remained a problem obtaining fuel for cooking. And they also had no cooking utensils, not a single pot. These problems were, fortunately, amenable to characteristic communist solutions.

The first was that the authorities had determined, in the interests of public hygiene, to send to the village a supply of spittoons.

To say the least, these weren't much prized by the villagers. The deportees, however, seized upon them to store food, and to cook with. When Ludwik had carried the fat back from the drowned ox, it had been in a spittoon. It hadn't been easy, because the spittoons had a hole, but it was just about possible.

Ludwik also found a socialist answer to the immediate fuel problem. In addition to spittoons, the Soviet authorities decided that what the farmhands really needed was a firmer grasp of communist ideas. They therefore provided a large, and unrequested, supply of a book entitled *A Short History of the Communist Party of the Soviet Union*. Written in Kazakh. This supply turned out to exceed demand for it, as the demand to read it was zero. Ludwik learned, through experimentation, that one volume burned just long enough for him to cook a spittoon-worth of 'glue'. He commandeered a large part of the farm's stock.

While Ludwik was collecting dung and burning socialist books, Lusia had returned to her labours in the fields. One day was very much like another. Waking early in the morning, washing, working very hard for a small piece of bread, exchanging precious belongings for a little extra food; receiving evening visits from the political police checking on their presence and that they hadn't been stealing or saying disobliging things about Stalin; lying in bed listening to the wolves coming onto the farm to hunt, falling asleep dreaming of Dolu and Herburtów street. And then waking up and starting all over again.

The field brigades each had a leader, but Lusia was regarded as too defiant to be given this job, too uninterested in pleasing the farm management. Generally the supervisory role was given to a Polish woman who was keen to show the superior work ethic of her compatriots and thus drove them rather hard. Lusia regarded this as oppressive and faintly ridiculous.

Her one shift in charge of a brigade demonstrated amply why

she was not brigade leader more often. The harsh Polish taskmaster fell ill one day and Lusia was given temporary command. Immediately she heard the news, she told her team to follow her to the field, taking with them whatever domestic work they had to do. 'We will try to do as little as possible, girls.'

The job that day was weeding, a fairly straightforward task on the face of it. But Lusia was, as Ludwik later described it, 'very untutored in matters agricultural'. The other members of her brigade weren't any better. Looking out at the fields, none of them could tell which plants were the crop and which the weeds. Lusia declared that it stood to reason that there would be more crop than weed, so they would pull up whichever there was less of. Her team went through field after field, uprooting all the crop and leaving only weeds.

It might have proved a horrible error. The Soviets were inclined to see almost anything as proof of sabotage. And certainly that would apply to the destruction of fields of valuable crops. Indeed, it might be considered sufficiently serious as to merit the death penalty, certainly a lengthy prison term. One thing saved Lusia and her friends. While they would have been punished, so would everyone else who had anything to do with it. The brigade leader who was ill would have been suspected, so would her supervisor, so would the farm manager. It was in absolutely nobody's interest to report the mistake.

So it was that the farm grew field upon field of weeds, harvested them, and put them into sacks as seeds for the next year. And nobody said a word.

———————

Along with the hunger, the work and the disease, Lusia and Ludwik also felt keenly the isolation. The letters from the family were the one source of news from the outside world. And this news had to be imparted with care, because the letters might well be opened, and their contents read by the secret police.

The Finkelsteins were keen to hear about friends back home, but Dorotea was not able to provide them with many glad tidings. The trains that had taken Lusia and Ludwik to Kazakhstan had arrived back in Lwów in early June, ready to deport more Poles. Most of the June wave consisted of people who had fled Western Poland when the Nazis had taken it over. They had found themselves in the Soviet zone and decided that they wished to go back home, Nazis notwithstanding. The Soviets had asked them to register for their return, and then used this list to fill the trains heading back to Siberia. They were joined on the cattle trucks by further Lwów residents regarded as counter-revolutionaries, for whatever flimsy reason.

On 1 July 1940, Dorotea reported to Lusia on the scale of this deportation and some names that might be familiar. 'On 29th of June Tysia left with the family and Mundia with his own relatives in your direction. The company was numerous and good.'

This guarded way of providing the information was typical. For instance, when Dorotea wanted in the same letter to tell Lusia that a friend's son had been arrested and sent to prison, she wrote: 'Karol B, Lucia's son, has been where Dolu is for the last two months.' And when she wished to inform her that the Soviets had captured another friend, she wrote that the 'victorious Red Army took Czerniowce, so Irenka has also been liberated'.

In March 1941, Dorotea's husband Szymek went to see Professor Bartel, the mathematician and former Prime Minister of Poland, who still lived in Herburtów street. Dolu had lent him a little money before the war, and Lusia suggested trying to get some of it back. Szymek reported that the professor was not there because 'he broke his leg and is in a hospital'. Maria Bartlowa, his wife, had returned 300 rubles and promised a further 200. She had 'words of appreciation and praise for you and Dolu', and said she had even sent a letter, although this did not appear to have arrived. Bartel had not broken his leg, nor had he been sent to hospital. Szymek was referring to the professor having been shipped to Moscow, where Stalin was trying to persuade him to cooperate with the Soviet regime.

Apart from members of Lusia's extended family, and news of their activities and their rows, the name that appears most often in the correspondence from Lwów is that of Ania. She appears to be a most turbulent individual. 'I cannot be silent about the incident between Ania and Adas,' reads one letter. 'They are fighting all the time because Adas wants to seize her apartment. He even found an accomplice. But she is a good opponent. In this apartment all the windows are broken and most of the furniture is also destroyed.'

Earlier, there had been some depressing news about someone called Frania who had 'died last month', coupled with the puzzling information that 'Ania is still fighting and sending birds to destroy something but it is still not enough'. This was made even more perplexing by subsequent information that Frania, despite having died, was embroiled in a lawsuit. 'Ania argued with Frania and they are involved in litigation, while Gicio is starting to be sick because Ania teases him a lot.'

Lusia may have shared this confusion at first, but after two or three such references she would surely have realised that 'Ania' is code for England. 'Adas' refers to Hitler, while his 'accomplice' is Stalin. The news about the death of Frania and the sending of birds is information that France has been overrun and that Britain continues to fight on in the skies. Frania's litigation is mentioned after the British destroyed the French navy to avoid it falling into German hands. Many French people had reacted to Churchill's decision with fury.

Wishing to encourage Lusia to stay strong in the face of all her trials, the foreign news being sent is upbeat. The letters repeatedly describe 'Gicio' – code for Germany – as being in trouble, while Ania 'has never been as healthy as she is now'. This sort of reassuring message was even included in a letter admitting that 'Gicio visited Alusia Gottlieb': in other words, that Germany had invaded Holland and Belgium. The Dunkirk retreat was also glossed over, with Lusia being told that 'Ania will take care of everything'. All of this, of course, was hopelessly optimistic, as probably both the readers and the writers of the letters appreciated.

There is also an irony in the bullish assessments that Lusia was being provided. If Germany had been defeated by Britain early in the war, Lusia and Ludwik would have been doomed to live and, before too long, die under Soviet rule.

During the period in exile, the family made many appeals – some in letters sent directly to Stalin – for Lusia and Ludwik to be allowed to move off the farm and to a nearby town. Wilhelm and Dorotea collected doctors' certificates citing Lusia's difficulties in childbirth, and Ludwik's supposed asthma, as reasons to be granted relief. None of these appeals even received a reply. If Soviet rule had continued unchallenged, it is reasonable to assume that nothing would have changed for Lusia and Ludwik. As it was, they were saved by a turn in the conflict that the letters do not anticipate.

On 22 June 1941, Hitler launched Operation Barbarossa, and invaded the Soviet Union.

———————

There was one further subject on which the letters were both unconvincingly cheerful and maddeningly vague. It was the subject that Ludwik and Lusia cared about most. What had happened to Dolu?

Since the moment he walked out of the apartment to sign some forms, they hadn't heard a word from him. And the only things the authorities had told Lusia about Dolu had been lies. So in all her correspondence, Lusia asked anxiously after her husband.

In the early letters from Lwów, there was at least a little bit of news, even though it was heavily disguised. On 25 June 1940, Nasio and his wife Fila wrote to say that 'Lulu's friends Dolek and Bronek were here in Lwów at Aunt Kazia's, now the older one left and the younger one stayed'. This meant that Dolu (Dolek in the code) and Bernard (Bronek) had been imprisoned in the Brygidki prison on Kazimierzowska street (Aunt Kazia). Dolu (the older one) had since been moved, while his younger brother Bernard was still there. In this and other letters, stung by Dorotea and Wilhelm's accusation that he was withholding support from his relatives, Nasio was keen to emphasise that he had been looking after the Finkelstein brothers by bringing them underwear, blankets and money.

Shortly after this there was news that Dolu was in Kiev, although this was still a rumour. The family hadn't heard from him directly. And in October, with Lusia clearly pressing to know more, Dorotea wrote: 'Lusia, I swear on everything dear to me that I know nothing about Dolu, he didn't have a trial yet.' Without a trial, he wouldn't be able to send any post and inform them of his whereabouts.

After this, the letters from Lusia's siblings became even less informative. They said that they didn't have 'any news from Dolu himself', but that other families had been in the same position, and then suddenly, just as their hopes were evaporating, had received a letter. Don't worry, Lusia; don't worry, dear sister.

There was a reason for their evasiveness, and for using formulations such as 'news from Dolu himself'. For the family had in fact received news about Dolu, just not from him. They had been visited by a Jewish employee of a prison where Lusia's husband and Ludwik's precious father had been held. He broke the terrible news to them. Dolu was dead. What had happened to so many in captivity had happened to their dear Dolu, and this man had witnessed his death. After this he had helped wash the body of Adolf Finkelstein to prepare him for burial.

They thanked the witness for bringing them this news, paid him for helping the undertaker, and grieved for their brother-in-law. Almost every day brought news of this kind to Lwów, but it never prepared families for news of those they loved. Dolu had always seemed so vigorous, so on top of things, it was hard to accept that he had just gone.

Lusia needed to stay strong, and her hope of seeing her husband again and reuniting him with his son was one of the things keeping her going. The family decided not to tell Lusia and Ludwik of the great tragedy that had befallen them.

MUM

Alfred's War

When news reached Alfred in June 1943 that Grete and their daughters had been arrested, he was in New York City. He had been there for almost three years, working for British intelligence and the American State Department, helping them fight the information war against Germany. And trying his best to save his family.

He had been in partnership with the intelligence agencies since almost the moment that he had left his family in Amsterdam and opened the Jewish Central Information Office in London on 1 September 1939. When Britain declared war on Germany two days later, its government quickly realised it knew almost nothing about the Nazi regime that it was now fighting. They hadn't done background research of even the simplest kind. They needed Alfred.

The British government lacked quite basic information. Who ran Nazi Germany's major institutions? What did these people think? What did they want? Where did they work? What did they look like? What did they wear? Alfred and his staff in Manchester Square were almost the only people outside the German government itself with the knowledge and documents to help answer these questions. It wasn't long before the Office was being described by one of the heads of British wartime intelligence as 'by far the most useful of the outside sources of information available to us'.

And after a few extremely rocky months – the ones that gave Grete sleepless nights and depleted the Wieners' savings – this appreciation produced solid financial support. At first it came from the Ministry of Information. Later, when the Political Warfare Executive was established, it became the main source of the Office's funding. The money paid for help not just for the PWE, but also for the Foreign Office, the secret activities of the Special Operations unit and the BBC.

The relationship with the government was never a simple one. Officials expected obedience for their money, and neither Alfred nor his staff were very good at that, valuing their independence. The new funders also didn't like the Office's name: they didn't like it being called the Jewish Central Information Office. It made it too obvious that the British were getting their information on the Nazis from Jews, with their focus on Jewish persecution, one that didn't reflect the government's policy or message.

From the beginning, the Office's new clients avoided using its real name, calling it instead 'Dr Alfred Wiener's office'. But, as one of the staff put it, this was 'a rather clumsy designation which did not easily commend itself to the miscellaneous, light-tongued merchants of information then hovering over Manchester Square'. One of these merchants eventually started calling it the Wiener Library, and the name stuck.

Alfred never much cared for it. He was relaxed about the idea that the office provided more than 'Jewish information'. That was no less than the truth, and had been for some time. But the new title was an Americanism, and, most of all, he didn't like his name being emblazoned on the office nameplate and stationery. It offended against both his secretive methods and his personal modesty. In the end, however, he had to accept that everyone was using the designation whether he liked it or not.

Despite the tensions, the relationship between the Library and the government was highly productive. There was an initial flurry of activity as the government got to grips with the basics, and then the Library's staff were on hand to help both with the general propaganda effort and with crises as they arose.

When, for instance, in May 1941, Hitler's eccentric deputy Rudolf Hess flew to Scotland on his own in a quixotic attempt to negotiate with the Duke of Hamilton, the Library was there to explain who Hess was and what he thought. There was an honest, but mistaken, view among some in government that Hess was a moderate who had been driven to act because of his opposition to Nazi policy. Before 4 p.m. on the day after Hess's arrival, ministers had on their desks a Wiener Library dossier amply demonstrating the extent of the Deputy Führer's extremism and explaining who the British were really dealing with.

Six weeks later, when Hitler invaded the Soviet Union, the Wiener Library was available to explain the economic and political importance to the Germans of the non-aggression pact they had abandoned. This briefing material helped the BBC with its initial reports on the German invasion, and was also used by the Foreign Office.

The information the Wiener Library provided had direct military and propaganda importance too. Before the famous Dambusters bombing raid, it provided useful intelligence on the Möhne Dam. And when Germany was carpeted with Allied leaflets or bombarded with broadcasts, much of the information used came from the Library too.

All this was accompanied by more general briefing, with the Library distributing bulletins designed to help ministries understand the enemy better. There were reports, for instance, on Nazi humour, on Nazi stage management, on Nazi racism towards people of colour, and on the Nazi honour code.

Naturally, the Library continued its work on the persecution of Jews, providing anyone who wanted to read about it with some of the earliest reports of what was happening in Auschwitz, and collecting and distributing eyewitness accounts from those escaping concentration camps. But, in truth, this wasn't what its funders wanted or encouraged.

This lack of official interest and understanding about the Nazi treatment of the Jews would have many consequences. It would eventually play a big role in the fate of Grete, my mother and my aunts.

———

Germany's invasion of the Low Countries in May 1940 had dealt a profound personal and professional blow to Alfred.

The nature of the personal blow is obvious. It meant that his last frantic efforts to move his family to Britain had failed. His wife and children were now almost entirely cut off from him, and facing dangers which he understood only too well.

Just after the Germans bombed Amsterdam, Alfred was visited by one of his intelligence contacts, Robert Walmsley. 'Dr Wiener asked me to pardon his distress,' reported Walmsley,

> because he had not been able to get any news about the fate of his wife and family who were of course virtually in the front line. He could not, I remember, keep the tears out of his eyes, but nevertheless he insisted on continuing to discuss whatever it was that I had come to see him about . . . I greatly admired his fortitude.

Alfred had a second nervous collapse, as bad as the one in 1933, taking several weeks off his duties and being looked after by one of his staff. For the rest of the war, his desperation to do something to free his family competed with a strong feeling that the effort might be hopeless, putting him under an almost intolerable strain.

And in the meantime, there was work to be done. As Alfred began to return to health, he started to consider how the Library would continue to receive the newspapers, documents and books it needed in order to stay up to date.

While Holland had been neutral and the Amsterdam Office

remained open, it had provided a route for Alfred to get information and printed material out of Germany. Now this route had been closed. That was the professional blow. There were still other neutral countries, of course, and Switzerland was to prove highly important. But it seemed imprudent to rely on countries like Spain, Portugal and Sweden remaining free of German control.

Alfred came up with an alternative. What about establishing a supply line that went from Germany to neutral countries in South America, as well as the United States, before the material was sent on to Britain? He approached his government contacts, asking them to support a visit to the United States to sort this all out. And they agreed.

In early August 1940, Alfred arrived in New York, where he was to spend the rest of the Second World War.

The supply line was created relatively easily and quickly. But soon it became clear Alfred wouldn't be returning to London immediately. It was decided that it might be safer if some valuable parts of Alfred's archive on the Nazis were stored in New York and Alfred worked on them there. And both British and (eventually) American intelligence realised he might be helpful to them in America. This suited Alfred well, as he had found the tension in wartime London great, and it quite suited the London staff too, who rather liked the freedom they obtained by putting several thousand kilometres between themselves and their demanding boss.

In the USA, Alfred could engage in some of his favourite tasks – scouring secondhand bookshops for material for the Library, and keeping up correspondences with American-based Jews like Albert Einstein, with whom he had been in touch since the early 1930s. It all contributed to his recovery.

After staying for a short period in an apartment uptown on West End Avenue, Alfred soon settled into the sixteen-storey Hotel Century, in Midtown, at 111 West 46th Street, near Times Square. And he reunited with an old friend from the days of the

Centralverein, Hans Oppenheimer. Hans had emigrated to the United States in 1938 with his wife Hertha, changed his name to John, and taken an apartment in Queens. Together, Alfred and John – storing parts of the archive in Alfred's hotel room and parts in the basement of the Queens building – established an American wartime outpost of the Library.

Perhaps the earliest piece of intelligence Alfred provided to the British government from New York was a rather downbeat report, filed in the summer of 1940, on American public opinion of the war. In these early days of his premiership, Churchill already understood the central importance of American involvement and support. Alfred provided no encouragement. He told London that in New York there was 'no war enthusiasm whatever'.

Yes, New Yorkers wanted to see Hitler defeated, and understood the impact his victory might have, but Alfred had yet to meet anyone 'prepared now to make any serious sacrifices for England and the cause of the Allies'. Instead, he was constantly meeting people, even quite senior officials, 'who, I am sorry to say, consider England as liquidated'. They were not only 'fearful but absolutely certain of the fact that nothing can stop Hitler's enormous superior power'.

Alfred found America a 'strange country', and the American authorities reciprocated the feeling. Who was this German who seemed to have a large stock of Nazi documents in his hotel room and another stash in Queens? Parcels of Nazi newspapers arriving at the Oppenheimers' from South America and Switzerland prompted an FBI search of their apartment and an interrogation of Alfred and his colleagues. They were all questioned intensively and it took several months before the inquiries were finally over.

Eventually, the State Department began to see the value of his work. Alfred and John built a strong relationship with them, helping evaluate foreign-language publications, and interviewing newly arrived Jewish refugees. But most of Alfred's work continued to be for the British.

After Pearl Harbor, and America's entry into the war, every part of the new allies' effort needed to be coordinated. As a result, the British relocated some of their propaganda staff to the United States, with their operational centre in New York. The new team contained admirers and old friends who considered Alfred an 'invaluable asset', and he began to work closely with them.

Their main jobs were to help persuade the American media to support the war, explain who the enemy were, and report back to London on American public opinion. They also secretly took over shortwave radio stations broadcasting to the Middle East and in Yugoslavia. And they bought an agency that specialised in supplying copy to the foreign-language newspapers that were read by some American ethnic minorities. The provision of suitable material for such propaganda efforts was a particular speciality of Alfred's.

At the head of the Political Warfare Mission was the Queen's brother, the brother-in-law of King George VI, David Bowes-Lyon. Under him were Walter Adams, later director of the London School of Economics, and the historian John Wheeler-Bennett. The philosopher Isaiah Berlin was engaged in associated work.

All these men became Alfred's friends and supporters, with Berlin describing him as 'a remarkable man' and praising his 'single-minded devotion'. Alfred made sufficient impression on Wheeler-Bennett that the writer provided readers of his book on America with a lengthy portrait of a man he called 'a droll little Berlin Jew' with the 'puckish humour' of a German street urchin. The Briton had bonded with Alfred over the latter's stories of commanding 'two hundred and fifty camels' during the First World War, and found him 'delightful'. Although it is impossible not to note upper-class condescension in his descriptions of his friend.

Wheeler-Bennett records Alfred arriving to see him in New York some time early in the war, and, upon taking his seat in the waiting room, noticing a 'distinguished but highly sensitive Zionist lawyer', who was also patiently seated. Alfred carefully folded the newspaper he had been reading and crossed the room to address himself to this complete stranger with the ominous warning,

'Do not post your letters in der mail boxes. Der spies feesh them out mit feesh hooks,' before leaving without further comment.

'My Zionist friend,' said Wheeler-Bennett,

entered my office trembling with anxiety and bewilderment. 'Will you kindly inform me,' he asked in a shaking voice, 'how I am to communicate with my friends and with my office in London if I cannot safely make use of the mail facilities of this country?' I pacified and reassured him explaining that this was just Dr Wiener's little way, and when the Herr Doktor next came in I reproved him for undue hubris; he replied, 'Ach, Herr General-Oberst, he looked so gloomy, I only wanted to cheer him up a little.'

Maintaining his sense of humour in even quite grim circumstances was typical of Alfred, but his stay in New York was a difficult time for the 'droll little Berlin Jew'.

In the years before Grete and his daughters were arrested, he did get some news from them, but it was neither frequent nor expansive. A birthday letter from Ruth in 1941 filled him with joy. But when he sent Grete a telegram through the Red Cross in November 1942, it didn't arrive for six months. The reply from Amsterdam then took four months to get back to him in New York. All it contained was the information that his immediate family and various other relatives (Trude, Jan and Fritz, for instance) were well, and by the time that the telegram reached Alfred even that sliver of information was no longer true. Most of them had been arrested and some of them were dead.

From the moment that he heard of the German invasion of Holland, Alfred realised that time was against him. With every month, the threat to his family would increase. And he knew that however helpless he may have felt, Grete was more helpless still.

It was up to him. And he had two problems to solve. He had to find a country willing to let his family in, and, somehow, persuade the Nazis to let his family out. Each of these was hard enough by itself; solving them both at the same time was almost impossible.

The first thing Alfred tried was the most obvious. As soon as he knew that he was going to America, he sought visas for them all to come and join him there. Through one of his contacts in Switzerland, a woman called Camille Aronowski, he passed a message to Grete, and she registered the Wieners with the US Consulate in Rotterdam. They were listed as applicants for the 'German quota' of American immigrants. But the application went nowhere.

So he tried somewhere else – Cuba. For a while, this seemed more promising. In the summer of 1941, Aronowski managed to get a Cuban visa approval number (10894) from the Cuban Consulate in the Spanish city of Bilbao. There was even correspondence about organising transport, and Grete's boss, Gertrude van Tijn, got involved, as she was in charge of arranging such Jewish emigration as there was. In the end, however, she was only able to give them bad news, passed on to Alfred through her American contacts. Transport wasn't the problem; she could even find the money for the fare. The difficulty was exit visas, so that they could leave Holland. She would do her best to put the Wieners at the top of the very first list, she wrote, but that wouldn't be enough, for 'even those people who have everything in order cannot get their exit permits'.

Soon there was worse news still. Alfred had not been the only person to obtain these Cuban visas. Several thousand others had done the same thing. But it had all been a swindle, designed to take the money of people whose desperation exceeded their caution. In April 1942, the President of Cuba invalidated all visas that had been issued to citizens of German-occupied countries.

More productive – but only because they could hardly have been less productive – were Alfred's efforts to provide Grete and the girls with visas for British-controlled Palestine, and try to get them out that way. In December 1941, there had been an exchange in which sixty-seven German citizens resident there had been allowed by the Allies to go back to Germany, and forty-seven Palestinian Jews who had been stuck in Poland were allowed to go back to Palestine. It provided a faint hope that larger swaps might be possible.

Through a friend living in Palestine, Alice Plaut, and through Van Tijn, Alfred helped Grete apply for immigration certificates to Palestine. In practice, this merely meant that they were placed on a list as being eligible for an exchange, if there ever was one. The certificates were initially given to those who had lived in Palestine, or had blood relatives there. Eligibility had then been expanded to those with some links to Palestine or a record of service to the Jewish community. This last group were designated 'veteran Zionists', an ironic category in which to place the Wieners, given Alfred and Grete's political history.

The Dutch list of Palestine certificates was one of many lists of such certificates, and guaranteed nothing. It was to play an important role in the family's survival, nonetheless.

But not as important as the group of exiled Poles living in Switzerland who turned the Wieners into citizens of Paraguay.

Citizens of Paraguay

The document that saved my mother's life looks exactly as official papers should. It is contained within a light-blue hard cover, with the word PASSEPORT embossed in gold letters. When the cover is opened, and the document inside is unfolded, it is full of stamps and photographs and signatures. And these are all genuine, each provided by the appropriate authority. This visa is not a forgery of any kind.

About halfway down, however, it features a large and obvious lie. And one that everyone associated with it – the providers, the signatory, the associated government, the passport holders, every country expected to recognise the passport, including Germany – knew to be a lie.

How this document came to be created, and its success despite its transparent falseness, is the great stroke of good fortune of my mother's war.

It started with a discovery that had nothing to do with Jews or even with Nazis. It started with a discovery about Poles and the Soviets. A discovery made by a group of diplomats working under the direction of a man called Aleksander Ładoś.

When Poland was invaded by Germany and the Soviets in 1939, its government fled, establishing an administration-in-exile that was eventually based in London. Associated with this government were a number of diplomatic outposts, and one of them was in Bern, the capital of Switzerland. And at the head of the Swiss mission was Ładoś.

Ładoś was, in effect, the Polish ambassador to Switzerland, although he didn't have that title. Ribbentrop, Germany's Foreign Minister, had made it clear to the Swiss that if they recognised Ładoś as ambassador, Germany would withdraw its envoy. And the Swiss – just as the Dutch had been before they were invaded – were very concerned about preserving their neutrality. So Ładoś became chargé d'affaires.

Swiss concern about neutrality was to have a greater impact on Ładoś than merely denying him the title that his position merited. It meant that the Swiss government was extremely sensitive about his activities where they might antagonise the Germans. Especially where that might involve encouraging refugees to make their way to Switzerland. Especially when those refugees were Jews.

Camped in the Consular Section of the Polish Embassy, Ładoś gathered together a team that was to become known as the Ładoś Group, which would be responsible for saving the lives of certainly hundreds, and possibly thousands, of people. The deputy head of the Legation was Stefan Ryniewicz, while the de facto head of the Consular Section was a former cavalry officer called Konstanty Rokicki. The final member of the quartet was a short, gregarious, cigar-smoking Jew by the name of Juliusz Kühl. Kühl had been born in Southern Poland, but at the age of nine had come to live in Zürich. Alone of the four, he didn't have formal diplomatic protection, and both this and his immigrant status were later to make him vulnerable.

Each of these men played an important role in the rescue mission that was to develop, but if it hadn't been for the leadership of Ładoś, it wouldn't have succeeded.

In the months after the Soviet invasion of Eastern Poland, Ładoś's group was looking for a way to help Poles who wanted to flee the Soviet zone. And that is when they made the discovery.

Paraguay employed an honorary consul in Bern, a Swiss notary called Rudolf Hügli, and it seemed he would provide Paraguayan visas for money. All the Polish Legation had to do was supply him with photographs, personal details and quite a lot of cash. With these documents, Poles might be able to escape the Soviets through the Japanese city of Kobe.

The Ładoś Group tried this and it worked. Kühl would later say it saved around thirty people from the communists. Soon they were to embark on something much more ambitious.

With the Swiss government doing its best to stop them.

———————

Alfred wasn't, of course, the only Jew desperate to find some sort of accreditation for his family. With Hitler's invasion of the Soviet Union and the beginning of the Nazi Final Solution, Jews all over Europe were trying everything they could to get a passport, or a visa, or even just a letter from some foreign embassy. Something that suggested that they were under the protection of a country that the Germans hadn't yet invaded.

It would be wonderful, naturally enough, if they could actually escape to whichever country that was, but being able to go there was a secondary matter. The priority was to have papers that might allow them to travel somewhere, anywhere – or, more realistically, that might make the Germans pause before killing them. Holders of a foreign passport might, for instance, be interned, when without it they would have been sent to the gas chambers.

So foreign papers were what the Ładoś Group started to provide. Ładoś, in particular, appreciated the danger that Jews were in. The Polish government-in-exile was among the first to perceive the turn that Nazi policy had taken in 1942, and the Bern diplomats were determined to do what they could to help. So what they had done for a handful of Poles, they proceeded now to do for thousands of Jews. The Paraguayan papers – and other Latin American documents – that they produced wouldn't prove enough to save all the people who were named on them. But for everyone who received them, they were better than nothing. And for some, my mother included, they were decisive.

Here's how the operation worked. To start with, the diplomats approached three Jewish community leaders and asked them to join the Ładoś Group. One was a man called Abraham Silberschein, a lawyer, politician and Polish Jew, who had arrived in Switzerland for a Zionist conference three weeks before the outbreak of the war, and when the fighting started, had decided to stay. He began working on aid for refugees, through which he met and later married another refugee aid worker, Fanny Schulthess-Hirsch. The third community leader was called Chaim Eiss. He was one of the founders of the Agudath Israel movement of orthodox Jews, and its main representative in Switzerland.

These three, and a network of helpers, provided the diplomats with the necessary details of Jews who they might be able to assist with a Paraguayan passport. And they also provided much of the necessary money, with the assistance of Polish government funds, some American donors and the wealthy Sternbuch family, Swiss Jews who lived near Lake Geneva.

While the information was being collected, one of the consular employees, usually Kühl, would visit the Paraguayan consul Hügli in his nearby office to collect blank passports and negotiate the fee. Because each passport might cover more than one person, the amount Hügli charged for each one would vary, between 500 and 2,000 Swiss francs. In other words, they could cost as much as an ordinary worker might earn in half a year.

It turned into quite an enterprise for Hügli. He sold the Poles at least 1,000 passports, providing accreditation for more than 2,000 people. At first he was able to use the blank forms he had in storage, but eventually he had a local bookbinder print him some more. For each one, he received at least a thousand times the cost of printing it.

The business having been transacted, Kühl would take the forms back to his colleagues, and then the team would work late into the evening, filling in blanks with details written in capital letters. Usually it was Rokicki who was the scribe, and his handwriting can be found on the vast majority of surviving Ładoś Group passports.

Printed across the top, in French, were the words: 'In the name of the Republic of Paraguay'. Underneath, it declares that the consul of the Republic of Paraguay based in Bern 'hereby invites all authorities and employees responsible for the maintenance of public order and general security to allow the bearer of this letter to pass freely and without hindrance'.

Rokicki would then fill in the names of the bearers, who might well be a whole family. Pictures of the holders would also be attached, accompanied by a written description of the adults. The details of eye colour, height and face shape were made as bland and imprecise as possible, so that if one of the intended recipients died before their papers arrived, someone else might be able to use them instead.

Then came the obvious lie. In the space left for the place of origin of the passport holder, Rokicki would write PARAGUAY. As he was fully aware, none of the people being accorded this designation had the slightest connection to Paraguay.

At the bottom, the Poles wrote in a date of issue and the length of time before expiry, after which the passport was ready for official validation. Kühl would take it to Hügli once more, who would sign it on the front and the back, and stamp it in various places.

The one thing that the consul did not do was inform the Paraguayan government of what he was up to. Nor did anyone tell the Swiss.

As Kühl began distributing the passports to Jews in Nazi-occupied Poland – smuggling them into the territory, sometimes paying bribes to German officials – news of their existence unsurprisingly began to spread.

Although the Paraguayan consul was the main provider of passports to the Ładoś Group, other Latin American diplomats also got in on the act. The racket filled the pockets of the Swiss representatives of Honduras, of Haiti and of Peru. The prospect of getting their hands on a Ładoś passport was one of the few sources of hope for Polish Jews, and eventually for Jews in other parts of Europe too.

In the Warsaw ghetto, Władysław Szlengel wrote a poem called 'Passports', with words such as:

> I'd love a Paraguayan passport,
> freedom and riches there lie,
> ah, it would be great to belong to
> a country that's called: Paraguay.

The final stanza reveals that, while the poet would like to be a citizen of Paraguay, it is really just a means to allow him to 'live then in peace in Warsaw, / The fairest – this none can deny'.

But the more Jews who knew about these documents, the more susceptible to exposure to the authorities it made the Ładoś operation.

In December 1939, Switzerland's Foreign Minister, Marcel Pilet-Golaz, had posed for a picture for the *Schweizer Illustrierte* magazine sporting a Hitler-style moustache and side-parting. That he thought this would prove appealing gives an indication of his country's politics at the time. His attitude was broadly shared by the police chief, Heinrich Rothmund, who in the same year had warned against the country becoming 'Judaized'.

If either of these men found out how the Ładoś operation worked, they were bound to try to shut it down. This almost happened before the Group had properly got going. In 1941, Hügli's supervisor, Paraguay's consul general, Walter Meyer, tried to inform the Swiss that his employee was charging large fees for irregular documents. Meyer told Karl Stucki, the head of the Swiss consular service, who in turn sought to inform the police. By a stroke of good fortune, the letter that he sent got lost in the post on its way to Police Chief Rothmund.

In April 1943, the Group's luck ran out. The Swiss Attorney General's Office caught a German spy. They arrested him because of unrelated espionage activities. But it so happened that one of the spy's targets, a rabbi called Shaul Weingort, had been among those helping the Ladoś Group identify recipients. As a result, when the Swiss prosecutors interrogated the spy, one of the things he told them was the existence of the rescue mission.

This information set off a disastrous chain of events. In May, the police raided the homes of other volunteers, including Chaim Eiss, finding in his possession envelopes full of passport photos and personal details. By confiscating these, the Swiss police doomed all the people to whom the details belonged. Reporting to the Foreign Ministry on what they had found, their information reached Karl Stucki. The head of the Swiss consular service finally realised that his earlier letter had gone missing, and Stucki weighed in with his concern that Hügli was engaged in nothing more than a moneymaking scam. The Foreign Minister gave the instruction that the police must restore order. The passport ring must end.

Then the police realised that something was missing. The helpers they had arrested had money, photographs, personal details and letters from Jews pleading for help. What they did not have were blank passports. The Jews they arrested couldn't have been acting on their own, because they didn't have the blanks. Nor could Hügli, because he didn't have the personal details. There had to be some link between the two. Someone else must be involved.

It wasn't long before the trail led the police to Abraham Silberschein, Fanny Schulthess-Hirsch, and finally the rest of the Ladoś Group. They kept the first two in solitary confinement for a week as they pressed them on the details of the scheme. For both of them, and for Kühl, the situation was perilous. They were foreigners living in Switzerland on licence, they didn't have diplomatic immunity and they could be expelled.

Ładoś also faced peril. There was a chance that his credentials might be withdrawn. But he remained robust. He energetically defended the operation and the members of his Group. He told the Swiss that he couldn't understand why they were becoming involved in a matter that need concern only Paraguay and Poland. It didn't endanger the Swiss in any way. All he wanted them to do was to turn a blind eye. This, after all, was about saving lives, and how would the Swiss look if they thought it worth sending people to their deaths because someone was breaking some petty regulations? Subtly, he hinted at public exposure.

His arguments were only partially successful. The Swiss decided that they didn't need to punish the Ładoś Group. Ładoś and Kühl could stay working at the Polish Embassy; Silberschein and Schulthess-Hirsch could remain in Switzerland. But the Swiss Federal Council determined that Hügli's credentials were to be withdrawn. The other Latin American consuls who sold passports suffered the same fate.

Hügli signed and stamped his last passports in the autumn of 1943. He dated them from the end of December 1942, in order to pre-empt any suggestion that he had validated them after he had lost the power to do so.

And then the escape route was closed.

The passport which accompanied my mother to Belsen is a classic Ładoś Group creation. Details of the Wiener family are provided in Rokicki's distinctive capital lettering. There are pictures of Grete and her three daughters, with Grete's photograph showing her worn and sad. The birth dates and names are all correct, although my mother's name is misspelled 'Miriam'. Grete is described as having brown hair and brown eyes, with a normal nose, a normal mouth, normal teeth, and being of average height, when in fact she was notably tall. And, of course, the paper contains the standard lie that the Wieners came from Paraguay.

Just above Hügli's signature, the passport is dated 30 December 1942, providing a hint that it was actually signed in late 1943, just as the passport operation was being wrapped up. And above that is the assertion that the document is valid for two years, with its threat that the passport's usefulness might come to an end before the war did.

Even when you know the story of its creation, to hold this document in your hands is to wonder – how exactly did Alfred get hold of it? And what exactly was the use of such an odd concoction?

DAD

Amnesty

As night fell on 21 June 1941, Wehrmacht soldier Alfred Liskow waded into the River Bug and started swimming.

Liskow was a communist sympathiser, and wanted to alert the Red Army that his fellow Germans were assembled in vast numbers for a dawn attack on the Soviet Union. Yet when his information was passed to Stalin, the Soviet leader was unimpressed. He ordered Liskow be shot for spreading disinformation.

It was one of forty-seven different warnings received by Soviet intelligence about the imminence of Operation Barbarossa. But when the German attack actually happened, Stalin was stunned. After issuing an initial flurry of instructions he retreated to his dacha, and remained out of communication for a week as the disaster unfolded.

Even in Siberia, in as isolated a place as the Baskermelte ranch, the news of the German invasion didn't take long to arrive and make an impact on Lusia and Ludwik. Lusia's days of working the fields came to an almost immediate end. This was for a practical reason, not a political one. The vast majority of the men in the village were drafted into the army, and no one was left who could read or write Russian. So Lusia, with her impressive command of languages, received a promotion. She would be the farm bookkeeper.

Unfortunately, as my father would put it, while 'her language was splendid, her command of arithmetic [was] rather eccentric'. This was not because she was innumerate. It was more a feature of her personality. She had no respect for petty rules or pointless conventions and might wave away inconvenient facts. As one of the great ladies of Lwów, she had been a popular guest, but not a popular bridge partner. She didn't care in the slightest whether she won or not, and thought anyone who did care about it ludicrous. Unsurprisingly, she was now extremely cavalier about Soviet figures.

Ludwik spent his days sitting by the window of the office, checking his mother's arithmetic to make sure that her imaginative maths didn't land her in too much trouble. He soon learned that even without Lusia mangling things, most of the bookkeeping on a Soviet farm consisted in providing higher officials with falsified numbers.

The utility of the work, however, was hardly the point. It meant working inside, in relative comfort. In July, it kept Lusia and Ludwik out of the sun during the day. But it didn't change their accommodation, and winter would come before too long and bring with it, once more, misery, hunger and perhaps even death.

As Hitler's armies swept east, driving the Soviets out of places like Lwów and heading towards Russia, Stalin realised that he needed help. And the British were willing to provide it.

Churchill's strategy for winning the war involved gaining support from powerful allies. Certainly the Americans, and preferably the Soviets too. He had always been a fierce opponent of Bolshevism but, as he later wrote, 'If Hitler invaded Hell I would make at least a favourable reference to the Devil in the House of Commons.' The Soviets had reserves of manpower that might hold up the Nazi advance.

For Stalin, the 'hyenas of capitalism' were a source of money and raw materials and he would need them, particularly having lost the economic advantages that had come from his earlier deal with Hitler.

So, on 12 July 1941, less than three weeks after the beginning of Operation Barbarossa, the Soviet Union and Britain signed an agreement in Moscow committing them to take common action against Germany. The British signatory was the country's ambassador, Sir Stafford Cripps. For the Soviets, the agreement was signed by Vyacheslav Molotov. It hadn't been two years since Molotov had signed the Molotov-Ribbentrop Pact with Germany.

One of the consequences of joining the Allies was that Stalin had to come to some sort of accord with the Poles. After all, protecting Poland was the reason Britain had given for entering the war. This was difficult for Stalin, because the Soviet position was that the Polish government had ceased to exist. Indeed, that assertion had featured in *their* argument for entering the war. But he accepted that he had little choice.

The Poles weren't happy about the idea of an accord either. A fierce debate broke out in the Cabinet of their government-in-exile. Stalin had arrested their families and friends, killed their fellow citizens and stolen their property. He was no ally. He wasn't willing, even now, to guarantee the position of Poland's postwar borders. But General Władysław Sikorski, the Prime Minister of the exiled Poles, saw that they had even less choice than Stalin. Based in London, they were utterly reliant on the British. And Churchill viewed alliance with the Soviets as essential.

A negotiation began. The central issue was the fate of all the people that the Soviets had arrested and imprisoned since they first invaded Poland. The Poles insisted upon their release, and the Soviets eventually agreed. The term used was an 'amnesty', which was itself a cause of controversy. 'Amnesty' implied that the prisoners had been guilty of a crime and remained guilty, an implication that many Poles justifiably found offensive. But the Soviets were not about to admit to any previous wrongdoing.

Uneasily, the two sides reached accord, and on 30 July 1941 the

Soviet ambassador in London, Ivan Maisky, and General Sikorski signed a pact, with the amnesty at its core. Two weeks later, the amnesty was issued and work began in earnest on the other main element of the pact. A Polish army was to be created, raised from the ranks of freed prisoners, to be led and managed by Poles, but to fight on the Eastern Front under Soviet command.

And the Poles hoped that this army might be led by the more than 10,000 Polish officers who had been captured in the fighting in 1939. People like the Finkelsteins' friend Major Ignacy Schrage. The Polish government-in-exile had been asking after these officers for months and getting nowhere. Now that there was to be an amnesty, and an army, surely the officers would reappear and take their rightful place at the head of this new Polish army.

Stalin knew that this was not going to happen.

———

As soon as the Red Army had entered Lwów in 1939, the Soviets had broken the promises that they had made to the city's defenders. 'Surrender and you can all go free.' 'Your privates can go home, and your officers will be allowed to leave Poland.' They never had any intention of allowing this. The words were hardly out of the mouths of the Soviets when they began arresting the Poles.

Although many privates were captured in these first days, they were never the real target. The Soviets did transport them to prison camps, but quickly decided that they had too many of them, and let them go. The officers were a different matter. Them, they kept.

Being arrested had been a brutal experience. Ignacy and his fellow officers had been roughly searched by young Soviet conscripts who took their belts and packs, tore off wedding rings and confiscated watches, ripped off epaulettes and stole cap badges, all the while shouting at them about the ruling class. Some Poles had been shot on the spot.

Those that were still alive, then spent days travelling. Marching on foot, bumping along in trucks, waiting at railway stations, stuffed into carriages, heading deep into the Soviet Union, leaving all hope of Poland behind.

Eventually, 15,000 Poles, mainly officers but also some other Polish professionals – politicians, doctors, engineers, journalists – were divided between three prisoner-of-war camps administered by the NKVD. Two of the camps were in Russia, with one in Kozelsk, near Smolensk, and one in Ostashkov, near Kalinin. The third was Starobelsk, near Kharkov in Ukraine, and this was where Ignacy was sent, along with most of the other officers from Lwów.

Starobelsk was not ready for the thousands of men it now received. It was a freezing cold monastery with few facilities. It had no latrines, no kitchens, only standpipes with cold water; its walls were crumbling, its roofs had holes in them. But at least it now had eight generals and hundreds of colonels and majors to organise things. They set about trying to put some of this right. They managed to improve their surroundings a little, but they still had to cope with inadequate rations and with the fact that many of them had been arrested in summer clothes. Winter came and no additional clothing was provided. They faced the snow, many of them, in shirtsleeves.

The repair work helped a little with the boredom. As did some evening lectures, which were allowed as long as they were not too blatant a provocation to the NKVD. Apart from that, there was little to do, save listen to hours of Soviet propaganda. It came from the forty-five loudspeakers that had been installed, which broadcast daily from 6 a.m. to 11 p.m. The prison administrators provided their Moscow superiors with the information that 'a large number of prisoners particularly enjoyed listening to Stalin deliver a lecture on the Soviet constitution'.

The other diversion, less welcome still, was interrogation. Each man could expect several interrogations, taking place at any time of day or night, sometimes lasting hours. The questioning could be relaxed or highly confrontational, political or very personal. And it wasn't obvious what the status of these interviews was. Were they ordinary intelligence-gathering encounters with prisoners of war? Or were they part of a criminal investigation of people who were now Soviet citizens, rather than captured officers of a country and an army that no longer existed? No one ever said.

In the many hours that these limited activities failed to fill, the officers engaged in petty arguments about personal slights, and enjoyed the circulation of rumours. As winter gave way to spring in March 1940, these rumours became increasingly optimistic. The Soviets were closing the camps. The officers would be freed. Ignacy would be able to go back to Lwów, back to Jadzia and Aldona.

And then rumour became reality. Each day, at about 10 a.m., Moscow would come on the line to the prison camps, and over the loudspeakers would be read the names of perhaps 250 officers. Off would go the NKVD guards to prepare these men to leave, and provide them first with a farewell meal and then with three herrings, 800 grams of bread and some sugar, food for the journey. The herring was wrapped in new pieces of paper, a luxury they had been without all these months. To everyone watching, this routine seemed to confirm that the men were about to be free, with the Soviets anxious that the freed men would speak well of their captors once they got home.

And then they departed, waving to their friends. The generals received an honour guard and, at Starobelsk, a military band played as they left. The NKVD joined in the farewell, assuring those leaving and those staying behind that they were indeed going home.

The moment that the officers left the gates, they experienced an entirely different atmosphere. There were new NKVD guards, now with truncheons, with machine guns, with dogs. The Poles were pushed into cars and then onto trains and off they went, destination unknown.

After a journey of about three hours, Ignacy found out his

destination. It was Kharkov prison. There was to be one further interrogation, the officers were all told. And so, not long after arriving, Ignacy was taken down some steps and into the cellars, his hands bound. He was escorted down a corridor to a door. His guard tapped lightly and asked, 'May I?' and from inside came the response: 'Come in.'

Stepping into the room, Ignacy encountered the jail commander and a prosecutor sitting at a table facing him. The prosecutor asked his name. 'Major Ignacy Schrage.' And then his date of birth. 'September 16th 1898.' To this the prosecutor responded, 'You may go,' and Ignacy turned to leave. As he did so, the jail commander called out, 'Hello,' stepped forward with a Soviet-manufactured 7.62mm pistol and shot Ignacy in the back of the head.

Then guards wrapped his head in his coat, so there wouldn't be blood on the floor, dragged his body out of the cell, put it on a truck, took it to a nearby wooded park, and placed Aldona's stepfather in a mass grave, piled with his fellow officers three or four bodies deep, one on top of the other. And over him they spread lime to speed up decomposition.

The officers from Ostashkov were killed in an NKVD jail in very much the same way, before being driven to a burial place. Those from Kozelsk were taken from the railway station at Gnezdovo onto a bus, and then into a wooded area just west of Smolensk, known as the Katyn Forest. Here, they too were shot, and their bodies buried in nearby open pits. When the graves were discovered later in the war, with 5,000 bodies in them, their location gave its name to all the 22,000 murders of officers and other Poles which took place that spring of 1940. They all became the Katyn Massacre.

By the end of May, the massacre was complete. Before Jadzia and Aldona reached Siberia, almost certainly Ignacy had already been murdered.

The true story of the killings would not be acknowledged for decades, and the Soviets would lie about them again and again. But the murders were not a bureaucratic error made by an over-zealous underling without the permission or knowledge of his superiors. The decision to kill the officers had been agreed in a memo that had been sent on 5 March 1940 by the head of the NKVD, Lavrentiy Beria, to Stalin and signed by both of them, and by various other Politburo members, including Molotov.

The Polish officers were, said the memo, 'sworn enemies of Soviet authority [and] full of hatred for the Soviet system'. People like Ignacy were only waiting for their release to continue their counter-revolutionary activities. The NKVD should therefore 'try [them] before special tribunals . . . and apply to them the supreme penalty: shooting'. Beria added that 'examination of the cases is to be carried out without summoning those detained and without bringing charges'.

In the summer of 1941, after Hitler's invasion, Stalin and his officials offered reassurances that the officers would reappear, though it would – the Poles must understand – take them some time to travel from their faraway prisons, given war conditions. They would need to be patient. For now, the Soviets faced the problem of providing leadership for the Polish army they had agreed to establish.

There was, fortunately, one suitable person they hadn't killed. General Władysław Anders, former commander of the Nowogródek Cavalry Brigade, had been severely wounded in the fighting in September 1939 and had ended up in hospital in Lwów just at the time that so many others had been arrested and deported. After he recovered, he spent the next year being moved from one Soviet prison to another, but he had never been held with the main groups that had been shot in the Katyn Massacre.

By this piece of luck, he was still alive in July 1941 and avail-able for service. Before too long, a startled Anders, a starved and browbeaten prisoner in the NKVD's Lubyanka prison in Moscow, found himself the recipient of a surprise visit from Beria. He was to be released, Beria told him, for he had been appointed commander of a new army. He would be allowed to recruit any amnestied Poles he thought fit for service.

Shortly afterwards, an emaciated Anders – wearing a shirt and trousers but no shoes and barely able to walk – departed the Lubyanka in an NKVD-chauffeured car. The prison governor carried Anders' suitcase of belongings to the car, although later the General realised it wasn't his, containing only someone else's swimming trunks.

Within a month, Anders, though still walking with a stick, had recovered sufficiently to start planning his new army.

In early September 1941, two Soviet police officers arrived at the Baskermelte ranch and asked to speak to Lusia, Ludwik and the other deportees. They had come, they said, to tell them about the amnesty and to provide them with Polish certificates of nationality in exchange for their Soviet documents. They were all free to go. And they could go anywhere. So long as it wasn't a major city, a so-called 'town of the first category'.

That, however, was it. There was no money to go anywhere, no offer of transport, no prospect of work. And all these points were impressed upon Lusia by the Kazakhs and the Soviet officials running the farm. They wanted her to stay, partly because she had now become a valued office worker, but also because they could see that she had become the leader of the deportees. If she went, the others would probably go too.

'Look, living in town is very tough,' they told her. 'Here, you are now an official. Whenever there's anything in the shop, we'll sell it to you. In the town, you might even have to pay for water. Here, water is free.' And on it went.

As terrible as the winter had been in Baskermelte, and would be again, and as modest as the promise of free water might seem, the choice being put before Lusia was a real one and not easy to make. Leaving the farm meant leaving a place where she and Ludwik were at least known and had work and accommodation, even if it was their freezing, broken-down shack. Many deported Poles left farms and work camps that September only to die on the Siberian plains searching for a better life that they couldn't find.

Perhaps it was at this moment of decision that Dorotea's wisdom was shown most clearly. Lusia's sister had not passed on what she had heard about Dolu's death. So Lusia could still dream of finding her husband and fulfilling the vow she had made, that one day she would reunite Ludwik with his father. She could only do that if she now gambled on the freedom she had been offered. Perhaps if her siblings had been more frank, she might have chosen to stay put.

As it was, she was very firm in her interview with the senior political officer of the village. He told her she was such a skilful person, so valuable to the farm, that she must be of working-class stock. And she replied that she was the daughter of a landowner and the wife of a capitalist and she kept going until he agreed that she had better leave. With her she took the Pirgo sisters, the Countess and the largest portion of the other deportees.

Lusia decided it wouldn't be a good idea to move far away, for now. It was her view that the longer you spent on the Soviet railway system the more likely you were to have your luggage stolen and to lose what little you had left. The idea of aimlessly travelling without much of a clue where you were going didn't seem to have much merit. So she decided they should set off for Semipalatinsk, the only remotely local town. From there, she could look for Dolu.

It took four days in an ox wagon to reach their destination. And when they arrived, it was all as the farm officials had warned her. No work, no food, nowhere to sleep. For the first nights, they slept in the open, on the pavement of Babinska street. Then they had a piece of luck of a very Soviet type. The occupants of the houses in Babinska street became the victims of a wave of arrests.

With their husbands at the Front, the local women had been engaging in black-market trading, with the acquiescence of the authorities. Suddenly this permission had been withdrawn, and everyone involved had been taken away, eventually to land in Soviet prison camps, leaving their homes empty and their jobs vacant. The same sort of arbitrary act that had left Lusia sleeping on the street in a town thousands of kilometres from Lwów, now produced for her somewhere to live and a way of feeding herself and Ludwik.

Together with Dorota and Ewa Pirgo, Lusia rented a room in 30 Babinska street. It was expensive, small and damp, and it didn't have any furniture, but it was better than the pavement, so it would have to do. After a couple of days, Lusia led the sisters on a night raid. From the nearby railway siding the women purloined the door of a goods wagon. This they propped up on bricks, and it served as a bed for Ludwik and Lusia.

As important as the new accommodation was the fact that Lusia could now find a job. She was employed in the railway canteen, sorting potatoes. It was mind-numbing and tiring, all day on her feet separating good potatoes from rotten ones. But it was a highly desirable position because it meant that, in a town where there was almost no other food, there were potatoes to steal. As Ludwik described it, Lusia went to work 'in an old dressing gown and returned with a bosomful of potatoes'. It is how they managed to live.

But, as always, Lusia was determined Ludwik would do more than live. Round the corner from 30 Babinska street was the First Turkestan-Siberian Railway School. As soon as they moved from sleeping on the pavement to sleeping on the goods-wagon door, Lusia sent her son back to school.

Ludwik was almost twelve years old by now, but was put in a class with eight-year-olds, because his Russian was still poor. It wasn't long before he was fluent, and he became a favourite of the teacher. And she became a favourite of his. His few weeks with Vera Ivanovna were more notable for her kindness than for her pedagogy.

Ivanovna's sympathy for Ludwik had been obvious from the moment he joined the class, and it was not solely the product of his studiousness. During the Bolshevik Revolution, both her parents had been shot in front of her, and later her daughter had died of starvation during the famine caused by Stalin's policy of farm collectivisation. There were unhappy people like Vera Ivanovna all over the Soviet Union. Her experiences were quite common.

What was less common was her willingness to help others. Helping people could be dangerous, because whoever you helped might later be designated a criminal, or an enemy of the state, and your earlier assistance might be interpreted as collusion. But Vera Ivanovna was willing to take a risk. She gave Ludwik a pound of honey on one occasion. And more remarkably still, she broke the school rules to provide him with bread. The school only permitted pupils to have bread if they paid for cabbage soup at lunchtime. This was vastly too expensive for Lusia and Ludwik, so the teacher allowed him to have bread without it.

For this reason above all, my father's experience of the First Turkestan-Siberian Railway School was a good one, though a typhus epidemic brought his experience of Semipalatinsk's education system to an end after a few weeks. He would go off happily to Vera Ivanovna's class in the morning and come back to Lusia in the afternoon. And each day he would ask her the same question. When would they hear from Dolu?

Lusia, of course, did not have an answer. But she did, at least, know how she would set about finding out what happened. Working in the railway canteen she saw, every day, a sad sight. The platforms were full of families of deported Poles waiting for trains that might carry amnestied Polish prisoners. Whenever one pulled in, the families would start shouting into the carriages, asking if anyone had heard of their relatives. Lusia could see it was hopeless.

She was sure that if Dolu had survived, he would wish to join the army that she knew was being established by General Anders. So she wrote letters to the two places where Anders was setting up camp. And added her name and address to a poster containing messages from other families in Semipalatinsk which was also sent to the new army's main base.

She remained unaware of the news about her husband that her siblings had kept from her. But before long her searching, and Ludwik's waiting, came to an end. For they finally learned the whole of Dolu's terrible story.

What Happened to Dolu

On 10 April 1940, the night when the militiamen had taken Dolu from Lusia and Ludwik 'to sign that we left the apartment in good order', he hadn't gone far. Just to Kazimierzowska street, round the corner from the opera house, a few minutes walk from the old Finkelstein apartment in Akademicka street. Here, right in the centre of Lwów, behind high walls, was the Brygidki prison.

It was to be a night of fear and confusion. For every newly arrested person, arrival meant registration, the taking of photographs, and a most humiliating search, conducted while they were naked, unwashed fingers probing the inside of their mouths, prisoners made to squat so it could be seen if anything was hidden between their buttocks or in their anus. Before their clothes were returned, anything – shoelaces, braces, even underwear with elastic – was removed that could conceivably be used to kill themselves.

All this was done without any explanation, often without a word being said save for curt instructions to turn this way or that. And then, shuffling along in shoes without laces, holding up their trousers to protect their dignity and avoid tripping, the new arrival was assigned a cell and pushed in. And as the door closed behind them, they appreciated properly for the first time that they were now a prisoner.

By the end of that first night, Dolu's tiny cell had forty people in it. And there was a good chance, each time the cell door opened, that someone would come in whom Dolu knew, a friend, a professional associate. Within days, this group had been turned into an undifferentiated mass of dirty bodies, shoved together so tightly it was hard to lie down, unshaven, sweating profusely, people fainting from thirst.

Ailments and discomforts suffered by one person were quickly a burden to everyone else. If someone had diarrhoea, or dysentery, everyone suffered in the small cell with one slop bucket for a toilet, especially those required to sleep by it. In the battle between lice and prisoner, the lice always seemed to have the upper hand. They spread typhus, a major cause of the deaths that now began to reduce the prison population.

In some cells, the social mix – and particularly the mix between ordinary criminals and political prisoners – produced almost unbearable tensions, with loud arguments and fistfights. This, at least, Dolu was spared during these early weeks in Brygidki. The particular circumstances of his arrest meant his cellmates were almost entirely political prisoners with a similar background to him. For as long as it lasted, this proved a comfort. To fill the time, the prisoners held lectures. Dolu gave his on economic conditions in Poland before the war.

Dolu was to spend the first two months like this in Brygidki, and at first there was no indication of where this imprisonment would lead, how long it would last, or what it was for. Every so often he would be allowed out of the cell to wash, or for a brief period of exercise, perhaps twenty minutes of walking in a circle. It was a chance to see who else was being held, and he twice caught sight of his brother Bernard from a distance. But when washing or exercising were over, he was returned to the cell without further words.

Then, after a few such silent and disorientating weeks, things did change. The interrogations began. It was the start of an ordeal that lasted for months.

Before a prisoner could be interviewed, their resistance first had to be weakened. One tool was sleep deprivation. The lights in Dolu's cell stayed bright all night, making it almost impossible to sleep even when he wasn't facing nighttime interrogation. If a prisoner did manage to doze off, they would be woken if they covered their faces, or if their hands strayed under the blanket. Sleeping during the day was also forbidden. The other tool to break down resistance was thirst. Dolu was fed salted fish without water.

When the guards called a prisoner for interview, they would usually shout out the first letter of the prisoner's surname. 'F', when it was Dolu's turn. All those with a surname beginning with 'F' would then stand, and give their first name and patronymic. After which, Dolu – 'Adolf Maksayevich' – would be led away. This elaborate dance was to prevent those in other cells learning who else was being held in the prison.

Dolu was rarely escorted directly to his interrogators. He would usually first be taken to a small cubicle, a tightly confined space, and be made to wait there. And through the walls he could hear someone taking potshots. Whether these were real executions, or shots fired in order to intimidate him, he had no idea.

The pattern of the interrogations was quickly established. There would be long periods of open questions, seemingly aimless ones. The NKVD was trying to draw a social map of Poland, collecting whatever data they could. But there were other, more pointed questions, with an aim more apparent to the person being questioned. The object was to prove Dolu guilty of 'strengthening the might of capitalist Poland'. Something that wasn't hard, because he absolutely was guilty of strengthening the might of capitalist Poland.

The questioning wasn't, however, very professional. Dolu sometimes had the impression that his interviews were training sessions for new interrogators. This impression was almost certainly wrong. What gave these confrontations their rather amateurish quality is that those quizzing him didn't really need any proof in order to charge him with a crime. The whole thing was a sham.

This didn't make it any easier to endure. The encounters could be very rough indeed. Every prisoner experienced shouting, almost all experienced violence, it was common to hear torture and beatings from the next-door room. And this went on night after night, month after month.

In the middle of June, the venue of the interrogations changed. Dolu was moved to Kiev and, after a further six weeks, to Poltava. Then in August 1940 he was transferred to Starobelsk, to the cold monastery prison that had been Ignacy Schrage's final home before his murder. In total, a journey of more than 1,200 kilometres.

Each prison had its own particular characteristics. Kiev, for instance, was dirtier even than Brygidki. Starobelsk had been somewhat improved by Ignacy's fellow officers, who left behind their scribbled messages on the walls, and also better amenities. But the regime was harsher, with prisoners allowed exercise only once a week, for half an hour at a time.

Yet in all of them, the basics were the same – the overcrowded cells, the salted-fish diet, the lack of water, the typhus and dysentery, the lack of sleep, the endless questioning. And the grotesque injustice.

Towards the end of 1940, after a little over three months in Starobelsk, Dolu was ordered to line up with his fellow prisoners. And the local NKVD chief pronounced verdicts and sentences for each of them in turn. There had been no trials, no consideration of evidence and, while confessions were preferred, no opportunities for formal pleas. A troika of officials had met without Dolu present and declared him guilty of one of the crimes that they had invented for the purposes of imprisoning pretty much whoever they wanted.

'You have been found guilty of being a socially dangerous element, Article 54-13 of the Ukrainian Criminal Code,' Dolu was informed. 'The maximum sentence is fifteen years. You've been sentenced to eight.' The numbers, like every other part of the procedure, were entirely arbitrary. But the officials may as well have said straight away that he had been sentenced to death. Dolu had just turned fifty. The chances of him surviving for eight years in a Soviet prison camp – or Gulag, as it is known – were effectively zero.

However bad these last seven months had been, things now became sharply worse.

Before living in hell, it is necessary to travel there. And this was to be an almost unimaginable torture. Dolu was taken to a cattle truck, shut in with the other prisoners, and sent, as Ludwik and Lusia had been, on a journey lasting three weeks. The prisoners were transported almost 3,500 kilometres to the north, to the virgin forests of the Komi Republic, on the edge of the Arctic Circle.

Yet while my father and grandmother had travelled in April and May, Dolu was being transported in the last days of December and early weeks of January. The temperature sometimes dropped to minus forty-five degrees Celsius. And he had almost no clothes to keep him warm. The fur coat he had worn when arrested had, naturally, been confiscated. He was now in his shirtsleeves, protected only by the blanket Nasio Landes had brought him in the early days of his imprisonment.

When Lusia and Ludwik were deported, the standing orders had included an instruction to bring a month's supply of food. Dolu, after his months in prison, was travelling without any supplies at all. He was therefore reliant entirely on a ration of salted fish, provided erratically, whenever the guards could be bothered. And being bothered was not a speciality of Soviet guards. Why should they put themselves out for the enemies of the people? Even when this salty food was forthcoming, it was rarely accompanied with water. The prisoners might go for days without any water at all. Whenever the train stopped, and they could reach out, Dolu and his fellow prisoners ate snow.

By the time that Dolu arrived in the forests of the north, many of his fellow passengers were dead – starved, frozen, taken by disease. The rest of them tumbled out of the cattle trucks, with night blindness from malnutrition a common complaint. But they all knew what they were now seeing.

'Gulag' is an acronym for the main camp administration, but it has come to be used to describe the camps themselves. Just as good a term, however, is 'concentration camp'.

Dolu had been taken to a place where the state concentrated those they had designated as enemies of the people, and where they worked many inmates to death and executed others. The best estimate is that eighteen million people experienced the Gulag between 1929 and 1953. And during the most intensive period of the Second World War, one in four prisoners died every year.

Each Soviet prisoner, as they left the train and entered a camp, will have passed underneath a sign above the gate. 'With Just Work I Will Pay My Debt to the Fatherland,' said one. Or, more starkly, 'Through Labour – Freedom.' The words that hung over the gates of Auschwitz too. Arbeit Macht Frei.

The Gulag was where political enemies were liquidated and where criminals were detained. It was the threat that eliminated dissent and the calamity that overtook anyone who dared catch the eye of officialdom. And, at the same time, it was a business venture intended to aid the Soviet economy. Millions of people put to work as slave labourers, as loggers and farmers and miners and builders.

Where Dolu had now been sent to work as a logger was not a single camp. It was a complex of camps centred on the town of Ukhta, and he was destined to circulate round a number of them. Some prison camps were big enough to boast permanent barracks and latrines and an exercise square, others were merely temporary encampments, with accommodation in ditches and snowdrifts. All promised a miserable and short life.

Each day, brigades of prisoners would be sent into the forests to cut down trees, to drag the trunks to the river, to load them on barges. There might be two hours of walking to arrive at the place of work, and at the end of the day, two hours walking back. Dolu arrived in January, when this walking had to take place in snow that might come up to his knees, and the snow had to be navigated in boots that had been inherited from a dead prisoner and were coming apart.

Dolu's main job was to be a packhorse. He was roped to the felled tree trunks and had to drag them from the forest down to the river. The physical load was almost impossible. For a man in late middle age, lately employed in an office, the burden was intolerable. The prisoners almost all found the relentless work and the biting cold hard to bear. They would become desperate for rest. There are reports of forestry workers using their axes to cut off their fingers so they might be allowed to stop. But cutting off your fingers yourself wasn't necessary as your fingers might just freeze anyway.

For the *zeks* – as the prisoners were known – the most important relationship was between food and labour. A brigade leader would agree with the camp administrators a quota of logging work to be completed by the end of the day, and would report back later on whether each member of his team had met their portion of the target. If a prisoner fulfilled their work norm, they would be fed. Yet the food was never enough to give the prisoner the strength to meet tomorrow's norm. As their capacity to engage in hard physical work went down, their food ration went down further. It was a vicious circle that could only end in death.

There was, of course, nothing scientific about the calculations of the norms and, in particular, nothing rigorous about the measurement of their fulfilment. The Soviet accountancy that Ludwik had observed on the collective farm held in the Gulag too. Absurd targets were set in order to make the target-setters look enthusiastic, and absurd outcomes were duly reported. The work a prisoner did might not relate all that closely to the amount that was recorded. All this meant that Dolu needed a good relationship with his brigade leader and other workers.

What prevented this was that he was a political prisoner. There was a clear hierarchy in the Gulag, and socially dangerous elements like Dolu were at the bottom of it. The camps were dominated by the *urki* – the common criminals. The *urki*, unlike the political prisoners, were not considered enemies of the state, so they were given clear preference by the guards. And their contempt for the politicals – 'fascists', 'yids' – could be used by the authorities as a weapon of camp control.

The criminals made the lives of the politicals even more of a misery than they were already. It wasn't just the *urki*'s brutal treatment of their fellow brigade members, or their distorted reports of work norms. They beat people, they took food, they stole property, they forced others to steal property, they raped, they forced others to rape. If a political prisoner found a dry place to sleep or a warm place to stand, they would be pushed away. When the political prisoners were allowed to take a rare bath, and returned to their clothes, they would find the clothes had gone. When the shared underwear was distributed, the politicals ended up with the torn rags at the bottom of the pile.

When the *urki* were about, a political couldn't rest for a moment. And the *urki* were always about.

For Dolu, so good at dealing with people, this savagery was hard to cope with. More than anything else, it made his life in the Gulag a severe trial. It wasn't long before he had lost any possessions he still had, even Nasio's blanket, even the underwear Nasio had brought to him when he was in Brygidki. All of it stolen by the *urki*.

By the end of March 1941, he was beginning to buckle. The hard physical work exceeded his capacity. And he fell victim to repeated bouts of dysentery, bad enough to produce fever and diarrhoea, but not necessarily considered bad enough to allow him to be excused logging duties. He was heading where so many had gone before, into a state of exhaustion so bad that one lost all sense of oneself and was pulled inexorably towards death.

Yet he retained one advantage. Surrounded by criminals whose sole skill was thievery, and camp administrators who were almost illiterate, Dolu was educated. Unlike many of his guards, he could read and he could write; unlike some of his fellow political prisoners he could also count, being able to draw up accounts and understand what he was preparing. He was also able to speak Russian.

Together, these skills won him the most coveted of all camp positions: a desk job. In April 1941, he became a camp bookkeeper. He would no longer have to slog through the forests and drag logs. And a desk job came with something else: a desk. Working in the forests had, at its best, meant sleeping in the barracks, in large groups, unprotected at night, prey to the *urki*. Now Dolu would be able to sleep in the office, using his desk as a bed.

And that is where he was – working in the Gulag office in the town of Ukhta – when news of the amnesty arrived in the middle of August 1941. Dolu and his fellow Polish Gulag prisoners were to be released, and a representative of General Anders' new army arrived, seeking to recruit them. They were relatively lucky. In some camps, the news of freedom took months to arrive. In others, the news was ignored by the Gulag administrators.

Not everyone wanted the offer now being made. It was possible to carry on working in the Gulag as free men, helping the slave-labour business function. And one of Dolu's friends urged this course upon him. This man was a dental technician and pointed out that, as a result, he had a free supply of alcohol. The two of them could sell this alcohol for extra food, he suggested. 'Don't go,' he said. 'You'll not be better off elsewhere.'

Dolu was starved, physically broken, only falteringly recovering from illnesses which had nearly killed him. The idea that this life

– bookkeeping in a concentration camp, scrapping for crumbs, selling dental spirits on the black market, sleeping on desks – would be his future, that he would actually choose such a life, struck him as impossible, ridiculous, unthinkable.

Besides, he was being given the chance to find his family, and to serve Poland. He wasn't about to give that up for the false security of employment in a Gulag.

He refused his friend's offer, and the jobs that the Gulag administrators pressed upon him, and took pride in trying to persuade as many others as possible to join him. He was sure he was doing the right thing, but the departure itself, on the morning of 7 September 1941, was nevertheless unnerving. The Poles were expelled from the prison and made to lie down on the railway tracks. It was a horrible moment. Dolu feared that the Soviets were about to run a train over them. But then, as if it had been nothing, they were told their transport had arrived and they could leave.

Dolu's destination was Totskoye, the main camp of the Anders army. It was 1,600 kilometres to the south, but with the Soviet Union fighting a desperate war against the Germans, the journey took sixteen days. To be among so many Poles was a joy, but it was also sobering. At Totskoye, he saw a mass of people who looked nothing like a military force. They were all like him. Drawn, malnourished, disease-ridden, exhausted, dressed in rags. Their only asset, a determination to show the Bolsheviks that the Poles had fighting spirit. From this, Anders was supposed to create a military force.

And Dolu had one last obstacle to overcome before he could take his place in it. The fact that he was a Jew.

His admission interview had gone smoothly through questions about his skills and military history, until finally the question of his ethnicity arose. 'Jewish,' he responded. Why, then, did he want to join the Polish army? 'Because I am an officer in the reserve, and it's my war.' All right then, replied the admitting officer, 'but we'd better put you down as a Pole'.

The Soviet Union had not relinquished its claim over Lwów or the other territories in the east that it had invaded. It didn't recognise Dolu's former home as part of Poland. There had been a vote. Lwów was now Lviv, and Lviv was in Soviet Ukraine. The communists were willing to allow ethnic Poles to join the Polish army, but someone who wasn't a real ethnic Pole, as far as they were concerned, but merely a Jew, couldn't join up simply because they were Lwówian. There was no such place as Lwów any more. There was only Lviv and Lvivians – and Lvivians were Soviet citizens. The Soviets were Anders' paymasters, they fed his officers and their dependants. And they made the rules.

But they didn't always enforce them. With this one lie shared between two Poles, Dolu had made it into the Anders army.

At first he did not have a role, but then the camp quartermaster general saw Dolu's army application. And he knew exactly who it was from. The Iron King of Lwów. Dolu would be put in charge of supplying food to the camp.

Totskoye was chaotic. Tens of thousands of people had arrived, with more coming every day. Some people had their families with them, most did not. Nobody seemed to know how to find anyone else. When letters arrived from stranded exiles desperately seeking their relatives, the best that could be done was to stick them on the post office wall and hope that someone would see them.

On 15 October 1941, one of the many newly-minted officers in Poland's new army of exiles was reading the post office's message board when he gave a cry of delight. Lusia Finkelstein of 30 Babinska street, Semipalatinsk, was seeking her husband.

Second Lieutenant Adolf Finkelstein had found his wife. She had survived. And so had he. The man who claimed to have seen him dead, and been paid for washing his body, had been a fraudster.

Reunion and Freedom

Dolu would tell Lusia that the moment when he saw her name on the post office wall was one of pure joy. 'There was no end to my happiness. Just imagine, after more than one and a half years I suddenly found a trace which [allowed] me to re-establish connection with my beloved family, the only treasure I have got.'

In truth, the moment had been clouded with anxiety. For while the list had said that Lusia was looking for him, it hadn't included any news about Ludwik. Dolu feared the worst. And it took him weeks to discover that his son was still alive.

Dolu's first telegram to Semipalatinsk, relaying to Lusia and Ludwik the news that he had survived and was in Totskoye, arrived relatively promptly. After that, husband and wife exchanged a series of communications which all went missing. It was almost the middle of November 1941 before they were able to share their news properly.

It was just one of many reminders that while they were still alive, and no longer prisoners, they were all still stranded in a foreign land, far from home, far from each other, and far from safe.

Dolu was able to send a little money and, importantly, a certificate that he was in the army. But he couldn't bring his family to him. The camp couldn't accommodate them. And he couldn't go to them, because they were 2,500 kilometres away. It would take at least three weeks to get there and back, and he didn't have the leave. Their reunion would have to wait.

In the meantime, winter was approaching. When Dolu first wrote, Lusia had replied that the weather was 'beautiful and warm'. Very soon she was reporting that it was 'snowing and freezing'. And soon it got worse still. Within a couple of months, Lusia and Ludwik had to endure temperatures of minus forty-five degrees lasting for weeks, with fuel hard to come by. The snow was too heavy, and their clothes too thin, to go outside. The days dragged.

Food was a bigger problem. When the money from Dolu had first arrived, Lusia was overjoyed. She told Ludwik that they would dine in the finest restaurant in all of Semipalatinsk. So they did. In they went, and a waiter took my grandmother's coat and they sat down. Each was given a large and fancy looking menu card. Yet as they requested items, they were told that unfortunately this or that was off the menu today. Eventually, Lusia asked: 'Well, what do you have?' Just bones and cocoa, came the reply.

Bones and cocoa, they soon came to realise, was quite an abundant list. There was almost nothing in the town to buy. The few things that could be obtained on the black market were ferociously expensive. Even with the occasional remittance from Dolu – which couldn't be relied upon because the mail was so poor – money started to run low. Lusia's job sorting potatoes came to an end and she couldn't find any new work, even as a labourer, in a town teeming with refugees.

As Dolu was now a 'Soviet' officer, Lusia applied for an allowance as his wife. She was told that none would be forthcoming, as only families with two or more children were eligible. She did, however, receive a small bread ration and, whenever the weather didn't prevent it, the right for her and Ludwik to use the army canteen. The queues for this were enormous. Even once you got in, you would have to stand behind someone's chair, waiting for them to finish. Often there would be four people in front of you.

Lusia asked Dolu if perhaps he could send some food. 'It would be useful,' she wrote, 'to have something for our thin child, maybe a bit of fat, because here I cannot even dream about this.' And some would arrive, when it wasn't stolen on the way.

But mostly they went hungry. Lusia hung a bag over their bed to keep their precious bread supply safe from rats. Ludwik spent much of his days lying on the converted goods-wagon door, staring up at the bread bag, and dreaming of the moment when Lusia would next open it to give him a morsel.

———————

At least, however, it was better than the farm. Lusia was clear about that. Anything was better than the farm. And at least they knew where Dolu was. Many others in Semipalatinsk were nowhere near as fortunate.

Lusia had been reunited in the town with old friends from Lwów, all anxious to find family members. In her first letter to Dolu, she asked if he had any news of Marian Helm-Pirgo, whose sisters had been sharing a room with Lusia and Ludwik since the first days of the shack on the farm. And, now that she was back together with their old friend Jadzia Schrage and Ludwik's companion Aldona, Lusia wanted to know if anything had been heard about Ignacy.

Dolu was able to reply with good news for the Pirgo sisters. Their brother Marian was his good friend. They met almost every day in the Totskoye officers' mess. When he had told his friend that his sisters were safe, he had received an embrace of happiness and relief.

But for Jadzia and Aldona, all he could offer was that he knew that all the officers in Starobelsk had been transferred out before Dolu got there himself. 'So far, none of them have come here [Totskoye]. Therefore, Jadzia should stay calm because all of them are still missing and the search for them is ongoing. Probably because of the long distance they will be found a little later.' He still thought the fact that none of the officers had reappeared was good news. What the Soviets had actually done to them was impossible to imagine.

Even as little news as this – news that there was no news – was more than many people had. Lots of separated Polish deportees were destined to wander the Soviet Union without any idea how to find each other. And some families who had managed to stay together in captivity were separated in the early days of freedom. They got onto crowded Soviet trains without food or water. At a station, someone would get off to find provisions and, without warning, the train would suddenly leave, stranding someone who might never be seen again. This was a remarkably common fate.

If the Finkelsteins were to be together, it would have to be carefully planned.

At the end of December 1941, Dolu was called to the army headquarters and informed that a new camp for Anders and his troops was to be established in the Soviet Union, 2,100 kilometres to the south and east of Totskoye. It would be in a place called Yangiyul, in Uzbekistan, near Tashkent. Dolu would be sent ahead to help set it up. On 2 January 1942, he received his commission to carry out this task, signed by General Anders himself, and two days later he was on a train heading south. Just before he left, he sent Lusia a letter. 'I have decided one thing. Immediately after I have settled, I will bring you to me . . . we will reunite, and God willing, we will return together to our beloved fatherland.'

Being in the advance party meant Dolu could lay claim to the best accommodation, or at least somewhere a family could live. He'd identify a place, get it ready and send for them. And being an officer meant he could dispatch someone to collect Lusia and Ludwik, rather than require his wife and son to navigate the hazards of the railways by themselves.

It took almost two months, but one night in late February 1942 there was knocking on the door and windows of 30 Babinska street. It was well past midnight, and that was not a good time to receive a knock on the door in the Soviet Union. There is an old Soviet joke about a couple's terror when such a knock comes, and the relief they feel when it is only the neighbours letting them know that the building is on fire. Lusia didn't open her door before she had shouted, 'Who is it?' and received the reply, 'A Polish soldier.'

The soldier was Senior Rifleman Wojczek Kieloch, Dolu's emissary. It was, said Ludwik, 'my moment of liberation'. Kieloch was beautifully dressed, wearing a leather belt and fine uniform, and most important of all, he was carrying three kitbags of provisions. There was plenty of bread, numerous tins of canned food, some apples, a small bag of tea, a large drum of boiled sweets. As well as ten bottles of vodka and a bottle of aftershave to use for bribes. My father thought the rifleman 'a knight in shining armour'. The moment he saw the food that Kieloch had brought, Ludwik picked up a knife, ran to the bed, cut down Lusia's bag of bread and ate its entire contents.

Dolu had warned Lusia by letter that Kieloch was 'a very decent man, but not very clever'. She and Ludwik, he said, would have to keep their wits about them over the coming days. But Kieloch would nonetheless 'be of huge help to you. He will arrange for everything, carry your luggage, watch over you at night in the carriage to make sure you are not robbed, and he himself will take a nap during the day. He will get you hot food at stations and Russian tea etc etc.' For Lusia, after all her days fighting for herself and for Ludwik, such protection seemed like a miracle. In the coming days, they would be very grateful indeed for their escort.

Semipalatinsk station was packed, heaving with people. It was not, however, heaving with trains. There was only one train on the Turkestan-Siberian railway to Tashkent and it was obvious it was going to be a long wait for it to arrive. They would all have to camp out on the platform. And to do that, they would have to obtain a delousing certificate.

This was Kieloch's first job. Getting such a certificate required all three of them to attend a delousing station, but such a visit was out of the question. If you wanted to be covered in lice, the best way to achieve that was to attend a delousing station. Kieloch used the more hygienic method of a cash bribe to acquire a three-day certificate.

A three-day certificate, however, expired too quickly. Lusia and Ludwik were still waiting for a train, sleeping in the waiting room, hovering on the platform, four days later. Kieloch had to hand over more cash for further certification.

Finally, the train appeared. Immediately the crowd on the platform pressed forward, everyone desperate for a place. Kieloch cleared a path, using the bottles of vodka to persuade people to make way for his charges. It was during this scrum that he parted company with the aftershave that my father always satirised as 'The Breath of Stalin'. Some lucky train guard got it. And Lusia and Ludwik, with their protector, pushed their way onto the train. It was so full that people had to be shoved in through the windows, but the vodka, or perhaps the aftershave, obtained a door for Ludwik, Lusia and Kieloch to squeeze through.

Inside, they found a small corner in which to squat. And there they stayed for a further four days. Towards the end of the ride, as Dolu had anticipated, someone did indeed try to rob them as they changed trains, and Kieloch prevented it. They made it onto the last leg of the journey luggage intact, spirits rising, a one-hour train ride from Tashkent to Yangiyul. A one-hour ride to Dolu.

It was the beginning of March 1942. It had been almost two years since Lusia had last seen her husband, since she and Ludwik had watched his father leave their apartment to sign some papers. Almost two years since he had disappeared and they had been deported. So much had happened since Lusia had stared out onto the empty steppes of the Soviet Union and sworn that one day she would bring her son safely back into the arms of his father.

They had all starved, they had all been worked to the point of death, they had all endured misery and cold and loneliness and fear. There had been beatings and slave labour and intimations of death. And for much of that time they had endured these privations without knowing who still lived, without knowing if their trials would ever come to an end.

But now, here Dolu was. It was Ludwik who saw him first, catching sight of him from the train. His father in uniform, to his son's eyes so gallant, so beautifully turned out, so handsome. And on the station platform Dolu took his boy to him and hugged his Lusia tight.

———————

The moment of reunion had been wonderful. And not just for the family. For the whole community of stranded Poles. It was so rare for soldiers to find their families again and to bring them safely to camp, that there was a special Polish guard at the station. On the platform, and in Yangiyul, there was an atmosphere of celebration that, with so many lost, someone had been found.

Uzbekistan was warm, there were fruit orchards, they were well-supplied with food. After a few days, they all travelled with Dolu's new outfit, the First Signals, to the army base at Veliko Alekseyevskaya, very near Yangiyul. Here, accommodation – a room in a peasant's hut – had been arranged. On the journey, Ludwik sat with Dolu on the back of the truck, perching on piles of uniforms that he, as quartermaster, was transporting. Ludwik revelled in his father's company and his undivided attention. Lusia, meanwhile, sat in the driver's cab and reflected that, for the first time in these years of exile, she didn't have to keep her eyes on her son. For the first time, there was someone else to take care of him.

Ludwik remembered their stay in the south with the army as 'a very pleasant time'. He had friends there to keep him company. And Lusia decided that he should learn English and started to teach him. But in reality things were more difficult – and the situation more perilous – than they appeared to a twelve-year-old.

The Polish army could be very rigid. Dolu's fellow officers were distrustful of him as a former reservist and as a Jew. Petty arguments would break out over the slightest things. He was twice challenged to a duel, once because someone was offended at the way he handled the distribution of army bibles. Receiving a challenge sent 'as an officer and a gentleman on his honour', Dolu replied, 'as a middle aged businessman and a Jew, please stop being so ridiculous'.

He did, however, have some protection. His old friend, the one-time mayor of Lwów, Stanisław Ostrowski, had survived imprisonment in Moscow and was now Captain Ostrowski, the regiment's medical officer. It helped socially to have the support and friendship of this most aristocratic of Poles.

Yet such social and professional tensions, however irritating they were, were easily overcome by a family that had recently experienced so much worse. More concerning was the overall position of the Anders army.

There were three problems, all related to the fact that the Poles were still in the Soviet Union, still living in the country which had invaded their homeland and taken them captive.

The first problem was that Stalin wanted the Anders army to fight immediately, while Anders insisted that they weren't ready. They weren't fit, they weren't trained, and they weren't properly armed. The climate in the south was better than it had been in Totskoye, but contagious diseases were endemic. As one set of soldiers was recovering from the ill health caused by captivity, another set was falling ill. Many were still dying. Not to mention that, even if they had been battle ready, there was hardly a Pole who wished to risk their life fighting under Soviet command.

This led to a second problem: that of supply. The army had grown to 80,000 people. Feeding them all was very hard, something that Dolu experienced directly, as he had been personally responsible for it. His army reference later described his contribution to tackling the problem as remarkable, particularly his 'business tactics' when it came to dealing with the Soviets. 'Under the harshest conditions imaginable [he] gave everything that an iron will, extraordinary energy and self-sacrifice could give to the service,' his captain attested.

But as 1942 progressed, Stalin was increasingly reluctant to provide food to a force that wasn't fighting. He told the Poles that the Japanese war was interrupting wheat supplies to the Soviet Union, and he would therefore be reducing the rations for the Anders army to enough for just 26,000 men. If this happened, tens of thousands of Poles would be unprovided for and die.

On 18 March 1942, just as Ludwik and Lusia were establishing their new home in Veliko Alekseyevskaya, Stalin met with Anders in Moscow to discuss their differences. While Stalin relented a bit, the best he was willing to offer was rations for 44,000 men. When Anders asked how he would feed the other 40,000, Stalin replied that they would have to go and work on collective farms. This was how fragile Dolu, Lusia and Ludwik's new life was, even now.

The eventual outcome of the argument between the two men was heavily influenced by the discussion of a different matter altogether. The third problem for the Anders army. Where, Anders asked Stalin, were the 10,000 missing officers? A few months earlier, in a meeting with the Polish ambassador, Stalin had actually picked up the phone, made out as if he was calling the NKVD, and announced that they were telling him that all the missing officers had been released and were sure to turn up soon. So now Anders wanted to know where they were.

Stalin said he really didn't know. He certainly had no reason to hang on to them himself, he said. Perhaps Hitler's invasion was to blame. 'It may be that they were in camps in territories which have been taken by the Germans and come to be dispersed.'

But even as brazen a liar as Stalin began to tire of coming up with answers to the questions. He'd signed the order, Ignacy and his fellow officers had been massacred, they weren't coming back, and he knew that eventually that would become clear. His desire to avoid being pressed further gave him an incentive to agree to Anders' proposal that his army and its dependants be evacuated to Iran and join up with the British. At the 18 March meeting, Stalin agreed that 40,000 should go.

The problem was that the British didn't really want them, certainly not all of them. Especially those who weren't soldiers. They were particularly worried about thousands of children being dumped on them without permission.

One extraordinary British diplomatic telegram sent from the Cairo ministry – a full-blown British government ministry looking after British interests in the Middle East – was quite frank about the calculation.

To put matters brutally if these Poles die in Russia the war effort will not be affected. If they . . . pass into Persia, we, unlike the Russians, will not be able to allow them to die and our war effort will be gravely impaired. Action must be taken to stop these people from leaving the U.S.S.R. before we are ready to receive them . . . however many die in consequence.

A Foreign Office colleague responded to this document by saying that this paragraph, 'though no doubt true will, I fear, read rather oddly to the future historian. It might perhaps have been omitted.'

Anders did not see this telegram, but he understood that, however horrifying the sentiment, what it said was indeed true. Stalin didn't care if the Poles starved. Unlike with the British, it would be no embarrassment to him. He'd like to get rid of the Anders army leadership and all their pesky questions, but he'd happily keep some Poles to fight on the Eastern Front and let their dependants starve as slave labourers. The General could see he would have to get everyone out.

Eventually, working with the Polish government-in-exile based in London, Anders wore down Stalin and overcame British resistance. The army and its dependants would cross the Caspian Sea to Iran. They would stay together under Anders' command and fight alongside the British. It was a remarkable feat of persuasion by Anders, an achievement brought about by great strength of character, and political skill of a high order.

Even at this late stage, the Finkelsteins had almost been trapped in the Soviet Union. That they were not, they owe to Anders.

On 15 August 1942, it was the turn of the Finkelsteins to join the great evacuation of the Anders army.

Dolu went with the troops, leaving Lusia and Ludwik to make one last Soviet train journey by themselves, a distance of 1,700 kilometres west from Uzbekistan to Krasnovodsk in Turkmenistan. There they would board a ship to Iran. The station was eight kilometres from the harbour and the day was burning hot, the sun pitiless. At one point, they briefly found shade, and ducked into a hut, only to find themselves in a morgue, surrounded by the bodies of those who had died of heat exhaustion and disease.

Eventually, they bribed an NKVD officer to give them a lift on a lorry. It meant surrendering to him most of their remaining belongings, but they wouldn't have been able to carry them anyway. At this point, it really didn't matter any more. All Lusia and Ludwik wanted to do was to get out of the Soviet Union before someone changed their mind, or they fell ill, or their ship left without them. They hardly cared what they left behind.

They arrived at the harbour to find a large crowd assembled and an officer reading out the names of those people allowed to board. It seemed that there were two lists. List A for ethnic Poles and List B for Jews. Dolu may have registered for the army as a Pole, but now their Jewish surname had been noticed by the Soviets. There were hundreds of people on List A. Lusia and Ludwik were the only passengers on List B.

Lusia sized up the situation quickly. She announced loudly, 'List B comes first.' She turned to a Russian soldier standing guard and said, 'Carry my bags, please,' before sweeping up the gangplank with Ludwik. They obeyed. List B came first. The elegance of her former years and the tough conditions of Siberia had forged a formidable individual. No one was ready to say no to her.

The ship they boarded, the *Zhdanov*, was named after one of the more monstrous of Stalin's comrades. It was a ramshackle affair, packed with thousands of people, many suffering dysentery, others seasick, and with almost no sanitary facilities. It took two days to cross the 800 kilometres to Pahlevi on the far shore. It was a hellish journey, one final hurrah for the Soviet Union. But they had made it, free at last from Stalin and his rule. Everyone on board had a feeling of escape, of triumph over an enemy that had tried so hard to destroy them.

The *Zhdanov* was too big to take them right onto the beach; so, a little way out, the passengers were decanted into small boats, and then they had to abandon those too, and clamber into the sea.

This was how they reached Iran. Surrounded by her fellow Poles, followed by the son that she had fought so long and successfully to keep alive, Lusia Finkelstein waded through the water to the beach, taking the last steps to freedom, as all around her compatriots sang a hymn.

'Lord Who Has Saved Poland in Ages Past.'

MUM

Westerbork

The Nazi security services were pleased with themselves: '102,000 of the 140,000 Jews have now gone. The round-up on 20 June was a big success,' their Amsterdam headquarters reported to its superiors. 'The Dutch population does not agree, but did not oppose it.'

The June 1943 operation which swept up my grandmother, my mother and her sisters was one of the biggest so far. It carried off 5,542 people, the bulk of those Jews who still remained in south and east Amsterdam that summer. Among them were the rest of our close family – Grete's sister Trude, her husband Jan and my mother's only first cousin, Fritz. Jan's sister, my mother's Aunt Else, was also arrested. The only member of the family to escape was Else's daughter Marion, who somehow managed to evade capture and go into hiding. As did Betty, of course.

The whole thing had been very well-organised, hence the Nazi officers congratulating each other. They had managed to keep it secret until the last moment, making their swoop more effective. The aim of the operation was to gather together the Jews on their lists, add in those they came across by chance or who were betrayed by neighbours, register their prisoners at collection points, and then transfer them all to Westerbork camp. From there, they would be sent to the gas chambers.

That Sunday in June was very hot, unusually so for Holland, and Mirjam, Eva and Ruth sweltered in the three layers of clothing their mother had insisted that they wear. By the time they left the pavement outside their house, it was 10.30 in the morning; they had been waiting for an hour or more, and the sun was becoming unbearable. Carrying their heavy rucksacks, they then had a fifteen-minute walk under guard to the Daniël Willinkplein, the square designated as their collection point.

'There was no chance of running away or anything,' Mirjam later observed. 'We were guarded by people with rifles and pistols and so on. They would not have hesitated to shoot anyone down.'

There are photographs of the Jews walking to the Daniël Willinkplein that day, adults with children in tow, old people with their bags, shuffling down the street, crossing the main road, standing in the big broad square with its tall block of flats and trees at one end and its large expanse of grass with no shade at all.

The pictures were taken from surrounding houses by Dutch residents who were quite used, by now, to the sight they were seeing. Some of them watched from their rooftops with binoculars. At one of the collection points, Olympiaplein, where the SS officer responsible for the deportations, Aus der Fünten, was personally directing operations, Jews stood with their rucksacks, waiting to go on the first leg of the journey to their death, while their fellow citizens of Amsterdam carried on using the square for their normal Sunday sports matches.

The wait in the Daniël Willinkplein was relatively brief. The family was registered by some of the few remaining employees of the Jewish Council, and then ushered into one of the empty tramcars lined up on one side of the square. The irony that Jews were forbidden to be on trams was not lost on the passengers. Within half an hour they were at Amsterdam Muiderpoort, the railway station to the east of the city.

The station was crowded and chaotic, the atmosphere one of barely suppressed panic. David Cohen arrived during the afternoon, pleading the case of this or that individual, and getting nowhere. 'The ghastliness of the scenes enacted by these desperate people devoid of all hope was indescribable,' Cohen said.

Mirjam and the family were taken directly from the trams onto cattle trucks and the door shut behind them. Inside, the temperature was overpowering. 'Excruciatingly hot,' as Ruth described it. They all sat on the floor, tightly packed, without water, without sanitation. Children screamed, adults fainted from the heat, many were in tears, all were afraid.

The train remained in the station for ages before it left, and then proceeded agonisingly slowly. Whenever my mother talked of it later, she would always finish the description with the observation that she had only been in the truck for a few hours. And then add: 'Ludwik had been for three weeks in one of those cattle trucks, so that really was nothing in comparison.' This provides a better insight into her personality than it does into the discomfort everyone experienced.

At 8 p.m., the Wieners arrived in Westerbork.

My mother always felt badly about what she did now. She cried. And she didn't stop crying. Not for days.

'I must have been scared,' she reflected later.

My poor mother. If I think about it now, it must have been terribly hard for her. I suppose [it was] a sort of hysterics, basically. But I felt displaced . . . Eventually, I settled down. But I was ten years old, old enough to know what was happening. I suppose the fact of being away from home, taken away, very worried adults, a sort of a mêlée of people around me and so on, was probably more than I could really cope with. Though on the whole I was quite a reasonably good child, but I do remember that.

The place they had arrived in was a 'desolate, windswept peat bog' in the north of the country, still in Holland but close to the German border. They were in a transit camp, a prison to be held in until they could be transferred somewhere else. And in most cases, the transfer was to be to a site of mass murder.

When the Jewish community had been forced by the Dutch government to help build and pay for Westerbork as a place for new refugees to Holland to live, Grete's boss, Van Tijn, had been quite pleased by the job that had been done. Newly built wooden barracks, with proper heating, for single people; some private apartments for families; areas for craft activities; a children's village, and so on. And even after the Germans had taken over in July 1942, some of these facilities remained.

Yet, by June 1943, Westerbork was run-down, rat-infested, filthy and overcrowded. There could be no question of new inmates having any privacy, even if they were in families. Accommodation was in vast barracks with three-tiered metal bunk beds along the sides, and there were toilets outside without doors. Everyone was living on top of each other, for as long as they stayed.

Except for the people Ruth called 'the old-timers'. Those Jews, mainly German refugees who had been homeless and sent to the camp by the Dutch when it had first opened, now found themselves in the strongest position. They occupied the family cottages, and ran the camp administration. Ultimately, of course, the Nazi officers were really in charge, the old-timers were safe only as long as they did what they were told, and even then no Jew was ever really safe from immediate deportation. But, within the constraints of a dreadful policy over which they had no control, the old-timers had a lot of power. They had a significant say not just in the way the camp ran but also in the fate – the life or the death – of individuals.

It was with the old-timers that Grete and her daughters registered on arrival that first Sunday, 20 June 1943. Registration meant giving names and addresses and birth dates over and over again; it meant handing over your ration cards and valuables and having whatever money you had with you – in Grete's case eighty-three guilders, about £500 in today's money – counted, and later having it confiscated by the Lippmann-Rosenthal bank, the German-controlled bank which was used to steal Jewish assets; and it meant being assigned a barracks. Initially the Wieners would be in Barracks Number 65, at the back of the camp. It was for women and children only, and they would share it with 1,000 people. Soon they would be moved to Number 58, with similar properties.

But along with these routine matters, under the spotlights and amid the clatter of typewriters recording the details of hundreds of others, registration involved pleading for your life.

It was at registration that the clerk recorded reasons why deportations to the East – transportation to death – should be delayed. Families needed to provide valid exemptions if they could, and ensure that these were noted. Life in Westerbork was a constant fight to stay off the death lists, using whatever argument, personal relationship, document or force of personality might work. And that fight began at registration.

Behind all this, lay Heinrich Himmler.

By the end of 1942, with German forces bogged down at Stalingrad, Himmler had started to believe that the war was not going as well for Germany as Nazi propaganda would have it. And he begun to wonder if, perhaps, it might be a good idea if he could sell some Jews. In other words, he began to wonder if he couldn't exchange some Jews for money, or weapons, or for Germans stuck in Allied countries who might want to come home and fight for the Reich.

He even discussed the matter with Hitler. 'I have asked the Führer with regard to letting Jews go in return for ransom. He gave me full powers to approve cases like that, if they really bring in foreign currency in appreciable quantities from abroad,' he wrote in a note to himself on 10 December 1942.

There was a huge amount of self-delusion in this plan. Himmler thought the Allies much more amenable to negotiations than they would prove, which should have been obvious to him from the beginning. And he was also constantly trying to persuade himself and others that he was really a humane individual, even though he would order the commandant of Westerbork to help him make Europe Jew-free, and in the summer of 1942 had personally gone to watch the gassing of the first 1,000 Dutch Jews sent from the camp to Auschwitz.

Whatever the confusion in his thinking and motives, what it meant for the Jews arriving in Westerbork in June 1943, like Grete and the girls, was that their deportation might be delayed if they could show that they had some possible exchange value to the Nazis.

The registration card that Grete succeeded in having signed on that first night made three claims – one certainly untrue, one dubious, the third true but, as it turned out, shaky.

The untrue claim was that Alfred was an American citizen. While he was in New York, he certainly did not have citizenship, and the family's application to join him had gone nowhere.

The dubious claim related to someone called Erich Puttkammer, a Dutch banker with strong Nazi links. Puttkammer was involved in trying to negotiate exactly the sort of exemptions in exchange for foreign currency that Himmler had discussed with Hitler. Presumably, Grete thought Alfred might be able to lay his hand on such money and had initiated negotiations. There is certainly no evidence of money having been paid, or of the family having access to the sort of resources Himmler had in mind. The mention on the registration card – just the name Puttkammer, referred to twice but without further elaboration – is the only evidence of it in any of the Wiener papers. And the Puttkammer stamp often didn't work anyway.

The most important note on the card – because it was true and there were documents to prove it – is that the family was, at that point, eligible for a 'Palestine exchange'.

The origin of this exemption was arcane. Palestine had long

been a home for an orthodox Lutheran sect, known as the Templers. When the war had started, some of the men in the sect had returned to Germany in order to fight. They had then approached Himmler asking him to help them reunite their families. As the Templer families lived under British rule, reuniting them required an exchange of people between the Germans and the Allies. And in May 1941, Himmler had agreed to try to set one up.

The numbers involved had been tiny, but they had given people like Van Tijn an idea. If they created lists of Jews with certificates of their eligibility for a Palestine exchange, the certificates might delay their deportation, as the Germans might regard them as potentially useful. The certificate holders might never go to Palestine, but it could still save their lives, at least for a few months, just by keeping them off the trains to the gas chambers.

This is exactly what Alfred and Grete had achieved by making sure that Grete and the girls were on the Palestine list. They had not yet received confirmation of their certificates, but being eligible and having made the request were enough for now. On the family's registration card was typed: 'Remark: Temporarily put on hold Palestine Exchange current request.'

When the family had been arrested, my Aunt Ruth had taken with her the 1943 pocket diary that she had won in a magazine competition. As children do, she had, on receiving it, immediately filled in the front section – her name and address, her telephone number (90257), her shoe size (39/40), and whom to contact in an emergency (Auntie Trude and Uncle Jan Abraham at the House Marion) – added in a few birthdays (14 March Aunt Else, 16 March Papa, 1 April Uncle Jan, and so on), and had then left it unused.

Now she started making entries, and carried on doing so over the next nineteen months. She used a pencil that became blunt over time, and the space in the diary for each day was small. In addition, after a year she needed to fit a second note in for the same date. So the entries were terse, but they nonetheless provide an important record of the family's concentration camp experience.

Her first note, for 20 June 1943, records the bare facts of their arrest, their transfer ('very warm – long wait') and their 'arrival in Westerbork'. The next entry, for Tuesday, 29 June, explains in just six words what Westerbork was for. 'Transport with 2000 people sent away.' And then a week later, Tuesday, 6 July: 'Another transport sent away. Aunt Else and Juultje [a schoolfriend] are in this group.'

There was a rhythm to life in Westerbork. A terrible one. On Sundays, the camp commandant, Albert Gemmeker, would call together a group of his officers and some of the camp old-timers, and inform them of the number of Jews he had been instructed by his superiors to deport 'to the East' – to send to the gas chambers, though he never said that – that week. He asked for an update on the number of prisoners in the camp, the number claiming exemptions, and therefore the number available for deportation. And if there were more available prisoners than needed for his quotas, he would instruct those drawing up the lists how they should prioritise.

There weren't any rules governing this. Sometimes Gemmeker would exempt pregnant women and bedridden prisoners from deportation as a matter of course, sometimes he would say they were exactly the sort of people who should be deported first. It was worse still when the number of prisoners available was smaller than his quota required. Then Jews would have to be sent even if they had exemptions that previously protected them. When there was a quota to fill, no one was safe, whatever was on their registration card.

Once the meeting had considered some further logistics – when the deportation trains would leave, permissible bags, provisioning and so forth – the attendees were dismissed to start work on organising the transports and preparing the lists.

As Monday progressed, rumours swept the camp. How many would go this week? What had Gemmeker decided about his priorities? Which exemptions would still hold? Frenzied pleading and bargaining began as each family tried to ensure that, at least for this week, they might be spared. And as the day wore on, and it became more obvious who was staying and who was leaving, and that the time for arguing had gone, this frenzy gave way to a feeling of despair.

Then, on Monday night, in each barracks, the final list for deportation was read. 'The scenes that followed defy imagination,' said one eyewitness. 'The piercing shriek of a mother almost demented with panic, the sobbing of children, the stricken looks of the men, the anguished cries of those whose dear ones were to be torn from them – all this sends a shudder through one's very bones.' For others, there was a sense of relief, sometimes expressed inappropriately in dances of joy, almost always mixed with a feeling of guilt.

This my mother witnessed over and over again. This scene, Monday after Monday, for all the months that the family were in Westerbork.

By early the next morning, the train trucks had arrived. The biggest change that the Germans had made when they had taken over Westerbork was to extend the railway line right into the centre of the camp. This saved all the prisoners an hour-long walk both to and from the station with their luggage. But convenience for the passengers was not, of course, the motivation of the Germans. It was built so that they could more smoothly and securely transport people to their deaths.

Everyone was confined to barracks on Tuesday mornings until the trains were full and had left. Except, naturally, for those who were on the list, whose names would again be read out at 7 a.m. and who would then process, three abreast, to the trucks. By this point, there was generally a sense of calm resignation among those about to depart. Gemmeker would be on the platform, consulting with his officers, presiding urbanely as if he was seeing off travellers on an ordinary journey.

The passengers were loaded into goods wagons, with one barrel of water and one barrel as a toilet. People were packed in and sometimes, if they had difficulty walking, thrown on top of the other passengers. Obscenely, the railway company charged for a ticket. It was half-price, and paid for out of the Jewish assets that the Nazis had stolen.

The other people allowed to leave the barracks were those pressed into service as helpers, assisting old people onto the transports. After she turned sixteen on 4 August 1943, Ruth was forced to do this. And she understood what she was being made to do. 'It was very hard, very hard.'

'I had to help with one of those transports every Tuesday,' she said.

There was a transport to what they called the East. You didn't quite know where, although you had a very good idea by that time. Certainly I did . . . I had to help people with their belongings get on this train . . . and had to pretend they were going on a trip, and wished them a good journey and went through all that . . . We knew that they were more or less going to a certain death. You didn't have any evidence of that, but by that time rumours had been spread around enough.

Everyone hoped, of course. Everyone wondered if the rumours could really be right. Everyone tried persuading themselves that they couldn't really be true. Everyone tried telling themselves that they at least might be all right. But really, they knew.

After the war, Commandant Gemmeker, so often seen smiling benignly on the platform, claimed that 'naturally' he had no idea where the Jews – more than 100,000 people – were being taken; no idea that he was sending them to their deaths. The court appeared largely to accept his account. He was sentenced to ten years, but was released in 1951, returned to his home in Dusseldorf and lived there until he died more than thirty years later.

To which the best response is that, even in her attic hideaway, Anne Frank knew. 'Friday 9 October 1942 . . . what must it be like in those faraway and uncivilized places where the Germans are sending [the Jews]? We assume that most of them are being murdered. The English radio says they're being gassed.' And the House of Commons knew, after Foreign Secretary Anthony Eden had informed them on 17 December 1942 that the Germans 'are now carrying into effect Hitler's oft repeated intention to exterminate the Jewish people in Europe'.

The world knew. And Ruth knew.

———

'Tuesday July 13th 1943. Transport to Poland with Uncle Jan, Aunt Nuti and Fritz.'

In this short sentence, unaccompanied by any description or hint of emotion – for what could possibly be said? – Ruth recorded in her diary one of the family's greatest tragedies. The inclusion of Grete's beloved sister Trude and her family on one of the Tuesday deportations. My mother's only aunt, uncle and cousin. Without any documentation to protect them, it is surprising that they lasted in Westerbork even as long as they did. But in the list for the fourth transport to depart since their arrival, the names of the Abrahams were read out in their barracks on the Monday night.

The next morning, Trude – Aunt Nuti – sat down and wrote her sister and her nieces some final words. In neat lettering, inscribed on a small piece of folded lined paper, they were delivered to Grete in Barracks Number 58, just as the train was departing.

They are words that know and do not know what is about to happen, words that accept and deny, words full of hope when there was no hope left, words of love when love was all they still had.

Dear little sister,

I'm sitting on my bed, booted and dressed in three layers of clothes, awaiting breakfast. And I feel serene. I'm so firmly convinced that everything will go well and that we will find each other again, healthy and in better places, because you know, looking at what I've experienced in my life, everything always turns out all right.

I promise you one hundred per cent, I will take care of myself, Jan and Fritz will do the same, and all of you will too.

A first miracle, the d. . . [diarrhoea] is suddenly gone, last night already, what do you say about that?

At first, all of us were unable to sleep and we started reading again at 12 o'clock. Then I slept quite well until 3 o'clock. Since half past three it's been busy here. Ruth M quite forcibly gave me a jar of mayonnaise and a little tin of toothpaste, it's so touching how she cares.

Please stay well, I hope to see you soon, either in the little house here or in the big house in A'dam.

Greetings and kisses to my beloved three [my mother and her sisters], they are indescribably sweet and good, and I am so happy about their love.

I kiss you, my dear, a thousand times in my thoughts, you know that the two of us belong together and will find each other again, wherever in the world. Of that I am sure.

Your Nuti

On a separate piece of brown paper, Jan added his own words of love. 'One more thing, heartfelt greetings to you and the children, and thank you, Jan.' Before adding, 'Fritz is doing well.'

Until quite late in her life, my mother thought that the Abrahams had been taken to Auschwitz, and that is how the family told the story. But Trude, Jan and Fritz had died somewhere else.

In total, eighty-three trains left from Westerbork to go to the death camps. The majority headed to Auschwitz; but between

2 March and 20 July 1943, nineteen transports went to the Sobibor extermination camp in Eastern Poland. It is not obvious why there was a period of using this different camp. A likely explanation seems to be some sort of contest between senior Nazis over how many Jews each of them could kill and how efficiently.

More people died in Sobibor than in almost any other camp, and its very ruthlessness is the reason why it is not better known. Some of those sent to Auschwitz were not killed immediately, but were instead put to work. Those who did not die were able to tell their story as survivors. In Sobibor, no one was put to work. Arrivals were almost all taken directly to the gas chambers. The lifespan of a Jew arriving in Sobibor was around three hours. The number of Jews sent from Westerbork to this camp was 34,313, and only eighteen of them returned home at the end of the war.

These eighteen were among a handful of people selected on arrival at Sobibor to go elsewhere. They did not witness what happened in the camp itself. So if there had not been an uprising in the camp in October 1943, there would have been no survivors of Sobibor, nobody at all who could testify as to what had happened there. And the Nazis burned almost all the documents about it.

But as it is, there is just enough witness testimony to allow a picture to be painted of Sobibor. Of how it was designed to look completely innocent from the outside, so that victims wouldn't suspect anything upon arrival. Of how there were three areas to the camp, all built around a railway line bringing deported Jews from Westerbork and other transit camps. Of how the first area housed guards brought in to manage the march to death; a second area was where prisoners undressed and their luggage was sorted; and a third, with additional barbed wire, was where the gassings took place.

The camp was staffed by around twenty German SS officers and a contingent of something like a hundred former prisoners of war from Ukraine, Estonia, Latvia and Lithuania, who were collectively known as 'Ukrainians'. These were volunteers – often choosing this murderous task over starvation – who had been drilled at the Trawniki training camp to carry out the guard work in extermination camps. Whether or not they had been pressed into service, they proved fanatically loyal to the Nazi killers and appallingly brutal.

The Ohio car-worker John Demjanjuk, who in the 1980s was wrongly accused of being 'Ivan the Terrible' of Treblinka, was, it transpired, in fact a Ukrainian guard at Sobibor. All that it proved possible for the courts to establish from his identification documents was that he had been present in Sobibor between the end of March and the end of September 1943. But this was enough to convict him, in May 2011, of having been an accessory to the murder of 28,060 people. For nothing other than murder took place in Sobibor. The dates of Demjanjuk's presence mean that among the deaths he was found guilty of assisting were those of Trude, Jan and Fritz.

The moment that the trains from Westerbork arrived, the guards, shouting abuse and commands, would throw open the wagon doors and drive out the prisoners with clubs, whips and rifle butts. Then the able-bodied were divided from the disabled.

The people who couldn't walk were loaded onto carts and told that they were going to hospital. The carts travelled 200 metres to a pit surrounded by shrubs, where they were pulled off the cart and shot. Those who could walk were marched to the area set aside for undressing, the men separated from the women. And there they were given a lecture by a white-coated officer of the SS, who told them that after such a train journey they needed to have a shower. They were going to be put to work and for this they had to be clean. Leave your valuables. No need to bring towels and soap. Everything would be provided. Sometimes they would even be asked if they had any questions.

Then the victims would enter the third part of the camp, naked, and be directed to a large shed where men waited with scissors.

The men would grab hold of the prisoners' hair and within half a minute they would have hacked it all off, to be collected and sent for processing at a firm near Breslau which paid half a Reichsmark per kilo.

Once this was done, they were herded – clubbed or whipped – into the gas chamber, 700 or 800 people packed into twenty-five square metres, the gas was pumped into the sealed room and, after half an hour, the doors could be opened. Everyone was dead. The bodies were pressed together so tightly that they were still upright.

This is how Aunt Trude, Uncle Jan and cousin Fritz died on Friday, 16 July 1943.

In June 2010, when she was seventy-seven years old, my mother sent an email to all her children, nephews and nieces. As it was something – writing us a note about the Holocaust, unprompted by us – that she had never done before, and didn't do again, we were all quite struck by it. She wanted to remind us all about her Aunt Nuti. It had just been the anniversary of Nuti's birth. Not a special anniversary, as she had been born in 1893, 'not a shattering event', wrote Mum, 'but it made me think of her and her family and how little I knew her'.

Jan's sister, Aunt Else Lazarus, had gone to the gas chambers just before her brother. Else's daughter Marion had died too. She had daringly hidden in a wardrobe on the night that everyone else had been arrested, and had gone into hiding in Amsterdam. But in May 1944, she had been betrayed and had eventually been deported to Auschwitz. At the end of January 1945, she died on one of the so-called 'death marches', when the Nazis forced Auschwitz prisoners to flee with them as the Russians approached the camp. They shot those who couldn't keep up, and left the bodies by the side of the road.

An entire family, Mum said, were 'wiped off the face of the earth'. She was writing about Nuti 'not to cause horror and dismay but to bring a spark of her existence back'. She recalled Fritz's dark curly hair. Who else was going to?

The Transfer

The main objective of life in Westerbork was simply to stay in Westerbork. And after the trains had departed on a Tuesday morning, those left behind always felt a sense of relief. They were dazed, they were often mourning friends or family who had just been taken, but they knew they had a few precious days free from danger before the weekend, when the whole cycle began again.

The day before Trude, Jan and Fritz were put on the train 'to the East', a letter arrived for Grete from Geneva, through the Red Cross, telling her that the Palestine exchange certificate had been granted for her and the girls. The timing was important. Grete's distress at her sister's prospective departure was so great that she had contemplated volunteering to join Trude. She knew what deportation meant, but whatever they had to face, at least they would be together. 'If we hadn't been there – us children – she would have definitely gone with them,' my mother said.

Now, with the certificate seemingly assured, Grete realised that, however overwhelmed she might feel at being parted from Trude, her duty was to try to save Mirjam, Eva and Ruth. And perhaps, with the certificate, she would be able to.

Which made what happened next all the more devastating. On Saturday, 17 July, just a few days after Trude's deportation, a letter from the camp commandant was read out in all the barracks.

Grete with her beloved sister Trude in 1919

Grete in the late 1920s

Jan van Eijckstraat before the war. The first set of doors on the left led to the Wiener family apartment and the Jewish Central Information Office

Before the war: Betty from Amsterdam with my mother on her lap (as well as Eva and Ruth and a playmate in the foreground)

After the war: Betty from Nottingham with my sister Tamara on her lap

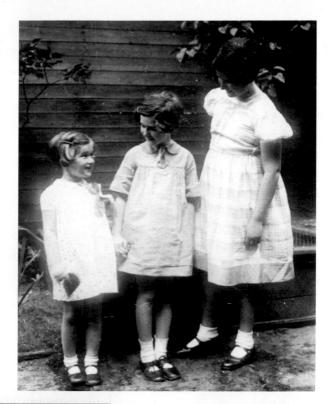

The Wiener girls in 1939. Left to right are Mirjam, Eva and Ruth

Trude Abraham with her son Fritz

One of the family's yellow stars

Two Montessori school girls: Mirjam (left) and Anne Frank

The Wiener girls in America a few months after their release
(left to right Eva, Mirjam and Ruth)

The leader of the passport effort: Aleksander Ładoś

(Top right) The blue cover of the Paraguayan passport

The inside of the passport filled out for the Wieners, stating they are Paraguayan

Camille Aronowski with Mirjam in the 1950s

A painting by Eva of Alfred reading *The Times* in Golders Green

Alfred in his study in the Wiener Library
in Manchester Square in the early 1950s

Alfred shows President
Theodor Heuss his name
on an SS list, 1958

Mirjam's picture taken by
Harry Borden outside
our dining room in Hendon

The Palestine list exemption no longer held. Anyone who had one should prepare themselves for the possibility of deportation. The move made about 1,200 more people eligible, and soon the reason for it became clear.

On Monday the 19th, Ruth recorded in her diary: 'Critical situation for us regarding the Tuesday transport – not enough people to make up the total.' Gemmeker was 700 Jews short.

Grete spent that day in frantic attempts to keep the family off the list. She had Alfred's war medals, and it is possible that they may have helped. There was the fact that he was currently living in the United States, which could have been made to sound more than it was. But the most likely assistance was that she was a German Jew, and so were the old-timers compiling the list. More than that, Grete had a record of helping other German Jews.

Shortly after the family arrived in the camp, Ruth's diary recorded that Grete had told the girls 'to say Uncle Erich and Aunt Vera to the Cohns'. In other words, to give Mr and Mrs Cohn the honorary title of Uncle and Aunt in order to stress the friendship of the Cohns and the Wieners. The Cohns were old colleagues of Alfred's, and people Grete had assisted as refugees in Amsterdam. In Westerbork, Erich Cohn had become one of the old-timers most involved in the compiling of Gemmeker's lists, which is why the girls had been told to be friendly to them. It is certain that Grete would have approached him at this crucial point. On the other hand, Ruth later noted that the Cohns had been 'rather distant and not helpful. A great disappointment to Mother!'

So perhaps the vital assistance in keeping the family from the list had come from someone else, another old-timer. Perhaps it had just been luck. Whatever was the case, on Tuesday, 20 July, Ruth was able to write: 'Thank G-d we are not being sent away.' Then she added: 'Mother becomes ill.'

For as long as one wasn't sent off to die, it was just about possible to live in Westerbork.

There was just about enough food, just about enough warmth, just about enough protection from disease. It was a life lived in fear, a life lived in public, and a life lived in captivity. But it was, just about, a life.

Westerbork was a dusty, grey-black colour, cold in winter and full of flies in summer. It made little stabs at normality. There was, for instance, a camp store. It had hardly anything in it, certainly not any food. The girls remember buying some toothpaste – or was it a toothbrush? – and having the amount credited against the money that had been taken from them on the first evening.

Although washing and going to the toilet all had to be done in public, there was, at least, occasional access to hot water, and there were tickets that allowed you to go to the bathhouse once a fortnight or so. There was a camp laundry too, although opportunities to use it were so limited that most washing had to be done in the barracks basins whenever you could.

There was limited contact with the outside world, with letters and packages allowed in and even some correspondence allowed out. Alfred could not be in touch directly, but there was communication from his associates in Switzerland. They sent chocolate, and sardines, and a little bread from time to time. The packages were withheld, before arriving in batches. As there was no privacy in the camp, the contents were shared.

One 'package' the Wieners received was less welcome. A few days after the family was arrested, a removal van with the words 'A. Puls Amsterdam' painted on the side had appeared outside the apartments at 25 Westerscheldeplein, their old home. It belonged to the removal firm of the Dutch Nazi Abraham Puls, whose company would visit the homes of arrested Jews and confiscate the belongings they had left behind. It was known as being 'Puls-ed'.

The removers were particularly keen on stealing book collections, and took all of Alfred's. As he never put a bookplate or markings in any of his volumes – his reverence for books was such that he thought writing or sticking things in them was a desecration – he was not able to retrieve any of them after the war, even though some were still in a Nazi warehouse.

But A. Puls Removers did send victims a suitcase of possessions to Westerbork, a very typical Nazi manoeuvre designed to conceal crime behind a respectable veneer. My mother remembers that the items they chose to send were random and useless. Only the suitcase itself was of any practical use.

A postal service was just one of the ways the camp contrived to seem normal. Westerbork also had a hospital. In the autumn of 1943, Mirjam and Eva fell ill with infectious hepatitis. It was serious for both of them, but Westerbork boasted quite good medical facilities. They 'carefully made sure that we got better', said Mirjam.

They gave us sugar – it was supposed to be good for the liver. I don't know whether nowadays they do such things. But they put us into an . . . isolation ward until we were better. Although what on earth they did that for – the mind boggles. Why not just chuck you in the next wagon, you know? But that's the Germans for you. It's amazing.

One answer to Mirjam's questions is that Gemmeker was keeping up a pretence. Definitely to the inmates, perhaps to himself as well. Westerbork was just a holding camp, and people were being sent to the East to work. So of course there was a hospital and medical care. The other answer was the one that my mother hit upon. The mind boggles. It's amazing.

Perhaps the oddest feature of Westerbork, odder even than the hospital, was its theatre. This allowed the organisation of variety shows, featuring Dutch and German Jewish comics, singers and actors, who formed themselves into a company. Gemmeker was very proud of this. He would show up for rehearsals and provide his artistic input, and he invited fellow senior Nazi officers to come to the camp for special first night productions. He would protect the artistes from deportation for a while, but many of them ended up being gassed in Auschwitz anyway.

For the inmates, the skits and singalongs provided moments of distraction from their troubles and fear. They featured gentle jokes about life in camp, about the joy of receiving packages, and so on. 'Nothing anti-Nazi,' said Ruth, 'you wouldn't be able to do that.' They 'were a lot of fun', added Eva. Mirjam didn't attend. She may have been too young.

The other distractions were work and schooling. Although perhaps 'schooling' is putting it a bit strongly. As Mirjam described it: 'It was allowed to gather some children together and do a little bit of reading or to sing songs.' Years later, the memory of these songs would sometimes return to her unbidden, and she would sing them to her family, still word-perfect.

Ruth, however, wasn't allowed to attend the classes. In June 1943, she was little more than a month away from her sixteenth birthday, and, like Grete, she had to work. The family had arrived just in time for the potato harvest, so she was sent out of the camp each day to do unpaid labour on local farms. The ground was soggy clay, the work was 'gruelling' and lonely, and she had to wear overalls and extremely uncomfortable wooden shoes. The only compensation was that at least it was something to do, something to keep you absorbed.

She felt the same when, after the harvest, she was assigned to work in the laundry. This again was very hard work. Ruth had to manipulate the mangle and a huge heavy iron, and be part of an assembly line folding sheets without let-up during a shift that lasted all night. Most of the laundry was for the German officers, but working there did mean that Ruth could wash the family's clothes and bedding more often. And, as autumn came, nights in the laundry kept you warm.

What upset Ruth, however – and my mother didn't feel quite the same, because she was younger, because there had been the pretence of classes – was that while she was washing the Nazis' clothes and picking their potatoes, she was missing out on her education. She had loved school. She loved learning. The loss obsessed her. She thought later that perhaps this obsession was an attempt to suppress other fears.

She tried her best to replace what she was missing. Her old teacher from the Joods Lyceum, Jaap Meijer, destined to become a famous writer and historian, was in the camp and living in a barracks near to Ruth's. She went to him for lessons in Hebrew and Jewish history. They worshipped together as well. It was still possible to have services in Westerbork on the major Jewish holidays.

Yet Ruth pined for school and teaching and the teenage life she was being denied.

———————

For Grete, it was profoundly painful to watch her children suffer. She tried her best not just to help them survive, but to console them, as my mother cried at the crowds and strangeness of Westerbork, or as Ruth cried over her lost prospects and her education. There was little Grete could do, little she could say, to put it right, but she tried.

On the night before Ruth turned sixteen, her mother somehow provided her with carnations – Ruth never knew how – and also wrote her a letter of love and support, one which captured Grete's hope for the future. But also showed how hard things were for her, without Alfred and with Trude now gone too.

My beloved child,

Tomorrow you will be 16 years old; no longer a child but a young woman, a very young woman. A new stage of life is about to begin for you.

In more normal times, we would have celebrated this new

beginning with everything good and beautiful; with many wonderful and useful, and also not so useful, gifts, with good food and drink, with cake, fruit, ice cream and chocolate; and above all, together with all our loved ones and friends.

That all this is impossible fills me with great regret, but you know, my dear, it is like this for everyone now, and we must hope that we will be able to catch up on it all one day.

My own 17th birthday was so wonderful and harmonious, and I would have wished the same for you. And I promise you that I will do everything in my power to make it up to you and Ev and Mirjam for all the current hardships.

My child, I have so much to tell you on your birthday, and because some things are so difficult to say, I am writing to you.

Above all, I have to say today (which you may not fully understand) how much your development in the last year has delighted me. It is a wonderful and pleasurable experience for a mother when she sees her child develop abilities and qualities that she wished for them to have. It is a much deeper happiness than that of the birth of the child. And how much does a mother actually contribute to that!?

Today I stand before you and must thank you, my dear, big girl! You were a true support to me in the difficult last few weeks, from the moment you got out of your nice, warm bed, early in the morning on that terrible 20th of June, and helped me so capably and understandingly. And then your behaviour here, under such terrible circumstances, your starting a new kind of work, your love and trust that you have shown to me, my dear, how grateful I am to you for everything!

You see, I had to write this to you, because if I said it to you, in your modesty you wouldn't want to listen. Tomorrow Papa will think of you with love and longing. I wish the day would come when I can give him back his daughters. I am very unhappy, you know, that he could not experience these 3 years of your development! How amazed and happy he will be to have you back.

And Aunt Nuti, Uncle Jan and Fritz are thinking of you! How far away everyone is that belongs to us. We should not even think about what was done to us. And we must be glad that the four of us are together.

My dear, I hug you and kiss you, I pray for you that you remain healthy and so beautiful and pure, that our dear God may reward your loving and childlike willingness, that he may give you much joy, and above all, the opportunity to develop your abilities. For that is the greatest happiness in life for every thinking person, the development of one's own personality.

Don't be sad that you can't continue learning like you did at school, that's all to come. You know, I also only did my Abiturium [the German equivalent of A levels] after years of interruption, and then went on to study further. I think you have the optimism to do that. I was so upset to see you crying tonight. My dear, let me do the crying.

Look, I am so tired, so worn, so sick from everything I had to go through in the last few years, and I am therefore probably often too serious, too heavy, too sad for you. You should not worry about that. Perhaps the time will come for me too when I can laugh again. Don't be angry with me, my dear child, if I have sometimes burdened you with my worries. Tomorrow we all want to think of a good future that will bring us all together again, with Papa and with the Abrahams.

Hopefully the cake will also arrive, and some gifts too, which were supposed to come today. First of all, take the carnations from me, put them on the table and take them as a symbol of the beauty and joy that I long for in the rest of your life.

I hug and kiss you, little big woman, I hope you understand me and have a little idea of how much I love you.

Mutti

When Ruth died in 2011, at the age of eighty-four, a mother
of two and grandmother of three, her son found Grete's letter in
the drawer by her bedside.

————————

In her diary for Monday, 22 November 1943, Ruth recorded a
camp meeting to which she and Grete were summoned. It was
with someone called 'Miss Slottke'. Ruth described arriving at
7 p.m. and being kept waiting until 11.30. After which she added,
'[we] are then told that the transport on the next day will not
take place. (This was supposed to have been a "good" transport
to the Exchange Camp in Celle).'

What going to Celle really meant was going to Bergen-Belsen.

In the spring of 1943, Himmler's interest in holding Jews as
hostage had found concrete expression in the creation of a special
kind of concentration camp. The German Foreign Office shared
Himmler's view that it might be possible to exchange Jews, with
its particular interest being swaps for Germans interned by Britain
and America.

In March that year, it sent a memo to the Reich Security Main
Office, the office of the police and SS who worked under Himmler,
asking that

About 30,000 Jews . . . who appear suitable for possible
exchange be held available for this purpose. It [the Foreign
Office] requests that care be taken that these persons are not
deported for the time being. In case the above-mentioned
exchange negotiations come to nothing, the deportation of
these Jews can still take place later.

The proposal was agreed. And, within a month, Himmler had commissioned a senior SS officer to create an exchange camp to corral the chosen people. The result was the establishment of the Belsen exchange camp.

By the summer of 1943, the camp had begun to receive Polish Jews, sent there with documents that suggested they might have exchange value. And by the autumn, the SS had begun to look for similar people among the Dutch and German Jews in Westerbork. That was what Gertrud Slottke was doing on that Monday night in November when she had summoned Grete and Ruth.

After the war, Slottke would claim that she had just been a secretary, and indeed until February 1942 she had merely been a stenographer in one of the Dutch security offices. But then she began to work for Wilhelm Zöpf, the Nazi officer charged by Eichmann with implementing the Final Solution in the Netherlands. In this role, she acquired the power of life and death.

For it was Slottke's job, one that she was enthusiastic about, to advise on which exemptions should be accepted and which rejected. And she did not like to do this sitting in her office. She was too diligent for that. She came down to the camp and involved herself personally in the picking and choosing.

Those who had the misfortune to encounter her, described Slottke as being friendly enough in their meetings and always to the point. But they also recalled her as being 'a nightmare come to life', 'a witch', 'an apparition' and a 'bat-like presence'. When Slottke eventually faced trial in 1967, it was obvious she saw herself rather differently – as the real victim, subject to a gigantic miscarriage of justice.

Slottke's November visit had come to nothing, but she was back at the beginning of January, once again reviewing documents and considering exemptions. And this time, for the Wieners, the review would change their circumstances entirely.

Death in Westerbork was only a matter of time. Ruth's diary is stark. 'Saturday August 14th 1943: Another transport arrives from Amsterdam . . . Dineke Roosevelt [a classmate] is among them . . . Monday August 16th: Met Dineke . . . Tuesday August 24th: Another transport ["to the East"] – Dineke among them. I become ill for four days . . . Monday August 30th: We are on the "transport list" again, but manage to get off . . . Tuesday August 31st: Yet another transport – Jenny [classmate and friend] is included.' Stay in the camp and one day their luck wouldn't hold. Slottke provided the one chance to leave, without leaving for the gas chambers.

What Slottke was looking for was evidence of any form of dual citizenship. If she found it, she would instruct the holder to prepare to leave for Belsen. And the reason why Ruth had the impression, recorded in her diary, that this was a 'good' camp, was that Slottke extolled its virtues. The food was good – even kosher, she claimed, if they wanted it. 'She sounded like a travel agent, trying to talk us into a vacation trip,' said one of my mother's camp contemporaries. It was all very odd, as she wasn't asking for volunteers. If she decided you were going to Belsen, that's where you would go.

Grete had the Palestine documentation that had helped before, but what did the trick this time was a set of papers more recently acquired. Somehow, the Wieners had become citizens of Paraguay.

Early in January 1944, in their barracks, Grete received a small piece of brown paper, about two inches by one and a half inches, with carbon-copied instructions and names typed in. She 'and her daughters Eva and Mirjam' – Ruth, as an adult, received a separate summons – would be sent to the exchange camp on 11 January.

Camille

Towards the end of November 1943, a forty-three-year-old woman called Camille Aronowski, who was working as a secretary in Bern for a local door manufacturer, received an unexpected visit from the Swiss police.

The authorities had found out, they said, that she had been buying large quantities of Nazi newspapers and collecting examples of fascist propaganda before sending them abroad. Curious – and worried that the activity might be some form of espionage or might endanger Swiss neutrality – the federal prosecutor's office had asked the police to investigate. And here they were.

Who was she, they wanted to know. And what was she up to?

Camille was happy to answer. There was nothing misleading about her apparent profession. She really was just a secretary for a door company. Before that, she'd worked for a printing manufacturer in a similar role. Collecting Nazi newspapers wasn't what she did for a living.

She'd been born Camille Weill, married a Polish lawyer called Samuel Aronowski, and had two children with him. After five years, Sam had left to live in Warsaw, only coming back after the Nazi invasion of Poland. Within a few weeks he had died, and now here she was, still in the old marital home, with her mother sharing the premises. Together with a Polish refugee child she had taken in. She lived a perfectly ordinary life.

And the newspapers?

That was simple to explain. Her much younger sister, Yvonne Weill, was secretary to the well-known local lawyer Georges Brunschvig, Camille related. When, ten years ago, he was starting out on what was to be a stellar career, Brunschvig had sued the publishers of the *Protocols of the Elders of Zion*. And Camille had become friends with one of the other members of the prosecution team – Alfred Wiener.

It was Alfred for whom she was buying the papers. He would send her notes listing the publications he was after, with a particular emphasis on official German Nazi party newspapers that were available in Switzerland. It was one of those notes, in fact, that had triggered the police investigation. She would buy them, bundle them up, visit the Bern post office or the Franke bookshop, and post them off to the home of John Oppenheimer in Long Island, New York.

Camille told the police she had sent about 150 packages of books and 400 bundles of newspapers over the last couple of years. She'd kept pretty precise records.

The officers were satisfied with what they heard. The conclusions of their report were benign.

The entire Aronowski family, including the persons living in the same household, have a good reputation and have never given the security or criminal police of the city of Bern cause to deal with them, with the exception of violations of traffic regulations . . . It should be noted that Mrs. Aronowski is considered intelligent and fluent in multiple languages . . . The outlook of Mrs. Aronowski is probably Swiss, or at least the investigations did not reveal any clues that could give rise to any remarks concerning her outlook.

With this, the police declared their intention to leave Camille alone. And they did.

What they did not ask Camille, and what she did not tell them, is what else she had been doing to help Alfred. Had they done so, the conclusions of their report might have been less favourable.

From the moment the Germans had invaded Holland, Camille had been Alfred's chief aide in the desperate search for visas for Grete and the girls. Based in a neutral country, it had been easier for Camille to make applications. So it was she that had facilitated the failed attempts to obtain US visas, and she who had been caught up in the Cuban visa scam, paying money for a stamp that proved invalid.

But in the summer of 1943, the weeks after Grete and her daughters had been arrested, Camille had finally got somewhere. And the result was a letter she sent on 3 July addressed to 'Frau Dr. Margarethe Wiener, z.Zt.Konzentrationslager Westernbork, b/ Amsterdam, Holland'.

By the time Grete received it, the letter had been opened by the censors. It was taped along its left-hand side, with small ink-stamped swastikas over the new seal. And perhaps anticipating that it would be read by the authorities, Camille had been careful how she expressed herself.

> Dear Dr Wiener,
>
> I have just learned that you have been taken to the Westernbork camp with your children and your niece Betty. This must be based on a mistake, because thanks to the efforts of your relatives you should get a foreign passport.
>
> I ask for immediate notification of your exact data, first names, birth dates, etc. so that I can send you the necessary papers immediately.

Alfred is fine and I hope that you are all in the best of health too.

Hoping to find out more from you soon, I remain, with best regards and wishes also from Alfred,

very warmly

Yours, C Aronowska.

Camille was revealing in this letter that there was much she didn't know about the Wieners' situation. She misspelled 'Westerbork', and even 'Margarete' (people often spelled it 'Margarethe' with an 'h', as that is the more common German spelling, but Grete always spelled her full name as 'Margarete'). And she clearly didn't know that Betty was no longer with the family.

But she probably did know that Betty was not Alfred and Grete's niece. She had phrased her letter that way because the passport she was promising to send was for a single family, and for Betty to be included she would have to be represented as a relative.

The document Camille was seeking to provide was one of the Paraguayan passports that the Ładoś Group had been creating, one of the ones that the Polish official Juliusz Kühl had been obtaining, having negotiated the fee with the Paraguayan consul.

Abraham Silberschein, the Polish Jew with whom the diplomats had been working, had kept a record of those people he had identified as possible recipients and passed on to the others in the Ładoś Group. And there was a record too of those from whom the Group had raised money to pay off the consul. But Camille's name was not in either of these files. Because her route to the passports had been different to almost anyone else's.

While Camille was already a forty-three-year-old widow by 1943, her sister Yvonne was still in her twenties, and had become engaged to a Pole living in Switzerland. That winter, Yvonne had married, and Camille had become the sister-in-law of Juliusz Kühl. The only known photograph of the Ładoś Group together was taken at the wedding of Yvonne and Juliusz. This is how Camille was able to secure the precious passport: she had been given it by Juliusz.

It was a good thing the Swiss police hadn't worked out this entanglement with the passport ring that they so detested. Who knows what trouble that might have caused.

This extraordinary chain of relationships, coincidences, inventiveness and bravery linked Alfred's years in Switzerland suing the publishers of the *Protocols* with his family becoming citizens of Paraguay.

On 29 July 1943, Camille wrote again to Grete. By now she had the name of Westerbork right, and was spelling 'Margarete' correctly too.

Dear Margarete

Thank you for your lines from 25 June. I hope that by now you have received my letter of 3 July. I reported to Alfred immediately and received your dates of birth provisionally from him, as we hope to be able to send you your passports soon.

Now I need to have from you as soon as possible:

Exact personal descriptions (hair colour, eyes, face size, constitution, etc.), as well as passport photos of all of you, several copies if possible, so that the passports can be filled out and sent to you.

I would be happy if I could take care of the children through the Red Cross and I am taking steps in this regard. Above all, I must have your passport photos as soon as possible.

Alfred is fine and, like me, intervened at the Palestine

Office so that you could be put on the exchange list. You will have received the message from Geneva by now.

Is Betty with you? I should have her data too.

I close in the hope that you are in good health and with best wishes for all of you.

Very warmly,
Yours, Camille.

With this information – the usual requirements to enable the Poles to fill in one of the blank passports – Camille was soon able to send the Wieners their new papers. They arrived in Westerbork in the late autumn, a few weeks before Slottke's first visit.

The passport was one of the very last that the Ładoś Group managed to complete and get Hügli to sign. Just a few more weeks and it would have been too late.

Belsen

On the afternoon of Sunday, 15 April 1945, after the Nazis had agreed a local ceasefire, British troops entered the camp of Bergen-Belsen. They were totally unprepared for what they found. For the rest of their lives, they would be haunted by that moment. Some of them could never talk about what they saw, while others could talk of little else.

There were corpses everywhere. Inside the wires, between the wires, in the huts, between the huts, in the gutters. The stench was unimaginable. There were signs of newly filled-in mass graves, and an open pit half full of bodies. And alongside the dead were the half-alive. Thousands of naked, or half naked, people lying on the floor, so many that it was impossible to lie at full length. They lay because they were too weak to stand. Many were weak from disease, primarily typhus. Others were weak from hunger.

There was no water, no sanitary facilities, no food. This is what had happened to Himmler's camp of hostages. This was how his failed idea of swapping thousands of Jews for Germans who wanted to come home and for resources had ended.

When the Wieners had arrived in January 1944, there hadn't been thousands of people in Belsen. In fact, as Mirjam observed, 'it was almost empty'. The family had been on the first train from Westerbork, with its contingent of Dutch Jews joining only a small group of mainly Greek Jews who had arrived in Belsen the previous summer. Prisoners who had built the camp could be seen through barbed wire in a separate adjoining section.

Though Grete, Ruth, Eva and Mirjam had travelled in an ordinary passenger train, sent on their way with Slottke's promises about Belsen's sterling qualities, the moment that they disembarked, the reality of where they had been sent began to make itself clear.

They had journeyed overnight, leaving Westerbork at about 6 p.m., stopping continuously, crossing the border into Germany at around midnight, seeing out of the windows the rubble to which Allied bombing had reduced Bremen. And at 8.30 in the morning they had finally arrived in the small railway station at Celle in Northern Germany. At least this wasn't Poland, at least they hadn't been tricked. But this was the only cause of relief. As the train pulled in, the platform filled with members of the Waffen-SS, each accompanied by a barking, snarling guard dog, and shouting, 'Raus! Raus!' as they opened the carriage doors.

The railway station was about an hour's walk from the camp and the prisoners set off on foot, carrying their own luggage. Even from a distance, as they approached, they could see barbed wire and watchtowers and hear more barking dogs. The word my mother would use most often to describe Belsen was 'bleak. It was terribly bleak.' Ruth immediately realised how different it was to Westerbork. 'I felt a little scared of the whole ambience, if you can call it that. The whole atmosphere was just horrible.' Eva was frightened too. All Grete could do was tell them that they should keep their spirits up, that it would be all right. She stayed strong. She had to.

Their stay in Belsen began with something that was to prove one of its most prominent features. Standing and being counted. On this occasion, it was only for a couple of hours, but it would often last much longer than that. Belsen in January was freezing, and none of the prisoners was dressed to stand around for long periods. This time – because it was relatively short, because they weren't yet at the point of starvation – everyone could just about cope with the roll call, before being allocated barracks. But eventually, being counted would become a torture for all of them and result in death for many.

The Belsen camp was divided into sections, with new parts being added as 1944 progressed, and the barbed wire constantly moving. But in January, the section that the Wieners had arrived in was the heart of the complex. It was known as the Star Camp, because its inhabitants wore civilian clothes with a large yellow star attached. They also weren't tattooed and their heads weren't shaved.

Mirjam was sure that this had been important for their survival.

You put somebody in prison pyjamas; you stamp them with a number – they are only known as a number – and you shave off all their hair so everybody looks the same; [it] takes away completely all identity and it's the first step to the grave basically. And that they didn't do to us . . . because there must have been in their minds there was the possibility of exchanges and it wouldn't look good if one had a number stamped on one . . . I think that made a big, big, difference.

The clothes they were allowed to keep were, by this point, too small for them. Ruth, for instance, had outgrown her own shoes in Westerbork and had to wear a pair of her mother's, which were much too big for her. All their overcoats had sleeves finishing inches above their wrists.

But, though the clothes wore out, becoming increasingly ragged, the discrepancies in size didn't get any worse while they were in Belsen. As Mirjam said: 'Children just stop growing if you don't feed them.'

———

Belsen was always cold. It was cold outside, it was cold where they slept, it was cold in the workplaces. There was a stove in the

301

barracks, but it gave off little heat. At night, as the temperature dropped, there was warmth only from the other people sleeping nearby in the straw on the wooden bunks. As the camp filled, there were two or sometimes three to a bunk.

Crowded together, it was hard to keep clean; everyone was soon covered in lice and there was little in the way of washing facilities, particularly as the year wore on. What there was involved a long walk across the camp and then splashing yourself with cold water in the already freezing outdoors, an unattractive proposition. The toilets were just holes in a wooden plank above a pit. In the evenings, families would sit in the barracks trying to squash any lice they found in the seams of their clothes. It was hard to see them in the half-light and the moment one lot were eradicated, another would appear. The task was fruitless.

The German way of running camps was to put one Jew in charge of another. Each barracks had an inmate who was given the job of hut leader. They would organise roll calls, make sure the barracks was clean, arrange for a party to collect the barracks' food from the kitchen, supervise its distribution, pass on all commands and ensure rules were obeyed. The hut leaders would be punished if they failed in any of these tasks. Ruth's diary for Friday, 6 May 1944, reads: 'Mrs Mainz (barracks leader) has to go to the prison cell because she miscounted our numbers earlier in the week.' Then, less than a week later, on Thursday 12 May, she wrote: 'Mrs Mainz back in cell because of counting errors.'

Above the barracks leaders was placed another Jew, a particularly unpleasant, short, stocky Greek man called Jacques Albala. He was 'very much in cahoots with the Nazis themselves', said Mirjam, and 'had a terrible reputation'. According to Ruth, 'he could bellow and roar as much as the Germans could. He was pretty fierce . . . he wanted to, I guess, establish himself. And he had a couple of underlings. They almost acted like Nazis themselves.'

The only thing to be said in Albala's favour is that when, as Ruth noted on 22 December 1944, he was 'deposed' by the SS, things actually got worse. The replacement was a group of Aryan convicts. Hanna Lévy-Hass, one of the Wiener family's fellow prisoners, reflected in her diary upon how corrupt Albala had been, and then said of the new leaders that

> they are true creatures of the devil . . . Cold, cruel, sadistic – had I not seen with my own eyes the obscene delight they take in beating us, I would never have thought it possible . . . Yesterday, December 30, two [Jews] were clubbed to death . . . The Kapos beat the women as well, or, even worse, force them to become prostitutes.

As in Westerbork, the adults all had to work. Grete cleaned the barracks, their own and that of others, including that of the German guards. Ruth was at first assigned to work in the kitchens, but two days later she was moved to the so-called 'shoe commando'.

It was a fortunate move. The kitchen involved getting up at three in the morning, being counted, and marching across the camp in rows of five. Although, theoretically, you could eat as much food as you liked while you were working, in practice it was inedible. The kitchen's main ingredient was turnips and eating them raw made you ill.

Some people were assigned to work in the kitchens that served the SS officers. There you might be able to get your hands on such delicacies as a raw carrot. But this was almost worse. The temptation to smuggle the carrots out, which was strictly forbidden, was too great. A distant relative of the Wieners did exactly that, stealing carrots for his starving young son. He was caught, made to stand overnight for twelve hours by the barbed wire fence, and in the morning he and his family simply disappeared. They were never heard from again.

The shoe commando was less dangerous, with slightly better hours. The 'factory', as it was jocularly referred to by the workers, processed the shoes of the Jews that the Nazis were killing. The shoes were sent to Belsen from all over Europe, and would be collected from the freight trucks, and assembled in a huge pile. From this men, based in one room, would pick up the shoes of dead children, separate the soles from the uppers and pass the latter through to the women's room.

At a large table, Ruth would sit with her fellow inmates, using a little knife to pick apart the uppers. In front of the group were military helmets to use as bowls, and into one they would place buckles, into another the laces, and so on. Then the stolen leather of murdered Jews was taken away and recycled to assist the German war effort. One of Ruth's co-workers said that life in the shoe commando was 'indescribable. Dirty, airless, dark, cold . . . the filthiest job there is.'

Although supervision was brutal and beating frequent, the workers could talk. Ruth sat with girls her age and talked about the future, though the future would be denied to many of the people in the shoe commando. So it was sociable, but it was hard and cold and workdays were long. Everyone would be woken at around 5.30 in the morning, there would be an attempt at washing, the distribution of rations, and then roll call and a march to work. Shoe-sorting would begin at seven. There would be a break at midday for a meal and then work would carry on until seven in the evening. This continued six and a half days a week. After work, there was always a further extended roll call. And quite often Sunday afternoons, the only rest period in the week, would be taken up by a particularly lengthy count.

While Grete and Ruth worked, Mirjam and Eva were left behind in the camp to do 'basically nothing', as Mirjam described it. 'One wasn't allowed to gather together. We did a bit of sort of helping with people who had small children.' She would sometimes go to the back of the camp with a spoon because the empty lunch churns would be there. The children would see whether they could find some leftover turnip scrapings. 'And I would look back at the camp and there was nothing there. It was all empty.' She understood later that this was her mind playing tricks on her. Even at work times, Belsen was never empty. But she struggled to remember anyone else being present, anything else really, save for the bleakness.

We sat around a lot doing nothing basically because the thing was to conserve one's energy. If you're hungry, you don't do anything, you know . . . You haven't got the energy to play, though no doubt being children I suppose we did pick up pebbles and play five-stones or something like that.

But one other activity my mother did recall clearly. Being counted. Albala, and then later the convicts, assisted the German soldiers as they rounded up the Jews in the camp, marched them to the Appellplatz – the 'roll-call square' – and arranged them in a large rectangle in rows of five. The Nazis favoured doing this late at night, they liked to do it when it was particularly cold, they enjoyed doing it when it was raining. The prisoners would be in thin shirts, sometimes in socks without shoes. The square would turn to mud. And the German officers, in their greatcoats and their high leather boots, would count and count and count.

If someone was late, they might be beaten, and the count would start again. Mirjam particularly recalled a German soldier who was widely known as William Tell, a pun on his name (Wilhelm) and counting (Tell). He would push prisoners and kick them and shout at them. And then he would announce, often with a smirk, that a mistake had been made and the count would need to start again. Sometimes this might go on for four hours, sometimes even more. People would collapse and die and be left in the mud until counting had finished. Later, a cart would arrive and take away the corpses.

What was this counting for? No one was going anywhere, nobody could escape. Even straying near the barbed wire could – and sometimes did – get you shot dead. So the counting wasn't really a security procedure. It was about control and the establishment of authority. There isn't a single memoir of Belsen that fails to mention the suffering it inflicted.

The other thing that every account mentions is the hunger. The reason that my mother went to the back of the camp with a spoon in the afternoons is that she was starving. Prisoners could often be seen rummaging through garbage to find anything edible and eating it with gusto, any sense of disgust having vanished.

In the morning, prisoners were issued with 350 grams of bread, which had to last them for 24 hours; in the middle of the day, there was a bowl of turnip soup, essentially water with a few pieces of vegetable floating in it; and, in the evenings, an occasional further bowl of soup. Once a week, a ration of sixty grams of margarine and a small spoonful of jam was distributed. Very occasionally there was something different – an eventuality remarkable enough for Ruth to mention it in her diary. That there was pea soup for dinner on 16 April 1944 was sufficiently exciting for it to be accompanied with an exclamation mark. A month later, there was spinach with potatoes. Rolled oats are mentioned once, as is macaroni.

The Wieners tried to save a little of their bread, to spread it out a bit, but it was hard to keep it safe. There was theft. And one morning the family woke up to find their rations had been hollowed out by a rat. Mostly they were too hungry to keep anything back anyway.

Grete's former boss, Van Tijn, produced a report, based on her own stay in Belsen, estimating that for each person 'there was a deficiency of about 1000 calories daily'. Yet Van Tijn had left the camp in July 1944 and was writing a month later. After this, the food rations had begun to get worse as the camp filled and the German administrators struggled to cope. There were frequent days when there was even less food than usual or none at all, sometimes as punishment, sometimes because there simply wasn't any to be had. Usually the former was a device to disguise the latter. By the end of 1944, Ruth's diary more often recorded rations being withheld than it did the odd additional sauerkraut.

Years later, when they had children of their own, Mirjam and Ruth realised something else about the food in Belsen that they hadn't appreciated at the time. Grete had starved herself to feed them. As Ruth put it: 'What are you going to do when your children say they are hungry?'

The more the inmates of Belsen starved, the more they talked about food, dreamt about food, even wrote about food. With a blunt pencil, Grete put down on paper some of her favourite recipes, and I found them among my mother's papers when she died. Simple things like omelette ('Burns easily!'); plum dumplings ('From yesterday's boiled potatoes (cold!), mix well, 2 eggs, enough flour to make dumplings, a little bit of salt, roll out, cut into four square pieces, wash plums well, dry them, take out the stones, put in salted water, sprinkle with brown butter'); stuffed bread ('Cut the top off a white loaf, leave a lid, hollow out the inside, do not damage the crust, stuff with cooked vegetables or cooked meat, a lot of fat or with fruit (eg preserved apricots)').

It is possible that Grete wrote these out so that her children would know how to cook her signature dishes. And there is a recipe for what she called 'risotto', idiosyncratically involving frying the rice with finely chopped meat, which my mother indeed used to make. But almost certainly the real reason Grete wrote them out was to remind herself of what food was, to savour the tastes even if just in her head, to remember the past, to imagine the future. As long as they survived and she saw her children to freedom. As she was determined she would.

Aside from dreaming about food the Wieners did what they could to lighten the darkness. Birthday celebrations, for instance. On 26 March 1944, Grete turned forty-nine, and one of her friends gave her three potatoes. The family fried them and were also able to make a bread pudding with saved rations that the rats hadn't got to. For Mirjam's eleventh birthday on 10 June, Ruth somehow managed to make a leather belt, and they also found some rhubarb (Ruth's diary doesn't say where from) to make a pudding with.

Ruth's birthday in early August also featured a belt, and a leather brooch from a friend, made from shoe scraps. She wrote that she 'had real porridge!' It is telling that by 15 September 1944, when Eva celebrated her birthday, there were gifts (a facecloth, a little bag) but not a celebratory meal. In fact, no meal at all. The words 'No Bread' appear in the diary, underlined.

There were also friends, particularly the Neuburger sisters, Marion and Erika. Like the Wieners, they had been born in Germany, fled to Amsterdam, belonged to the same synagogue and religion classes as Anne and Margot Frank, and had been sent to Belsen rather than Auschwitz or Sobibor because they had obtained Latin American passports. Ruth wrote in her diary for Saturday, 19 March 1944, that she and Erika 'published' a newspaper, though she didn't elaborate on what this was, or keep a copy.

The other consolation was religion. Some Jews in the camps lost their faith, or didn't have much to begin with. Many European Jews responded to the Holocaust by hiding their identity even from their children. But others clung to their Jewish identity even more tightly. That was certainly the case with Grete and with Ruth, maybe less so Eva. My mother would remain strongly attached to Judaism for the rest of her life.

In Westerbork, it had been possible to study Judaism and to celebrate the festivals, including ushering in the Sabbath and lighting the candles on a Friday evening. In Belsen, such gatherings were banned, with guards leading surprise raids to see if they could catch their prisoners in acts of worship. On important Jewish festivals such as Yom Kippur, the Nazis would deliberately schedule particularly lengthy roll calls, or communal showers. In any case, there usually wasn't the oil or wax for candles, and if there was, you wouldn't waste it. There was also no question, for most, of fasting on the Day of Atonement. Yet despite this, there were some furtive Jewish ceremonies, with evening readings in the dark, sometimes on the Sabbath, sometimes on special festival days.

In the summer of 1945, Ruth wrote of what these ceremonies, and the more open ones in Westerbork, had meant to her, to the family and to other inmates:

Through the snow we walk home from our work. Our backs are bent over, our eyes look tired. It is cold, biting cold.

But look what is happening. Suddenly there is a change within us. We are whispering one word: Fridaynight. This word changes us; we walk straight through the gates, which will be locked behind us. As we enter our barracks, we see our friends sitting around the table and waiting for us. Everything is ready to celebrate Erev Shabbos [Sabbath Eve].

Soon the lights will go out and we will sit in darkness. No, not tonight. Tonight the candles will burn and we will pray and sing. One of us starts to hold the service, another one makes a speech. While we listen to them, we forget everything around us: for tonight we are free. Then we start singing the old songs, which were brought to us from our fathers, and to them from their fathers and so on. We sing louder and louder with laughing faces and shining eyes.

Little by little the candles are burning down, we go into our beds in complete darkness, but on our faces is a smile and in our hearts is a light. Tomorrow a new day will come, a day with hard work and little rest, but this light will give us the strength to go on living, as it did, and will do, as long as there are Jews on earth.

'Monday, June 6th 1944 Invasion in France!!' News about the progress of the war spread quickly in Belsen. A guard might speak out of turn and the rumour mill would do the rest. Ruth's diary shows that the inmates knew of D-Day on the day it happened.

There had been rumours about an Allied assault for at least a month before. And, in May, Ruth began to report air-raid alarms, which then appear in the diary with increasing frequency. That the war was now going badly for the Germans was, naturally, a source of encouragement to the camp inmates. But its immediate practical impact on them was disastrous.

The Star Camp for exchange prisoners, in which the Wieners were held, was, of course, only one of a number of compounds separated by barbed wire. Next door had originally been a convicts' compound, and there was also a compound for citizens of neutral states, and one for a group of Hungarians in the middle of a separate exchange attempt. From the spring of 1944, as the configuration began to change, the prisoners' compound started to be used as a so-called 'recuperation camp'. Jews were brought there from other labour camps when they were no longer able to work, with the first group being tubercular prisoners who had been labouring on what became the V-2 rocket.

There was no recuperation in the recuperation camp, naturally. Not a single doctor – even a prisoner-doctor – had accompanied the invalids to Belsen. And when they got there, there was no one to look after them, no blankets even, and no hot food. The invalids generally did not last long upon arrival.

And then, in the summer of 1944, the Nazis began to erect a new section of Belsen altogether, known as the 'women's camp' and initially housed in tents behind the shoe 'factory'. In November, this tent city was blown away in a heavy gale, leaving its inhabitants in this hail and the rain with a few shared blankets as protection. Eventually, they were moved inside, staying in the kitchens and the shoe barracks, before they could be rehoused in half-built huts with even less light and comfort than the standard accommodation.

Germany's deteriorating military position impacted upon Belsen in three ways. The first is that it made the success of Himmler's hostage plan even more unlikely. The Allies, always reluctant to make any kind of deal with the Nazis, became even less attracted to it as victory started to get closer. This meant both that the inmates of the Star Camp did not leave, and that the Nazis became less interested in looking after them.

The second, even more serious, impact was that the Nazis began to evacuate other concentration camps which they thought would be overrun by their enemies. They moved these Jews towards the middle of Germany, with Belsen being an obvious destination. In the late autumn of 1944 the Germans began to move people out of Auschwitz-Birkenau, and dismantled the gas chambers and crematoria there. Many of the survivors were marched to Belsen, with many dying on the way.

Although there are few records to help establish exactly how many people arrived in Belsen after the summer of 1944, it is clear that it numbered in the tens of thousands. From being almost empty at the beginning of the year, by December there were about 15,000 people in the camp. By the end of March 1945, there were nearly 40,000 in the camp and in total there were around 50,000 deaths in Belsen.

Among those who came from Auschwitz, and were housed in the tents, were Margot and Anne Frank. Ruth was told that some Dutch people had arrived in Belsen, and she went to see who might be on the other side of the barbed wire. She took Mirjam with her and they were excited to see familiar faces. On 20 December 1944, Ruth wrote in her diary: 'Margot and Anne Frank in the other camp.' The new arrivals were mostly barefoot and had no coats. Ruth recalled that the Franks looked 'pretty horrible'.

In Erika Neuburger's 2008 account of her time in Belsen (something she rarely spoke about otherwise), she mentions being good friends with Hanneli Goslar, the close companion of Anne Frank, who was also in the Star Camp. Perhaps it was through Erika that Eva got to know Hanneli as well.

In the only testimony she left, given in 1958, Eva recalled having been part of 'a secret agreement' with Hanneli, who had discovered the Franks were in the next-door camp.

> We got together at night, and mother [Grete] threw something that she had saved over the wire. It was a little bit of food for the Franks, because they were starving. Another woman caught the morsel and ran away with it, thanking heaven. Margot and Anne were crying and really in grief.

Eva dictated her story to an eleven-year-old girl writing a school project. Almost everything in the account that the girl wrote down is consistent with Mirjam and Ruth's story, and consistent with the broader historical record as well. The details of this story, however, may not be quite right. Grete, for instance, was very ill by December, and it seems unlikely she would have been throwing things to anyone, especially at night. And existing accounts of food being thrown to Anne do not suggest Margot met Hanneli. Although, as there was straw tightly packed into the barbed wire where the encounter took place, Eva may not have been aware that Margot wasn't there.

But it does seem likely that the broad thrust is true, because Erika told a very similar story of going with Hanneli to meet Anne in the dark and throwing her 'some of our Red Cross food'.

The third way in which Germany's collapsing war effort affected Belsen is that, at the same time as the camp population grew, its leadership became less capable of looking after it. In so far as they cared. That there was less food available was partly the result of the breaking down of supply lines. The collapse of the sanitary system and the lack of basic facilities and hygiene, however, were primarily caused by the indolence and callousness of the camp's SS officers.

The result was that the prisoners began to sicken and die, particularly from typhus, typhoid and dysentery, made worse by attending endless roll calls in all sorts of weather. There was no one to look after the sick, and no medicines. And soon there was no one to bury them either.

As Hanna Lévy-Hass wrote in her diary:

January 1945: General malnutrition. It is as much as we can do to move. Nobody is able to walk upright, in a normal way; they all drag themselves along, swaying from side to side. Whole families die in the space of a few days . . . Death has now finally settled among us, our most faithful companion, ever present . . . One begins to mistake the dead for the living. Not that there is much difference. We are skeletons that can still move, whereas they are skeletons that cannot. But there is a third category – those who lie stretched out on their bunks, still breathing slightly but unable to move.

The deaths and illnesses came closer and closer to the Wieners. A friend of Ruth, whose father had already died, woke up in her bunk to find her mother dead beside her. Erika and Marion's mother, Irene, got an infection from the dirty shoes they were picking apart in the shoe commando. It degenerated into blood poisoning and there was no medical assistance available. On 28 November, she died.

A week before that, on 21 November 1944, Ruth wrote in her diary: 'Mother gets certificate from chief medical officer to declare her unable to work or be at roll call.' Weakening since the earliest days of Westerbork, possibly ill from typhus, feeding her children before she fed herself, Grete now found it hard to leave her bunk.

And then, as Belsen descended further into what its official historian has described as an inferno, Gertrud Slottke, the woman who had sent the Wieners to Belsen with the promise of a better life and the possibility of freedom, reappeared.

The Exchange

As food ran low and sickness advanced, there had been, in the summer of 1944, one shaft of light in the darkness for Mirjam and the family. Ernst Mös, an adjutant of Eichmann, had come to Belsen and assembled all the holders of South American passports.

The visit of Mös, the Wieners knew, might change everything, or mean nothing. In June, Eva had seen Heinrich Himmler himself marching through Belsen, and reported a combination of curiosity and fear watching 'that little, but big powered, man'. At the end of that month, whether connected to the visit or not, there had then been an exchange, with a few Belsen Jews winning their freedom. So far, it constituted the only fruits of Himmler's entire Belsen plan. And it had involved a small number of those who held Palestine certificates.

The Germans had, of course, agreed to two earlier swaps of Jews for the Christian Templers in Palestine. It was what had given Van Tijn the idea of creating the longer Palestine list, of which the Wieners had been part. And, in June 1944, there had been one final swap. Those doing the deal were worried that there weren't enough Templers left in Palestine, or Palestinian Jews left in German controlled territory to make it work. So, in the end, a small exchange involving 222 people from Belsen had been possible, with Dutch Jews providing the numbers.

Van Tijn herself had been among the 222. The Wieners had not been. Indeed, there isn't any suggestion in any of their papers or testimony that they were considered for this exchange. The public documentation doesn't shed any light, either, on why some certificate holders were selected and others were not. In July, there were sixty-six British passport holders involved in another such exchange. But there didn't seem to be any serious prospect of a further Palestine swap.

So, by August, the Paraguayan passports seemed to provide the one slender hope of escape, the one chance of not being consumed by the inferno. And the visit of Mös that month did seem to be a sign, however slight, that such hope was not entirely forlorn.

After he had convened the passport holders, Eichmann's man had left without saying anything more. But things didn't fall entirely silent. Over the coming months, Ruth's diary is studded with references to the South American passports. A further visit by Mös in September, this time with Slottke; news of 'a list' of South Americans being compiled in November; and then, at the end of that month, 'more rumours about a South American list'. Yet, ominously, the words 'ill' and 'sick' also appear in Ruth's entries, and Grete's health was deteriorating every day.

Then, on 19 January 1945, Mös returned, again with Slottke. And Ruth wrote in her diary: 'We are called.'

———

The Belsen exchange which freed my mother can be thought of as a miracle. For in many ways it was.

The number of Jews rescued by exchanges during the Second World War was tiny, a few thousand in all. And Himmler's grand plans for swaps involving tens of thousands of people came to almost nothing, save the death and misery of Belsen's collapse. In 1944, Belsen had acted as the stopping place for the Hungarians who were on their way to an exchange and kept in a different compound, but of the Star Camp Jews there had just been the release of the two groups, involving 288 people in total.

In 1945, there was only one further exchange, involving 136 Jews. For Mirjam, Ruth, Eva and Grete to be four of them, out of the 50,000 who died in Belsen and the millions that died in the Holocaust, was indeed a miracle.

Miraculous-seeming too, is that their escape happened when time was running out. Their exchange came at the very last possible moment. Germany was losing the political and military capacity to make such decisions; the Allies were sweeping to victory and had other concerns. Yet the months ahead for anyone who stayed in Belsen were horrible and lethal. The chances of my mother surviving until the camp was liberated were not good.

The family possessed fraudulently created documents supporting not merely false, but obviously ludicrous, claims to Paraguayan citizenship, documents which said on their face that they expired in December 1944. The Germans were quite aware of the questionable nature of their papers. Yet still these documents set them free. This too appeared to be a miracle.

And, of course, there were all the unlikely personal elements. Not just the heroic Polish passport operation, but that Alfred had met Camille Aronowski through his work on the Bern Trial, that Camille's sister had been married to Juliusz Kühl, a member of the Ładoś Group, and that they had received the passports before being sent to the gas chambers, something that had been close to happening many times.

Yet what happened to my mother was not really a miracle. That there were such small numbers who were swapped, and that it happened so late, is closer to a scandal than a miracle. And every step towards freedom that Mirjam took was the result less of serendipity than of victory in a hard-won political battle.

The idea that the Nazis were engaged in genocide, or that they had an obsessional interest in the Jews, is now obvious. It should have been obvious to the Allied leadership at the time. And not just because Alfred had been trying to explain the Nazi view of Jews since the 1920s. There had been numerous reports to Allied governments during the war on what was happening to the Jews, not least from the Polish government-in-exile.

And there had been that time, in December 1942, when the British Foreign Secretary, Anthony Eden, had read to the House of Commons a declaration that hundreds of thousands of Jews were being transported to Eastern Europe, that Poland had become a 'Nazi slaughterhouse', that ghettoes were being created and then emptied, and that 'none of those taken away are ever heard of again', having been worked to death or 'deliberately massacred in mass executions'. After Eden finished, the House stood in silence as a show of respect and a mark of the horror of members at what they had been told.

Yet despite this evidence, and despite the fact that they were advertising it themselves, Allied governments appeared not to understand what they were seeing or what they were saying. They regarded themselves as engaged in a general war against Germany, with the Jews simply one ethnic group facing oppression. Lots of people needed help, was their view. The Jews could not jump the queue. As Roswell McClelland of the US War Refugee Board would say in the months after the conflict in Europe ended: 'We did not, and indeed do not generally now, grasp or believe the truly diabolic character of the Nazi revolution.'

This attitude led Allied governments to reject any idea of special rescue efforts or exchanges for Jews until it was too late for most of them, and almost too late for my mother. The Germans did seem to want to get back some of their nationals who had been captured, or in some other way were stranded, in Allied-occupied territories. Himmler was particularly keen. There were deals to be done.

There was a natural concern that any exchanges might send the Germans something, or someone, that would aid their war effort. This made it extremely hard to find any interned or imprisoned German whom the Allies were willing to swap for anyone, Jew or not.

But what the Allies feared most about the idea of rescuing Jews from the Nazis is that the effort might be successful. Hitler might suddenly decide to let millions of Jews go, and the Allies would have to look after them. Even if it were just tens of thousands, what would they do then?

As the head of the British Foreign Office's refugee department put it in a note in 1943: 'Once we open the door to adult male Jews to be taken out of enemy territory, a quite unmanageable flood may result. (Hitler may facilitate it!)' In December of that year, the British opposed a plan for evacuating Jews from France and Romania because they would find 'disposing of' 70,000 Jews too hard.

The British had a particular concern that Jews might go to Palestine, making relationships with the Arabs even harder than they already were. But the Americans shared the resistance to receiving Jewish refugees, with President Franklin D. Roosevelt already sensitive to the accusation that he gave special preference to Jews, and employed too many of them. His opponents had dubbed his New Deal, the 'Jew Deal'.

Connected with this simple idea of preventing a load of Jews from coming to countries that didn't want them, there were a number of practical concerns. One of these was how to transport any Jews that Hitler chose to release. The US State Department continually reiterated that it could not divert shipping in order to aid refugees. There was a view within the department, seriously held by reasonably senior people, that the Jewish organisations pressuring the Allies to rescue the Jews, had actually been created by the Nazis. The German idea, these US officials thought, was to cripple the war effort with the demand for ships. The assistant chief of the US State Department's visa division said that Hitler was 'really behind the [Jewish] pressure groups'.

There were two other concerns with a particular impact upon Mirjam and the family. One was that both the British and Americans feared that the Germans would use exchanges to send over spies. The State Department and the Foreign Office engaged in a quite extraordinary discussion in the spring of 1941 in which the British expressed surprise that so few Jewish refugees had been exposed as spies, believing that this must be due to a failure to investigate them properly.

This culminated in the US Embassy in London writing to Washington that one of its diplomats remembered reading 'of a special "school" which the Germans had set up in Prague for the purposes of "making Jews out of non-Jews"'. Here, 'instruction in the Hebrew language and the Talmud, and alteration of features were included in the curriculum'. From Washington came the response that one of their officials had heard something similar. 'He remembers, in particular, that the results of the plastic surgery practiced were remarkable.' Perhaps he'd read it in a newspaper or seen it in a moving picture. He wasn't sure. Almost certainly the diplomats had read a piece of gossip that had been planted by the State Department itself the previous year, and was now being reported back to it as fact.

There was a particular concern that Latin America would be a route for such spies, since there was so much false documentation circulating. And, indeed, my mother and her sisters would later be suspected of being foreign agents.

But the problem that the Allies had with the Latin American papers held by the Wieners and others was not just that they might be used by spies. It was that, as the State Department was still saying internally as late as March 1944, accepting falsely issued documents might undermine the whole passport system. It was 'fraudulent and improper', and the idea that recognition might save hundreds of lives was an 'oversimplification'. As a result, the department boasted that 'we prevailed upon some of the other American republics to stop it, to prevent its recurrence, and to take steps to invalidate documents already issued'.

So the American and British governments were not simply stalling on rescue efforts, not simply failing to conclude satisfactory exchanges that might free imprisoned Jews. They were actively working to undo the efforts of Aleksander Ładoś and his group, actively trying to invalidate the documents that Alfred and Camille Aronowski had obtained, actively seeking to remove the protection of the one piece of paper that stopped Grete and her daughters going to the gas chambers.

Not that the Paraguayan government needed much encouragement to abandon the Jews. During these years, its national police chief had a son. He named him Adolfo Hirohito.

———————

But at the beginning of 1944, around the time the Wieners were moved from Westerbork to Belsen, things had begun to change. Henry Morgenthau, Jr., decided that enough was enough, and he was going to see President Roosevelt and do something about it.

Morgenthau, Roosevelt's Treasury Secretary, played a very important role in winning the war. He had urged the President to prepare for it while FDR was still temporising, he had raised the money in taxes and debt for the fight, and he had been the early architect of the US aircraft programme. Morgenthau was also Jewish, and the most important voice for Jews in the administration. What he now did with that voice ranks alongside the greatest of his wartime achievements.

Certainly it was the one that impacted the Wieners most directly.

Morgenthau had long opposed the State Department view that rescuing or exchanging Jews was bad policy. He wasn't too impressed by the British position either, describing one of their communiqués on the Jews as 'a satanic combination of British chill and diplomatic double talk, cold and correct and adding up to a sentence of death'. But he had found it difficult to make any headway. Roosevelt didn't have much interest in the topic; the British were unmoved. Then, at the end of 1943, Congress gave Morgenthau leverage. It became obvious that unless the President came up with a rescue plan for Jews, he would be forced to do so by the House of Representatives and the Senate.

On Sunday, 16 January 1944, Morgenthau went to see FDR, carrying with him a short report on the way Roosevelt's administration was acquiescing in the murder of Jews, and also bringing to the President a demand. The government must set up a commission charged with rescuing as many Jews as possible. The meeting took place in the early afternoon, and lasted just twenty minutes. Roosevelt listened to Morgenthau's summary of the situation and, aware of the pressure from Congress, agreed to his proposal. On 22 January, the President issued an executive order to establish the War Refugee Board.

It is too much to say that the Board's creation represented a turning point in American policy. It only had thirty staff and its work was still hampered by the State Department, many of whose officials disapproved of its existence and of its policy. But its creation did mean that, for the first time, the Allies had an agency actively seeking opportunities to move Jews out of harm's way.

Children hidden in Vichy France, for example, were moved to Switzerland before the Nazis could find them. A refugee camp was established with the Board's help in a former military barracks in Philippeville, Algeria. And the Board also set about seeing whether there were any unexploited opportunities for exchanges involving Jews.

Quite early on, it realised that the Paraguayan passports created by the Ładoś Group represented just such an opportunity. In other words, at last there was an agency with a policy of trying to save Grete and the girls and others like them, and a plan for doing so.

In early 1942, the United States had instigated a round-up of Germans living in Latin American countries. The idea was that deporting these people would protect the security of the Americas in general, but, once the round-up had taken place, no one was quite sure what to do with the people they had collected. Some were used in early exchanges for Americans stuck in Nazi-occupied territories. But there was always the concern that any Germans that the Allies sent home might help the Nazi war effort. So the exchanges stalled, and thousands of Latin American Germans ended up stuck in internment camps, including a large number in a camp in Crystal City, Texas.

These were people who, the Board realised, might be available to be swapped for Jews possessing Latin American passports, however dubiously obtained. That is, if the Jews with those papers weren't killed before anybody got round to negotiating their release. For until well into their stay in Belsen, the security offered by the Wieners' Paraguayan document was very fragile indeed. The Nazis had begun killing those who held them.

At the end of 1943, both the Allies and the Paraguayan government were making it quite clear that they didn't recognise the papers. The Swiss had put an end to the Ładoś Group's operations, and Hügli, the Paraguayan consul in Bern, had been sacked. The Nazis had long known that the papers were falsely issued, but that wasn't the point. If the Allies were willing to acknowledge the holders as genuine, then the holders had exchange value. Without that acknowledgement, their value disappeared.

So the Nazis started to kill them. Towards the end of 1943, they gathered in Belsen 1,700 Polish holders of what were called *promesas*, letters from consuls promising passports to follow. And they sent them to Auschwitz. A riot erupted on the Auschwitz rampway, but every single person was murdered. In March 1944, the Nazis began to move Poles with Latin American passports out of an internment camp in Vittel in occupied France, where they were being held. They too were destined for Auschwitz and death.

News of the plight of the Polish Jews, the people Ładoś had started off trying to help, reached the Jewish communities in Allied and neutral countries and campaigning began in an effort to assist them. Ładoś himself led the charge, sending telegrams to whomever he could, obtaining the help of the Vatican, arranging for the Polish government-in-exile to use all its contacts to prevent disaster. The US War Refugee Board was sympathetic, but the State

Department resisted strongly, still hung up on the fact that the papers were false. 'We are being placed in the position of acting as nurse-maid to persons who have no claim to our protection,' wrote the first secretary of the US legation in Bern.

In the end, it was Morgenthau who resolved the crisis. A delegation of orthodox rabbis from New York had hurried to Washington, and the oldest of them broke down in tears in Morgenthau's office, weeping and weeping. The Treasury Secretary responded by getting the State Department on the phone and insisting that they act.

Before long, the change of policy that had begun with the formation of the Board was complete. The USA had successfully pressed the Paraguayans to recognise the passports, on the understanding that they weren't under any obligation to allow the holders actually to live in Paraguay; they had also arranged for the Paraguayans to agree that the passports would continue to be valid even when the expiry date had passed; and, after Morgenthau's intervention, they had prevailed upon the Germans to acknowledge this new policy and to stop sending the holders to their deaths.

This all came too late for the Poles, but for many of the Dutch Jews in Belsen, for the Wieners, it was a life-saver. At least for a time. It meant that their passports wouldn't be confiscated; it meant that they wouldn't immediately be sent to the gas chambers.

Yet every day in Belsen was a day closer to a different death. As the camp collapsed, Latin American passport holders were dying of disease and starvation along with everyone else. The War Refugee Board, with Roswell McClelland in its Bern office as the main instigator and organiser, was working frantically on ways of including the Belsen 'Latin Americans' in some sort of exchange involving the pool of Germans interned in Crystal City, Texas. But time was running out.

It was very hard to agree anything, and any exchange would inevitably prioritise any full US citizens that the Germans were holding. All the arguing had held things up, and it was still going on as 1944 turned into 1945. But eventually, there had been a breakthrough in negotiations. There would be a swap, taking place in Switzerland, involving about 800 people going in each direction. And a handful of them would be Belsen inmates. That was why Mös and Slottke were in the camp on 19 January 1945. That was why Ruth and Mirjam and the family had been called.

By lobbying for the passports to be recognised, Aleksander Ładoś had done one last service for the Wieners, acted one last critical time to save them.

Despite all the rumours, being summoned by Mös and Slottke had been worrying as well as promising. With the Nazis, who really knew? 'We didn't know what was happening, but we were very frightened,' Eva recalled. 'We thought we were on the list to be killed, because anything could happen now.'

And this fear would persist until freedom was secure. It was a well-founded fear too, given what had happened in 1943 to the Poles who had Latin American *promesas*, given the way that they had opened the train doors at their destination and found themselves on the rampway to the gas chambers. Nevertheless, the Wieners hoped. All they could do was hope.

On the morning of 20 January 1945, the morning after that first call, the barracks door flew open, there were boots stamping on the floor, a call to attention, and then an instruction: 'Everyone holding a North American or South American passport must report immediately to the chief doctor to determine your fitness for exchange.'

Mirjam always thought that the medical exam was designed to exclude anyone whose condition would reveal to the Allies how bad things were in the camps. This, after all, was one of the main reasons why the prisoners hadn't received a tattoo. But, in so far as disguising the privations of the camp was the aim, it was bound to fail. The condition of all Belsen inmates, the Wieners included, was terrible by this point. A Swiss Jew who would witness Mirjam and her fellow survivors disembark from their journey to freedom observed: 'I have already seen much misery, but I have never before encountered such shadowy, emotionally and physically broken figures, as on this transport. They moved past me like so many ghosts.'

The greater reason for the exam was probably a practical one. The Nazis didn't want people to die on the journey. It would be a nuisance. They'd have a body on their hands. Perhaps it could be left for the Swiss to deal with, but if a prisoner died, the Germans would also have the wrong number of people to exchange. The difficult negotiations had ended in the strict rule that the swap would be one for one – one person from Crystal City sent to Germany for every one person set free by the Germans.

Whatever the reasoning with which the Nazis had contented themselves, for the Wieners the prospect of the examination was a grim one. For nearly two months, Grete had hardly been able to leave her bunk. Objectively, it was hard to imagine any sort of examination that she would pass. But Grete saw things differently. It had been five years since she had watched Alfred fly off from the airport in Amsterdam, and she had fought every day since then. She had fought to protect her children against oppression, she had fought to give them some sort of childhood despite everything, she had starved herself so that they would eat. She would not fail now. Salvation was in sight. She would not let the girls down now.

Her daughters helped her from the bunk and together they approached the roll-call square, where a table had been placed. At the table sat the medical director and his assistant in white coats. They had in front of them pens with which they made checks on typed papers and cards with blue circles. The doctor had a hooked nose, an overbite, and also a kindly look in his eyes that fooled nobody about his true character. Slottke was present as well.

As Mirjam described it: 'One often sees these scenes in films . . . we had to walk past him [the medical director]. And he would decide who would or would not go to wherever it was we were going.'

There were hundreds of passport holders in line and many would fail the test. Marion and Erika Neuburger were in the queue with their father Wilhelm, their mother having died already. But when their turn came, Wilhelm – who had typhoid and diarrhoea – was too obviously ill. They were not allowed to join the exchange, and shortly afterwards Wilhelm died. His daughters remained in Belsen almost until the end, and barely survived the infamous 'Lost Train'.

When it was the turn of Grete and the girls, they were asked the same questions as everyone else. What were their names? Did they understand what was happening and wish to participate in the exchange? And are you sick? A question asked with greater intensity of those most obviously ailing. Somehow Grete managed to answer all these, and hold herself upright, and walk past the table, and pass the medical exam. 'Next!' called out the doctor, ticking off the Wieners from his checklist. It was a supreme moment of courage and fortitude, the greatest Grete had shown in those five years, and she had shown many. The family was told to start packing.

The train would leave the next day, on 21 January, but before that came yet another unsettling experience. The exchange-Jews were told they would be given a shower. They were taken to the bathhouse and told to strip. By this stage of the war, almost everyone knew what that might mean. Mirjam recalls being oblivious, but noticing the fear of the adults. There was relief, even laughter, when water came out of the showerheads.

After that, the prisoners were fed, and this time, though they were served soup, the food was more substantial than the normal turnip water. Said Mirjam: 'It had actual pieces of potato in it. That, a child remembers.'

There was one additional, strange ritual before the family boarded the train from Belsen. The Wieners were given their money back. On the first night in Westerbork, Grete had handed in all the family's cash and valuables and had been given a receipt. Since then, unknown to them, a careful account had been kept, with sums removed for personal items (the toothpaste from the Westerbork store, and stamps for their letters) and also collective items (to recompense the Nazis for running the camps, and transporting people to their deaths, and so forth). Now, ludicrously, the remaining amount was handed back to Grete as if the whole transaction was the most ordinary thing in the world.

Finally, at about four in the afternoon, the time came for departure. There were about 300 Jews in the exchange group, and they were loaded onto the back of lorries, heading towards the railway station at Celle. It was cold, as the lorry backs were open to the elements, but it was better than walking. And the sight that greeted them on the platform more than made up for any discomforts on the journey. For the train that stood there was not formed of cattle trucks. It was a Red Cross passenger train, with large red crosses on the side and on its top, to avoid it being the target of Allied bombing.

The train was warm inside. Properly heated. And they flopped down onto seats with soft cushions. Gertrud Slottke passed through the carriage, handing out scissors for them all to cut off the yellow stars on their clothing. They would be travelling to Switzerland, it was explained.

At the border in Konstanz would be another Red Cross train, this one with the Germans who had been interned by the Americans. These would mostly be German-born civilians. People who had been trapped in North or South America by the war, rounded up as alien elements. People whose one way of reuniting their families and leaving internment was for all of them – husbands, wives and children – to go to Germany, even if their families had never been there before. When the Wieners' train arrived at the border, it would halt alongside the train of Germans, there would be a check and the Germans would go off into Germany. The Jews would then be free.

Today, a train journey from Celle to Konstanz might take about eight hours. The Wieners' train from Belsen took three and a half days to reach its destination. There were many stops, as the lines had been destroyed and there needed to be emergency repair work. There was also an initial diversion to Berlin, to collect the interned Americans who would make up most of the numbers in the swap. The devastation of the city, apparent through the carriage window, shocked the Wieners, despite their experience of seeing Bremen a year earlier.

Grete sat in her seat, drifting in and out of consciousness, her weakness apparent, as the train made its way steadily to safety for her and for the girls. Outside, the weather grew worse, it was freezing, snow fell, but still the train slowly progressed.

And then came one final, heart-stopping moment. As the border approached, the Germans concluded that they had too many prisoners for the proposed exchange. Of the 306 people who had left Belsen, only 136 were needed. Some people would have to be removed from the train. Left, as Eva and Mirjam thought, to walk back to Belsen in the snow; left, essentially, to die. Ruth thought it was more likely that they'd be sent at the very last minute to a civil internment camp. And Ruth was right. Those taken from the train would be housed somewhere with better conditions than Belsen. But still in captivity. Still with the threat of Nazi murder at any moment.

An SS man, 'one of these SS officers with their high boots and so on', as Mirjam put it, came through the carriage, pointed to the girls, and said: 'Off.' Ruth responded: 'But we can't. My mother is too sick to move.' There was a pause. The man shrugged and said, 'All right. Stay,' and passed on.

No wonder Mirjam always saw her survival as a miracle.

———————

So it was that near midnight on 24 January 1945 the Wieners crossed the border to Switzerland and to freedom. Grete had triumphed. She had protected her girls through the long years of Nazi occupation and terror, kept them alive through the valley of death, given them every last crumb of food, and seen them to safety.

In New York, Alfred was waiting for news. Camille Aronowski, based in Switzerland, had learned of the prospective exchange and informed him. Now he received an erratically spelled telegram through the Red Cross:

DR ALFRED WIENER III WEST 46TH STREET NEW YORK YOUR WIFE MARGARETHE WIENER WITH CHILDREN RUTH EVA MIRJAM WIENER FROM CAMP BERGENBLELSEN GERMANY ARRIVED SWITZERLAND CHILDREN IN GOOD HEALTH.

Then came these final lines:

MARGARETHE WIENER PAST AWAY AFTER ARRIVAL ON WEAKNESS JEWISH FUNERAL 26 JANUARY AT KREUZLINGEN.

DAD

The Dock at Southampton

In that first joyous correspondence, when Dolu, Lusia and Ludwik all found each other again in the Soviet Union in 1941, they had rushed to provide assurances that they were all healthy. Dolu, in particular made great play of it.

'I went through prisons and labour camps,' he wrote in the very first letter to reach them.

It was hard, very hard, but I came out of it without any damage to my physical health and without breaking down mentally . . . I went through a good slimming programme, but I feel healthy, and everyone in the camps and those here now, cannot believe I'm already 50. Everyone thinks that I am at least 10 years younger. I am telling you this to make sure that you don't worry.

He made a similar point in a number of other letters, and perhaps he was indeed only saying it so that Lusia wouldn't worry. Or perhaps, as it seems to me from the correspondence, he really believed it. Whatever the case, it wasn't true. The Gulag had broken Dolu. He lived for almost nine years after he was freed; but as surely as if his death had happened in the snow while pulling logs to the river, the Gulag killed him.

When the Anders army had arrived in Iran, with Lusia and Ludwik wading ashore in August 1942, the first days had been miserable. Rain started falling, and there was no shelter. Hundreds of Poles died of disease and exhaustion. Ludwik developed a high temperature and Dolu tended him carefully, stretching over him an officer's rubber cape. After a few days, the rain cleared, Ludwik improved, and they were moved, first to a tented encampment and then, at last, to quarters in Tehran.

Ludwik would always remember the first experience of their new life. 'We went to a restaurant! I could not believe the fact that there, in that restaurant, you sat down and somebody served an enormous basket of bread, tomatoes and cucumbers, which is normally what Persians do, and you could order anything you liked!'

Almost as soon as this meal was over, there was a painful parting. Dolu went with the Anders army to aid British operations in Iraq, and the family was again separated for the best part of a year. But despite this wrench, in Tehran Lusia and Ludwik were able to resume a civilised life, one lived in peace, one lived without danger. Ludwik was able to restart his education. He reached the age of thirteen, old enough to have a bar mitzvah, a victory given all that had happened, even if there wasn't much of a Jewish community to celebrate it with.

In Iran there was a welcoming local people, there was food, there were hot showers, there was a sense of community. There were shady trees and classrooms pitched underneath them, there were shops and exotic local drinks, and a café-restaurant for Poles, serving Wiener schnitzel and offering its customers mountains of cakes. The camp they lived in initially was pretty basic, but soon they found a room in a house. And Lusia found a job. She would teach English at the Polish cultural centre. In one way or another, she would carry on teaching English to foreign-language speakers until she retired in her seventies.

In the summer of 1943, Dolu received a new posting. He was in his fifties, and it was determined that he could no longer be a fighting soldier. As he spoke good German, and had expertise in accounting and administration, he was asked to help train people to administer German-occupied territories once the territories were recaptured. The staff courses were in Tel Aviv, so the whole family moved to Palestine.

They would stay there for the next four years, with Dolu mostly employed teaching the courses or helping the army with inventory control, and Lusia employed teaching English. When part of the Anders army went to Italy, fought in the battle of Monte Cassino, and integrated into the British Eighth Army, Dolu stayed behind in Palestine, as the administrative and combat sections of the Polish army divided.

But Dolu's army service was fitful. There were long periods in which he could not carry on, brought low by illness and depression. In Iraq he had suffered from jaundice, and in Palestine from high blood pressure. In 1946, he suffered his first heart attack. An old friend from Lwów who encountered Dolu in Palestine was shocked by the change he witnessed. 'I found him very emaciated and changed and in a very depressed state.'

He was getting old, he was miles from home, he had lost his wealth, he had lost his status. And he had also lost his beloved brother.

After their long imprisonment, after seeing him through the gloom in the Brygidki prison in 1940, and after all their years apart, Dolu had seen his sibling again for the first time as he marched past Bernard while disembarking in Iran. He'd had to keep going, eyes facing front. Only when the marching was over could they finally hug. Yet despite the cinematic nature of this encounter, it did not have a happy ending. For less than a year later, on 3 May 1943, Bernard, his health wrecked by his own Gulag experiences, died of typhus while helping build the Tehran railway. His death was on his fifty-first birthday.

In a letter to their sister Lola in New York, Dolu relayed the news and added: 'My dear sister, I mourn the death of our brother.

He was not only my brother, but my best friend, my co-worker and my honest business partner. I will never forget him and I will mourn his death for ever.'

———

Bernard's loss was not the only one that the family suffered at this time.

On 5 June 1941, seventeen days before the Germans invaded the Soviet Union in Operation Barbarossa, Lusia's sister Dorotea and her husband Szymek wrote the latest of their letters sending news from home, inventories of their most recent parcels, and messages of love.

Brother Wilhelm, the letter said, had run out of money and had nothing more he could sell; people in Lwów were suffering; and still more friends had been imprisoned or deported by the Soviets. Some tea, some rice and some elastic were on their way. 'Please write to us, love you, kiss you many times, Dorotea and Szymek.'

The letter was the last Lusia ever heard from her sister, or indeed from any of her siblings.

Operation Barbarossa brought freedom for Lusia, Dolu and Ludwik. Without it, they would all surely have died during the coming winter, or the one after. But Hitler's invasion was a disaster for all their relatives still living in Lwów.

In the family records, there is an eerie silence about the fate of Lusia's family, about what happened to the Diamantsteins. It is not mentioned in any of their correspondence, it does not arise in my father's oral testimony, there were no official documents in all of the many that my father left behind. Not one that tells of what happened to his aunt, uncles and cousins. It is as if this, alone in the story of my family's suffering, was too painful to talk about.

But sadly it is not hard to work out.

On the day of the German invasion, the Soviets started shooting their prisoners in Lwów. After an attempt to flee the Brygidki prison was prevented by the NKVD, they murdered thousands of political prisoners and those they regarded as having committed 'crimes against socialist property'. Though many of the murdered prisoners were Jews, the majority were Ukrainians. And, when the Soviets had finally departed, it was the Jews who were accorded much of the blame for the massacre.

The result was that even before the Nazis arrived in the city, a pogrom had started. Ukrainian militiamen using sticks and whips were beating Jews in the streets. Many Jews were forced to run the gauntlet, funnelled towards the prison by huge crowds, and made to clean and remove the bodies. Perhaps as many as 8,000 Jews were murdered.

Among the dead was Rabbi Ezekiel Lewin of the Tempel, the synagogue that the Finkelsteins used to attend. He had been offered sanctuary by Ukrainian clerics, to whom he had gone in order to ask them to restrain the population. But he had decided that his place was with his congregation, with his people. He had been seized on the streets, taken to Brygidki, and was shot there in front of his son. When the Germans entered the city, one of their early acts was to demolish the Tempel itself, first setting fire to it in order to destroy its contents and ornamentation, and then laying dynamite and blowing up the building.

At around the same time, the first Nazi killing squad arrived in the city and began shooting and hanging Jews. Within two months, 4,000 more had been killed.

By the end of their first week of occupation, the Germans had rounded up twenty-five university professors and seventeen other university employees as part of their campaign against Polish intellectuals. Among them was Dolu and Lusia's old friend from Herburtów street and the Scottish Café, the mathematician and former Polish Prime Minister Kazimierz Bartel. Mocked in prison for having treated communists and Jews kindly, forced to polish the boots of Ukrainian conscripts, he was finally shot on 24 July 1941 on the direct orders of Himmler.

Soon Jews were wearing special armbands and facing restrictions on how they travelled, the food they could eat, the work they could do, and the places they could go. A ghetto was established, and Jews were forced into crowded accommodation at excessive prices. On their way to their new homes, carrying their belongings in carts or on their backs, old and frail people were stopped, brought to nearby sandpits, and shot.

From the ghetto, many were deported to the gas chambers in Belzec, others were shot in the street or burned to death in their homes, and still others were sent to the Janowska forced labour camp. And then, in June 1943, the Lwów ghetto was liquidated. Jews were either killed on the spot or transferred to the Janowska camp and killed there. By the autumn, almost every Jew had been killed, with only a handful somehow escaping. In September 1943, the Nazi divisional headquarters for the territory noted: 'The Jewish question in the District of Galicia should therefore be considered in the main as settled.'

Exactly when, during this period, the Diamantsteins died, isn't clear. But Lusia was one of seven brothers and sisters, and by 1945 she was the only one left.

Lusia's brother Leopold had died just before the war, diabetes taking him at the age of forty-seven in July 1938. And her sister Róża had died in childbirth in 1910. The other siblings were all alive when Hitler invaded.

There is no record at all of what happened to Lusia's eldest brother, Mayer, his wife, their daughter and son-in-law, or their three grandchildren. Nor of her brother Oskar. This is not uncommon among the Jews killed in Poland after Barbarossa.

Of Wilhelm, her favourite brother, and her beloved Dorotea, there is at least something a bit more conclusive. Testimony provided to the Yad Vashem Holocaust archive by a man called Leopold Gatz records simply that Wilhelm was killed during the Holocaust. And Szymek's sister provided Yad Vashem with the information that Dorotea, Szymek and their daughter Halina had all been murdered in Lwów in 1944.

On each Yad Vashem record, alongside the names of the family who saved Lusia and Ludwik with their love and their parcels, are the words:

During the Shoah [Holocaust], Jews were murdered in a variety of ways, among them gassing, shooting, burning, drowning or burial alive, exhaustion through forced labour, starvation, epidemic diseases, deprivation of medical care and minimal hygienic conditions, and more. Some Jews took their own lives in order to escape arrest and further persecution, or to end their hopeless, relentless suffering.

Some time after the war, but before my parents met, Lusia drew up a family tree of the children, grandchildren and great-grandchildren of her parents, Izak and Sluwa Diamantstein. The tree named twenty-nine people. By the time she drew it, almost everybody on the tree was dead, most of them murdered. Lusia, Dolu and Ludwik had survived, of course. But there were also three other people who lived into old age.

Leopold Diamantstein's elegant and sociable wife Zosia, and her two boys Josek and Eduard had somehow managed to escape Lwów. Eduard had fought with the resistance and also escaped from a prison camp. With a little help from Dolu, and money from Zosia's brother, they eventually made it to Argentina. Zosia rebuilt their life there, working in couture. As a child, Aunt Zosia and her family were my only Diamantstein relatives.

When Lusia set out in a smart dress and coat with hat, gloves and handbag to shop at the Express Dairy in Hendon Central, the clothes she wore were often ones she had been sent by Zosia.

Even when things were at their worst, Dolu and Lusia never lost hope, more than that, never lost belief, that one day they would go home. They imagined themselves once more on one of 'our walks in the linden tree lane on Herburtów street'. Once more they would talk, as in better days, and always find so much to say to each other.

But neither of them were destined ever to return, not even to visit. And this included my father, though he outlived the fall of the Berlin Wall by more than twenty years.

Perhaps Dolu and Lusia's dream was always unrealistic. But this only revealed itself to them slowly, as the war progressed. And the first step towards that understanding came in January 1943. In that month, an intriguing story reached the ears of the head of a German signals regiment that had set up camp in the Katyn Forest. There were graves of Polish officers nearby, he was told. Some Poles had explored the area and found bones and military insignia. The officer ordered an excavation. The Germans had found one of the main burial sites of the Katyn Massacre.

The Nazis knew exactly what they had discovered, and its potential value to them. A clear example of Soviet crime, and the chance of a major propaganda coup. They wondered if perhaps they might be able to undermine Stalin, split the Allies and win support from Poles. They set about carefully exhuming the bodies, photographing and cataloguing what they found, and arranging for witnesses to see the mass graves and their contents.

The immediate response of the Soviets was to claim that the officers had been killed by the Germans. Obviously it was a crime that the Nazis would have been perfectly capable of committing, and the Nazi moral indignation about their find was grotesque. Equally obviously, the Soviet suggestion was absurd.

The Poles were quite well aware when and where their officers had disappeared, and who held them before their disappearance. In any case, the letters and documents found on the bodies all predated 1940, and corpses were found in winter clothes, making ridiculous a Soviet claim that they had been killed in the summer of 1941 by the advancing German army.

But any Polish hope that the Soviets would stop lying about Katyn, or that their Allies would take the Polish side, was soon dashed. When the Poles called for a Red Cross investigation, and the Germans did too, the Soviet press responded with headlines about 'Hitler's Polish collaborators'. And on 21 April 1943, Stalin informed Churchill and Roosevelt that he was furious about the Polish behaviour, and intended to withdraw recognition from the Polish government-in-exile. He proceeded to do so, and the withdrawal was announced five days later.

The anger, of course, was synthetic. Stalin knew perfectly well how the officers had died. He was taking the opportunity to remove a rival for the control of postwar Poland.

As for the Allies, they too knew what had happened. General Sikorski, the government-in-exile's Prime Minister, had lunched with Churchill on 15 April and told him that he believed the murders had been committed by the NKVD. Churchill had shown his agreement by remarking: 'The Bolsheviks can be very cruel.' But he wasn't about to break with his vital Soviet partner over Katyn. Indeed, he felt Soviet ruthlessness could serve the common cause, however distressing on this occasion.

Stalin now set about completing the job that he had begun with his invasion of Poland in 1940 and the Katyn murders.

He started installing a communist government in Poland which would keep that country in the Soviet sphere of influence. He was determined to exclude from any position in postwar Poland any Poles with nationalist or liberal democratic leanings. Particularly those who had been in London. He was much helped in this endeavour when Sikorski was killed in a plane crash after taking off from Gibraltar airport in July 1943. It robbed the government-in-exile of its most charismatic figure.

In the summer of 1944, the Polish Home Army, resistance fighters based in Poland but largely under the control of the

London Poles, helped the Red Army to liberate Lwów. Immediately, their officers were arrested and their units disbanded.

That same summer, the Polish resistance in Warsaw rose against the Germans in anticipation of the arrival of Soviet forces. Though they had been encouraged to rise by Soviet radio broadcasts, Stalin held back his army, leaving the Germans to it. As the German forces massacred the Poles, entering schools and bludgeoning children to death with rifle butts, Himmler rejoiced that the intellectual capital of Poland was being destroyed, wiping out a nation that had been in Germany's way for hundreds of years. This was precisely how Stalin saw it too, from a Russian perspective. The attitudes that produced the Molotov-Ribbentrop Pact persisted, even if the pact had not.

When the so-called 'Big Three' – Churchill, Roosevelt and Stalin – met in Yalta in February 1945 to discuss postwar arrangements, Stalin was intransigent on Poland. It was the subject of more argument than anything else. In the end, the Americans and British yielded.

The policies agreed at Yalta determined that there would be new boundaries for Poland. The whole country would shift west. It would take in a part of Germany, but to the east it would lose territory to Soviet Ukraine. Postwar Lwów, now Lviv, would be in the Soviet Union. And the Polish government, despite some woolly language about elections that Stalin accepted, would be dominated by the communists.

When Dolu and Lusia heard the news, they understood that they could not safely go home. Not to Lviv certainly, where Dolu would doubtless be almost immediately arrested and returned to the Gulag. And not to the new Poland either, where their prospects would not be much better. The only question was whether they would be forced to return there, simply because nowhere else would have them. The British might put the Anders army under the control of the Polish communist government, and insist upon its return to Poland.

After Yalta, General Anders and Churchill had a furious row, shouting loudly at each other; but once the anger had subsided, it was obvious that the British Prime Minister felt guilty about what had been agreed. He first told Anders, and then the House of Commons, that he very much hoped that the brave Poles who had fought under British command – a category to which Dolu belonged – would be offered British citizenship.

It was reassuring, but uncertainty remained. It was at about this time that Ludwik took Dolu to the railway station in Tel Aviv, as the latter headed off for a short assignment in Egypt. Dolu told Ludwik that he might not return. 'You must realise,' he said to his son, 'that if we are put under the communists, we're going to mutiny.' He would be arrested, he might be shot. Then he added: 'Look after your mother.'

It didn't come to this. The British delivered upon Churchill's promise. Members of the Anders army were allowed to join the newly formed Polish Resettlement Corps, which offered them a home in Britain. Ludwik wasn't entirely sure that he wanted one. He'd rather have stayed in Palestine, where he was making friends. Dolu briefly thought about it too, if they could get permission. But he was sick of war and sick of struggle, and life in Britain seemed to offer less of both those things. Though Ludwik was seventeen, it never occurred to him to stay in Palestine without his parents.

So, on Wednesday, 27 August 1947, Dolu, Lusia and Ludwik arrived by boat in Britain, with their first impressions formed by the rainy Southampton docks. They felt, said my father, 'demoralised and defeated as Poles'.

They had no money, they had no standing, they had no home. But they did, at least, have each other. And after all they had been through, they had nothing to lose and nothing to fear. They would start again. This would not be the end of the Finkelsteins, they felt sure. This would be their new beginning.

MUM

Three Skeletons

The transport from Belsen had arrived in the station at Kreuzlingen in Switzerland at 11.30 p.m. on 24 January 1945. There, the passengers changed trains to make a further short journey of about an hour to St Gallen, where accommodation had been prepared for them.

Mirjam and her sisters made this change, but they left their mother behind. After crossing the border, Grete had lost consciousness for the last time. She was taken to hospital in Kreuzlingen on a stretcher, and died there at just past midnight.

The girls were informed of her death in the morning. Despite seeing how unwell she was, they had still somehow expected her to survive. Her death seemed inconceivable after all that they had been through together. The news left them numb. It took them all a long time to realise what had happened, or what it meant. I think my mother was still gradually coming to understand it when she was an old woman, and dying herself. She would often remark how her mother had been only forty-nine years old. 'Yes; forty-nine and not yet fifty; no age, really.'

Grete's death, and that of two others on the transport, was one of the earliest pieces of direct evidence that the Allies received of the conditions in the camps. It caused Roswell McClelland of the War Refugee Board to report to Washington that 'there is every reason to believe that the extreme malnutrition from which the exchanges were suffering is far from confined to Bergen Belsen but is common to all German concentration camps and deportee work companies'. He urged the military authorities to prepare to find tens of thousands of people like this as they liberated areas from the Nazis.

The reason that the girls had not accompanied their mother to hospital, and had not been with her when she died, is that they were still under guard. The Swiss said that they were concerned about the spread of disease, but really their concern was that the refugees might abscond and then try to stay in Switzerland, which wasn't part of the deal at all, as far as the Swiss were concerned.

Grete was buried in Kreuzlingen at 3.30 in the afternoon of the 26th. Mirjam and Eva were not permitted to be present; but after a great deal of pleading, Ruth was allowed to travel to the funeral, guarded by a soldier with a rifle. The Rabbi, Lothar Rothschild, and the president of the congregation, Robert Wieler, had both known Alfred before the war, and the entire congregation joined in as the traditional service took place, and the Rabbi gave a eulogy.

Afterwards, Wieler and his wife invited Ruth back to their house, gave her dinner, allowed her to take a hot bath, and provided her with a change of clothing. They also gave her some clothes for her sisters which they had collected from other members of the local community. The Wielers commented upon the way that Ruth waited for them to eat before eating herself, even though she must have been extremely hungry. Ruth observed that Belsen had not managed to erase the way that Grete had brought them up.

The deal that the War Refugee Board had struck with Paraguay was similar to the one that it struck with Switzerland. The Swiss helped broker the deal, and it was accepted in return that the refugees wouldn't stay in Switzerland. In the same way, because Paraguay helped with the exchange by recognising the passports, the Americans would ensure that the passports would not entitle the refugees to go to Paraguay. Instead, they would be sent to the United Nations camp that had been established in Philippeville, Algeria.

So, on 30 January 1945, dressed in their new clothes and having burned their old rags to destroy any lice, the girls headed back to St Gallen for a train to the port of Marseilles. Journalists who saw my mother and her fellow passengers boarding the train noted the contrast between the American internees and the group from Belsen.

These people [the Belsen survivors] arrived here in a pitiful state: enfeebled, emaciated, aged, some critically ill . . . [they] climbed slowly down the steps to the platform as if they were old men. Children and women limped away, and the people even had to be put on the train on stretchers.

The train travelled down the Rhône-Saône valley through a war zone, an area littered with tanks and other military vehicles, and then, on arrival in the port of Marseilles, the group was divided. The Americans were taken to the *Gripsholm*, a Swedish ocean liner managed by the Red Cross and transporting wounded soldiers home to the United States. The Belsen survivors were taken to an Italian ship destined for Algeria, Mirjam and her sisters among them.

However, ever since Alfred had first learned about the exchange, he had been hard at work in New York, trying to persuade the authorities to allow his daughters to join him there. His early relationship with the State Department may not have been very good, but by now he was a trusted contributor to their work and had many contacts. Through them – and by paying $1,000 for the passage – he was able to obtain a place on the *Gripsholm* for the girls.

Just as the ship for Philippeville was about to leave, the sisters were collected and taken across to the liner bound for New York.

The *Gripsholm* would take almost two weeks to reach its destination. It went a long way off the normal course, to avoid submarines and mines and so forth. But it was a comfortable journey. The ship had kept many of its prewar fittings, and contemporary photographs show spotless lounges and beautiful dining areas. And the girls had normal tickets which allowed access to the leisure facilities and meals in smart surroundings (Dining Room C, Sitting 2, Table 158).

On the day that they set sail, an American army band was playing. Everyone was drunk, some literally, most giddy with joy. The food was plentiful, but so rich that it made them ill. Nevertheless, they gained a little weight. They needed to. Eva was five feet four inches tall and weighed only eighty pounds.

But there were many reminders that it was not a normal journey. The ship carried wounded soldiers home from war in what Mirjam said was 'a terrible state . . . the injuries of these poor young men, it was really quite appalling'. Enough to shock them despite their own state, and all they had seen in Belsen. One soldier had lost all four limbs. He told Eva that if only he had wrists, he would kill himself.

And there was also their rising apprehension about what might greet them in New York. The girls were, of course, unaware of the debate about exchanges like theirs, and of the arguments about the danger of espionage that had taken place between American officials. They knew nothing of rumours about spies receiving plastic surgery to look like Jews. But Ruth had picked up that they were likely to be questioned on arrival.

That's why, as arrival became close, she took her sisters back to their cabin near the top of the ship, on Deck A, just below the promenade deck, wrapped Alfred's war medals – his Iron Cross (second class) and Iron Crescent – in a handkerchief, opened a porthole, and threw them into the water.

Every hour I knew we were coming nearer and nearer, and then the great moment came. For a long time I stood on the deck, and suddenly at a great distance I saw the shore. Slowly we entered the harbour, passed the Statue of Liberty, the symbol of everything which America offers to us. I looked at the skyscrapers, the thousands of lights, which I had not seen for so long. I imagined hearing people, talking and laughing, seeing crowded streets and busy traffic. This is America, I felt, and in one of those buildings my father would live, and he would wait for us . . . And I was happy, very happy.

So wrote Ruth of the moment, on Wednesday, 21 February 1945, that the *Gripsholm* approached New York. Despite all that they had lost, and all that they had left behind, despite their fears of what the welcome might be for stateless refugees in wartime, despite their poor health and uncertain futures, the girls were elated.

Alfred had sent a loving note to them on the ship two days earlier, explaining that he would not be allowed on board, telling them that he was impatient to see them, warning them not to catch cold. His words sustained them through the coming days.

Before anyone could leave the *Gripsholm* in New York, the FBI and intelligence officers engaged in what the *New York Times* described as 'close questioning as a precaution against the admittance of enemy agents'. Of the 622 civilians on board, a couple of dozen were taken to Ellis Island for further interrogation. The Wieners were among them, having been kept waiting on board until five o'clock on the Friday afternoon.

It took two days for the intelligence and immigration services to satisfy themselves that the three young Jewish girls were not spies. Alfred had reassured his daughters that the officials would be friendly, and would release them quickly. And he had sent them some chocolate, some pencils and some *hopjes*, a traditional Dutch caramel sweet. Nevertheless, it was an ordeal. 'My sisters and I were frightened again,' Eva explained, 'because the doors were locked. We thought we were in another camp in America.'

On the Monday morning, they were released. They were taken by boat to a pier in New York's harbour and then by car to the Bureau of Immigration in Columbus Circle, where their papers would be issued. They were told to sit on a bench in a long corridor.

A few moments later, a man appeared. Bald, distinctive big ears, slightly formal. He just stood there. The girls were not told of his arrival, nor he that his girls were already present. The final test of their truthfulness had been whether they recognised their father and he recognised them. Eva saw him first. 'Daddy! Daddy!' she shouted, and they ran towards him.

The girls had to swear an oath that he was their father and their father had to swear an oath that these were his girls, and then Alfred took his daughters by the hand, as Grete had been determined that one day he would, and together they walked out onto the streets of Manhattan. They turned down Fifth Avenue. And, Eva would remember, 'everyone stared at us. We were three tall skeletons and one short, little, old man.'

PART THREE

AFTER

DAD

The Lady of Hendon Central

Despite the fact that he eventually found that he admired Britain – he liked its orderliness and felt it well-governed – Dolu was not to experience a new dawn.

His plan was to revive his business career. He had thought the old Finkelstein property in Vienna might be sold, and the money help put them back on their feet. But he discovered that the apartment block had been destroyed in the war. And the small amount of Finkelstein money deposited in London had been, perfectly reasonably, used by his sister Lola years earlier to make good her escape from Vienna and create a new life in America. His only other hope – family support – proved equally unavailing.

His aunt, Maks' sister, Antonia Thorn, was living in Golders Green, in northwest London, and her son, Jules, had made his fortune in electrical goods and was well on his way to becoming Sir Jules. Dolu and the family were able to stay with Antonia for the first year after arriving, but that was all. Dolu's anticipation that his cousin might lend him money to re-establish himself was to be disappointed.

He approached Jules first with ideas to set up in the building trade and later with a proposal to create an estate agency. He was sure he would be able to pay any loan back quickly and that the money would be a drop in the ocean for Jules. But he was told that it wasn't a good moment for Jules's business, and no loan was forth-coming. Soon Dolu was, in any case, too ill to start new ventures.

In the spring of 1948, Dolu had begun seeing the doctor, complaining of repeated chest pains. Then, in April 1949, less than two years after arrival in Southampton, he suffered a major heart attack from which he never really recovered. The doctors struggled to help him, trying also to treat his anxiety and depression. But nothing worked, and on 27 June 1950 his coronary heart disease finally killed him. He was a few months short of his sixtieth birthday.

His doctor was clear why his patient had died so young. 'His heart and nervous condition were caused by his dreadful experiences during the war years . . . In my opinion these experiences were responsible for Mr. F's illnesses and early death.'

So, living in a small house on the main road through Hendon Central, died the Iron King of Lwów, a man who had lost everything except the love of his family and the respect of his friends.

———————

That love was considerable and durable. Lusia was forty-nine years old when Dolu died and never married again, or took another partner. She was devastated to lose her husband, and decades later could sometimes be seen, sitting alone, thinking of him and their life together, eyes moist.

Indeed, for a while after Dolu died, she was totally lost. She hadn't any plans, she hadn't a big social circle, she had hardly any money at all. She wasn't eligible for a widow's pension, and she and Ludwik had only his small university study grant. For several months, they lived on that and on National Assistance, and she planned to become a kitchen assistant at the Johnson and Son's chemical works on the Hendon Way.

Gradually her toughness reasserted itself, and she found her feet again. The labour exchange informed her that there was a language school in nearby Golders Green looking for a part-time teacher.

Soon she was working twelve-hour days teaching the neighbour-hood's au pairs to speak English. Known by them all as 'Mrs Finn', and able to speak their languages fluently, she was very popular with her pupils and her employer.

Inevitably, Dolu's death intensified the already intense bond between Ludwik and his mother. In a letter sent while working away from home on May 1953, my father first provided some rather banal news about his day and then finished with this:

> Forgive me darling for being so unpoetical . . . You are so much part of me that I cannot really feel that you are far away and instead of writing a proper letter to you I am just having a chat. I'm also convinced that a letter from me to you and from you to me could not really be written down in any language on earth, for communication between me and you is after all half that peculiar slang of ours, half thought transfer. Please then read this letter and do not be a harsh judge of form and style. You shall learn from this letter what is happening to my body, my heart and soul are with you as ever . . . Your loving and devoted Ludwik.

It is to the credit of both Mirjam and Lusia that Ludwik's marriage did not disrupt this relationship, or produce tension between mother and daughter-in-law. They loved each other unconditionally. And Granny was loved by all of us, her grandchildren, as well.

Lusia never recovered her fortune, but she lived comfortably round the corner from her son and family. And she recovered her poise. By the time she died of old age in 1980, she had become, as she had been in her youth, once more an imposing social figure, her company much sought after, her wit appreciated, her conver-sation enjoyed, her elegance admired.

Among the many dozens of letters my father received on her death was one that said: 'She was so dignified and gentle . . . we shall always retain the memory of a person for whom the title "lady" was invented especially.'

MUM

The Man on the President's Conscience

The reunion between Alfred and his daughters in New York was relatively brief.

At the end of November 1944, Alfred had received a letter from his friend and colleague, David Bowes-Lyon, the Queen's brother. And it contained unwelcome news. The British Political Warfare Mission in Washington, which Alfred had been supplying with books and briefings, no longer needed his services.

He was told that the liberation of German-occupied territories meant that the Allies now had their own supplies of material. 'The Department has instructed me to inform you that it will terminate its financial support for your activities in the United States at the 31st January, 1945.' Alfred should cease buying books for the mission, and he would doubtless wish to close his New York office and dispose of its stocks.

Bowes-Lyon was most anxious that his instructions were not taken by Alfred as 'implying any lack of appreciation of your very valuable services . . . we are all most grateful to you for the devoted service you have given'. Nevertheless, the letter was firm, indeed curt, and strongly implied that funding for the Library in London would soon be coming to an end as well. As was indeed the case.

The letter offered to facilitate Alfred's return to London by sea, suggesting he do so as soon after 31 January 1945 as possible, and he had made arrangements with the mission to do just that. And then, in the last week of that month, he had heard about the Belsen exchange, and that his wife and children were to be free.

He delayed his departure from America, but he couldn't delay it long. It had been made clear to him that he should leave New York as soon as possible. He wasn't working for the British government any more, and he wasn't an American citizen. His whole professional life was about to collapse, and he would be left without any money. The Library would be closed and its employees out of a job. An archive he thought invaluable would be lost. He had to go to London and try to prevent this calamity.

Nor, realistically, could he bring his daughters back to London with him. It was hard enough to find transport for himself with the war still raging, let alone find transport for them. And what would he do with them in London? How would he care for them? Even if he could find help, life was very difficult in wartime Britain. He decided that he would return to London in March, and find others to care for the girls in America.

However compelling the logic when it is rehearsed, the decision still seems an odd one. He didn't see his daughters for a further two years. At the very least, it shows the priority work always had for Alfred. But his daughters never questioned it. They loved him without reserve. Once or twice someone would venture a criticism of Alfred's decision to my mother, and receive a very dusty answer indeed.

Alfred looked after them in his hotel room for a few days. 'He took us to a cafeteria,' marvelled Mirjam. 'You know, it was as if we'd landed on the moon. It was quite, quite extraordinary.' And then, before leaving in early March, he took them to stay with a Quaker family in their large, comfortable house in Hastings-on-Hudson.

Richard Day, an eminent paediatrician, and his wife Ida had three daughters who were around the same age as the Wieners.

Mirjam remembered hearing them play music together and feeling as if she had gone to heaven. It had been so long since they had enjoyed music in that way. And the youngest Day girl, Kate, said of the Wieners that 'my mother became very attached to them'. Ida described them as 'very traumatized, very needy, and like all institutionalized children, very receptive to love. Seeing them change, almost day by day, was wonderfully rewarding.'

Kate recalled one other thing. In 1952, the Days hosted Hilde Speer. The daughter of the Nazi leader Albert Speer had won a competition to study in America. Though Hilde – who became a fierce anti-Nazi, and later devoted herself to returning stolen Nazi art to Jews – remembered Ida Day as extremely kind, Kate remembered her mother as being uncharacteristically sharp with their guest, and one day shouting at her about her faults. 'I did wonder whether the very strong feelings my mother had had for the three Wiener girls had something to do with the anger she showed that day to Hilde.'

Later in 1945, Mirjam and her sisters moved to Newark, Delaware, to stay with a Jewish family; and later still they split up for a while, with Ruth going to live in New York City, acting as a home help and going to school, while Mirjam and Eva lived with Quakers in Concord, New Hampshire.

Almost immediately, all talk of the war and of the Holocaust stopped. The three girls, who had survived Belsen, lost their mother, and were apart from their father, simply went to school and tried to resume their lives. 'One didn't talk about it actually,' said Mirjam. They were just left to get on with it.

In the middle of March 1945, one of Alfred's friends had taken them to the dentist and then, according to the letter she wrote to Alfred a couple of days later, to see 'Miss Schultz, a psycho-analist with whom they had a very nice chat. When we left, she passed a remark that unfortunately I forgot. Afterwards we went back to the Eclair Conditorei to buy some cake.' And this was the sum total of the therapy they received.

At school, the other girls asked Mirjam more about Holland

than anything else. 'Did we wear wooden shoes and did we live in a windmill,' was the most frequent inquiry. Mirjam felt much more mature than her fellow pupils and it distanced her from them a little, though she was always able to make friends. In Ruth's school yearbook, the words describing her were telling:

> Ruth had dignity that this ditty,
> Can't explain – it's the same
> As her warm and lovely eyes,
> Laughing, yet so very wise.

The teachers mostly shared this lack of insight. About six weeks after arriving in New York, Ruth wrote a remarkable school essay entitled 'My First Impressions of America'. It told of her suffering in concentration camp, the death of her mother, the way she dreamt about her friends who had been murdered. Her written English, even so soon after arrival, was near-perfect. The teacher underlined the phrase 'I thought of my mother, who died after departing the camp', and added a querulous question mark above it. She awarded Ruth the grade A/B–.

At her graduation from the Robert Louis Stevenson School in 1946, Ruth was the Salutatorian of her class. She gave a speech about all the knowledge that school had given her. The independence, the understanding of life. And she added that her listeners might want to think about oppressed children who studied, when studying was forbidden. 'Imagine, people risking their lives in order to learn, hardworking and hungry people, spending their evenings studying. Many of them have not returned, but those who have survived, have expressed their desire for an education. They appreciate school more than any of us.'

She did not let her audience know that she was talking about herself.

This general obliviousness about the Holocaust, about what had really happened, whom it had happened to, and its true significance, was also encountered by Alfred on his return to London.

As the letter from Bowes-Lyon had prefigured, in April 1945, on his first visit to his Whitehall sponsors, Alfred was informed that all government subsidy to the Library would cease in three months. There had been a row over who would pay for his passage from New York and there was no budget to pay his salary even for these three months.

A perfunctory letter from Foreign Secretary Anthony Eden thanked the Library for its help during the war and, as a goodwill gesture, the government offered a monthly subscription of fifteen guineas. Apart from that, Alfred and his colleagues were on their own.

It seemed that people could not imagine why it might be useful to keep together books and documents about Nazism. They couldn't see why anyone would need to study racist ideology or research the crimes of the Holocaust. This failure of comprehension afflicted even those who engaged with the subject. Even these people were not much help to the Library. Understandably, perhaps, they were more interested in direct help to survivors and the millions of refugees that the war had produced. Others donated to the nascent Jewish state. Books and documents were a relatively low priority.

Alfred would, therefore, spend the rest of his life finding inventive ways to raise funds, and keep the Library alive. It turned out that he was good at it. He had an eye for a possible donor, or an influential backer. His wit and erudition charmed people. And he was tireless. Nonetheless, the Library lived from hand to mouth for decades. There were many moments when it looked possible that it wouldn't continue. It always had to tend what funds it did have very carefully.

Crucial to survival was Alfred's identification of a wealthy and willing patron. Leonard Montefiore was a member of a moneyed Jewish dynasty and shared Alfred's commitment to German Jewry as well as his intellectual interests. He provided vital financial support, and persuaded others to do so too. Eventually, money was also forthcoming from the German government. But any stability they attained would only last for a short period, and there were various crises, including some months when the Library was homeless.

In 1946, Alfred created a Wiener Library Board, giving it a formal legal footing it had lacked. David Bowes-Lyon agreed to serve, as did the Marquess of Reading, and, of course, Montefiore. But one other member was to prove particularly significant.

Having read in the newspaper in 1946 of a newly elected back-bench Labour MP who had visited Nazi war trials, Alfred searched him out. He introduced himself and the work of the Library. The man he met, and proceeded to befriend, was James Callaghan, destined to have one of the greatest British political careers of the postwar era, and to be the only man to have held all four great offices of state – Chancellor, Home Secretary, Foreign Secretary and, finally, Prime Minister.

Callaghan would remain a friend for the rest of Alfred's life, and a friend of the Library for the rest of his own. In 1980, the year after he stopped being Prime Minister, he agreed to head an endowment appeal and threw himself into the task. His support saved the Library at one of its most difficult moments. Callaghan's official biographer, Kenneth O. Morgan, accords a special place to the statesman's involvement with the Library among his many achievements. 'The Wiener connection was important to Callaghan,' he writes, 'as it was to his generation. It shows him at his most genuine and idealistic.'

Callaghan understood in 1945, and in the decades after, the value of a dispassionate and comprehensive collection of material on the Holocaust. He also appreciated that few others shared this understanding. In a meeting between him and Alfred in 1949, the future Prime Minister advised his friend that government assistance would be 'extremely difficult' to come by. He suggested that the Library seek funds from the trade unions by producing a memorandum about German industry. He thought that there would be little interest in funding research on the continuing dangers of nationalism, 'as much as one might regret it'.

Yet all the while, as they fought to keep the Library going, events were beginning to vindicate Alfred's work. And the most important of these events were the Nuremberg trials. In October 1945, the Allied powers indicted the surviving Nazi leaders, including many of the figures directly responsible for the crimes against both of my parents – Göring, Ribbentrop and Arthur Seyss-Inquart, the Reich Commissioner of the occupied Netherlands. The Allies needed evidence to determine the charges and secure convictions. And Alfred had been collecting the evidence.

The Wiener Library played an important role in the trials, helping provide the investigators with documents, and helping the lawyers interpret what they had found in the papers that had been recovered from the Germans. When the first main trial was over, and most of the indicted Nazis had been executed, General de Baer, a United Nations war crimes commissioner, indeed the chairman of the commission's Facts and Evidence Committee, thanked the Library publicly. 'Documents which could be found nowhere else were available there. The help it has given has been invaluable in the preparation of charges against the leaders of Nazi Germany.'

The Library was rewarded with the right to send an observer to the trials and was given one of the sets of Nuremberg trial documents, a sufficiently large collection that it required a room of its own to store.

In 1960, when Eichmann was arrested and put on trial in Israel, the chief investigator made a visit to the Library one of his earliest tasks. He too sent thanks for its help, and apologised for how much assistance he had required. Again the Library was offered trial documents as a reward, and observer status. But a sign of its money troubles is that it was unable to afford to take up the invitation to travel to the trial.

It was also involved in less high-profile investigations, both official proceedings and journalistic endeavours. For example, a rumour about the infamous Dr Joseph Mengele, the Auschwitz physician, torturer and murderer, required the Library's participation. It was said that he was in South America, but nobody was sure what he looked like. The Library had a picture.

Alfred found vindication too in the emergence of the new field of Holocaust studies. He was able to help historians as they tried to understand what had happened, and in particular the way that the murderous policy of the Nazis had been a deliberate attempt to eradicate the Jewish people. For years he had been working to get people to understand who the Nazis were, and what they thought. Finally he succeeded, changing fundamentally the common understanding of the war.

The important early books on the genocide, such as Gerald Reitlinger's *Final Solution*, all give credit to Alfred and his archive. One of the leading historians of the Nazi ascendancy, Alan Bullock, would later say that Alfred's name would 'long be remembered for the services he has rendered to scholarship'. An open letter from academics in 1980, published in *The Times*, declared that without the Wiener Library, the current state of research into the history of national socialism would be 'unthinkable'.

In 1953, under the guidance of Alfred's close associate Eva Reichmann, the Library had also begun the first proper collection of Holocaust eyewitness statements, building on those taken after Kristallnacht. This too was a pioneering effort. Among the statements was one from Betty Lewin. Slightly oddly, Alfred didn't ask his own daughters to contribute, even though my mother was still living with him.

The publication of the most famous Holocaust book of all also involved Alfred. Otto Frank, his old friend from their Amsterdam days, had published his daughter Anne's diary. Otto consulted Alfred about how to publicise the book, and later about how to prove the authenticity of the diary, which ultimately became the subject of a court case.

Otto's second wife had a daughter living in London and he visited Britain frequently. Whenever he did, the two men would meet, sometimes in Alfred's home, where Mirjam remembered meeting him too, and sometimes at Otto's hotel, Clarendon Court in Maida Vale.

As well as Anne and Margot, Otto had lost his first wife in the Holocaust. And though the sadness never left him, nor the drive to educate people about what had happened, Otto had rebuilt his life, found contentment in his work, and was happy in a new relationship.

And all this was true of Alfred too.

On 3 January 1947, Mirjam, Ruth and Eva set off for London to join Alfred in his flat above the Queensway ice-skating rink near the centre of town. The family were all together again, at least those that had survived. It was the first time that the girls had lived with their father for almost seven years.

Alfred soon moved. The flat was too full. But not full of people. The flat was too full of books. Partly because he was an obsessive collector, and partly because he traded books to supplement his fairly small salary, Alfred filled every room with volumes. Eventually, a building inspector, possibly worried about the rink below, told him that the weight of books was too great for the structure. Alfred had to choose between the flat and the books. He chose the books.

He bought a house on Middleton Road in Golders Green, Number 25, a good deal further out from the city centre and requiring a commute to work. But the compensation was that he could keep on buying books. Mirjam used to see him off on a weekend to go book-shopping, and sigh with relief when he came back in a taxi with only a small shopping bag. Then another taxi would pull up with the books in it.

While Alfred was busy book-shopping and saving the Library, Mirjam went back to school, Eva to art college, and Ruth to study for a BA at the University of London. Within two years, Ruth had met Paul Klemens, a physics PhD student and fellow refugee. By 1950, they had married and moved to Australia. The next year, Eva moved to Israel and then to America, having married Ted Plaut. Ted was the son of Alice, the friend of Alfred's who had helped him obtain the Palestine certificates. Alice had been determined that one of her sons would marry one of Alfred's daughters. Rather against the odds, she had succeeded.

And then, in 1953, also against the odds given his commitment to work and books, Alfred met someone too. On a liner, returning from a visit to her brother's chicken farm in Israel, Lotte Philips had asked Alfred, returning from a holiday, if he had a watch and could tell her the time. Before long, they were partners; Lotte became Lotte Philips-Wiener and moved into Middleton Road. Mirjam turned twenty that year and was grateful to have someone else to help with caring for her father, whose own domestic skills had not improved. Fortunately, she got on well with Lotte, and remained extremely close to her after Alfred's death. She was very much part of our family and loved as such.

What had happened in Germany had shaken Alfred profoundly. It had challenged every belief he had held. After the war, for instance, he embraced wholeheartedly the idea of a Jewish state in Israel. But he still maintained his belief in the 'other Germany'. Small in number and ineffective they might have been, but hadn't some Germans heroically resisted the Nazis? Hadn't the churches, for instance, opposed the regime?

He began to return to Germany, making visit after visit, seeking to tell young Germans what had happened and to spread to them the ideals of this 'other Germany'. He would return from these encounters with shining eyes, feeling that this new generation would create a democratic, modern postwar Germany. Their enthusiasm and commitment made him feel that his idealistic view of Germany had contained truth within it, even though his own generation had betrayed him so badly.

His visits were greatly appreciated in West Germany, where they were viewed as exceptionally generous and open-minded, and a symbol of hope for the country's future. In March 1955, Chancellor Konrad Adenauer, the country's great postwar leader, personally recommended that Alfred receive Germany's highest civilian decoration – the Grand Cross of Merit of the Federal Republic of Germany. The award marked Alfred's seventieth birthday, and in a press statement it was announced that he had received the distinction both for the work he had done fighting national socialism and also for his work with German youth.

There were some friends of his who felt he should not accept such an award from Germany. He did not agree. I suspect he felt that this new medal could stand in place of the ones his daughters had thrown from the *Gripsholm*.

He wasn't naive about the country. As he put it in an interview:

I don't fall around the neck of the Germans. I am sad when I realise that Nazi officials are working for the German Government . . . I must admit that I am a little disappointed with the Germany of today. What happened [t]here was a unique catastrophe. One expected a unique reaction. One expected deeper feelings. They were not there.

Nor had he forgotten what he had suffered personally. Indeed, what he was still suffering:

The crimes the Nazis committed lie not only in the ghostliness of the concentration camps, which are now well-known. There are the invisible crimes of which the effects are still felt: the families who have been torn apart for ever. My own wife is dead, a victim of the Third Reich. One of my daughters lives in America, another in Australia. Children, through acts of 15 years ago, have become strangers to their parents.

But he was always very careful about generalising. He thought that the Nazis had generalised about the Jews. He was happy to receive an award on the recommendation of Adenauer. As he was, a little over three years later, to play host to the liberal President of the Republic, Theodor Heuss.

In October 1958, Heuss made the first state visit to Britain by a German head of state since the Kaiser in 1907. It went smoothly, although there were some MPs who felt he should not have been received. Near the end of the trip Heuss visited his old friend Alfred at the Library, now in Devonshire Street, in Marylebone.

Alfred pointed out the President's name on a list of 'important people dangerous to the Nazi regime' that had been compiled by Himmler and the SS. The document shocked Heuss, and the moment of him being shown it, with the President removing his cigar and mopping his brow, became a symbol of the visit and made all the papers. There were big pictures, and headlines like 'The Moment of Horror' and 'Library of Doom'. The *Daily Mail* profiled Alfred, dubbing him 'The Man on the President's Conscience'.

By 1960, Alfred's health was beginning to fail. He retired from the Library – in truth a semi-retirement, as only death could really end his working life – in 1961, when he was seventy-six. Announcing his intention, he emphasised the need to tackle the broader problem of racism.

We have always believed that it is no good to isolate anti-semitism from all other forms of intolerance and hatred in human relations, and that one cannot successfully combat anti-Jewish prejudice, while ignoring the colour bar or other manifestations of racialism. In the Library today we pay attention not only to antisemitism and Nazism but to fascist and racialist movements as well.

After a year or two, he was only able to contribute to this work by correspondence. Increasingly he was bed-bound or, at most, capable of sitting in an armchair, reading.

On 4 February 1964, Alfred died, just short of his seventy-ninth birthday, with Lotte and my mother and father by his side. The news appeared in most of the leading newspapers in Britain, America and especially Germany. 'Alfred Wiener, Kept Nazi Data', was the heading of the *New York Times* report. The President of the Federal Republic of Germany, Heinrich Lübke, thanked him publicly for his 'magnanimity'. The Chancellor, Ludwig Erhard, said that Alfred would long be remembered in Germany and that he had been one of the most important of all of its émigrés.

When he had been reunited with his daughters in 1945 and they had told him that they had disposed of his war medals in the water by the Statue of Liberty, Alfred had been upset. This seems puzzling. Why on earth would he want German *anything*, let alone military insignia? Surely he could understand that in the circumstances, it wasn't worth taking even the tiniest risk for a few pieces of German metal.

But throwing away his medals denied two things that were central to Alfred. He believed in the power of truth. Discovering the truth, revealing the truth, helping people understand the truth, that was his life's work.

In 1945, he was still awaiting the vindication of his belief that was to come. It's not hard to see why he found it depressing, this man with his faith in truth, that the truth of his service and his war decorations was something that had to be hidden.

Yet although this was part of the explanation for his reaction, it was the smaller part. What will have loomed larger for Alfred, even over the denial of truth, was the denial of his German identity. The indication that in what lay ahead for him, being German was something better consigned to the depths.

By the time that he died, Alfred had accepted his exile from Germany. At least from a practical standpoint. The Library and his life were in London, and he never seriously thought about going back. One of the few concessions made to him when the Library's funding was cut so unceremoniously in 1945 was that his years in New York would count as British residence. As a result, he qualified for naturalisation, and in 1946 he became a British citizen.

He had settled in London quite well, and appreciated Britain's way of life and its institutions. One of his obituaries described him as regarding *The Times* as 'second only to the Bible'. As a present, he would routinely give copies of George Mikes' comic gem, *How to be an Alien*. This little book, by a Hungarian exile, is humorously affectionate about Alfred's adopted country. But also sees his fellow countrymen from the perspective of an outsider.

Alfred's real feelings may be intuited from the fact that he asked for the psalms and prayers at his graveside to be read in Hebrew and German. In the prayer hall, the eulogy was in German too, and among the large crowd of mourners were the German ambassador and his wife. On Alfred's coffin rested a wreath from the Federal President in black, red and gold.

Alfred Wiener died as he had lived – a self-confident Jew and a German patriot.

MUM & DAD

Friday Evening

Between 1949 and 1956, Mirjam kept a diary. The entries were short, the contents, in general, unremarkable.

The life that the diary portrays provides hardly a hint of the ordeal its author had been through a short time before. The only occasion that is touched upon is in a description of a holiday in Switzerland, taken in August 1951. Museums are visited ('had a very nice day'), Mirjam goes swimming, takes a long walk, and sees a French film; and then, on 27 August, comes: 'Arrived in Kreuzlingen in morning. Went to Mammie's burial ground. Mr Wieler showed me Kreuzlingen in car. Slept at hotel.' And that is it.

Then, on Sunday, 22 April 1956, appear the words: 'Outing, George, Joyce, Ludwig.' It isn't long before my father's name, correctly spelled, is appearing more frequently than anyone else's.

My Mum had met my Dad.

It had been a meeting of the B'nai B'rith Youth Organisation in Seymour Place in central London which had resulted in their first encounter. It was Ludwik's first visit; Mirjam was membership secretary. He was twenty-six years old and she was twenty-two. Between the two of them, they had lived in ten countries.

We always used to tease my father about his choice of first date. He had taken my mother to an exhibition being held by the Institute of Physics. Yet, now that I think about it, this was a joke we children would make. My mother didn't join in. She almost certainly found the exhibition very interesting. And someone who thought it a good place to go on a date was probably just what she was looking for. To a child of Alfred and Grete Wiener, such an intellectual choice of entertainment probably didn't seem all that eccentric.

They had found a perfect match for each other. My father wasn't a great one for mysticism, but he definitely felt his relationship with my mother was fated.

My father died without knowing about the involvement of Poles in my mother's survival, but I don't think he would have been surprised. He always thought that he and Mum were meant to be a couple, and even took to speculating how they would have met if the war hadn't thrown them together.

He might not have been surprised to discover that his own father, Dolu, and Ładoś had been together in school in Lwów, in the IV Gymnasium, one year apart. Their names are listed on the same page of the school yearbook. In this small but vital way, my parents' stories brushed lightly against each other, just as Dad imagined they must.

———————

Ludwik had been set on a career in engineering ever since his days of collecting dung to solve the heating problem in Kazakhstan. By 1956, my father was working for the National Coal Board, in its research department. He was spending quite a bit of his time underground, developing and testing scientific instruments. One task was to try and find a way of measuring the hardness of coal, so as to gauge its suitability for new means of extraction. The experience led him to the view that the field of instrumentation was insufficiently scientific. It became his life's work to put that right.

Within a few years, he had completed a master's degree in physics and become an academic. He was destined to be a professor of measurement and one of the staff central to the development of City University, now part of the University of London. Shortly before his death City named a laboratory after him. And on the institution's 125th anniversary it officially named him 'an icon' of the university.

In the meantime, on Sunday, 21 July 1957, at the West London Synagogue, he and Mirjam had married. It had been a relatively small affair. Alfred had given them a little money and told them to do what they liked with it. They'd spent some on a tea, and the rest on a honeymoon in France.

After the honeymoon, they had returned to live with Lusia on the Hendon Way, until they had enough money to move out. Eventually, they moved round the corner, and then round the corner again to 9 Cheyne Walk, with Lusia buying their old house from them. After all their travels, my parents spent their entire married life in one place. They were married for fifty-four very happy years, until my father died in 2011. My mother died in 2017, and she did so in her bed in their house in Hendon.

My mother and Lusia were, in many ways, quite different people. Lusia had been brought up as a grand lady and Mirjam certainly had not; Mirjam was very forgiving and tactful, while Lusia didn't mind saying pretty much anything and was capable of holding a grudge (she never bought any Thorn products after Jules failed to lend Dolu money, for instance); Lusia had an 'artistic' approach to numbers and a quirky intellect, while Mirjam was equally clever but very much a scientist.

Yet somehow the two of them got on. They both loved Ludwik and they determined to love each other. Lusia's example inspired Mirjam to behave in a similar way to her own daughters-in-law and to my sister's husband.

Even more profound was the influence of Alfred on Ludwik.

My father took to Alfred straight away, and vice versa, and the two would spend hours reorganising Alfred's books. Although Ludwik remarked that they did very little actual organising. They would bring a pile or two from one room to another, before Alfred would be distracted by the contents of one of the volumes. He would then insist that they sit down, have a cognac, and discuss it.

As a wedding present, Alfred told Ludwik that he could select 300 books from the Middleton Road collection. He stipulated only that my father should take a multi-volume biography of Bismarck, because no properly stocked library would be complete without one.

The result was that Alfred's intellectual obsessions gradually became my father's too. Having taken only a mild interest in Judaism before – none at all in Lwów, a little in Palestine – he soon became completely absorbed. To Alfred's books he would add thousands of his own. And most of them were Judaica. The biblical prophets particularly engaged him. You could start studying the prophet Isaiah in my parents' dining room and not stop for a year.

He never became devout, but studying Judaism became his main hobby and the celebration of Jewish festivals one of his principal recreations. Like Alfred, he even contemplated becoming a rabbi, though in his case in retirement, before concluding that some of the practical duties would be beyond him.

My mother and her sisters remained close, even though the geographical distance between them did its best to disrupt that. As did cancer. Eva died in 1977, having achieved success as an artist, a happy marriage with Ted, and two daughters, Julie and Karen. She was only forty-six and it is hard not to speculate about the impact her starvation as a teenager might have had upon her body.

Ruth and Paul continued to visit, and receive visits, until everyone was too old to travel. Their children, Michael and Susan, are still a much-loved part of our lives.

As Paul was a physicist – like Ludwik, a professor – and one of the pioneers of the 'Star Wars' missile system, there was always plenty to converse about. The small talk was of nuclear power (my mother was a strong advocate, as well as my father) and nuclear missiles. Ludwik, sharing Dolu's belief that you should contribute to the defence of your country, had become Chief Regional Scientific Adviser for London in his spare time. It was his job to help lead preparations in the event of a nuclear conflict, for which he received an OBE. His experience of the Soviets made him a strong opponent of unilateral disarmament, a political position he thought almost mad.

Meanwhile, Ruth and Mirjam had both become teachers, with Ruth teaching French for twenty-four years in Connecticut middle and high schools. When Grete had died, Mirjam had called Ruth 'Mummy' for a period. As they grew older, the relationship became more one of equals, but I don't think my mother ever lost the sense of looking up to Ruth, and admiring her.

Mirjam always felt that although they had shared all their experiences, it had all been harder on Ruth. Ruth had been almost six years older, more able to appreciate what was happening, forced to accept more responsibility. And she had missed more of her youth, lost more opportunities.

Ruth didn't quite see it that way herself, at least not after it was over. Looking back on that time in relative old age, she said: 'My daughter told me that she sometimes can feel that I have this sadness in me, and I said I don't know if I ever did, I think I came out of it pretty well.'

The silence about the Holocaust that my mother first experienced in school in America continued for decades. Once in a while, she and my father would go to dinner at the houses of friends that they had made in this country – neighbours, parents of children that I or my siblings were playing with, engineering colleagues – and the party would stumble upon the topic. There would be a stunned reaction, a gap in the conversation, and then talk would resume. After she became a maths teacher, she discussed it once or twice in the staffroom with the English teachers who were studying Anne Frank with their classes; but beyond that, nothing much.

She talked about it to us, if we asked. And we often did, because what child doesn't like to hear about their parents before children came along? Mum told the stories quite gently, with a conscious attempt, I think, not to horrify us. I didn't know any better, so I didn't appreciate how remarkable it all was. Even quite recently, when a friend wanted to see the yellow star my mother kept, I was slightly surprised. In my head flashed the thought, 'Doesn't everyone have one?' before I realised that was absurd.

Then, in the 1980s, she began to be asked to give talks. To Jewish groups at first – my synagogue's Hebrew classes, for example – and then to schools. Eventually, she became part of an organised effort to talk to young people, and did so quite frequently. She even gave a talk in Downing Street when the Chancellor asked her to come and meet his children; and, on another occasion, told of her wartime experiences to the Prime Minister and his wife in Number 10.

The media became interested too, and she gave interviews on radio and to newspapers. The BBC found out that she and Albert Speer's daughter had both lived with the Day family, and they made a documentary in which Mum went to Berlin on a cold December afternoon in 2004 to meet Hilde.

My mother shared her story and the two women got on well. But Mum had not asked her about Albert Speer. When she returned to London and I asked her how it had gone, she replied: 'I thought Hilde came across as a very sensitive and fine person. And she has obviously been much affected by her paternity. My opinion of her father is very low indeed. But it's not her fault. She is a victim too. I did not want to confront her. He was her father. Her letters are addressed to "lieber Papa". He was her Daddy.' She paused and added: 'Perhaps you will think I am a coward.' I assured her that I did not.

But while interest in my mother's story gradually increased, and what she had experienced became better understood, none of this happened to my father. The public interest in Stalin's crimes didn't come. It has never come. Nobody invited Dad to tell his story in schools. Nobody spoke of the Katyn murders, hardly anyone knows of the Polish deportations. If anyone, even now, points to similarities between communism and fascism, it is regarded as a rather crude thing to do.

When the seventy-fifth anniversary of the Nuremberg trials was celebrated in 2020 as the birth of international justice, it wasn't much commented upon that every crime the tribunal had determined that the Nazis were guilty of, the Soviets were guilty of too.

The Nuremberg defendants had been charged with crimes against peace (the Soviet invasion of Poland was a crime against peace); they had been charged with crimes against humanity (the Soviet deportation of my father and the enslavement of Dolu were crimes against humanity); they had been charged with war crimes (the murder of Ignacy Schrage and his fellow officers were war crimes); and they had been charged with a conspiracy to commit these crimes (the Molotov-Ribbentrop secret appendix and the Beria Katyn memo are among the many documents that prove Soviet conspiracy).

The Soviets even succeeded in bamboozling the other powers into charging the Nazis for the Katyn murders at Nuremberg, although the effort was so embarrassing that it fizzled out, and wasn't mentioned by the judges at the end of proceedings.

After Nuremberg, Eastern and Central Europe were swallowed by the Soviets. And with the Jews having been massacred and the remaining Poles driven westwards, what had been Lwów became, finally and permanently, almost entirely Ukrainian Lviv. The Soviets smoothly moved into Herburtów street, closed off the road to all except senior officials, and used Number 12 and neighbouring houses as residences for Soviet leaders like Leonid Brezhnev and his other comrades to stay in when they came to Lviv from Moscow.

The silence over the Soviets' crimes had its consequences. There has never been a reckoning over what they did. They have never been forced to see what they did as shameful. It has allowed Vladimir Putin to write his own version of Russian and Ukrainian history, and that in turn has helped him justify, at least to himself, the latest war against the people of my father's city. Once more, the news tells of bombs falling on Lviv.

So the crimes against my parents are regarded in very different ways. For my parents, however, the correspondence between their experiences was simply a fact.

And I think one secret to their long and happy marriage is that they processed their experiences in the same ways. Together they held, I think, to two principles, one public and one personal.

The personal one was that while they had the right to act as victims, it wasn't a right they were going to exercise. That's what my mother meant when she said, in the caption for her photo in the book *Survivor*, that she wanted to be seen as a person first rather than a survivor. To be defined as a victim is to be trapped. Despite all the apparent political power of victim status, often justified, they could see that it was still enfeebling.

My parents did not forget, and 'forgive' isn't the right word either. What they did, instead, was to transcend what happened to them. Because for all that we were different from other families, my parents were determined that we wouldn't just exist, we would *live*. And to do that we couldn't be victims, even though, by any objective standard, my parents had been.

They always wanted to look to the future, rather than dwell in the past. My father travelled all over the world as a professor. Because he spoke so many languages, he was in great demand at international conferences. Many of those were behind the Iron

Curtain. Dad felt strongly that science was international, and that knowledge was a tool against oppression. So he spoke often in Poland and East Germany, and even in Russia. Though when he did that, he lied to Lusia about where he was going.

Yet he never went back to Lviv, or Lwów, as he always insisted upon calling it. When I asked him why, he said: 'Because the property is there, and we are here, and it is better that way.' He would happily talk about his childhood, but he didn't want to be its prisoner.

Then there was their public view. While never excessively political, my parents brought up their children to be engaged with the world. My sister Tamara became a civil service permanent secretary, and my brother Anthony, Chief Scientific Adviser for National Security and then President of City University, where our father had once taught. After all, how could any of us think that politics didn't matter?

Politics had murdered my grandmother, and dozens of other members of my family. Politics had exiled my grandfather and stolen his precious German citizenship. Politics had almost starved my mother to death and frozen my father in the Siberian wastelands. Politics had sent my other grandfather to pull logs like a packhorse, and put my aunt to work as a forced labourer. Politics had stolen every brick of property they had, every book, every piece of cutlery. Politics had stolen my parents' youth, it had killed their teachers, it had robbed them of their education and murdered their schoolfriends.

So, yes, politics matters. And our politics is the one we inherited from Mirjam and Ludwik. For protecting civil rights under the law; defending liberal norms; supporting a Jewish state while integrating into the country that had taken us in. For moderation against extremism. For reason over irrationality. For optimism and resilience tempered by the memory of dictatorship and oppression, but never overwhelmed by it.

And for the quiet institutions of a stable society and a peaceful state. As my grandmother Lusia used to say: 'While the Queen is safe in Buckingham Palace, we are safe in Hendon Central.'

———————

This Friday, we are once again at my sister's house, celebrating the arrival of the Sabbath. Present are the children of Mirjam and Ludwik, their partners, and all of their grandchildren, now eight in number.

When my parents died they left us with each other, a family tied strongly together, the greatest gift they could bestow.

We light the Sabbath candles as Grete once did, and as Ruth and Mirjam and Eva did in the concentration camps. The priestly blessing is given and there are blessings for the bread and the wine. We read them as my father used to, and as Alfred used to before that.

We sing the grace after meals and the Sabbath songs, and we take our place in the long line that came before us and in the long line that will come after us.

Our family has survived. Love has conquered hate.

In the battle with Hitler and Stalin, the victory belongs to Mum and Dad.

Acknowledgements

Seven or eight years ago, I put a CD in a disc player and found that it didn't work. If it had, I don't think I'd have been able to write this book.

I'd asked Ben Barkow, then director of the Wiener Holocaust Library, to send me a short audio clip of my father which had appeared in one of their exhibitions. But when it arrived, it didn't work. It wasn't long before I realised why. It was a DVD. Instead of talking for a couple of minutes about his experiences, my father had given a four-hour-long video account.

The interviews with my father and my mother conducted by Bea Lewkowicz of the Association of Jewish Refugees were crucial to this book. I – and historians of all kinds – owe her a huge debt of gratitude for the interviews that she has conducted with many survivors of oppression.

Sending me the DVD is only one of the reasons I am grateful to Ben Barkow. His life of Alfred Wiener is an excellent piece of work and he has kindly read this manuscript and offered many helpful comments. But I also know how much my mother admired his leadership at the Library.

Ben's successor, Toby Simpson, has also been wonderfully helpful. He's always been ready to offer advice and identify papers I should be aware of. The Library is both skilled and fortunate to have in him, as in Ben, a leader my grandfather would have thought in every way worthy of the job. Other staff at the Library, including Christine Schmidt and Roxzann Moore, have been of great assistance. The Library welcomes visitors to its Russell Square home in London for its frequent exhibitions, events and tours.

Among the things Toby did for me was to identify and persuade the talented Anna Norpoth and Tessa Bouwman to help with translations from the German and Dutch respectively, and in particular of Ruth's papers. I'm grateful to them both. As I am to Natalie Perman for her work on Alfred and Grete's correspondence. And to Anna Withers who read Grete's thesis and articles and provided me with a brilliant summary of my grandmother's thinking.

My cousin (Lola's granddaughter) Nina Price, who has been a valued supporter of this project convened a family group to discuss the Finkelstein story, which, together with my siblings, included Nina's mother Renate Rainer, her brother Andrew Rainer, and Bernard's grandchildren Chris Meddows-Taylor and Ellen Hanson. This provided both insight and motivation.

Nina's other great help was in connecting me to the extraordinary Margaret Omanska. Margaret and her husband Zbig managed to decipher and translate more than ninety letters sent to Kazakhstan by Lusia's siblings. It was an amazing effort. Letters sent between Dolu and Lusia after they found each other were translated by Zuzanna Sojka, whose endeavours were fantastic. I found the work with Zuzanna, Margaret and Zbig, people who share a commitment to telling the story of the exiled Poles, very moving.

Thank you to my friend Dmitry Sitkovetsky for translating the inventory of Lusia's possessions.

Reading Philippe Sands's masterpiece, *East West Street*, I realised that he too was a Landes from Lwów. We are, we are certain, cousins. And he has been a most generous relative. His intellectual insights, of course, were invaluable. He also accompanied me to our home city, introduced me to Ivan Horodsky (who assisted with research on Lwów) and to Sofia Dyak. Sofia did much to help me understand her city's history and, most importantly, persuaded Andriy Khudo to allow me to visit 12 Herburtów street where he now lives with his family. Andriy was very kind to agree, and proved a most welcoming host. Thanks also to Inna Zolotar for guiding me on an excellent walking tour of Lviv.

I am grateful, as should all historians of the Holocaust be, to Ambassador Jakub Kumoch for his research on Aleksander Ładoś, and his valiant efforts to obtain for Ładoś the recognition that he deserves. Thanks also to his colleague Jędrzej Uszyński and to Jürgen Buch for helping me find documents that completed Camille Aronowski's story. Her change of name at the end of the war to Camille Arnaud, the name I always knew her as holding, had nearly prevented me from finding out how she had been able to obtain the passports.

Other historians and researchers have been generous with their time. Bernard Wasserstein, having written his excellent book on Gertrude van Tijn, *The Ambiguity of Virtue*, assisted me with establishing what Grete was doing for the Jewish Council. Jan Zajaczkowski shared with me many things he discovered about Dolu and the Finkelsteins. Thanks also to Alexandra Wenck, Gerald Steinacher, David Ferriero, Max Paul Friedman, Janine Stein, Ed van Rijswijk, Marcel Weyland, Anne Applebaum, Ryland Thomas, Marc Bernstein and Jack Malvern.

Special thanks to Nico Knapper, for sharing his memories of his friend Sammy Cohen; to Hephzibah Rudofksy; to Jack Santcross; to Warren Grynberg; to Noemie Lopian and her family; and to Olivia Marks-Woldman and Karen Pollock for all that the two of them do for Holocaust survivors, including my mother.

Sonja Schneidinger shared precious memories of her mother Erika Neuburger; and our dear friend Marion Rosenberg of her mother Aldona Paneth and of the Schrages.

Over many lunches, my friend Robert Harris gave me advice on how to structure the book and how to keep my notes in order. The occasions were a privilege and the advice essential. He also passed on Tom Stoppard's warning that just because something is true, it doesn't mean that it is interesting.

Jonathan Haskel, David Edmonds, Tim Rice and Matthew Gould read the book and gave me very useful feedback. Thanks also to Phil Collins, Oliver Kamm, Sue Haskel, Simon and Alexis Blum, Stephen Pollard, Dominic Lawson, David Aaronovitch, Iain Martin, Robert Shrimsley, Andrew Cooper, Greg Clark and George Osborne.

This book wouldn't have appeared without the guidance of my agent, Toby Mundy, who is very very good at what he does. It has also benefited hugely from the editing in the UK of Arabella Pike and in the USA of Kris Puopolo. Thanks also to the William Collins' team, particularly Kit Shepherd, Katy Archer, Katherine Patrick and Sam Harding.

My *Times* colleagues, especially the former editors John Witherow and James Harding, the current editor Tony Gallagher, and my comment colleagues Mike Smith, Roland Watson and Richard Preston deserve thanks for their support and intellectual stimulation. Nicola Jeal, Henry Zeffman, Robert Crampton, Damian Arnold and Georgia Heneage have all been very encouraging.

And then there is my family. Michael Klemens, Ruth's son, carefully preserved her papers and has always been a very special cousin. As has his lovely sister Sue and her husband Dan Root.

Ted Plaut, Eva's husband, and the last of that generation, died during the writing of the book, aged ninety-seven. But not before many helpful discussions. I am also grateful to his daughters Julie and Karen and his granddaughter Laura.

Thanks also to my cousin Cecilia Bianchi and her mother Viviana Stupnicki. And to my father-in-law Henry Connor, with whom I enjoyed many long discussions about the book as I wrote it.

My sister Tamara and my brother Anthony share this story, have been endlessly encouraging, and are wonderful people. My debt to them is too great to be properly expressed. They married respectively Michael Isaacs and Judith Fishman, the partners they deserve.

Acknowledgements

Anthony and Tamara would agree that no book on our family would be complete without thanking our Hendon neighbours Nurit and Geoff Heath. My parents adored them and so do we and they are a part of us.

Aron Finkelstein, my middle son, helped me with the onerous task of organising and scanning the Finkelstein and Diamantstein family correspondence. I thank him and his brother Isaac also for their love and support during this project.

My eldest son, Sam Finkelstein, has been by my side at every stage of this book. A relentlessly exacting inquisitor and (I'm proud to say) a talented editor, there isn't a paragraph that hasn't benefited from his comment or correction. He worked incredibly hard on it. His efforts have been heroic.

And my partner in everything that I do, my beautiful, clever and perceptive wife Nicky, has been vital to this venture too, always probing to ensure the story was clear and readable. Robust but also encouraging. And also willing to endure almost endless conversations about Finkelsteins and Wieners.

Telling my parents' story has been a duty, a privilege and, given their ultimate triumph, a pleasure. My dearest hope is that nobody in our family ever has cause to write another book like it.

Notes

Introduction

'The very first of America that I saw': Mirjam Wiener, 'A Dutch Girl's Appreciation of America.', undated (c.1945–6), Wiener Family Papers.

'a wife and mother first, and a survivor last': Harry Borden, *Survivor: A Portrait of the Survivors of the Holocaust* (Cassell, 2017).

Part One: Before
Alfred and Grete

columns of troopers . . . took over government buildings: Nigel Jones, *Hitler's Heralds: The Story of the Freikorps 1918–1923* (Lume Books, 2020).

remonstrated with him about antisemitism: Eva G. Reichmann, 'Alfred Wiener – The German Jew', *The Wiener Library Bulletin*, vol. 19 (1965), pp. 10–11.

his belongings secured to its roof: Jones, *Hitler's Heralds*.

without the slightest hesitation or reservation: Ben Barkow, *Alfred Wiener and the Making of the Holocaust Library* (Vallentine Mitchell, 1997).

the country of barbaric pogroms: Entry for 'Paul Nathan', Fred Skolnik (ed.), *Encyclopedia Judaica: Second Edition*, vol. 15 (Thomson Gale, 2007), p. 11.

A severe bout of dysentery: 'Alfred Wiener', short autobiography, undated (probably August 1940), Wiener Family Papers.

'When he pronounced the very name "Potsdam"': Reichmann, 'Alfred Wiener'.

Bentschen, Alfred later recalled: Alfred Wiener, 'Some Informations Regarding The Jewish Community And The Jews At Bentschen', 1953, Wiener Holocaust Library, London, ref. no. 1656/1/1/455.

'he was driven by a veritable awe': C. C. Aronsfeld, 'Dr. Alfred Wiener: Death of the Library's Founder', *The Wiener Library Bulletin*, vol. 18, no. 2 (1964), pp. 13–14.

In his early twenties, he had spent time travelling: Barkow, *Alfred Wiener and the Making of the Holocaust Library.*

The Jews of Germany had moved into the big cities: Jay Howard Geller, *The Scholems: A Story of the German-Jewish Bourgeoisie from Emancipation to Destruction* (Cornell University Press, 2019).

'A mighty antisemitic storm': Alfred Wiener, 'Prelude to Pogroms? Facts for Thoughtful People' (1919), in *The Fatherland and the Jews: Two Pamphlets by Alfred Wiener*, Ben Barkow trans. (Granta, 2021), pp. 45–69.

an uncannily farsighted publication: Michael Berkowitz, introduction to *The Fatherland and the Jews*, pp. 3–43.

'sexual intercourse with Jews and other roundheads': Ausschusses für Volksaufklärung leaflet, quoted in Alfred Wiener, 'Prelude to Pogroms?'.

'we will shortly free ourselves, completely and mercilessly, from these bloodsuckers, the Jews': Max Beyer, quoted in Alfred Wiener, 'Prelude to Pogroms?'.

As a volunteer for Hamburg War Aid: This organisation's work is described by Christoph Strupp, 'Hamburg in the First World War', *Cahiers Bruxellois – Brusselse Cahiers*, vol. 46, no. 1 (2014), pp. 189–201.

'A huge mass meeting . . . at Würzburg': Jewish Telegraphic Agency, 'Call Mass Meeting to Counteract Ritual Murder Agitation', *Jewish Daily Bulletin*, 8 May 1929.

three quarters of the 600,000 Jews living in Germany: Alfred Wiener, 'The Centralverein deutscher Staatsbuerger juedischen Glaubens – Its Meaning and Activities', 1945, Wiener Holocaust Library, London, MS 143.

factions from the left and right tried to seize power: Jones, *Hitler's Heralds*.

Grete's PhD . . . was one of the victims: 'Margarete Wiener', short biography, Alfred Wiener, undated (probably August 1940), Wiener Family Papers.

'the danger of racism and Nazism not only for world Jewry': Wiener, 'The Centralverein deutscher Staatsbuerger juedischen Glaubens'.

'feared neither hecklers nor rioting Nazis': E. G. Lowenthal, '35 Jahre – Vertrauen und Freundschaft, Alfred Wiener: Wesen, Wandlung, Worte', *Allgemeine Wochenzeitung der Juden in Deutschland*, 21 February 1964.

the community took to the courts: Donald L. Niewyk, 'Jews and the Courts in Weimar Germany', *Jewish Social Studies*, vol. 37, no. 2 (1975), pp. 99–113.

Such attacks on any religion were against the law: Dennis E. Showalter, 'Jews, Nazis, and the Law: The case of Julius Streicher', *Simon Wiesenthal Center Annual*, vol. 6 (1989), pp. 143–163.

a significant burden on the Nazis: Niewyk, 'Jews and the Courts in Weimar Germany'.

So alarmed was Alfred: Ibid.

'Here lay one of the secrets': Eva G. Reichmann, 'Trauer um Alfred Wiener', *AJR Information*, vol. 19, no. 3 (1964), pp. 6–7.

even the Kaiser was actually a Jew: Alfred Wiener, 'German Jewry in Political, Economic and Cultural Perspective' (1924), in *The Fatherland and the Jews*, pp. 75–119.

'anti-semitism will come to an end prematurely': Barkow, *Alfred Wiener and the Making of the Holocaust Library*.

'the mistrust between Germans and Jews': *Die Welt*, quoted in Hans Lamm, 'Dienst am Recht: In memoriam Alfred Wiener', *Allgemeine Wochenzeitung der Juden in Deutschland*, 14 February 1964.

'if there were a Nobel Prize': Geller, *The Scholems*.

'conspiracy against the Ten Commandments': Aronsfeld, 'Dr. Alfred Wiener'.

baptism cleansed them of that smell: Randall L. Bytwerk, *Julius Streicher: Nazi Editor of the Notorious Anti-Semitic Newspaper* Der Stürmer (Cooper Square Press, 2001).

A Critical Journey through Palestine: Alfred Wiener, *Kritische Reise durch Palästina* (Philo Verlag, 1927).

'Almost everyone has their own plan': Margarete Wiener, general notes, quoted in Alfred Wiener, *Kritische Reise durch Palästina*, p. 18n1.

'The plight of the Jews of the East': Alfred Wiener, *Kritische Reise durch Palästina*.

'every effort to live with them in friendship': Ibid.

'one of the leaders of German antizionism': Ibid.

He was sharply rebuffed: Barkow, *Alfred Wiener and the Making of the Holocaust Library*.

Soon agreement was forthcoming: Ibid.

provide it with thirty-five cuttings: Leonidas E. Hill, 'Walter Gyssling, the Centralverein and the Büro Wilhelmstraße, 1929–1933', *The Leo Baeck Institute Year Book*, vol. 38 (1993), pp. 193–208.

Copies of *Der Stürmer* and Nazi anti-Christian literature: C. C. Aronsfeld, 'Aus der Frühzeit der Wiener Library: Erinnerungen an die Jüdische Informations-Zentrale in Amsterdam', *Gedenkschrift für Bernhard Brilling*, eds. Peter Freimark and Helmut Richtering (Institut für die Geschichte der deutschen Juden, 1988), pp. 246–256.

'Hitler was sitting in that exact chair': Barkow, *Alfred Wiener and the Making of the Holocaust Library*.

He took Planck through some of the latest violent incidents: Alfred Wiener, 'Unterredung mit Herrn Staatssekretaer der Reichskanzlei Dr. Planck', July 1932, Wiener Holocaust Library, London, ref. no. 796/1.

she would get a *schultüte*: Ruth Klemens, video interview, 29 October 2001, Visual History Archive, USC Shoah Foundation, University of Southern California, Los Angeles, interview 51777, tape 1.

the CV offices were raided: Julius Brodnitz, 'Niederschrift von Julius Brodnitz', April 1934, Wiener Holocaust Library, London, MS 219.

demanded to see Brodnitz: Ibid.

'when he [Göring] spoke': Alfred Wiener, 'Unterredung mit dem persoenlichen Referenten des Herrn Reichsinnenministers von Gayl, Herrn von Steinau-Steinrueck', July 1932, Wiener Holocaust Library, London, ref. no. 796/2.

These would have to be destroyed: Julius Brodnitz, diary entry 3 March 1933, cited in Anna Ullrich, 'Eine Frage der Erwartung? Der Centralverein und die Wahrnehmung und Einschätzung der nichtjüdischen Deutschen', *Was soll aus uns werden?' Zur Geschichte des Centralvereins deutscher Staatsbürger jüdischen Glaubens im nationalsozialistischen Deutschland*, eds. Regina Grundmann, Bernd J. Hartmann and Daniel Siemens (Metropol Verlag, 2020), pp. 45–80.

destroyed the work of five years: Ibid.

'In a discussion held on 3 March': 'Der 5. März: Ein Wort an die deutschen Juden', *CV Zeitung*, 9 March 1933.

'My police are not a Jewish protection force': Kurt Sabatsky, 'Hermann Göring', undated, Wiener Holocaust Library, London, ref. no. 874/13.

On 25 March, the Reich Minister: Ibid.

a 'reception in dictatorial posture': Brodnitz, 'Niederschrift von Julius Brodnitz'.

Göring made his visitors stand: Ibid.

'Anyone who means well for Wiener': Ibid.

'According to the ruling of the laws and regulations': Alfred Wiener, 'Zwischen Himmel und Erde', *CV Zeitung*, 1 June 1933.

Dolu and Lusia

The award-winning design of the villa: Ludwik Finkelstein, video interview, 16 October 2006, Refugee Voices: The AJR Audio-visual Testimony Archive, London, interview 130, tape 1.

Maks . . . had made his way to Vienna: Ibid.

The emperors' policy: Christoph Mick, *Lemberg, Lwów, L'viv, 1914–1947: Violence and Ethnicity in a Contested City* (Purdue University Press, 2016).

Lemberg became Lwów: Ibid.

This pattern persisted: Ibid.

hauling their water from public wells: Ibid.

'iron girders, iron plate, gas pipes [and] waterworks': Advertisement for Finkelstein i Fehl, *Spis Abonentów sieci tele-fonicznych Państwowych i Koncesjonowanych w Polsce (z wyjątkiem m. st. Warszawy)*, (Wydawnictwo państwowego przedsiębiorstwa 'polska poczta, telegraf i telefon', 1939), p. 626.

'for me a truly unforgettable experience': Finny Ziegler, letter to Ludwik Finkelstein, 14 April 1980, Finkelstein Family Papers.

And he was fussed over: Ludwik Finkelstein, interview, tape 1.

'I had friends from school': Ibid.

and allowed her to ride his horse: Correspondence with Marion Rosenberg, 2021.

The respect in which all held Major Schrage: Ludwik Finkelstein, 'Hidden Tales from Polish History', *Manna*, no. 97 (2007), pp. 12–14.

first proper election since the days of Austrian rule: Mick, *Lemberg, Lwów, L'viv*.

And the candidate with the most votes of all: Lwów city council election result notice, 27 May 1934, State Archive of Lviv Oblast.

Malopolska Pipe Centre in Lwów: Amalia Finkelstein, 'Eidesstattliche Versicherung: Lebenslauf und Schilderung des Verfolgungsvorganges des verstorbenen Herrn Adolf Finkelstein', affidavit for Finkelstein compensation claim, 15 March 1966, Finkelstein Family Papers.

'The Iron King': Jerzy Janicki, *Ni ma jak Lwów: krótki przewodnik po Lwowie* (Oficyna Literatów 'Rój', 1990).

Each year, about 200,000 people: Stefan Mękarski, *Lwów: A Page of Polish History* (Koło Lwowian, 1991).

'I was treated there as a member of the family': Monika Schneider, 'Eidesstattliche Versicherung', draft affidavit for Finkelstein compensation claim, 1966, Finkelstein Family Papers.

When the university hostel . . . Dolu stepped in: Gustaw Bodek, 'O konstruktywną pomoc społeczeństwa', *Księga pamiątkowa: wydana z okazji 70-lecia istnienia Towarzystwa Rygorozantów we Lwowie 1868/9–1938/9*, eds. Fryderyk Auerbach and Dawid Fysz (Towarzystwo Rygorozantów we Lwowie, 1939), pp. 46–51.

'numerous attempts to resolve the dispute had no impact': 'Dzięki rozumnej inicjatywie r. Finkelsteina przeprosił się prez. Kammer z wiceprez. Schleierem', *Krzyk*, 9 March 1935.

'I managed to find a solution': Adolf Finkelstein, letter to Amalia Finkelstein, 22 February 1942, Finkelstein Family Papers.

'occupying an honoured place': Entry for 'Adolf Finkelstein', Herman Stachel (ed.), *Almanach żydowski* (Kultura i sztuka, 1937), p. 480.

'I remember that I was always offered pretzels': Ludwik Finkelstein, interview, tape 1.

the Zionists were foolish to argue against improving the lot of Poles: Ibid.

early donors for a 'United Polish Land' monument: 'Wykaz wpływów', *Morze*, vol. 7, no. 1 (1930), p. 14, http://dlibra.umcs.lublin.pl/Content/26489/czas2595_7_1930_1.pdf [accessed 9 November 2022].

full Jewish participation in the life of the nation: Emanuel Melzer, *No Way Out: The Politics of Polish Jewry, 1935–1939* (Hebrew Union College Press, 1997).

Jewish stores and factories closed in mourning: Jewish Telegraph Agency, 'Polish Jews Set Four Weeks of Mourning for Pilsudski', *Jewish Daily Bulletin*, 17 May 1935.

'hit him on the nose and it bled': Ludwik Finkelstein, interview, tape 1.

12,000 joined in the procession: Mick, *Lemberg, Lwów, L'viv*.

'Jewish Academic Youth! Don't give up hope': Adolf Finkelstein, 'Nil Desperandum', *Księga pamiątkowa: wydana z okazji 70-lecia istnienia Towarzystwa Rygorozantów we Lwowie 1868/9–1938/9*, p. 16.

at Number 5 lived Kazimierz Bartel: Przemysław Włodek and Adam Kulewski, *Lwów: przewodnik* (Oficyna Wydawnicza 'Rewasz', 2006).

'Our treat,' recalled Molotov: Roger Moorhouse, *The Devils' Alliance: Hitler's Pact with Stalin, 1939–1941* (The Bodley Head, 2014).

'There is one common element in the ideologies': Ibid.

An Amsterdam Childhood

'What a great joy it was last night, when your letter arrived!': Margarete Wiener, letter from Margarete and Alfred Wiener to Ruth, Eva and Mirjam Wiener, 16 August 1938, Ruth Wiener collection, Wiener Holocaust Library, London, file 1962/1/5/2.

as much of an impression on her grandchildren as the treats: Ruth Klemens, video interview, 29 October 2001, Visual History Archive, USC Shoah Foundation, University of Southern California, Los Angeles, interview 51777, tape 1.

'Wide Jewish Street': Bernard Wasserstein, *The Ambiguity of Virtue: Gertrude van Tijn and the Fate of the Dutch Jews* (Harvard University Press, 2014).

The Wieners could join their fellow immigrants on: 'Beethovenstraat', Joodsamsterdam, 29 April 2016, https://www. joodsamsterdam.nl/beethovenstraat/ [accessed 7 November 2022].

'Books, books and books again': Ruth Klemens, interview, USC Shoah Foundation, tape 1.

messages, poems and mottos penned by family and friends: Poesie books, 1939–1942, Ruth Wiener collection, Wiener Holocaust Library, London, ref. no. 1962/1/2/1–2.

Jacqueline later became well known as: Theo Coster, *We All Wore Stars: Memories of Anne Frank from Her Classmates*, trans. Marjolijn de Jager (Palgrave Macmillan, 2011).

'Noble be Man': Johann Wolfgang Goethe, 'The Godlike', trans. John S. Dwight, *The World's Best Literature,* eds. John William Cunliffe et al. (Warner Library Company, 1917), vol. 11, p. 6446.

'Modern, and a trifle anarchic': Sophia van Emde, quoted in 'Childhood', Herman Hertzberger official website, 29 September 2017, https://www.hertzberger.nl/index.php/en/component/ content/article/2-uncategorised/228-childhood [accessed 7 November 2022].

Grete attended the teacher conferences: Ruth Klemens, interview, USC Shoah Foundation, tape 2.

using one belonging to the Theosophical Society: 'Consecration of the Liberal Jewish Synagogue in Amsterdam', Anne Frank House, 7 September 2020, https://www.annefrank.org/en/ timeline/33/consecration-of-the-liberal-jewish-synagogue-in-amsterdam/ [accessed 7 November 2022].

'vain and unimaginative': Wasserstein, *The Ambiguity of Virtue*.

'A certain haughtiness of manner': Ibid.

'it was possible to do so safely': Ibid.

up the stairs to the third floor of my mother's home: C. C. Aronsfeld, 'Aus der Frühzeit der Wiener Library: Erinnerungen an die Jüdische Informations-Zentrale in Amsterdam', *Gedenkschrift für Bernhard Brilling*, eds. Peter Freimark and Helmut Richtering (Institut für die Geschichte der deutschen Juden, 1988), pp. 246–256.

Alfred kept . . . the 1938 Vienna phone book: Correspondence with Ben Barkow, 2021.

'out of Germany through normal channels': 'Achievements and Aspirations', *The Wiener Library Bulletin*, vol. 1, no. 1 (1946), p. 1.

heroic quantities of cigars and cigarettes: Aronsfeld, 'Aus der Frühzeit der Wiener Library'.

'unmistakably the boss': Ibid.

'counter the Nazi slanders and Dr. Goebbels' attempt': Alfred Wiener, 'The Wiener Library', *A.J.A. Review*, vol. 5, no. 2 (1953), pp. 7–11.

'What are the non-German countries doing?': Aronsfeld, Aus der Frühzeit der Wiener Library'.

The Truth on Trial

Georges Brunschvig embarked on his usual routine: Hadassa Ben-Itto, *The Lie That Will Not Die: The Protocols of the Elders of Zion* (Vallentine Mitchell, 2020). The author had access to Georges Brunschvig's private papers, and this chapter draws heavily on her account of Alfred's interventions.

'one of the most important of the 20th century': Hadassa Ben-Itto, quoted in Steve Boggan, 'The Anti-Jewish Lie That Refuses to Die', *The Times*, 2 March 2005.

'must be one of the most fascinating trials': Harry Woolf, foreword to Ben-Itto, *The Lie That Will Not Die*.

'When the day's proceedings were over, they met in the dark': Obituary of Alfred Wiener, *Aufbau*, 14 February 1964.

several of the most interesting with him in his little suitcase: C. C. Aronsfeld, 'Aus der Frühzeit der Wiener Library: Erinnerungen an die Jüdische Informations-Zentrale in Amsterdam', *Gedenkschrift für Bernhard Brilling*, eds. Peter Freimark and Helmut Richtering (Institut für die Geschichte der deutschen Juden, 1988), pp. 246–256.

Sergei Aleksandrovich Nilus had published a book: Howard Falksohn, 'The Lie That Won't Die: Alfred Wiener and the Bern Trial of *The Protocols of the Elders of Zion*', *AJR Journal*, vol. 21, no. 3 (2021), pp. 14–15.

and set religions against each other: Entry for 'Protocols of the Elders of Zion', Holocaust Encyclopedia, United States Holocaust Memorial Museum, 1 April 2010, https://encyclopedia.ushmm. org/content/en/article/protocols-of-the-elders-of-zion [accessed 7 November 2022].

'terrible' Jewish power of the purse: *The Protocols and World Revolution* (Small, Maynard & Co., 1920), quoted in Ben-Itto, *The Lie That Will Not Die*.

combine to destroy industrial prosperity: Ibid.

He had bought the *Dearborn Independent*: Steven Watts, *The People's Tycoon: Henry Ford and the American Century* (Vintage, 2006).

'Everything was blamed on the Jewish conspiracy': Ben-Itto, *The Lie That Will Not Die*.

'I still think this is a phony war': Henry Ford, quoted in Watts, *The People's Tycoon*.

'I regard Heinrich Ford as my inspiration': Adolf Hitler, quoted in Ben-Itto, *The Lie That Will Not Die*.

reprinted more than thirty times: Randall L. Bytwerk, 'Believing in "Inner Truth": The Protocols of the Elders of Zion in Nazi Propaganda, 1933–1945', *Holocaust and Genocide Studies*, vol. 29 (2015), pp. 212–229.

'when an event had aroused so much interest': Ben-Itto, *The Lie That Will Not Die*.

showing they were pawns of the Jews: Falksohn, 'The Lie That Won't Die'.

'a potpourri of antisemitic stereotypes': Michael Hagemeister, '*The Protocols of the Elders of Zion* in Court: The Bern Trials, 1933–1937', *The Global Impact of* The Protocols of the Elders of Zion*: A Century-Old Myth*, ed. Esther Webman (Routledge, 2011), pp. 241–253.

the Jewish Central Information Office produced a daily digest: Falksohn, 'The Lie That Won't Die'.

'nothing more than ridiculous nonsense': Ben-Itto, *The Lie That Will Not Die*.

Some academics find the account a little confused: Hagemeister, '*The Protocols of the Elders of Zion* in Court'.

extensively distributed and read in the Middle East: Ben-Itto, *The Lie That Will Not Die*.

Trapped

a 'stay at home Mom': Ruth Klemens, video interview, 29 October 2001, Visual History Archive, USC Shoah Foundation, University of Southern California, Los Angeles, interview 51777, tape 1.

'a refugee should henceforth be considered as an undesirable element': Bernard Wasserstein, *The Ambiguity of Virtue: Gertrude van Tijn and the Fate of the Dutch Jews* (Harvard University Press, 2014).

'great gratitude', and praising the 'great devotion': David Cohen, on behalf of the Committee for Jewish Refugees, letter to Margarete Wiener, 10 January 1939, Wiener Family Papers.

'After Kristallnacht, it was clear': Jay Howard Geller, *The Scholems: A Story of the German-Jewish Bourgeoisie from Emancipation to Destruction* (Cornell University Press, 2019).

in the woods, penniless and starving: Wasserstein, *The Ambiguity of Virtue*.

'My first contact with him,' remembered Bondy: Louis Bondy, letter to C. C. Aronsfeld, 18 February 1964, quoted in Ben Barkow, *Alfred Wiener and the Making of the Holocaust Library* (Vallentine Mitchell, 1997).

'we are talking past each other in English': Margarete Wiener, letter to Alfred Wiener, 8 December 1939, Wiener Family Papers.

a list of people who had been stripped of citizenship: 'Bekanntmachung', *Deutscher Reichsanzeiger und Breukischer Staatsanzeiger*, 28 August 1939.

those living abroad 'who have damaged German interests': 'Gesetz über den Widerruf von Einbürgerungen und die Aberkennung der deutschen Staatsangehörigkeit. Vom 14. Juli 1933.', *Reichsgesetzblatt, Teil I: Jahrgang 1933* (Reichsverlagsamt, 1933), p. 480.

'We are now completely free!': Margarete Wiener, letter to Alfred Wiener, 3 September 1939, Wiener Family Papers.

'walking around without a winter coat and in cotton socks'?: Margarete Wiener, letter to Alfred Wiener, 31 October 1939, Wiener Family Papers.

'sliding downhill on a sleigh': Margarete Wiener, letter to Alfred Wiener, 29 December 1939, Wiener Family Papers.

'Sometimes I toss and turn during sleepless nights': Margarete Wiener, letter to Alfred Wiener, 8 December 1939.

'I'm not prone to anxiety and nervousness': Margarete Wiener, letter to Alfred Wiener, 13 November 1939, Wiener Family Papers.

'the constant tension makes me tired': Margarete Wiener, letter to Alfred Wiener, 30 August 1939, Wiener Family Papers.

'helping at the Committee for some hours a day': Margarete Wiener, letter to Alfred Wiener, 17 October 1939, Wiener Family Papers.

'the Dutch at least [do] not expect a German invasion': Wasserstein, *The Ambiguity of Virtue*.

'most people outdo themselves': Margarete Wiener, letter to Alfred Wiener, 13 November 1939.

'to stay here for the sake of the children': Ibid.

secure visas for them to come to Britain: Ruth Klemens, interview, USC Shoah Foundation, tape 2.

'a warning from a significant quarter': Alfred Wiener's notes attached to Josef Bettelheim, 'Die letzten Tage des Jewish Information Büros', July 1955, Wiener Holocaust Library, London, ref. no. 1656/3/9/110ab.

A Knife in the Back

'and that's when life changed entirely': Ludwik Finkelstein, video interview, 16 October 2006, Refugee Voices: The AJR Audio-visual Testimony Archive, London, interview 130, tape 1.

'a small rain from a large cloud': Adolf Finkelstein, letter to Amalia Finkelstein, 23 August 1939, Finkelstein Family Papers.

their 'Devils' Alliance': Roger Moorhouse, *The Devils' Alliance: Hitler's Pact with Stalin, 1939–1941* (The Bodley Head, 2014).

'I remember standing by the radio': Ludwik Finkelstein, interview, tape 1.

the blood of civilians who had been attempting to escape: Julius Margolin, *Journey into the Land of the Zeks and Back: A Memoir of the Gulag*, trans. Stefani Hoffman (Oxford University Press, 2020).

'reliable' and 'loyal' Dolu: Stanisław Ostrowski, 'Zaswiadczenie', character reference for Adolf Finkelstein, 9 November 1944, Finkelstein Family Papers.

'to help the Poles defend themselves': Ludwik Finkelstein, interview, tape 1.

the Soviet troops were greeted with flowers: Jan T. Gross, *Revolution from Abroad: The Soviet Conquest of Poland's Western Ukraine and Western Belorussia* (Princeton University Press, 2002).

'the Polish government has disintegrated': Roger Moorhouse, *First to Fight: The Polish War, 1939* (The Bodley Head, 2019).

cross the Polish frontier at dawn: Ibid.

its existence was 'probable': Katherine R. Jolluck, introduction to Margolin, *Journey into the Land of the Zeks and Back.*

'a knife inflicting a death blow': Stanisław Ostrowski, *W obronie polskości Ziemi Lwowskiej; Dnie pohańbienia 1939–1941: wspomnienia* (Pokolenie, 1986).

'cemented in blood': Moorhouse, *The Devils' Alliance.*

his advice was to leave straight away: Ostrowski, *'Dnie pohańbienia 1939–1941'.*

Among these prisoners was Major Ignacy Schrage: Ludwik Finkelstein, 'Hidden Tales from Polish History', *Manna*, no. 97 (2007), pp. 12–14.

He went home to Herburtów street: Ludwik Finkelstein, interview, tape 1.

buried his service revolver in the garden: Ludwik Finkelstein, oral testimony.

followed Ostrowski everywhere with a revolver: Ostrowski, *'Dnie pohańbienia 1939–1941'*.

'Of course, there is Copenhagen too': Margolin, *Journey into the Land of the Zeks and Back.*

'torn uniforms, dirty coats, hands and faces': Gross, *Revolution from Abroad.*

'we were waiting for ideals': Ibid.

'a spectacle of confusion and unrest': Margolin, *Journey into the Land of the Zeks and Back.*

bread, or vodka, or basically anything: Ibid.

terrorising the local population, shooting at will: Ludwik Finkelstein, interview, tape 1.

different sides in an ethnic war: Gross, *Revolution from Abroad.*

the communists were wearing red armbands: Christoph Mick, *Lemberg, Lwów, L'viv, 1914–1947: Violence and Ethnicity in a Contested City* (Purdue University Press, 2016).

And Dolu did: Ludwik Finkelstein, interview, tape 1.

moved the First Secretary of the Communist Party of Ukraine: Edward Crankshaw, *Khrushchev* (Bloomsbury, 2011).

the neighbours of Nikita Khrushchev: Jerzy Janicki, *Ni ma jak Lwów: krótki przewodnik po Lwowie* (Oficyna Literatów 'Rój', 1990).

'the dead or broken bodies of innumerable comrades': Crankshaw, *Khrushchev.*

'Trotskyite-Bukharinite-Fascist-Spying Filth': Ibid.

'unswerving Bolshevik and Stalinist': *Bilshovik Ukrainy*, no. 7 (1938), quoted in Crankshaw, *Khrushchev.*

'wipe from the surface of the earth': *Krasnaya gvesna*, 23 September 1939, quoted in Crankshaw, *Khrushchev*.

Only one, a Lwów lawyer called Vinnickenko: US Department of State, 'Soviet Deportation of the Inhabitants of Eastern Poland in 1939–1941', confidential P-66020 report (London), December 1943, in Tadeusz Piotrowski (ed.), *The Polish Deportees of World War II: Recollections of Removal to the Soviet Union and Dispersal Throughout the World* (McFarland and Company, 2004), pp. 211–223.

a commission sent to Moscow and Kiev: Gross, *Revolution from Abroad*.

The normal waiting time for a loaf of bread: Mick, *Lemberg, Lwów, L'viv*.

supervisors, and supervisors over the supervisors: Margolin, *Journey into the Land of the Zeks and Back*.

The camp bed in the front room and the sheet partition: Ibid.

her son, daughter-in-law and grandson moved in: Ludwik Finkelstein, interview, tape 1.

'no doubt this list of "anti-Soviet elements"': Piotrowski (ed.), *The Polish Deportees of World War II*.

'Accounting must embrace all persons ... opposed to the socialist order': People's Commissar for Internal Affairs of the Lithuanian SSR, 'Excerpts from NKVD Instructions Relating to "Anti-Soviet Elements"', Order No. 0054, 28 November 1940, in Piotrowski (ed.), *The Polish Deportees of World War II*, p. 203.

'university professors, teachers, doctors': US Department of State, 'Soviet Deportation of the Inhabitants of Eastern Poland in 1939–1941'.

'In the Soviet Union there are only three categories of people': Gross, *Revolution from Abroad*.

if the head of the family was arrested: Piotrowski (ed.), *The Polish Deportees of World War II*.

the number was more than 400,000: Gross, *Revolution from Abroad*.

whatever they fancied while they were at it: Ibid.

Ludwik watched as they led Dolu out: Ludwik Finkelstein, interview, tape 1.

'exact details of where your husband is': Ibid.

Overrun

Mirjam remembered standing in the street: Mirjam Finkelstein, video interview, 6 November 2006, Refugee Voices: The AJR Audio-visual Testimony Archive, London, interview no. 136, tape 1.

blaring 'every hour, day and night': Ruth Wiener, 'Mai 1940.', 5 June 1945, Ruth Wiener collection, Wiener Holocaust Library, London, file 1962/1/4.

Eva, has a different memory: Nora Hope Karan, 'An Unforgettable Tale', 1958, Tauber Holocaust Library, Jewish Family and Children's Services Holocaust Center, San Francisco, call no. ST.099. Eva Plaut gave extensive testimony to Karan, an eleven-year-old, in 1958; in 'An Unforgettable Tale', Karan recounts the family's story from Eva's perspective, whose character she assumes. Recollections and quotations attributed to Eva throughout this book are drawn from this record.

'mute but defiant': Alfred Wiener's notes attached to Josef Bettelheim, 'Die letzten Tage des Jewish Information Büros', July 1955, Wiener Holocaust Library, London, ref. no. 1656/3/9/110ab.

'A bitter argument ensued in the course of which': Bettelheim, 'Die letzten Tage des Jewish Information Büros'.

Zielenziger's son would always maintain: Ben Barkow, *Alfred Wiener and the Making of the Holocaust Library* (Vallentine Mitchell, 1997).

'a big caterpillar crawling along the ground': Karan, 'An Unforgettable Tale'.

she decided the best bet was to return home: Ruth Klemens, video interview, 29 October 2001, Visual History Archive, USC

Shoah Foundation, University of Southern California, Los Angeles, interview 51777, tape 2.

without even being able to attend its meetings: Bernard Wasserstein, *The Ambiguity of Virtue: Gertrude van Tijn and the Fate of the Dutch Jews* (Harvard University Press, 2014).

Joy and Glee

'Blackouts impressed us': Nora Hope Karan, 'An Unforgettable Tale', 1958, Tauber Holocaust Library, Jewish Family and Children's Services Holocaust Center, San Francisco, call no. ST.099.

'Each signed his own death warrant': Jacob Presser, *Ashes in the Wind: The Destruction of Dutch Jewry*, trans. Arthur Pomerans (Profile, 2010).

which was still among Ruth's papers when she died: *Lust en Vrolijkheid* Papers, 1941, Ruth Wiener collection, Wiener Holocaust Library, London, file 1962/1/2.

'And no, Paul and Harold Duizend did not come back': Eddy Posthuma de Boer, Kinderkroniek 1940–1945, quoted in 'Olympiaplein', Joodsamsterdam, 18 October 2022, https://www.joodsamsterdam.nl/olympiaplein/ [accessed 7 November 2022].

The twins were twelve years old: Entry for 'Harold Lodewijk Duizend', Joods Monument, https://www.joodsmonument.nl/en/page/199710/harold-lodewijk-duizend [accessed 7 November 2022].

murdered with her mother in the gas chambers at Auschwitz: Entry for 'Dorothee Julie Miloslawski', Joods Monument, https://www.joodsmonument.nl/en/page/199691/dorothee-julie-miloslawski [accessed 7 November 2022].

died in the arms of her thirteen-year-old daughter: Janine Stein, 'Remembering one', Londonmom blog, 17 April 2017, https://thelondonmom1.blogspot.com/2017/04/remembering-one.html?m=0 [accessed 7 November 2022].

Ursula's mother was one of them: Ursula Klau papers, United States Holocaust Memorial Museum, Washington, DC, accession no. 2006.410.2.

the history of the Amster family during the Holocaust: Larry Nelson, 'The Holocaust: Martin Amster Family Experience', *Israel Philatelist*, vol. 67, no. 2 (2016), pp. 53–57.

'I didn't want to take advantage of the injustice': Nico Knapper, 'Een gelukkige jeugd', blog post, 16 February 2013, http://www.nicoknapper.com/71448132 [accessed 22 October 2022].

The inhabitants of . . . Jan van Eijckstraat were murdered: Nammen en Nummers, https://www.namenennummers.nl [accessed 7 November 2022].

The Departing

cognac – 'a glass or two or three': Mark Roseman, *The Villa, The Lake, The Meeting: Wannsee and the Final Solution* (Allen Lane, 2002).

'a) the expulsion of the Jews': 'Translation of the Protocol: Minutes of discussion', 20 January 1942, in Roseman, *The Villa, The Lake, The Meeting*, pp. 108–118.

an undertaking that the 'amount will be paid': L. D. Frank, on behalf of the Jewish Council for Amsterdam, letter to Margarete Wiener, 18 March 1942.

a dial on the wall that only broadcast Nazi propaganda: Ruth Klemens, video interview, 29 October 2001, Visual History Archive, USC Shoah Foundation, University of Southern California, Los Angeles, interview 51777, tape 3.

The bookseller kept his promise: E. Stock, De Boekenbron, letter to Alfred Wiener, 4 October 1945, Wiener Family Papers.

all over Amsterdam reading 'Forbidden for Jews': René Kok and Erik Somers, *The Persecution of the Jews in Photographs: The Netherlands, 1940–1945* (W Books, 2019).

to go to school – without risking severe punishment: Jacob Presser, *Ashes in the Wind: The Destruction of Dutch Jewry*, trans. Arthur Pomerans (Profile, 2010).

'only the Germans could think of this': Mirjam Finkelstein, video interview, 6 November 2006, Refugee Voices: The AJR Audio-visual Testimony Archive, London, interview no. 136, tape 1.

'Once they slipped us some candy, and we felt pretty wonderful': Nora Hope Karan, 'An Unforgettable Tale', 1958, Tauber Holocaust Library, Jewish Family and Children's Services Holocaust Center, San Francisco, call no. ST.099.

children were considered Jewish if: Dienke Hondius, 'Memories of Segregation: Jewish Schoolchildren in Amsterdam, 1941–45', unpublished manuscript based on Dienke Hondius and Miep Gompes-Lobatto, *Absent: Herinneringen aan het Joods Lyceum Amsterdam, 1941–1943* (Vassallucci, 2001).

these accounts are somewhat 'polished' ones: Ibid.

she recalled singing groups and volleyball: Ruth Klemens, video interview, 19 March 1987, Fortunoff Video Archive for Holocaust Testimonies, Yale University Library, New Haven, CT, interview HVT-835, tape 1.

'And those that survive I am still in touch with': Ruth Klemens, interview, USC Shoah Foundation, tape 3.

'Her parents . . . put her into hiding with another family': Karan, 'An Unforgettable Tale'.

who failed to appear were Margot and Anne Frank: Anne Frank, *The Diary of a Young Girl: The Definitive Edition*, ed. Otto H. Frank and Mirjam Pressler, trans. Susan Massotty (Doubleday, 2001).

'she never had – to me – anything too special': Ruth Klemens, interview transcript, University of Connecticut interview with Ruth H. Klemens and Simon Konover, 30 April 1992, Center for Oral History, University of Connecticut Library, CT, MSS 1984.0025, ref. no. 39153013990074.

'Hopefully she would have been a belieber': 'Anger over Justin Bieber's Anne Frank message', BBC News, 14 April 2013, https://www.bbc.co.uk/news/world-europe-22146859 [accessed 7 November 2022].

'And I always looked up to her, as a matter of fact': Ruth Klemens, interview, USC Shoah Foundation, tape 2.

the dispatch of food parcels to Westerbork: Bernard Wasserstein, *The Ambiguity of Virtue: Gertrude van Tijn and the Fate of the Dutch Jews* (Harvard University Press, 2014).

Grete . . . decided not to: Ruth Klemens, interview, Fortunoff Archive, tape 1.

'to bring food for three days (rye bread': Wasserstein, *The Ambiguity of Virtue*.

'as the Jews of the Netherlands had never even imagined': Presser, *Ashes in the Wind*.

The first warning came early in the morning: The following accounts of the family's arrest have informed my own: Ruth Klemens, interview, USC Shoah Foundation, tape 3; Ruth Klemens, interview, Fortunoff Archive, tape 1; Ruth Wiener, '20 Juni '43', handwritten account, undated, Ruth Wiener collection, Wiener Holocaust Library, London, file 1962/1/4; Karan, 'An Unforgettable Tale'; Mirjam Finkelstein, interview, tape 1; Betty Lewin, '"Illegal Life" in Holland', spring 1955, Wiener Holocaust Library, London, ref. no. 1656/3/4/107.

Betty from Nottingham

Betty . . . was also secretly someone called Jo Bosch: The content of this chapter is largely drawn from Betty Lewin, '"Illegal Life" in Holland', spring 1955, Wiener Holocaust Library, London, ref. no. 1656/3/4/107.

Into Exile

how Soviet troops . . . should execute deportations: Deputy People's Commissar of Public Security of the USSR, 'Basic Instructions on Deportations', Order No. 001223, 11 October 1939, in Tadeusz Piotrowski (ed.), *The Polish Deportees of World War II: Recollections of Removal to the Soviet Union and Dispersal Throughout the World* (McFarland and Company, 2004), pp. 204–209.

'**to meet your husband in another part of the Soviet Union**': Ludwik Finkelstein, video interview, 16 October 2006, Refugee Voices: The AJR Audio-visual Testimony Archive, London, interview no. 130, tape 1.

'**Throughout the operations**': Deputy People's Commissar of Public Security of the USSR, 'Basic Instructions on Deportations'.

by this point 'somewhat hysterical': Ludwik Finkelstein, interview, tape 1.

given an inventory of the contents of the property: Jan T. Gross, *Revolution from Abroad: The Soviet Conquest of Poland's Western Ukraine and Western Belorussia* (Princeton University Press, 2002).

The list handed to Finkelstein Amalia Isaacovna: 'ОПИСЬ', 13 April 1940, Finkelstein Family Papers.

had become a gigantic traffic jam: Gross, *Revolution from Abroad*.

paralysed, say, or otherwise disabled: US Department of State, 'Soviet Deportation of the Inhabitants of Eastern Poland in 1939–1941', confidential P-66020 report (London), December 1943, in Piotrowski (ed.), *The Polish Deportees of World War II*, pp. 211–223.

'**They will disappear over there, as a field mouse**': Gross, *Revolution from Abroad*.

the other extreme, stifled to death: Piotrowski (ed.), *The Polish Deportees of World War II*.

the conditions were miserable enough: Gross, *Revolution from Abroad*.

Lusia was 'extremely agitated': Janina Jagodzinska, 'Entwurf: Eidesstattliche Versicherung', draft affidavit for Finkelstein compensation claim, 1966, Finkelstein Family Papers.

'**accommodate yourself to the old workers**': Ludwik Finkelstein, interview, tape 1.

The Island of Hunger and Death

'**We will allocate you to cow milking**': Ludwik Finkelstein, video interview, 16 October 2006, Refugee Voices: The AJR Audio-visual Testimony Archive, London, interview no. 130, tape 1.

In practice, there wasn't much difference: Roy D. Laird and Betty A. Laird, *Soviet Communism and Agrarian Revolution* (Penguin, 1970).

farmers stopped working or hid their produce: Anne Applebaum, *Red Famine: Stalin's War on Ukraine* (Penguin, 2017).

'an island of hunger and death': Amalia Finkelstein, letter to Adolf Finkelstein, 3 November 1941, Finkelstein Family Papers.

being like a 'lunatic': Dorotea Grüner, letter to Amalia Finkelstein, 24 September 1940, Finkelstein Family Papers.

'the first sharp pain of misery': Dorotea Grüner, letter to Amalia Finkelstein, 27 April 1941, Finkelstein Family Papers.

'my love was always greater for you, my sister': Ibid.

'otherwise we would have died of hunger': Amalia Finkelstein, letter to Adolf Finkelstein, 10 November 1941, Finkelstein Family Papers.

'I just sent you a 3rd parcel since the beginning of March': Dorotea Grüner, letter to Amalia Finkelstein, 24 March 1941, Finkelstein Family Papers.

'Lusia, what condition is the sausage': Dorotea Grüner, letter to Amalia Finkelstein, 14 January 1941, Finkelstein Family Papers.

'I met the postman in front of our house': Dorotea Grüner, letter to Amalia Finkelstein, 14 May 1941, Finkelstein Family Papers.

'today is a joyful day': Wilhelm Diamantstein, letter to Amalia Finkelstein, 30 May 1941, Finkelstein Family Papers.

'what kind of a simpleton, dimwit and boor he is': Szymon Grüner, letter to Amalia Finkelstein, 7 October 1940, Finkelstein Family Papers.

'A moron, that is all': Amalia Finkelstein, letter to Adolf Finkelstein, 18 November 1941, Finkelstein Family Papers.

'I see there is no end to your suffering': Dorotea Grüner, letter to Amalia Finkelstein, 24 December 1940, Finkelstein Family Papers.

Lusia and the Countess felt keenly that they were constantly dirty: Amalia Finkelstein, 'Toaleta Potockiej', *Sylwetki z Baskermelte*, notebook (undated), Finkelstein Family Papers.

'what is the difference between an anode and a cathode?': Ludwik Finkelstein, interview, tape 1.

Waking early in the morning . . . and starting all over again: Ludwik Finkelstein, interview, tape 2.

'very untutored in matters agricultural': Ibid.

counter-revolutionaries, for whatever flimsy reason: US Department of State, 'Soviet Deportation of the Inhabitants of Eastern Poland in 1939–1941', confidential P–66020 report (London), December 1943, in Tadeusz Piotrowski (ed.), *The Polish Deportees of World War II: Recollections of Removal to the Soviet Union and Dispersal Throughout the World* (McFarland and Company, 2004), pp. 211–223.

'On 29th of June . . . Irenka has also been liberated': Dorotea Grüner, letter to Amalia Finkelstein, 1 July 1940, Finkelstein Family Papers.

because 'he broke his leg' . . . 'praise for you and Dolu': Szymon Grüner, letter to Amalia Finkelstein, 12 March 1941, Finkelstein Family Papers.

persuade him to cooperate with the Soviet regime: Kazimierz Bartel, letter to Maria Bartlowa, 16 July 1941, quoted in Zygmunt Albert, *Kaźń profesorów lwowskich, lipiec 1941: Studia oraz relacje i dokumenty* (Wydawn, 1989).

'I cannot be silent about the incident between Ania and Adas': Wilhelm Diamantstein, letter to Amalia Finkelstein, 5 September 1940, Finkelstein Family Papers.

Frania who had 'died last month': Unsigned, letter to Amalia Finkelstein, 5 July 1940, Finkelstein Family Papers.

'Ania argued with Frania and they are involved in litigation': Szymon Grüner, letter to Amalia Finkelstein, 13 July 1940, Finkelstein Family Papers.

'Lulu's friends Dolek and Bronek': Ignacy and Fila Landes, letter to Amalia Finkelstein, 25 June 1940, Finkelstein Family Papers.

'I know nothing about Dolu, he didn't have a trial yet': Dorotea

Grüner, letter from Dorotea and Szymon Grüner to Amalia Finkelstein, 7 October 1940.

didn't have 'any news from Dolu himself': Wilhelm Diamantstein, letter to Amalia Finkelstein, 7 May 1941, Finkelstein Family Papers.

Alfred's War

The British government lacked quite basic information: Ben Barkow, *Alfred Wiener and the Making of the Holocaust Library* (Vallentine Mitchell, 1997).

'by far the most useful of the outside sources': Obituary of Dr Alfred Wiener, *The Times*, 6 February 1964.

they didn't like it being called the Jewish Central Information Office: Barkow, *Alfred Wiener and the Making of the Holocaust Library*.

'a rather clumsy designation which did not easily commend itself': 'Farewell to Manchester Square', *The Wiener Library Bulletin*, vol. 11, nos. 1–2 (1957), pp. 1–3.

the day after Hess's arrival . . . a Wiener Library dossier: Alfred Wiener, report on the work of the Institute from 1 December 1940 to 15 September 1941 ('The Big Report'), quoted in Barkow, *Alfred Wiener and the Making of the Holocaust Library*.

this wasn't what its funders wanted or encouraged: Barkow, *Alfred Wiener and the Making of the Holocaust Library*.

'Dr Wiener asked me to pardon his distress': A. R. Walmsley, letter to Christa Wichmann, 25 April 1983, quoted in Barkow, *Alfred Wiener and the Making of the Holocaust Library*.

looked after by one of his staff: Barkow, *Alfred Wiener and the Making of the Holocaust Library.*

a visit to the United States to sort this all out: Walter Laqueur, 'Dr. Wiener's Library 1933–1960', *The Wiener Library Bulletin: 50 Years of the Wiener Library*, Special Issue (1983), pp. 3–9.

correspondences with American-based Jews like Albert Einstein: John Oppenheimer, letter to Ruth Klemens, 14 March 1983, Ruth Wiener collection, Wiener Holocaust Library, London, file 1962/1/5/2. The correspondence with Einstein does not appear to have survived.

in New York there was 'no war enthusiasm whatever': Alfred Wiener, 'First Impressions in New York', confidential report no. 1, 20 August 1940, Wiener Holocaust Library, London, ref. no. 1071/13.

Alfred found America a 'strange country': Alfred Wiener, letter to Ruth Wiener, 31 March 1941, Ruth Wiener collection, Wiener Holocaust Library, London, file 1962/1/5/1.

an FBI search of their apartment and an interrogation: John Oppenheimer, letter to Ruth Klemens, 14 March 1983.

considered Alfred an 'invaluable asset': John Wheeler-Bennett, *Special Relationships: America in Peace and War* (Macmillan, 1975).

supplying copy to the foreign-language newspapers: David Garnett, *The Secret History of PWE: The Political Warfare Executive, 1939–1945* (St Ermin's Press, 2002).

'a remarkable man' . . . 'single-minded devotion': Isaiah Berlin, comments for *Wiener Library Endowment Appeal* leaflet (1980).

'a droll little Berlin Jew': Wheeler-Bennett, *Special Relationships*.

'cannot get their exit permits': Gertrude van Tijn, telegram to Morris Troper, 21 July 1941, Wiener Family Papers.

the President of Cuba invalidated all visas: Bernard Wasserstein, *The Ambiguity of Virtue: Gertrude van Tijn and the Fate of the Dutch Jews* (Harvard University Press, 2014).

Citizens of Paraguay

Ładoś became chargé d'affaires: Robert Kaczmarek (writer and director), *Passports to Paraguay*, English-language version (Institute of National Remembrance, 2020).

a former cavalry officer called Konstanty Rokicki: Jakub Kumoch (ed.) et al., *The Ładoś List: An Index of People to whom the Polish Legation and Jewish Organizations in Switzerland Issued Latin American Passports during the Second World War*, trans. Julia Niedzielko and Ian Stephenson (Pilecki Institute, 2020).

cigar-smoking Jew by the name of Juliusz Kühl: Mark MacKinnon, '"He Should Be as Well Known as Schindler": Documents Reveal Canadian Citizen Julius Kuhl as Holocaust Hero', *The Globe and Mail*, 7 August 2017.

saved around thirty people from the communists: Kaczmarek, *Passports to Paraguay*.

one of the founders of the Agudath Israel movement: Naomi Lubrich, *Passports, Profiteers, Police: A Swiss War Secret* (Jewish Museum of Switzerland, 2021).

accreditation for more than 2,000 people: Kumoch, *The Ładoś List*.

'I'd love a Paraguayan passport': Władysław Szlengel, 'Passports', trans. Marcel Weyland, *What I Read to the Dead* (Brandl & Schlesinger, 2012), p. 89.

warned against the country becoming 'Judaized': Lubrich, *Passports, Profiteers, Police*.

consuls who sold passports suffered the same fate: Ibid.

Amnesty

and remained out of communication for a week: Roger Moorhouse, *The Devils' Alliance: Hitler's Pact with Stalin, 1939–1941* (The Bodley Head, 2014).

She would be the farm bookkeeper: This chapter's account of Lusia and Ludwik's experience draws heavily from: Ludwik Finkelstein, video interview, 16 October 2006, Refugee Voices: The AJR Audio-visual Testimony Archive, London, interview no. 130, tape 2.

'her command of arithmetic [was] rather eccentric': Ibid.

'If Hitler invaded Hell': Winston S. Churchill, *The Second World War, Volume 3: The Grand Alliance* (Cassell & Co., 1950).

For Stalin, the 'hyenas of capitalism': Norman Davies, *Trail of Hope: The Anders Army, an Odyssey across Three Continents* (Bloomsbury, 2016).

Churchill viewed alliance with the Soviets: Ibid.

on the Eastern Front under Soviet command: Ibid.

Some Poles had been shot on the spot: This chapter's account of the events at Katyn owes much to: Jane Rogoyska, *Surviving Katyń: Stalin's Polish Massacre and the Search for the Truth* (Oneworld, 2021).

'a large number of prisoners particularly enjoyed': Ibid.

they spread lime to speed up decomposition: Allen Paul, *Katyń: Stalin's Massacre and the Triumph of Truth* (Northern Illinois University Press, 2010). Paul's description of the manner of the killings in Kharkov prison is based on the deposition Mitrofan Syromiatnikov, a militia officer at the jail, gave to prosecutors in the early 1990s.

'sworn enemies of Soviet authority': Lavrentiy Beria, letter to Joseph Stalin, 5 March 1940, in Tadeusz Piotrowski (ed.), *The Polish Deportees of World War II: Recollections of Removal to the Soviet Union and Dispersal Throughout the World* (McFarland and Company, 2004), pp. 209–211. Reprinted from Louisa Vinton, 'The Katyn Documents: Politics and History', RFE/RL Research Report, vol. 2, no. 4 (1993), pp. 19–31.

departed the Lubyanka in an NKVD-chauffeured car: Anne Applebaum, *Gulag: A History of the Soviet Camps* (Allen Lane, 2003).

only someone else's swimming trunks: Rogoyska, *Surviving Katyń.*

expensive, small and damp, and it didn't have any furniture: Amalia Finkelstein, letter to Adolf Finkelstein, 3 November 1941, Finkelstein Family Papers.

because his Russian was still poor: Ibid.

What Happened to Dolu

learning who else was being held in the prison: Anne Applebaum, *Gulag: A History of the Soviet Camps* (Allen Lane, 2003).

once a week, for half an hour at a time: Applebaum, *Gulag*, attributed to 'Karta, Kazimierz Zamorski Collection, Folder 1, File 1253'.

'Article 54-13 of the Ukrainian Criminal Code': Dave Obee, 'Researching Stalin's Victims', *FEEFHS Journal*, vol. 10 (2002), pp. 16–21.

'You've been sentenced to eight': Ludwik Finkelstein, video interview, 16 October 2006, Refugee Voices: The AJR Audio-visual Testimony Archive, London, interview no. 130, tape 2.

eighteen million people experienced the Gulag: Applebaum, *Gulag*, attributed to Edwin Bacon, *The Gulag at War: Stalin's Forced Labour System in the Light of the Archives* (Palgrave Macmillan, 1994).

one in four prisoners died every day: Applebaum, *Gulag*.

'With Just Work I Will Pay' . . . 'Through Labour – Freedom': Applebaum, *Gulag*, attributed to Yuri Chirkov, *A bylo vse tak* (Politizdat, 1991).

destined to circulate round a number of them: Ludwik Finkelstein, interview, tape 2.

your fingers might just freeze anyway: Julius Margolin, *Journey into the Land of the Zeks and Back: A Memoir of the Gulag*, trans. Stefani Hoffman (Oxford University Press, 2020).

used by the authorities as a weapon of camp control: Ibid.

Reunion and Freedom

'There was no end to my happiness': Adolf Finkelstein, letter to Amalia Finkelstein, 5 November 1941, Finkelstein Family Papers.

the weather was 'beautiful and warm': Amalia Finkelstein, letter to Adolf Finkelstein, 3 November 1941, Finkelstein Family Papers.

it was 'snowing and freezing': Amalia Finkelstein, letter to Adolf Finkelstein, 15 November 1941, Finkelstein Family Papers.

'to have something for our thin child': Amalia Finkelstein, letter to Adolf Finkelstein, 18 November 1941, Finkelstein Family Papers.

if anything had been heard about Ignacy: Amalia Finkelstein, letter to Adolf Finkelstein, 29 October 1941, Finkelstein Family Papers.

'So far, none of them have come here [Totskoye]': Adolf Finkelstein, letter to Amalia Finkelstein, 11 November 1941, Finkelstein Family Papers.

This was a remarkably common fate: Account of Sabina Kukla, *The Polish Deportees of World War II: Recollections of Removal to the Soviet Union and Dispersal Throughout the World*, Tadeusz Piotrowski (ed.) (McFarland and Company, 2004), pp. 86–87.

'we will return together to our beloved fatherland': Adolf Finkelstein, letter to Amalia Finkelstein, 4 January 1942, Finkelstein Family Papers.

an old Soviet joke about a couple's terror: Anne Applebaum, *Gulag: A History of the Soviet Camps* (Allen Lane, 2003).

'my moment of liberation': Ludwik Finkelstein, video interview, 16 October 2006, Refugee Voices: The AJR Audio-visual Testimony Archive, London, interview no. 130, tape 2.

Kieloch was 'a very decent man, but not very clever': Adolf Finkelstein, letter to Amalia Finkelstein, 22 February 1942, Finkelstein Family Papers.

'Under the harshest conditions imaginable': Eustachy Talarski, 'Ozwiadczenie', reference for Adolf Finkelstein, 16 January 1945, Finkelstein Family Papers.

enough for just 26,000 men: Norman Davies, *Trail of Hope: The Anders Army, an Odyssey across Three Continents* (Bloomsbury, 2016).

Stalin said he really didn't know: Jane Rogoyska, *Surviving Katyń: Stalin's Polish Massacre and the Search for the Truth* (Oneworld, 2021).

'To put matters brutally, if these Poles die': Minister of State, Cairo, telegram no. 897 to Foreign Office, 22 June 1942, British Library, London, ref. no. IOR/L/PJ/8/412/319.

'though no doubt true will, I fear, read rather oddly': F. K. Roberts, notes attached to telegram no. 897, 25 June 1942.

Westerbork

'102,000 of the 140,000 Jews have now gone': René Kok and Erik Somers, *The Persecution of the Jews in Photographs: The Netherlands, 1940–1945* (W Books, 2019).

'There was no chance of running away or anything': Mirjam Finkelstein, video interview, 6 November 2006, Refugee Voices: The AJR Audio-visual Testimony Archive, London, interview no. 136, tape 1.

using the square for their normal Sunday sports matches: Kok and Somers, *The Persecution of the Jews in Photographs*.

'The ghastliness of the scenes enacted': David Cohen, quoted in Jacob Presser, *Ashes in the Wind: The Destruction of Dutch Jewry*, trans. Arthur Pomerans (Profile, 2010).

'Excruciatingly hot': Ruth Wiener, '20 Juni '43', handwritten account, undated, Ruth Wiener collection, Wiener Holocaust Library, London, file 1962/1/4.

'Ludwik had been for three weeks': Mirjam Finkelstein, interview, tape 1.

'My poor mother. If I think about it now': Mirjam Finkelstein, interview, tape 2.

a 'desolate, windswept peat bog': Bernard Wasserstein, *The Ambiguity of Virtue: Gertrude van Tijn and the Fate of the Dutch Jews* (Harvard University Press, 2014).

'the old-timers': Ruth Klemens, video interview, 19 March 1987, Fortunoff Video Archive for Holocaust Testimonies, Yale University Library, New Haven, CT, interview HVT-835, tape 1.

Number 58, with similar properties: Mirjam Bolle, unsent letter to Leo Bolle, 8 July 1943, *Letters Never Sent: Amsterdam, Westerbork, Bergen-Belsen*, trans. Laura Vroomen (Yad Vashem, 2014), pp. 159–167.

'I have asked the Führer with regard to letting Jews go': Heinrich Himmler, quoted in Yehuda Bauer, *Jews for Sale? Nazi-Jewish Negotiations, 1933–1945* (Yale University Press, 1994).

an orthodox Lutheran sect, known as the Templers: A. N. Oppenheim, *The Chosen People: The Story of the '222 Transport' from Bergen-Belsen to Palestine* (Vallentine Mitchell, 1996).

filled in the front section . . . and had then left it unused: Ruth Wiener, 1943 diary, Ruth Wiener collection, Wiener Holocaust Library, London, ref. no. 1962/1/3/1.

Her first note . . . records the bare facts of their arrest: Ruth Wiener, transcription of Westerbork/Bergen-Belsen diary, 20 June 1943–21 January 1945, Ruth Wiener collection, Wiener Holocaust Library, London, ref. no. 1962/1/3/2.

When there was a quota to fill, no one was safe: Presser, *Ashes in the Wind*.

'The scenes that followed defy imagination': Unnamed eyewitness, quoted in Presser, *Ashes in the Wind*.

half-price, and paid for out of the Jewish assets: Wasserstein, *The Ambiguity of Virtue*.

'I had to help with one of those transports every Tuesday': Ruth Klemens, video interview, 29 October 2001, Visual History Archive, USC Shoah Foundation, University of Southern California, Los Angeles, interview 51777, tape 4.

sentenced to ten years, but was released in 1951: Presser, *Ashes in the Wind*.

'The English radio says they're being gassed': Anne Frank, diary entry 9 October 1942, *The Diary of a Young Girl: The Definitive Edition*, ed. Otto H. Frank and Mirjam Pressler, trans. Susan Massotty (Doubleday, 2001), pp. 54–55.

the Germans 'are now carrying into effect': Anthony Eden, United Nations Declaration, 17 December 1942, Hansard, House of Commons, vol. 385, col. 2083.

'Dear little sister, I'm sitting on my bed': Trude and Jan Abrahams, note to Margarete Wiener, 14 July 1943, Wiener Family Papers.

some sort of contest between senior Nazis: Jules Schelvis, *Sobibor: A History of a Nazi Death Camp*, ed. Bob Moore, trans. Karin Dixon (Bloomsbury, 2014).

The lifespan of a Jew arriving in Sobibor: Lawrence Douglas, *The Right Wrong Man: John Demjanjuk and the Last Great Nazi War Crimes Trial* (Princeton University Press, 2016).

only eighteen of them returned home: Bob Moore, foreword to Schelvis, *Sobibor.*

the Nazis burned almost all the documents: Schelvis, *Sobibor.*

present in Sobibor between the end of March and the end of September: Douglas, *The Right Wrong Man.*

'not a shattering event', wrote Mum: Mirjam Finkelstein, 'Tante Nutti a greataunt', email addressed to her children, nieces and nephew, also sent to Ruth Klemens and Ted Plaut, 24 June 2010, Finkelstein Family Papers.

in May 1944, she had been betrayed: Betty Lewin, '"Illegal Life" in Holland', spring 1955, Wiener Holocaust Library, London, ref. no. 1656/3/4/107.

and had eventually been deported to Auschwitz: Entry for 'Marion Lazarus', *Gedenkbuch: Opfer der Verfolgung der Juden unter der nationalsozialistischen Gewaltherrschaft in Deutschland 1933–1945*, Bundesarchiv.

she died on one of the so-called 'death marches': Entry for 'Marion Lazarus', Joods Monument, https://www.joodsmonument.nl/en/page/208231/marion-lazarus [accessed 7 November 2022].

The Transfer

'If we hadn't been there – us children': Mirjam Finkelstein, video interview, 6 November 2006, Refugee Voices: The AJR Audio-visual Testimony Archive, London, interview no. 136, tape 1.

The Palestine list exemption no longer held: Mirjam Bolle, unsent letter to Leo Bolle, 19 July 1943, *Letters Never Sent: Amsterdam, Westerbork, Bergen-Belsen*, trans. Laura Vroomen (Yad Vashem, 2014), pp. 168–171.

The move made about 1,200 more people eligible: A. N. Oppenheim, *The Chosen People: The Story of the '222 Transport' from Bergen-Belsen to Palestine* (Vallentine Mitchell, 1996).

'**Critical situation for us regarding the Tuesday transport**': Ruth Wiener, transcription of Westerbork/Bergen-Belsen diary, 20 June 1943–21 January 1945, Ruth Wiener collection, Wiener Holocaust Library, London, ref. no. 1962/1/3/2.

'**to say Uncle Erich and Aunt Vera to the Cohns**': Ruth Wiener, diary entry 11 July 1943.

most involved in the compiling of Gemmeker's lists: Ad van der Logt, 'Erich Gustav Cohn', Herinneringscentrum Kamp Westerbork, 5 June 2019, https://westerborkportretten.nl/bevri jdingsportretten/erich-gustav-cohn [accessed 7 November 2022].

'**A great disappointment to Mother!**': Ruth Klemens, 'Diary Notes', September 2008, Ruth Wiener collection, Wiener Holocaust Library, London, ref. no. 1962/1/3/6.

'**They gave us sugar**': Mirjam Finkelstein, interview, tape 1.

'**Nothing anti-Nazi,' said Ruth:** Ruth Klemens, video interview, 19 March 1987, Fortunoff Video Archive for Holocaust Testimonies, Yale University Library, New Haven, CT, interview HVT-835, tape 2.

They 'were a lot of fun': Nora Hope Karan, 'An Unforgettable Tale', 1958, Tauber Holocaust Library, Jewish Family and Children's Services Holocaust Center, San Francisco, call no. ST.099.

'**It was allowed to gather some children**': Mirjam Finkelstein, interview, tape 1.

the work was 'gruelling' and lonely: Ruth Klemens, interview, Fortunoff Archive, tape 2.

'**My beloved child, Tomorrow you will be 16 years old**': Margarete Wiener, letter to Ruth Wiener, 3 August 1943, Ruth Wiener collection, Wiener Holocaust Library, London, file 1962/1/5/2.

'**About 30,000 Jews . . . who appear suitable**': Quoted in Eberhard Kolb, *Bergen-Belsen: From 'Detention Camp' to Concentration Camp, 1943–1945*, trans. Gregory Claeys and Christine Lattek (Vandenhoeck & Ruprecht, 1985).

she acquired the power of life and death: Rachel Century, *Female Administrators of the Third Reich* (Palgrave Macmillan, 2017).

'a nightmare come to life': A. J. Herzberg, quoted in Jacob Presser, *Ashes in the Wind: The Destruction of Dutch Jewry*, trans. Arthur Pomerans (Profile, 2010).

'a witch', 'an apparition' and a 'bat-like presence': Presser, *Ashes in the Wind*.

subject to a gigantic miscarriage of justice: Century, *Female Administrators of the Third Reich*.

'She sounded like a travel agent': Barry Spanjaard, *Don't Fence Me In! An American Teenager in the Holocaust* (B&B Publishing, 1981).

Camille

'The entire Aronowski family': Report on Camille Aronowski's political views and activities, Bern Security and Criminal Police, 3 December 1943, Swiss Federal Archives, Bern, file C.16-04474 P.

'taken to the Westernbork camp': Camille Aronowski, letter to Margarete Wiener, 3 July 1943, Wiener Family Papers.

'Thank you for your lines from 25 June': Camille Aronowski, letter to Margarete Wiener, 29 July 1943, Wiener Family Papers.

Belsen

how his failed idea . . . had ended: Eberhard Kolb, *Bergen-Belsen: From 'Detention Camp' to Concentration Camp, 1943–1945*, trans. Gregory Claeys and Christine Lattek (Vandenhoeck & Ruprecht, 1985).

as Mirjam observed, 'it was almost empty': Mirjam Finkelstein, video interview, 6 November 2006, Refugee Voices: The AJR Audio-visual Testimony Archive, London, interview no. 136, tape 1.

'Raus! Raus!' as they opened the carriage doors: Mirjam Bolle, unsent letter to Leo Bolle, 18 January 1944, *Letters Never Sent: Amsterdam, Westerbork, Bergen-Belsen*, trans. Laura Vroomen (Yad Vashem, 2014), pp. 209–218.

'bleak. It was terribly bleak': Mirjam Finkelstein, interview, tape 1.

'I felt a little scared of the whole ambience': Ruth Klemens, video interview, 29 October 2001, Visual History Archive, USC Shoah Foundation, University of Southern California, Los Angeles, interview 51777, tape 4.

it was only for a couple of hours: Mirjam Bolle, unsent letter to Leo Bolle, 18 January 1944.

'You put somebody in prison pyjamas': Mirjam Finkelstein, interview, tape 2.

The task was fruitless: The Birnbaums, *For It Is a Tree of Life*, privately published account of their parents' experiences by the children of Yehoshua and Henni Birnbaum, undated, Sonya Schneidinger private collection.

The hut leaders would be punished: Tomi Reichental, *I Was a Boy in Belsen* (O'Brien Press, 2012).

'Mrs Mainz (barracks leader) has to go': Ruth Wiener, transcription of Westerbork/Bergen-Belsen diary, 20 June 1943–21 January 1945, Ruth Wiener collection, Wiener Holocaust Library, London, ref. no. 1962/1/3/2.

particularly unpleasant, short, stocky: Barry Spanjaard, *Don't Fence Me In! An American Teenager in the Holocaust* (B&B Publishing, 1981).

'in cahoots with the Nazis themselves': Mirjam Finkelstein, interview, tape 2.

'he could bellow and roar as much': Ruth Klemens, interview, USC Shoah Foundation, tape 4.

'they are true creatures of the devil': Hanna Lévy-Hass, diary entry December 1944 III, *Inside Belsen*, trans. Ronald Taylor (Harvester Press, 1982), pp. 49–50.

They were never heard from again: Ruth Klemens, interview, USC Shoah Foundation, tape 5.

life in the shoe commando was 'indescribable': Mirjam Bolle, unsent letters to Leo Bolle, 14 and 15 June 1944, *Letters Never Sent*, pp. 265–267.

left behind in the camp to do 'basically nothing': Mirjam Finkelstein, interview, tape 2.

any sense of disgust having vanished: The Birnbaums, *For It Is a Tree of Life*.

there was spinach with potatoes: Ruth Wiener, diary entry 15 June 1944.

Rolled oats are mentioned once, as is macaroni: Ruth Wiener, diary entries 22 and 18 May 1944.

'there was a deficiency of about 1000 calories': Gertrude van Tijn, 'Information regarding Bergen-Belsen on June 28, 1944', 12 August 1944, Records of the US War Refugee Board, 1944–1945, Franklin D. Roosevelt Presidential Library and Museum, Hyde Park, NY, series 1, box 5, http://www.fdrlibrary.marist.edu/_resources/images/wrb/wrb0126.pdf, pp. 106–110 [accessed 7 November 2022].

'What are you going to do when your children say they are hungry?': Ruth Klemens, interview, USC Shoah Foundation, tape 5.

'Burns easily!': Margarete Wiener, recipe sheets, undated, Wiener Family Papers.

she 'had real porridge!': Ruth Wiener, diary entry 4 August 1944.

because they had obtained Latin American passports: Erika Guggenheim-Neuburger, 'Der 2. Weltkrieg erlebt von Erica Guggenheim geb. Neuburger', digitised manuscript, 2008, Claims Conference Holocaust Survivor Memoir Collection, United States Holocaust Memorial Museum, Washington, DC.

'Through the snow we walk home from our work': Ruth Wiener, untitled note, 16 August 1945, Ruth Wiener collection, Wiener Holocaust Library, London, file 1962/1.

no blankets even, and no hot food: Kolb, *Bergen-Belsen*.

the Franks looked 'pretty horrible': Ruth Klemens, video interview, 19 March 1987, Fortunoff Video Archive for Holocaust Testimonies, Yale University Library, New Haven, CT, interview HVT-835, tape 2.

being good friends with Hanneli Goslar: Guggenheim-Neuburger, 'Der 2. Weltkrieg erlebt'.

'We got together at night, and mother [Grete]': Nora Hope Karan, 'An Unforgettable Tale', 1958, Tauber Holocaust Library, Jewish Family and Children's Services Holocaust Center, San Francisco, call no. ST.099.

straw tightly packed into the barbed wire: Melissa Müller, *Anne Frank: The Biography*, trans. Rita and Robert Kimber (Bloomsbury, 2013).

throwing her 'some of our Red Cross food': Guggenheim-Neuburger, 'Der 2. Weltkrieg erlebt'.

'General malnutrition. It is as much as we can do to move': Lévy-Hass, diary entries January 1945 V and VI, *Inside Belsen*, pp. 54–56.

what its official historian has described as an inferno: Kolb, *Bergen-Belsen*.

The Exchange

'that little, but big powered, man': Nora Hope Karan, 'An Unforgettable Tale', 1958, Tauber Holocaust Library, Jewish Family and Children's Services Holocaust Center, San Francisco, call no. ST.099.

The public documentation doesn't shed any light: A. N. Oppenheim, *The Chosen People: The Story of the '222 Transport' from Bergen-Belsen to Palestine* (Vallentine Mitchell, 1996).

A further visit by Mös in September: Ruth Wiener, diary entry 14 September 1944, transcription of Westerbork/Bergen-Belsen diary, 20 June 1943–21 January 1945, Ruth Wiener collection, Wiener Holocaust Library, London, ref. no. 1962/1/3/2.

news of 'a list' of South Americans: Ruth Wiener, diary entry 12 November 1944.

'more rumours about a South American list': Ruth Wiener, diary entry 26 November 1944.

Poland had become a 'Nazi slaughterhouse': Anthony Eden,

United Nations Declaration, 17 December 1942, Hansard, House of Commons, vol. 385, col. 2083.

'the truly diabolic character of the Nazi revolution': Roswell McClelland, 'Report on the Activities of the War Refugee Board through its Representation at the American Legation in Bern, Switzerland, March 1944–July 1945', 2 August 1945, Records of the US War Refugee Board, 1944–1945, Franklin D. Roosevelt Presidential Library and Museum, Hyde Park, NY, series 2, box 50, http://www.fdrlibrary.marist.edu/_resources/images/wrb/wrb1178.pdf, pp. 10–70 [accessed 11 November 2022].

'Once we open the door to adult male Jews': A. W. G. Randall, quoted in Bernard Wasserstein, *Britain and the Jews of Europe, 1939–1945* (Institute of Jewish Affairs, 1988).

'disposing of' 70,000 Jews too hard: Henry Morgenthau, quoted in Wasserstein, *Britain and the Jews of Europe*.

a particular concern that Jews might go to Palestine: Rainer Schulze, '"Keeping very clear of any 'Kuh-Handel'": The British Foreign Office and the Rescue of Jews from Bergen-Belsen', *Holocaust and Genocide Studies*, vol. 19, no. 2 (2005), pp. 226–251.

dubbed his New Deal, the 'Jew Deal': David S. Wyman, *The Abandonment of the Jews: America and the Holocaust, 1941–1945* (Plunkett Lake Press, 2018).

Hitler was 'really behind the [Jewish] pressure groups': Robert C. Alexander, 7 May 1943, quoted in Wyman, *The Abandonment of the Jews*.

was now being reported back to it as fact: Correspondence between H. Freeman Matthews and James Dunn, quoted in Max Paul Friedman, *Nazis and Good Neighbors: The United States Campaign against the Germans of Latin America in World War II* (Cambridge University Press, 2003).

It was 'fraudulent and improper': Willard F. Barber, memo, quoted in Friedman, *Nazis and Good Neighbors*.

He named him Adolfo Hirohito: Richard S. Sacks, 'Historical Setting', *Paraguay: A Country Study*, eds. Dennis M. Hanratty and Sandra W. Meditz (US Government Printing Office for the Library of Congress, 1988).

alongside the greatest of his wartime achievements: Peter Moreira, *The Jew Who Defeated Hitler: Henry Morgenthau Jr., FDR and How We Won the War* (Prometheus, 2014).

'a satanic combination of British chill and diplomatic double talk': Quoted in Wyman, *The Abandonment of the Jews*.

opportunities for exchanges involving Jews: Moreira, *The Jew Who Defeated Hitler*.

every single person was murdered: Eberhard Kolb, *Bergen-Belsen: From 'Detention Camp' to Concentration Camp, 1943–1945*, trans. Gregory Claeys and Christine Lattek (Vandenhoeck & Ruprecht, 1985).

They too were destined for Auschwitz and death: Charles E Dickerson, on behalf of the US Embassy in Lisbon, letter to Secretary of State and enclosed report, 31 July 1944, Records of the US War Refugee Board, 1944–1945, Franklin D. Roosevelt Presidential Library and Museum, Hyde Park, NY, series 2, box 54, http://www.fdrlibrary.marist.edu/_resources/images/wrb/wrb1217.pdf, pp. 28–33 [accessed 11 November 2022].

Ładoś himself led the charge: Robert Kaczmarek (writer and director), *Passports to Paraguay*, English-language version (Institute of National Remembrance, 2020).

'We are being placed in the position of . . . nurse-maid': George Tait, quoted in Wyman, *The Abandonment of the Jews*.

they had prevailed upon the Germans: McClelland, 'Report on the Activities of the War Refugee Board through its Representation at the American Legation in Bern, Switzerland'.

'We didn't know what was happening': Karan, 'An Unforgettable Tale'.

'Everyone holding a North American or South American passport': Irene Butter, with John D. Bidwell and Kris Holloway, *Shores Beyond Shores: From Holocaust to Hope, My True Story* (TSB, 2019).

'I have already seen much misery': 'A Transport of Misery', *St. Galler Tagblatt*, 31 January 1945, trans. in 'Press Cuttings Regarding the Exchange of Civilian Internees between Switzerland and Germany', *Testifying to the Truth: Eyewitnesses to the Holocaust*, https://www.testifyingtothetruth.co.uk/viewer/full text/106538/en/ [accessed 31 October 2022].

fooled nobody about his true character: Butter, *Shores Beyond Shores*.

'One often sees these scenes in films': Mirjam Finkelstein, video interview, 6 November 2006, Refugee Voices: The AJR Audiovisual Testimony Archive, London, interview no. 136, tape 2.

barely survived the infamous 'Lost Train': Erika Guggenheim-Neuburger, 'Der 2. Weltkrieg erlebt von Erica Guggenheim geb. Neuburger', digitised manuscript, 2008, Claims Conference Holocaust Survivor Memoir Collection, United States Holocaust Memorial Museum, Washington, DC.

those most obviously ailing: Butter, *Shores Beyond Shores*.

Mirjam recalls being oblivious: Mirjam Finkelstein, interview, tape 2.

'It had actual pieces of potato in it': Mirjam Finkelstein, quoted in Daniel Finkelstein, 'My Mother's Life with Anne Frank', *Daily Mail*, 18 January 2009.

The Jews would then be free: Jan Jarboe Russell, *The Train to Crystal City: FDR's Secret Prisoner Exchange Program and America's Only Family Internment Camp During World War II* (Scribner, 2015).

'YOUR WIFE . . . FROM CAMP BERGENBLELSEN': Rabbi Lothar Rothschild, telegram to Alfred Wiener, 3 February 1945, Wiener Family Papers.

The Dock at Southampton

'I went through prisons and labour camps': Adolf Finkelstein, letter to Amalia Finkelstein, 5 November 1941, Finkelstein Family Papers.

Hundreds of Poles died of disease and exhaustion: Evacuation of Polish citizens from Krasnovodsk: report on refugee camps in Persia, August–September 1942, The National Archives, Kew, ref. no. WO 204/8711.

'We went to a restaurant!': Ludwik Finkelstein, video interview, 16 October 2006, Refugee Voices: The AJR Audio-visual Testimony Archive, London, interview no. 130, tape 3.

Wiener schnitzel and offering . . . mountains of cakes: Norman Davies, *Trail of Hope: The Anders Army, an Odyssey across Three Continents* (Bloomsbury, 2016).

'I found him very emaciated and changed': Maurycy Morecki, 'Eidesstattliche Versicherung', draft affidavit for Finkelstein compensation claim, enclosed in Leon Stellman, letter to Amalia Finkelstein, 15 March 1966, Finkelstein Family Papers.

'My dear sister, I mourn the death of our brother': Adolf Finkelstein, letter to Lola Urbach, 19 May 1943, Urbach Family Papers.

'Please write to us, love you': Dorotea and Szymon Grüner, letter to Amalia Finkelstein, 5 June 1940, Finkelstein Family Papers.

the majority were Ukrainians: Jan T. Gross, *Revolution from Abroad: The Soviet Conquest of Poland's Western Ukraine and Western Belorussia* (Princeton University Press, 2002).

was shot there in front of his son: Ludwik Finkelstein, 'Hidden Tales from Polish History', *Manna*, no. 97 (2007), pp. 12–14.

laying dynamite and blowing up the building: Yevhen Nakonechny, Шоа у Львові (Piramida, 2006).

shot on 24 July 1941 on the direct orders of Himmler: Zygmunt Albert, *Kaźń profesorów lwowskich, lipiec 1941: Studia oraz relacje i dokumenty* (Wydawn, 1989).

'The Jewish question in the District of Galicia': Quoted in Christoph Mick, *Lemberg, Lwów, L'viv, 1914–1947: Violence and Ethnicity in a Contested City* (Purdue University Press, 2016).

'During the Shoah [Holocaust], Jews were murdered': Entries for 'Wilhelm Diamantshtein', 'Dola Tzila Gruener', 'Szymon Gruner Griner', and 'Halina Gruner', The Central Database of Shoah Victims' Names, Yad Vashem, Jerusalem.

'our walks in the linden tree lane on Herburtów street': Amalia Finkelstein, letter to Adolf Finkelstein, 20 November 1941, Finkelstein Family Papers.

he felt Soviet ruthlessness could serve the common cause: Jane Rogoyska, *Surviving Katyń: Stalin's Polish Massacre and the Search for the Truth* (Oneworld, 2021).

Himmler rejoiced that the intellectual capital of Poland: Diana Preston, *Eight Days at Yalta: How Churchill, Roosevelt and Stalin Shaped the Post-War World* (Picador, 2020).

He first told Anders, and then the House of Commons: Wiesław Rogalski, *The Polish Resettlement Corps, 1946–1949: Britain's Polish Forces* (Helion, 2019).

'if we are put under the communists, we're going to mutiny': Ludwik Finkelstein, interview, tape 3.

Three Skeletons

died there at just past midnight: Robert Wieler, on behalf of the Jewish Community of Kreuzlingen, letter to Alfred Wiener, 5 March 1945, Wiener Family Papers.

'Yes; forty-nine and not yet fifty': Mirjam Finkelstein, video interview, 6 November 2006, Refugee Voices: The AJR Audio-visual Testimony Archive, London, interview no. 136, tape 2.

'there is every reason to believe that the extreme malnutrition': William O'Dwyer, 'Report of the War Refugee Board for the Week of January 29 to February 3, 1945', Roswell and Marjorie McClelland Papers, United States Holocaust Memorial Museum, Washington, DC, accession no. 2014.500.1, series 5, file 3.

to erase the way that Grete had brought them up: Ruth Klemens, video interview, 29 October 2001, Visual History Archive, USC Shoah Foundation, University of Southern California, Los Angeles, interview 51777, tape 5.

'[the Belsen survivors] arrived here in a pitiful state': 'A Pitiful Picture!', *Volksstimme* (St. Gallen), 31 January 1945, trans. in 'Press Cuttings Regarding the Exchange of Civilian Internees between Switzerland and Germany', *Testifying to the Truth: Eyewitnesses to the Holocaust*, https://www.testifyingtothetruth.co.uk/viewer/fulltext/106538/en/ [accessed 31 October 2022].

Through them – and by paying $1,000 for the passage: Alfred Wiener, letter to Robert Murphy, 19 December 1956, Wiener Family Papers.

Eva was five feet four inches tall: 'The Wienerchen' (Eva, Ruth and Mirjam), letter to John F. and Hertha Oppenheimer, 5 April 1945, Wiener Family Papers.

and weighed only eighty pounds: Nora Hope Karan, 'An Unforgettable Tale', 1958, Tauber Holocaust Library, Jewish Family and Children's Services Holocaust Center, San Francisco, call no. ST.099.

'a terrible state . . . the injuries of these poor young men': Mirjam Finkelstein, interview, tape 2.

if he only he had wrists, he would kill himself: Karan, 'An Unforgettable Tale'.

'he would wait for us . . . And I was happy, very happy': Ruth Wiener, 'My First Impressions of America', 16 April 1945, Ruth Wiener collection, Wiener Holocaust Library, London, file 1962/1/4.

'close questioning as a precaution': 'Gripsholm Civilians Questioned Closely', *New York Times*, 24 February 1945.

'We thought we were in another camp in America': Karan, 'An Unforgettable Tale'.

'three tall skeletons and one short, little, old man': Ibid.

The Lady of Hendon Central

'responsible for Mr. F's illnesses and early death': Dr Emanuel Kost, medical letter for Finkelstein compensation claim, 26 May 1966, Finkelstein Family Papers.

'**Forgive me darling for being so unpoetical**': Ludwik Finkelstein, letter to Amalia Finkelstein, 18 May 1953, Finkelstein Family Papers.

'**a person for whom the title "lady" was invented especially**': Sylvia and David Lewin, letter to Ludwik Finkelstein, 4 March 1980, Finkelstein Family Papers.

The Man on the President's Conscience

'**any lack of appreciation for your very valuable services**': David Bowes-Lyon, letter to Alfred Wiener, 27 November 1944, Wiener Family Papers.

'**it was as if we'd landed on the moon**': Mirjam Finkelstein, video interview, 6 November 2006, Refugee Voices: The AJR Audio-visual Testimony Archive, London, interview no. 136, tape 2.

'**my mother became very attached to them**': Gitta Sereny, *Albert Speer: His Battle with the Truth* (Picador, 2017).

'**like all institutionalized children, very receptive to love**': Ibid.

'**the anger she showed that day to Hilde**': Ibid.

'**One didn't talk about it actually**': Mirjam Finkelstein, interview, tape 2.

'**Miss Schultz, a psycho-analist**': Alice Hamburger, letter to Alfred Wiener, 22 March 1945, Wiener Family Papers.

'**did we live in a windmill**': Mirjam Finkelstein, interview, tape 2.

'**Laughing, yet so very wise**': Entry for 'Ruth Weiner', Rita Weintraub (ed.), *The Stevenson Circus: Robert Louis Stevenson School*, yearbook, June 1946, Ruth Wiener collection, Wiener Holocaust Library, London, file 1962/1/4.

The teacher underlined the phrase, 'I thought of my mother': Ruth Wiener, 'My First Impressions of America', 16 April 1945, Ruth Wiener collection, Wiener Holocaust Library, London, file 1962/1/4.

'**They appreciate school more than any of us**': Ruth Wiener, 'Graduation Speech made on June 22, 1946', Robert Louis Stevenson School, 1946, Ruth Wiener collection, Wiener Holocaust Library, London, file 1962/1/4.

Alfred and his colleagues were on their own: Walter Laqueur, 'Dr. Wiener's Library 1933–1960', *The Wiener Library Bulletin: 50 Years of the Wiener Library*, Special Issue (1983), pp. 3–9.

'The Wiener connection was important to Callaghan': Kenneth O. Morgan, *Callaghan: A Life* (Oxford University Press, 1997).

'as much as one might regret it': Alfred Wiener, 'Unterredung mit Herrn James Callaghan, M.P.', undated memorandum about a meeting on 29 March 1949, Correspondence with James Callaghan folder, Wiener Holocaust Library, London, file 3000/9/1/253.

'The help it has given has been invaluable': Marcel de Baer, 'Nuremberg and the War Criminals', *The Wiener Library Bulletin*, vol. 1, no. 1 (1946), p. 3.

unable to afford to take up the invitation to travel to the trial: C. C. Aronsfeld, on behalf of the Wiener Library, letter to Ephraim Hofstadter, 17 March 1961, Wiener Library Archive: Pre-1963 Correspondence, Wiener Holocaust Library, London, ref. no. 3000/9/1/652/148.

The Library had a picture: 'Alfred Wiener, Kept Nazi Data: Founder of London Information Center Dies', *New York Times*, 6 February 1964.

Alfred's name would 'long be remembered': Alan Bullock, 'The Wiener Library: Congratulations to a Friend', *AJR Information*, vol. 15, no. 3 (1960), p. 5.

the current state of research . . . would be 'unthinkable': Richard Bessel et al., 'Wiener Library move', open letter, 18 March 1980, in *The Times*, 28 March 1980.

Clarendon Court in Maida Vale: Alfred Wiener, memo to Aronsfeld, Brügel, Kahn and Wolff, 15 July 1959.

his idealistic view of Germany had contained truth within it: Eva G. Reichmann, 'Alfred Wiener – the German Jew', *The Wiener Library Bulletin*, vol. 19 (1965), pp. 10–11.

The award marked Alfred's seventieth birthday: Alfred Wiener, letter to Konrad Adenauer, 5 April 1955, Wiener Family Papers.

friends of his who felt he should not accept: Mirjam Finkelstein, oral testimony.

'I don't fall around the neck of the Germans': Alfred Wiener, interviewed by Robert Muller, 'The man on the President's conscience', *Daily Mail*, 22 October 1958.

'The Moment of Horror': Jack Crossley, 'The moment of horror', *Daily Mail*, 24 October 1958.

'Library of Doom': Stefan Mendelsohn, 'Library of Doom: Little doctor's printed dynamite', *The Sun* (Sydney), 7 November 1958.

'it is no good to isolate antisemitism': 'Dr A. Wiener to Resign', *Jewish Chronicle*, 24 February 1961.

thanked him publicly for his 'magnanimity': Heinrich Lübke, 'Beileid zum Tode von Dr. Alfred Wiener', *Bulletin des Presse- und Informationsamtes der Bundesregierung*, 12 February 1964.

one of the most important of all of its émigrés: Ludwig Erhard, 'Beileid zum Tode von Dr. Alfred Wiener', *Bulletin des Presse- und Informationsamtes der Bundesregierung*, 13 February 1964.

regarding *The Times* as 'second only to the Bible': C. C. Aronsfeld, 'Dr. Alfred Wiener: Death of the Library's Founder', *The Wiener Library Bulletin*, vol. 18, no. 2 (1964), pp. 13–14.

On Alfred's coffin rested a wreath from the Federal President: Eva G. Reichmann, 'In memoriam Alfred Wiener', *Das Parliament*, 26 February 1964.

Friday Evening

my father should take a multi-volume biography of Bismarck: Ben Barkow, *Alfred Wiener and the Making of the Holocaust Library* (Vallentine Mitchell, 1997).

'I think I came out of it pretty well': Ruth Klemens, video interview, 29 October 2001, Visual History Archive, USC Shoah Foundation, University of Southern California, Los Angeles, interview 51777, tape 6.

every crime . . . the Soviets were guilty of too: Bronisław Kuśnierz, *Stalin and the Poles: An Indictment of the Soviet Leaders* (Hollis & Carter, 1949).

wasn't mentioned by the judges at the end of proceedings: Ann Tusa and John Tusa, *The Nuremberg Trial* (Skyhorse Publishing, 2010).

List of illustrations

Plate section 1:

Dolu and Bernard *(Finkelstein family collection)*
Dolu and Lusia *(Finkelstein family collection)*
Lusia and Ludwik *(Finkelstein family collection)*
Major Ignacy Schrage and Jadzia *(Finkelstein family collection)*
12 Herburtów street *(Myroslava Liakhovych)*
Ludwik and Dolu *(Finkelstein family collection)*
General Władysław Anders *(Farabola/Bridgeman Images)*
Dolu's commission *(Finkelstein family collection)*
Dolu, Lusia and Ludwik *(Finkelstein family collection)*
Ludwik and Lusia in Hendon *(Finkelstein family collection)*
Ludwik on Friday evening *(Finkelstein family collection)*
Lusia outside the family home *(Finkelstein family collection)*
Mirjam and Ludwik on their wedding day *(Finkelstein family collection)*
Mirjam and Ludwik on the beach *(Finkelstein family collection)*
Mirjam and Ludwik out to an engineering dinner *(Finkelstein family collection)*

Plate section 2:

Grete with her beloved sister Trude *(Finkelstein family collection)*
Grete in the late 1920s *(Finkelstein family collection)*
Jan van Eijckstraat *(Wiener Holocaust Library)*
Before the war: Betty from Amsterdam *(Finkelstein family collection)*
After the war: Betty from Nottingham *(Finkelstein family collection)*
The Wiener girls *(Finkelstein family collection)*
Trude Abraham with her son Fritz *(Finkelstein family collection)*
One of the family's yellow stars *(Finkelstein family collection)*
Mirjam *(Finkelstein family collection)*
Anne Frank *(United Archives GmbH/Alamy)*
The Wiener girls in America *(Finkelstein family collection)*
Aleksander Ładoś *(public domain)*
The blue cover of the Paraguayan passport *(Finkelstein family collection)*
The inside of the passport *(Finkelstein family collection)*
Camille Aronowski *(Finkelstein family collection)*
A painting by Eva of Alfred *(Finkelstein family collection)*
Alfred in his study *(Wiener Holocaust Library)*
Alfred shows President Theodor Heuss his name *(Wiener Holocaust Library)*
Mirjam *(Harry Borden)*

Index

Abraham, Fritz, 26, 66, 96, 98, 136, 267; death of at Sobibor (16 July 1943), 280, 281; deported to death camp, 277–9, 280

Abraham, Jan, 24, 25, 26, 66, 98, 146, 267; death of at Sobibor (16 July 1943), 280, 281; deported to death camp, 277–9, 280

Abraham, Trude (Aunt Nuti, Grete's sister), 24, 25, 26, 66, 96, 98, 134, 146, 267; death of at Sobibor (16 July 1943), 280; deported to death camp, 277–9, 280

Adams, Walter, 213

Adenauer, Konrad, 373, 374

Agudath Israel movement, 220

Albala, Jacques, 302–3, 305

Amster, Marion, 136, 139–40

Amsterdam: Anne Frank House, 149, 152–3, 154; apartment at 16 Jan van Eijckstraat, 67–8, 70–1, 73–4, 125–8, 135–6, 137, 145–6, 162, 163; Beethovenstraat (modern Jewish area), 66–7; De Boekenbron, bookseller, 147; fate of Jan van Eijckstraat's Jews, 137–42; First Montessori School, 69–70, 134, 150; Frank family in, 66, 68, 70, 146, 370; Franks go into hiding, 128, 149, 153–4, 170, 277; German occupation of, 128, 129–31, 132–42, 145–60; Grete and daughters remain in (1939), 93–9; 'Help for the Departing' team, 156–7; 'hunger winter' (1944-45), 174; institution of the Aryan Attestation, 135; Joods Lyceum (Jewish High School), 150–3; Joy and Glee Club, 135–41, 287; Liberaal Joodse Gemeente synagogue, 70; Marnixstraat prison, 169–70; Municipal Gymnasium senior school, 149–50; Municipal Lyceum senior school, 134; Nazi deportations of Jews from, 154–60, 165, 171–3, 267–9; and policy of 'evacuation to the East,' 151–2, 154–5; Vondelpark, 167; Weteringschans (Nazi prison), 170–2; Wiener family flees to (1933-4), 41, 65–6, 162, 163; Wiener family's life in 1930s, 65–71, 76, 88, 162, 163; Women's Swimming Club, 134

Anders, Władyslaw, 236–7, 241, 250, 251–2, 256, 260, 261–3, 334, 343

Anschluss (1938), 88, 89

antisemitism: barbaric Russian pogroms, 19, 81, 85; CV's fight against, 26–9, 30–3, 35–8; Évian Conference on Jewish refugees (1938), 88, 89; of Henry Ford, 81–3;

'Ford Tactic' on the *Protocols*, 82–3, 86; French in late-nineteenth-century, 85; increased levels in 1930s Poland, 58–9; Kristallnacht (9 November 1938), 88, 90, 91, 139; in Lwów of Great War era, 49; Nazi killing squads in Lwów, 337–8; Nazism's central confusion over, 144; pogrom in Lwów (June 1941), 337; in Polish universities, 58–9; *Protocols of the Elders of Zion*, 78–9, 80–7, 144, 294, 297, 316; ritual murder libel, 22, 26, 29; specific Nazi measures in Holland, 133, 146–60; in Weimar Germany, 17, 18, 21–3, 26–33, 35–8; yellow six-pointed star, 147–8, 164, 301, 327, 384; *see also* Holocaust; Wiener Library (Jewish Central Information Office)

Argentina, 339

Aronowski, Camille, 215, 293–8, 316, 320, 329

Aronsfeld, Caesar, 76

Asscher, Abraham, 130

Auschwitz concentration camp, 66–7, 138, 141, 142, 247, 272, 278, 281;

dismantling/evacuation of, 311; early reports on events at, 209; and Joseph Mengele, 370; Polish holders of *promesas* killed at, 322, 324

Austro-Hungarian Empire, 47–8, 49

Baer, Marcel de, 369

Bamberger, Hartog, 67

Bartel, Kazimierz, 52, 57, 59, 60, 112–13, 114, 200; murder of, 337

Bartlowa, Maria, 60, 200

BBC, 208, 209, 384

Belzec death camp, 338

Ben-Itto, Hadassa, *The Lie That Will Not Die*, 79, 83

Bentschen, Germany, 20

Bergen-Belsen concentration camp: British troops enter (15 April 1945), 299; daily life in, 300–9; deteriorating conditions in, 310–13, 316, 323, 324–5; as exchange camp, 290–1, 292, 299, 308, 310–11, 314, 315–16, 322; and fate of Amsterdam's Jews, 127, 138, 139, 140, 141–2, 326; Hungarians at, 310, 315–16; hunger at, 303, 304–5, 306–7, 308, 312–13; 'the Lost Train,' 138–9, 140, 326; medical exam for exchange prisoners, 324–6; rapid expansion from mid-1944, 310–13; roll calls at, 300–1, 304, 305–6, 308, 312; Star Camp, 301–10, 311, 315–16; Wiener family at, 4, 10, 300–13, 314–15; Wieners released from on exchange, 315, 316–17, 323–9, 347

Beria, Lavrentiy, 236–7, 385

Berlin: Academy for the Science of Judaism, 20; Betty Lewin's background in, 162, 174; Büro's office at Wilhelmstrasse, 36–8, 39–40, 74; Charlottenburg district of, 25–6, 42, 74; Jewish middle class in, 21, 24–6; Kapp putsch (March 1920), 17–18; wartime devastation of, 328; Wiener family life in, 25–6, 32, 39, 42, 76

Berlin, Isaiah, 213

Bettelheim, Josef, 126–7, 128

Bieber, Justin, 152–3

Bijllaardt, Tina van den, 156

Bitburg cemetery, West Germany, 4

Blüth, Ellen, 135, 136, 137, 139

B'nai B'rith Youth
  Organisation, 379
Bondy, Louis, 92–3
Borden, Harry, *Survivor*, 4,
  386
Bowes-Lyon, David, 213,
  363–4, 367, 368
Brezhnev, Leonid, 386
Brodnitz, Julius, 39–40, 41
Brunschvig, Georges, 78–9,
  81, 85, 87, 294
Buchenwald concentration
  camp, 139
Bullock, Alan, 370

Callaghan, James, 368–9
Central Association of German
  Citizens of the Jewish Faith
  (CV), 26–9, 30–3, 35–40,
  42, 74, 211–12
Chamberlain, Neville, 89, 93,
  94
Chichester, Lord, 99
Churchill, Winston, 212, 230,
  231, 341, 342, 343
City University, London, 381,
  387
Cohen, Abraham, 140–1
Cohen, David, 72, 73, 77, 89,
  91, 97, 268–9; as
  co-chairman of Jewish
  Council, 130, 147–8,
  157–8; and Jewish Central
  Information Office, 74,

91–2, 95, 126; wartime role
  of as controversial, 72,
  157–8
Cohen, Henriette, 140–1
Cohen, Jopie, 136, 137, 139,
  140–1
Cohen, Sammy, 136, 139,
  140–1
Cohn, Erich, 283
Cohn Strauss, Elfriede, 135,
  153
Colijn, Hendrikus, 91
communism, 32, 39, 62,
  114–15, 116, 181; Dutch,
  130; Polish, 111; *see also*
  Soviet Union
Crankshaw, Edward, 113
Cripps, Sir Stafford, 231
Crystal City, Texas, 322, 325
Cuba, 215, 295
Czechoslovakia, 89

Dambusters bombing raid, 209
Danzig, 61, 140
Day, Ida, 364–5, 384
Day, Kate, 365, 384
Day, Richard, 364–5, 384
Dearborn Independent, 82
Demjanjuk, John, 280
the Diamantsteins (Lusia's
  family), 336, 338–9;
  Wilhelm Diamantstein
  (brother of Lusia), 189–90,
  191–2, 203, 336, 338–9

Diels, Rudolf, 39
Dreyfus Affair, 85
Druijf, Estherina, 66–7
Duizend, Harold and Paul, 136, 137–8

East Germany, 5
Eden, Anthony, 277, 317, 367
Egyptology, 21
Eichmann, Adolf, 143, 291, 314, 315, 369
Einstein, Albert, 211
Eiss, Chaim, 220, 223
Erhard, Ludwig, 375
Évian Conference (1938), 88, 89

Fehl, Gustav, 46–7
Finkelstein, Adolf (Dolu, paternal grandfather of author): and army's move to Iran, 263, 334; arrest and disappearance of, 120–1, 177, 178, 179, 191, 202–3, 242–52; arrival in UK (27 August 1947), 343; asks Jules Thorn for help, 357–8, 381; belief in return to Lwów, 340; broken by the Gulag, 333, 335, 358; builds house on 12 Herburtów street, 45–6, 60–1; as businessman in Lwów, 50, 51, 54–5; character of, 55–6; commitment to modern Polish ideal, 53, 57, 60; death of (27 June 1950), 358, 359; false report of death of, 203, 238, 252; financially ruined by war, 115–16, 200, 343, 357; First World War service, 48, 49; and German language, 47; interrogations of at Brygidki prison, 243–5; life in Lwów, 45–6, 47, 50–7, 60–1, 380; life in UK, 357–8; Lusia looks for (1941), 238, 240–1, 252, 253; marries Lusia (1921), 50–1; name on list of "anti-Soviet elements", 117, 119; 'Nil Desperandum' (article, 1939), 59; in Palestine (1943-7), 335–6, 342–3; as Polish army reservist, 57, 106, 108, 111, 259; pride in his Jewishness, 56; reconnects with Lusia (late-1941), 252, 253–5, 333; released from Gulag due to amnesty, 250–1; reunion with Lusia (March 1942), 258–9; sent to Gulag in Komi Republic, 245–51, 333, 335; serves in the Anders army, 251–2,

253–5, 256–7, 259–64, 334–6, 342–3; serves on Lwów City Council, 54–7, 108, 111, 119; solo holiday in Krynica Górska, 106; transferred to Yangiyul (early 1942), 256, 258; in wartime Lwów, 107, 108, 111, 112–13, 114, 115–17; work in Gulag office, 250; works as logger at Gulag, 247–8, 249, 333

Finkelstein, Amalia (Lusia, paternal grandmother of author): arrest and deportation of, 121, 177–86; arrival in UK (27 August 1947), 343; background of, 50, 51; belief in return to Lwów, 340; chooses to leave Baskermelte (September 1941), 237–8; death of (1980), 359; Dorotea sends food parcels to, 190–2, 336, 339; draws up family tree, 339; endures Siberian winter, 192–6; forced labour on Soviet state farm, 187, 188–203, 229–30; journey to Iran (August 1942), 263–4; life in Lwów, 45–6, 47, 50–7, 60–1; life in UK, 7–8, 11, 339,

358–9, 381, 387, 388; looks for Dolu (1941), 238, 240–1, 252, 253; marries Dolu (1921), 50–1; office job at Baskermelte, 229–30; in Palestine (1943-7), 335, 343; personality of, 8, 50, 192, 263–4, 358, 359, 381; reconnects with Dolu (late-1941), 252, 253–5, 333; relationship with Mirjam, 359, 381; reunion with Dolu (March 1942), 258–9; in Semipalatinsk, 238–41, 253–5, 256–8; as teacher in London, 358–9; in Tehran (1942-3), 334–5; train journey to Yangiyul, 257–9; as unaware of Dolu's supposed death, 203, 238, 241, 252; in Veliko Alekseyevskaya (1942), 259, 261; in wartime Lwów, 107, 108, 112–13, 115–17

Finkelstein, Anthony (brother of author), 11, 387

Finkelstein, Bernard (brother of Dolu), 47, 51–2, 54, 107, 121, 179, 202–3, 243; death of (3 May 1943), 335–6

Finkelstein, Charlotte (mother of Dolu), 47–8, 117, 120, 177–83, 189, 191

Finkelstein, Karolina (Linka, wife of Bernard), 51, 179

Finkelstein, Ludwik (father of author): academic/professional career, 6, 380–1, 386–7; arrest and deportation of, 121, 177–86; arrival in UK (27 August 1947), 343; birth of in Lwów (6 December 1929), 52; childhood in Lwów, 46, 52–3, 56, 58; death of (2011), 381; endures Siberian winter, 192–6; at First Turkestan-Siberian Railway School, 239–40; forced labour on Soviet state farm, 188–203, 230–1; grandchildren of, 388; influence of Alfred on, 381–2; and intellectual matters, 6, 8, 10–11, 196–8, 230, 379–81, 382, 383, 386–7; journey to Iran (August 1942), 263–4; Judaism of, 10–11, 382; leaves Baskermelte (September 1941), 237–8; life in UK, 4–12, 358, 359, 379–84, 386–8; Lusia educates in Siberia, 195–6; meets and marries Mirjam, 359, 379–80, 381; never returns to Lwów, 340, 387; openness about experiences, 4–5, 387; in Palestine (1943-7), 335, 343; personality of, 4–7, 8, 9; practical plans for survival in Siberia, 196–8; rejection of victimhood, 386; reunion with Dolu (March 1942), 258–9; in Semipalatinsk, 238–41, 253–5, 256–8; in Tehran (1942-3), 334–5; train journey to Yangiyul, 257–9; in Veliko Alekseyevskaya (1942), 259, 261; victory over Hitler and Stalin, 388; view on nuclear disarmament, 383; in wartime Lwów, 105, 106–7, 108, 112, 115

Finkelstein, Maks (father of Dolu), 46–8, 51

Finkelstein, Mirjam (Mother of author): arrest and deportation of (20 June 1943), 158–60, 165, 267–9; arrival in New York (February 1945), 1, 351–2; arrival in Switzerland (24 January 1945), 328–9, 347–8; at Belsen, 4, 10, 299–313, 314–15; birth of in Berlin (10 June 1933), 42; childhood in Amsterdam, 65–71, 76, 88,

93–9, 125, 128, 132–6, 140, 145–58, 163–4; as citizen of Paraguay, 216, 217, 224–5, 292, 297–8, 314, 315, 316, 319–20, 322; death of (2017), 381; on death of her mother, 347; education of, 69–70, 134, 150, 151–2, 371; on Anne Frank, 152–3; friends offer to hide in Amsterdam, 155–6; gives talks on Holocaust, 10, 384; grandchildren of, 388; has hepatitis at Westerbork, 285; and intellectual matters, 9, 379–80, 381, 383; interrogated on Ellis Island, 351–2; joins father in London (1947), 371; journey to New York (February 1945), 349–51; Judaism of, 10–11, 308; life in UK, 4–5, 8–12, 359, 371, 372, 379–81, 383–5, 386–8; loss of German citizenship (1939), 94–5; meets and marries Ludwik, 359, 379–80, 381; meets Hilde Speer (2004), 384–5; on Nazi responsibility, 127; openness about experiences, 4–5, 384; personality of, 4, 8–11, 127, 381, 384–5;

photograph in Borden's *Survivor*, 4, 386; rejection of victimhood, 386; relationship with Lusia, 359, 381; released from Belsen on exchange, 315, 316–17, 323–9, 347; remains in Amsterdam (1939), 93–8; remembers Lazarus family, 281; scientific training, 9, 381; spoken voice of, 2, 5; summons to Belsen (January 1944), 292; teaching career, 9, 383, 384; train journey to Switzerland (21-4 January 1945), 327–9; as trapped in Holland (May 1940), 99, 210; in USA (1945-7), 364–6, 371, 384; victory over Hitler and Stalin, 388; in wartime Amsterdam, 125, 128, 132–6, 140, 145–58, 163–4; at Westerbork, 269–71, 272, 273–5, 282–92; on the yellow star, 148

Finkelstein, Nicky (wife of author), 2

Finkelstein, Tamara (sister of author), 2, 5, 8, 11, 387

Finkelstein and Fehl (business in Lwów), 46–7, 50, 52,

54–5, 57; nationalised by Soviets, 115

First World War, 18–19, 21, 22–3, 48, 49, 283

Fleischauer, Ulrich, 85

Ford, Henry, 81–3

France, 84–5, 106–7, 201, 321, 322

Frank, Anne, 66, 68, 70, 146, 308; at Belsen, 10, 311–12; diary of, 150, 152–3, 277, 370–1, 384; in hiding, 128, 149, 152–4, 170, 277

Frank, Edith, 66

Frank, Evelyne, 136, 139

Frank, Margot, 66, 70, 146, 149, 150, 152–4, 170, 308, 311–12

Frank, Otto, 66, 70, 154, 170, 370–1

Frankfurter, David, 79–80

Freemasonry, 85

Freie, Margrita, 149–50

Freud, Sigmund, 75

Fünten, Ferdinand aus der, 147, 157, 268

Gatz, Leopold, 338

Geller, Jay Howard, 90

Gemmeker, Albert, 274, 275, 276, 282–3, 285–6

gender roles, 25, 51, 129, 130

Germany: antisemitism in Weimar era, 18, 21–3, 26–33, 35–8; Beer Hall Putsch (1923), 28; hyperinflation in 1920s, 27; invasion of Poland (1939), 61, 107–8, 217–18; Jewish middle class, 21, 24–6; Kapp putsch (March 1920), 17–18; Kristallnacht (9 November 1938), 88, 90, 91, 139; Molotov-Ribbentrop Pact, 61–2, 106, 109, 231, 342, 385; Nazi era, 38–42, 73–7, 89–90, 91; Reichstag fire (February 1933), 39; Talmud Trial, 29; and Warsaw uprising (summer 1944), 342; Weimar Republic, 17–18, 25–32, 35–8; Alfred Wiener's love of, 19–20, 31, 372–4, 375–6; *see also* Berlin; Nazism

Goebbels, Joseph, 36, 76, 77

Goethe, Johann Wolfgang von, 'Das Göttliche,' 69

Göring, Hermann, 18, 39–41, 73, 74, 90, 144, 369

Goslar, Hanneli, 311–12

Graves, Philip, 82–3

Gripsholm (ship), 349–51, 373

Grüner, Dorotea (sister of Lusia), 51, 107, 184, 189–92, 194, 200–2; death of in

Lwów, 338–9; and Dolu's supposed death, 203, 238; sends food parcels to Lusia/Ludwik, 190–2, 336, 339

Grüner, Halina, 107, 191, 338–9

Grüner, Szymon (Szymek), 107, 189, 192, 200, 336, 338–9

Gyssling, Walter, 36

Hagemeister, Michael, 85
Hahn, Harald, 136
Haiti, 222
Hamilton, Duke of, 209
Helm-Pirgo, Marian, 193, 255
Hendon, 2–3, 7–8, 11–12, 339, 388
Hess, Rudolf, 209
Heuss, Theodor, 374
Heydrich, Reinhard, 143, 144–5
Himmler, Heinrich, 138, 145, 273, 337, 342; Eva watches at Belsen, 314; plan to ransom Jews, 271–2, 290–1, 299, 310–11, 314, 315–16
Hindenburg, President, 38
Hitler, Adolf: becomes Chancellor (January 1933), 38–9; belief in the *Protocols*, 83, 144; bomb plot against (20 July 1944), 38; Henry

Ford's influence on, 83; hatred of Jewish intellectuals, 21; invasion of Soviet Union (22 June 1941), 202, 209, 219, 229–31, 336; and Munich Agreement (October 1938), 89; personal cowardice of, 37; political emergence of, 28, 35–6; secret appendix to pact with Stalin, 61, 62, 106, 109–10, 385; *Mein Kampf*, 35–6

Holländer, Ludwig, 30–1

Holocaust: Alfred keeps Wiener Library alive postwar, 367–9; Alfred on personal impact of, 373; and Alfred's German identity, 19–20; Allied failure to grasp nature of, 209–10, 316–21; betrayals, 169, 172, 267, 281; Borden's *Survivor*, 4, 386; closure of Paraguay escape route, 224–5, 298; 'death marches,' 281, 311; debates about complicity of the Dutch, 71–2; 'evacuation to the East' as euphemism for mass murder, 145, 151–2, 154–5; fate of Lwów's Jews after Barbarossa, 336–9; and form-filling/

bureaucracy, 133, 154; general silence about in postwar West, 365–7, 383–4; and Himmler's plan to ransom Jews, 271–2, 290–1, 299, 315–16; Holocaust studies (academic field), 370; Jewish quest for foreign documentation, 219–25, 295–8, 319–20, 321, 322–4; Ładoś Group in Switzerland, 218–25, 296–8, 316, 319–20, 321, 322, 380; 'the Lost Train,' 138–9, 140, 326; mapping and counting of victims, 75; mass-murder process at Sobibor, 279–81; and Mirjam's Judaism, 11; Mirjam's talks on, 10, 384; mistake by Jewish Council leaders (May 1943), 157–8; Morgenthau and US Jewish policy, 320–1, 323; murder of Amsterdam's Jews, 66–7, 130, 137–42, 151–2, 154, 267, 271, 272, 274–81, 291–2; and 'Palestine exchange,' 216, 272–3, 282–3, 297–8, 314–15; processing of the shoes of murdered Jews, 303–4; right place to flee to as unknowable, 60; Wannsee Conference (January 1942), 143–5, 154; War Refugee Board in USA, 317, 321–2, 323–4, 347–9; Warsaw ghetto, 222, 342; widespread knowledge of by end of 1942, 277, 316–17; Wiener Library's eyewitness statements, 370; see also Auschwitz concentration camp; Bergen-Belsen concentration camp; Westerbork camp; Wiener Library (Jewish Central Information Office)

Hondius, Dienke, 151
Honduras, 222
Hügli, Rudolf, 218–19, 220, 221, 222–3, 225, 298, 322

Iran, 261–4, 334–5
Iraq, 334
Islam, 34
Israel, 84, 367, 369, 372
Israel Philatelist, 139
Ivanovna, Vera, 239–40

Janowska forced labour camp, 338
Jewish Council of Amsterdam: criticism of, 130, 157–8, 163; few remaining employees of (1943), 268; and Grete's wartime work,

129, 130–1, 146, 154–5, 163–4; levy imposed by, 146; moral dilemmas faced by, 129, 130, 147–8, 155, 157–8; Nazis order creation of (12 February 1941), 129–30, 135; refugee committee as answerable to, 130; workers exempt from deportation, 154–5, 163–4, 165

Jewish life/communities: in 1930s Amsterdam, 66–71, 72–3, 88–9, 90–1, 96–8, 162–3; community leaders in Switzerland, 220, 223–4, 296; education and gender, 51; and the German language in Poland, 47; in Lwów, 47, 49–50, 53–7, 58–61, 337; middle class in Germany, 21, 24–6; in Nazi Germany, 38–42, 73–7, 89–90, 91; in occupied Amsterdam, 125–8, 129–31, 132–42, 145–58, 164–5, 166–7; and Piłsudski's death in Poland (1935), 57–8; in Weimar Germany, 20, 21–9, 30–8; *see also* antisemitism; Judaism

Joly, Maurice, 83, 84, 85

Judaism: at Belsen, 308–9; family meals in Hendon, 11, 388; and German identity, 25, 31–3, 35; of Grete, 25, 70–1, 308; Grete's funeral in Kreuzlingen, 348; Liberaal Joodse Gemeente synagogue, Amsterdam, 70; of Ludwik, 10–11, 382; in Lwów, 53–4, 56–7, 337; of Mirjam, 10–11, 308; Pirkei Avot, 68–9; of Ruth, 135, 153, 287, 308, 309; survival of, 388; and 'Talmud Trial,' 29; in wartime Amsterdam, 135, 153; in Westerbork, 287, 308, 309; of Alfred Wiener, 20, 25, 31, 68–9, 70–1, 153, 382

Juliana, Queen, 139

Kahle, Paul, 21

Kapp, Wolfgang, 17–18

Katyn Massacre, 232–6, 255–6, 261, 340–1, 385

Kharkov prison, 235

Khrushchev, Nikita, 113–15, 180–1

Kieloch, Wojczek, 257–8

Kiev prison, 245

Kistryn, Mieczysław, 60

Klau, Bella, 138

Klau, Oscar, 138, 140

Klau, Resa, 138

Klau, Ursula, 136, 138–9

Klemens, Michael, 290, 382

Klemens, Paul, 372, 382–3

Klemens, Ruth (sister of Mirjam): arrest and deportation of (20 June 1943), 158–60, 165, 267–9; arrival in New York (February 1945), 351–2; arrival in Switzerland (24 January 1945), 328–9, 347–8; attends Grete's funeral in Kreuzlingen, 348; at Belsen, 299–313, 314–15; birth of (1927), 25; childhood in Amsterdam, 66–71, 76, 88, 93–8, 125, 128, 132–7, 140, 145–58, 163–4; childhood in Berlin, 26, 32, 39, 76; as citizen of Paraguay, 216, 217, 224–5, 292, 297–8, 314, 315, 316, 319–20, 322; diary notes at Westerbork/Belsen, 273–4, 277, 283, 290, 291–2, 302, 306–7, 308, 310, 313, 315; on the Frank sisters, 152, 153; as 'helper' at Westerbork, 276; interrogated on Ellis Island, 351–2; joins father in London (1947), 371; journey to New York (February 1945), 349–51; Judaism of, 135, 153, 287, 308, 309; letter from Grete on her sixteenth birthday, 287–90; loss of German citizenship (1939), 94–5; marries and moves to Australia (1950), 371–2, 382–3; released from Belsen on exchange, 315, 316–17, 323–9, 347; remains in Amsterdam (1939), 93–8; summons to Belsen (January 1944), 292; as teacher in America, 383; throws Alfred's war medals in sea, 1, 350, 373, 375; train journey to Switzerland (21-4 January 1945), 327–9; as trapped in Holland (May 1940), 99, 210; in USA (1945-7), 364–6, 371; in wartime Amsterdam, 125, 128, 132, 133–7, 140, 145–58, 163–4; at Westerbork, 269–71, 272, 273–5, 276, 277, 282–92

Klemens, Susan, 382

Klugerman, Jack, 139, 140

Knapper, Marianne, 136, 140–1

Knapper, Nico, 140–1

Kobe, Japanese city of, 219
Komi Republic, 246–9
Kozelsk camp (near
    Smolensk), 233, 235
Kristallnacht (9 November
    1938), 88, 90, 91, 139
Krynica Górska, Southern
    Poland, 106
Kühl, Juliusz, 218, 219,
    220–2, 223–4, 296–7, 316
Kuryłło, Adam, 60

Ładoś, Aleksander, 217–19,
    224, 320, 322–3, 324
Landes, Ignacy (Nasio), 183,
    189–90, 191–2, 202–3,
    246, 249
Landesberg, Markus, 59
Lazarus, Else, 146, 267, 274;
    death of at Auschwitz, 281
Lazarus, Marion, 146, 267, 281
Leeuw, Louis de, 66
Lévy-Hass, Hanna, 313
Lewin, Betty, 66, 67–8, 71,
    97, 129, 134, 148–9, 157,
    296, 370; in Amsterdam
    during last days of war,
    174; arrest of (20 June
    1943), 158–60, 165;
    arrested and interrogated by
    Gestapo (January 1944),
    168–72; background of,
    162–3; as 'Betty from
    Nottingham,' 161–2, 174;

escape from Nazis (20 June
    1943), 165–6; in hiding as
    Jo Bosch (1943-44), 166–8;
    as resistance hero, 174;
    second escape from Nazis
    (at Assen), 172–4; wartime
    work for Jewish Council,
    163–4, 165; works for
    Dutch resistance (as Jo
    Bosch), 164–8
Lewin, Rabbi Ezekiel, 337
liberal democracy, 2–3, 387–8
Liskow, Alfred, 229
London: Alfred's attempt to
    obtain visas for family
    (1940), 98–9, 210; Ford's
    Hotel, 92, 93, 95, 129;
    Hendon, 2–3, 7–8, 11–12,
    339, 388; Jewish Central
    Information Office moves
    to, 92–3, 125–6, 207;
    Polish administration-in-
    exile, 217–18, 219, 231,
    262, 317, 341–2; Wiener
    family together in (1947),
    371; Alfred Wiener in
    during war, 98–9, 125–6,
    129, 163, 207–10
Lübke, Heinrich, 375
Lwów (formerly Lemberg, now
    Lviv): becomes part of
    Soviet Ukraine, 115–16,
    252, 385–6; Brygidki
    prison, 242–5, 335, 336–7;

deaths of the Diamantsteins, 336, 338–9; Dolu and Lusia's life in, 45–6, 47, 50–7, 60–1; fall of to Soviets, 110–13, 232; fate of decided in secret agreement, 108–10; fate of Jews after Barbarossa, 336–9; Finkelstein and Fehl (family business), 46–7, 50, 52, 54–5, 57, 115; Finkelstein home at 12 Herburtów street, 45–6, 60–1, 116–17, 385–6; impact of First World War on, 49–50; IV Gymnasium school, 48, 380; Jan Kazimierz University, 51, 58–9; Jews flee to avoid Russians (1914), 49, 51; Khrushchev's crimes in, 114–15, 117–21, 242–52; lists of "anti-Soviet elements, 117–19; Ludwik never returns to, 340, 387; and outbreak of war, 105–6; pogrom in (June 1941), 337; Polytechnic, 58, 59; in postwar Soviet Union, 342; Red Army liberates (summer 1944), 341–2; Soviet mass deportations from, 119–21, 177–86; Soviets shoot prisoners (June 1941), 336–7; Tempel Synagogue, 53–4, 337; wartime bombing of, 105–6, 107; Zalewski confectionery shop, 52

Maarsen, Jacqueline van, 68
Maisky, Ivan, 232
Mauthausen concentration camp, 130, 142
Mazzucato, Aleksander, 60, 113
McClelland, Roswell, 317, 323, 347–8
Mehler, Jacob, 70
Meijer, Jaap, 287
Mengele, Joseph, 370
Meyer, Walter, 222–3
Mikes, George, *How to be an Alien*, 376
Miloslawski, Dorothee, 68, 136, 138
Miloslawski, Max, 138
Molotov, Vyacheslav, 61, 106, 109, 231, 236
Montefiore, Leonard, 367–8
Moorhouse, Roger, 106
Morgan, Kenneth O., 368
Morgenthau Jr, Henry, 320–1, 323
Mös, Ernst, 314, 315, 324
Munich Agreement (October 1938), 88, 89

Nazism: anti-Christian

literature, 37; antisemitism
in Weimar era, 26–33,
35–8; Beer Hall Putsch
(1923), 28; Büro's
monitoring of activities,
36–8, 39–40, 74; CV's
fight against, 26–9, 30–3,
35–8; economic boycott of
Jewish business, 72;
economics of, 24–5;
Gestapo, 168–9; Himmler's
plan to ransom Jews,
271–2, 290–1, 299,
310–11, 314, 315–16;
hostility to elites, 62; policy
of forced Jewish emigration,
144; revoking of citizenship,
94–5; the SS, 143, 147,
157, 172, 173, 268, 290–1,
328; Waffen-SS, 300,
302–3, 312; Wannsee
Conference (January 1942),
143–5, 154; *see also* Hitler,
Adolf
Nenza, Monika (Teta), 52
Netherlands: building of
Westerbork, 90–1, 270;
compliance of authorities
with Nazi persecution,
149–50; confidence over
wartime neutrality, 97;
Dutch behaviour towards
Jews before the occupation,
72–3, 74, 89, 90–2; Dutch

behaviour towards Jews
during the occupation,
71–2, 130, 133, 148,
149–50, 155–6, 284–5;
Dutch Jewish support for
new refugees, 72–3, 89,
90–1, 96, 129, 130–1,
139–40, 154–5; Dutch list
of Palestine certificates, 216;
Dutch Nazis, 130, 169,
171, 284–5; Dutch
resistance, 130, 164–8, 174;
German invasion of (May
1940), 62, 125, 163, 210;
German Jews flee to in
1930s, 66–7, 70, 71, 72–3,
90–1, 162; 'hunger winter'
(1944-45), 174; and policy
of 'evacuation to the East,'
151–2, 154–5; and return
of Jewish refugees to
Germany, 73, 77; specific
Nazi anti-Jewish measures,
133, 146–60; survival rate
of Jews in, 151; *see also*
Amsterdam; Westerbork
camp
Neuburger, Erika, 308, 311,
312, 326
Neuburger, Marion, 308, 326
New York City, 1, 207,
211–14, 272, 294, 350–1,
363–7, 375
Nicholas II, Tsar, 84

Nilus, Sergei Aleksandrovich, 80–1, 84

NKVD (Soviet secret police), 111, 115, 116, 119–21, 177–8, 233–7, 242–6, 261, 336–7, 341

Nottingham, 161–2, 174

nuclear power/weapons, 383

Nuremberg trials, 369, 385

Oppenheimer, Hans (John), 211–12, 294

Ostashkov camp (near Kalinin), 233, 235

Ostrowski, Stanisław, 108, 109, 110–11, 119, 260

Palestine, 33–5, 57, 215–16, 318; Finkelsteins in (1943-7), 335–6, 342–3; 'Palestine exchange,' 216, 272–3, 282–3, 297–8, 314–15

Paneth, Aldona, 53

Papen, Franz von, 38

Paraguay: fake passports, 217, 224–5, 296–8, 314, 315–16, 319–20, 321–3, 348–9; honorary consul in Bern, 218–19, 220, 221, 222–5, 322; and the Ładoś Group, 219–21, 222–5, 296, 320, 321; Nazi sympathisers in, 320; Wieners as 'citizens' of, 216,

217, 224–5, 292, 297–8, 314, 315, 316, 319–20, 322

Peru, 222

Philippeville, Algeria, 349

Philips-Wiener, Lotte, 372

Pilet-Golaz, Marcel, 222

Piłsudski, Józef, 48, 53, 57–8

Piotrowski, Tadeusz, 117

Pirgo, Dorota and Ewa, 193, 238, 239, 255

Planck, Erwin, 38

Plaut, Alice, 216, 372

Plaut, Eva (sister of Mirjam): arrest and deportation of (20 June 1943), 158–60, 165, 267–9; arrival in New York (February 1945), 351–2; arrival in Switzerland (24 January 1945), 328–9, 347–8; at Belsen, 299–313, 314–15; birth of (1930), 25; childhood in Amsterdam, 39, 65, 66, 70, 93–9, 125, 128, 132–7, 140, 145–58, 163–4; as citizen of Paraguay, 216, 217, 224–5, 292, 297–8, 314, 315, 316, 319–20, 322; death of (1977), 382; has hepatitis at Westerbork, 285; interrogated on Ellis Island, 351–2; joins father in London (1947), 371;

journey to New York
(February 1945), 349–51;
and Judaism, 308; loss of
German citizenship (1939),
94–5; marries Ted Plaut,
372, 382; released from
Belsen on exchange, 315,
316–17, 323–9, 347;
remains in Amsterdam
(1939), 93–8; summons to
Belsen (January 1944), 292;
testimony on time at
Belsen, 311–12; train
journey to Switzerland
(21-4 January 1945),
327–9; as trapped in
Holland (May 1940), 99,
210; in USA (1945-7),
364–6, 371; in wartime
Amsterdam, 125, 128, 132,
133–7, 140, 145–58,
163–4; at Westerbork,
269–71, 272, 273–5,
282–92

Plaut, Ted, 372, 382

Polak, Samuel, 66

Poland: administration-in-
exile, 217–18, 219, 231,
262, 317, 341–2; amnesty
(accord with Soviets, 30
July 1941), 231–2, 237–8,
240–1, 250–1; and Anglo-
Soviet agreement (12 July
1941), 231; antisemitism in

universities, 58–9; Bartel as
Prime Minister of, 52, 57;
creation of Polish state
(1918), 47; exiles in Siberia
'freed' (September 1941),
237–8; fate of decided at
Yalta (February 1945), 342,
343; fate of Jews after
Barbarossa, 336–9; and
Hitler-Stalin secret
agreement, 61, 62, 106,
109–10, 385; increased
antisemitism in 1930s,
58–9; invaded by Nazis and
Soviets (1939), 61–2,
107–9, 217–18, 385;
Khrushchev's crimes in
Eastern areas, 114–15,
117–21, 177–86, 242–52;
Lwów ghetto, 338; Nazi
discovery of Katyn, 340–1;
non-aggression pact with
Hitler, 57–8; officers as
prisoners of Soviets, 110;
Polish army in East (from
1941, Anders army), 232,
236–7, 241, 250, 251–2,
253–4, 256, 259–64,
334–5, 342–3; Polish
Home Army, 341–2; Polish-
Soviet War, 48; Soviet mass
deportations from Eastern
areas, 119–21, 177–86,
385; Soviet mass murder of

officers, 232–6, 255–6, 261, 340–1, 385; Soviet policy of disorder in, 112; Stalin's murdering of elite, 105, 232–6, 255–6, 261, 340–1, 385; Warsaw ghetto, 222, 342; *see also* Lwów (formerly Lemberg, now Lviv)

Polanska, Maria, 183

Pollack, Leo and Lina, 67

Poppelsdorf, Juda, 66–7

Posthuma de Boer, Eddy, 137–8

Potocka, Countess, 193, 195, 238

Potocka, Zosia, 193–4, 196

Potsdam, Germany, 19

Presser, Jacob, 152

Prins, Ralph, 135, 136, 137, 139

Protocols of the Elders of Zion, 78–9, 80–7, 144, 294, 297, 316

Puls, Abraham, 284–5

Putin, Vladimir, 386

Puttkammer, Erich, 272

Reading, Marquess of, 368

Reagan, Ronald, 4

Reichmann, Eva, 19, 30, 370

Reichmann, Hans, 36

Reitlinger, Gerald, *Final Solution*, 370

Ribbentrop, Joachim von, 61, 106, 109, 218, 369

Rokicki, Konstanty, 218, 221, 224

Roosevelt, Dineke, 292

Roosevelt, Franklin Delano, 89, 318, 320–1, 342

Rothmund, Heinrich, 222–3

Rothschild, Lothar, 348

Russian Empire, 19, 48, 49, 51, 80–1, 84, 85

Ryniewicz, Stefan, 218

Saulmann, Gertrud, (*see* Abraham, Gertrud)

Schrage, Aldona, 53, 179, 234, 235, 255

Schrage, Ignacy, 53, 54, 110, 179, 232, 233, 234–5, 255, 385

Schrage, Jadzia, 53, 179, 234, 235, 255

Schulthess-Hirsch, Fanny, 220, 223–4

Second World War: Anders army at Monte Cassino, 335; becomes inevitable in Nineteen thirty-eight, 88–90; D-Day landings (6 June 1944), 309–10; in Dorotea's coded letters to Siberia, 201–2; Dutch resistance, 130, 164–8, 174; German invasion of

Holland (May 1940), 62, 125, 163, 210; Germans sign unconditional surrender (7 May 1945), 138; Germany's deteriorating military position, 310–13, 316; Nazi invasion of Soviet Union (22 June 1941), 202, 209, 219, 229–31, 336; outbreak of, 61, 93, 94, 105–7, 207; Pearl Harbor and US entry (1941), 212–13; Polish resistance, 341–2; Stalingrad, 271

Semipalatinsk (Kazakhstan), 238–41, 253–5, 256–8

Seyss-Inquart, Arthur, 369

Sikorski, Władysław, 231, 232, 341

Silberschein, Abraham, 220, 223–4, 296

Slottke, Gertrud, 290, 291, 292, 298, 300, 313, 315, 324, 325, 327

Sobibor death camp, 138, 140–1, 142, 278–81

Soep, Rini, 136, 139

South America, 219–20, 222, 224, 292, 296, 297, 308, 314, 315, 323; Alfred's supply line through, 211, 212; Allied anxieties over spies in, 319; Allied efforts to block fake passports from, 319–20, 322; Nazis start to kill passport holders, 322, 324; US round-up of Germans living in, 321–2, 323–4, 325, 327; see also Paraguay

Soviet Union: amnesty (accord with the Poles, 30 July 1941), 231–2, 237–8, 240–1, 250–1; and Anders army, 232, 236–7, 241, 250, 251–2, 253–4, 256, 259–64; Baskermelte ranch, Siberia, 187–91, 192–202, 229–30, 237–8; collectivisation of agriculture, 187–8; fall of Lwów to, 110–13, 232; forced labour on state farms, 187–203, 229–30; the Gulag, 247–51, 333, 335; invasion of Poland (1939), 61, 108–10, 217–18, 385; and 'judicial processes,' 179–80; Khrushchev's crimes in Eastern Poland, 114–15, 117–21, 177–86, 242–52; Khrushchev's de-Stalinization, 113; lists of "anti-Soviet elements, 117–19; mass deportations from Eastern Poland,

119–21, 177–86, 385; mass murder of Polish officers, 232–6, 255–6, 261, 340–1, 385; Molotov-Ribbentrop Pact, 61–2, 106, 109, 231, 342, 385; Nazi invasion of (22 June 1941), 202, 209, 219, 229–31, 336; Polish exiles in Siberia 'freed' (September 1941), 237–8; Polish-Soviet War, 48; shooting of prisoners in Lwów (June 1941), 336–7; silence over crimes of, 385–6; and Warsaw uprising (summer 1944), 342; *see also* Stalin, Joseph

Speer, Hilde, 365, 384–5

Stahl, Artur, 45–6

Stalin, Joseph: agriculture collectivised by, 187–8; and the Anders army, 260–3; desire to destroy Polish nation, 180; ignores warnings about Barbarossa, 229; installs communist government in Poland, 341, 342; lack of public interest in crimes of, 385–6; looks to West after Barbarossa, 230–1; murdering of Polish elite, 105, 232–6, 255–6, 261, 340–1, 385; and Polish-Soviet War, 48; secret

appendix to pact with Hitler, 61, 62, 106, 109–10, 385; and Warsaw uprising (summer 1944), 342; at Yalta (February 1945), 342

Starobelsk camp (Ukraine), 233–4, 245

Sternbuch family, 220

Streamline Moderne (architectural style), 45–6

Streicher, Julius, 29

Stucki, Karl, 222–3

Der Stürmer (anti-Semitic journal), 26, 28, 29, 37, 77

Stutthof concentration camp, 140

Switzerland: Alfred and Grete's holidays in, 66; Alfred's contacts in, 87, 215, 284, 293–8, 316, 320, 329, 348; Alfred's supply line through, 211, 212; attitude to Jewish exchange refugees, 348–9; Bern Trial of the *Protocols*, 79, 80, 81, 83–7, 144, 294, 297, 316; concern about neutrality, 218, 293–5; elite antisemitic/pro-Nazi opinion in, 222–3; Jewish community leaders in, 220, 223–4, 296; Ładoś Group exposed (April 1943), 223–5, 322; Ładoś Group in, 218–25, 296–8, 316, 319–20, 321, 322, 380; Mirjam's holiday in (1951), 379; Nazi rally in the Bern Casino, 78; Paraguayan honorary consul in, 218–19, 220, 221, 222–5, 322; Swiss Nazi Party, 78, 79–80; Wieners arrive in (24 January 1945), 328–9, 347–8

Szlengel, Władysław, 222

Tel Aviv, 335, 343
the Templers (Lutheran sect), 272–3, 314
Theresienstadt concentration camp, 139
Thorn, Antonia, 357
Thorn, Jules, 115, 357–8, 381
Tijn, Gertrude van: at Belsen, 306, 314–15; as confident of Dutch neutrality (autumn 1939), 97; leaves Belsen in exchange (June 1944), 315; and 'Palestine exchange,' 216, 273, 314–15; and refugee committee in Amsterdam, 72–3, 89, 129, 130, 139–40, 148, 154–5, 158, 163, 215, 270; split with David Cohen, 158; wartime role of as

controversial, 72
Tobler, Theodor, 85
Totskoye (camp of Anders army), 251–2, 253–4, 256
Treblinka death camp, 280

Ukhta (town in Komi Republic), 247, 250
Ukraine, Soviet, 109, 113, 114–15, 252, 342, 385–6
Ukrainians: in Lwów, 47, 48, 49, 51, 112, 336–7, 385–6; Soviets shoot prisoners (June 1941), 336–7
United Kingdom: active work to undue efforts of Ładoś Group, 318–20; Alfred's postwar life in, 367–71, 372–6, 381–2; allies with Soviets after Barbarossa, 230; army in Middle East, 261–4, 334; attitude to Anders army, 262; declares war on Germany (3 September 1939), 93, 94, 106–7, 207; and Évian Conference (1938), 89; failure to grasp nature of Holocaust, 209–10, 316–21; fear of mass release/rescue of Jews, 318; Finkelsteins arrive in (27 August 1947), 343; Hess flies to (May 1941), 209;

knowledge of Katyn, 341; knowledge of the Holocaust, 277, 316–17; Nazi failure to defeat, 201–2; and Palestine, 89, 215–16, 315, 318; Political Warfare Executive, 208; Political Warfare Mission in USA, 213–14, 363–4; *Protocols of the Elders of Zion* in, 81; as wary of exchanges, 318–19, 320–1; and Wiener Library during war, 207–9, 211–14, 363–4, 367; *see also* London

United Nations war crimes commission, 369

United States: active work to undue efforts of Ładoś Group, 318–20; attitude to Jewish exchange refugees, 350, 351–2; British Political Warfare Mission in, 213–14, 363–4; enters war after Pearl Harbor (1941), 212–13; and Évian Conference (1938), 89; failure to grasp nature of Holocaust, 316–21; FBI investigates Wiener Library, 212; fear of mass release/rescue of Jews, 318; Hitler's view of, 144; Morgenthau and Jewish policy, 320–1, 323; policy on fake South American papers, 321–4; public opinion on war (1940), 212; round-up of Germans living in Latin American, 321–2, 323–4, 325; War Refugee Board, 317, 321–2, 323–4, 347–9; as wary of exchanges, 318–19, 320–3, 350, 351–2; Wiener daughters in (1945-7), 364–6, 371; Alfred Wiener in during war, 207, 211–16, 272, 294; Alfred Wiener's work with State Department, 207, 212; *see also* New York City

Urbach, Lola (sister of Dolu), 47, 107, 335–6, 357
Urbach, Robert, 107
Uzbekistan, 256, 259

V-2 rockets, 310
Versailles Peace Conference, 81
Vienna, 46, 47, 48, 51, 75, 107, 357
Vittel internment camp, France, 322

Walmsley, Robert, 210
Wannsee Conference (January 1942), 143–5, 154
Wasserstein, Bernard, 72

Weill, Yvonne, 294, 296–7, 316

Weingort, Shaul, 223

Weizmann, Chaim, 84, 97

West Germany, 4, 372–4, 375, 376

Westerbork camp: building of, 90–1, 270; daily life in, 271, 284, 285–7, 308, 309; deportation process, 274–6, 277–9, 291–2; fight to stay off the death lists at, 271, 272–3, 274–5, 282–4, 291–2; Grete's letter to Ruth on her sixteenth birthday, 287–90; as holding camp for gas chambers, 154, 163, 267, 271, 272, 274, 278–9; national monument for, 139; old-timers at, 270–1, 274, 283; transportations to, 139, 140, 154–5, 157–60, 163–4, 171–3, 267–9; Van Tijn's team send aid to, 155, 163–4; Wieners arrive in (June 1943), 269–71, 327; Wieners depart for Belsen (January 1944), 299–300, 320

Wheeler-Bennett, John, 213–14

Wieler, Robert, 348, 379

Wiener, Alfred (maternal grandfather of author): analysis of Nazi/far-right antisemitism, 21–3, 144, 316–17; attempts to obtain visas for family (1940-43), 98–9, 210, 214–16, 295–8; awarded West German Grand Cross of Merit, 373, 374; and Bern Trial of the *Protocols*, 79, 80, 81, 83–7, 144, 294, 297, 316; book collection stolen by Dutch Nazis, 284–5; on broader problem of racism, 374; and Büro's monitoring of Nazi activities, 36–8, 39–40, 74; collecting of Nazi material while in USA, 211, 212, 293–5; collection of Oriental antiquities, 67, 147; confrontation with Kapp (March 1920), 17–18; as constantly working, 26, 30–1, 76, 80, 88, 163, 364; critique of Zionism, 33–5; death of (4 February 1964), 375; family life in Berlin, 25–6, 32, 39, 42, 76; family remains in Amsterdam (1939), 93–9; financial problems after outbreak of war, 95–6, 128–9; First World War service, 18–19, 21, 283; at Ford's Hotel, London, 92, 93, 95; and David Frankfurter case, 79–80; friendship with Otto Frank, 370–1; and Henry Ford's antisemitism, 81–3; influence on Ludwik, 381–2; informed of Grete's death, 329; intellectual interests, 20–1, 24, 25, 34, 67, 68–9, 382; intelligence work during war, 1, 207–10, 211–14, 294, 363–4; Judaism of, 20, 25, 31, 68–9, 70–1, 153, 382; keeps Library alive postwar, 367–9; leading role in CV, 26–9, 30–3, 35–8; leaves Germany (summer 1933), 41–2; and legal strategy against antisemitism, 29, 79–80; life in Amsterdam (1930s), 65–71, 73–7, 162, 163; life in Nazi Germany (1933), 39–42; life in postwar UK, 367–71, 372–6, 381–2; in London during war, 98–9, 125–6, 129, 163, 207–10; loss of German citizenship (1939), 94–5; love of Germany, 19–20, 31, 372–4, 375–6; marries Margarete (1921), 24; meeting with Göring (3 March 1933), 18, 39–40, 73, 74; near obsession with books, 20, 67, 284–5, 371, 382; nervous breakdowns/ collapses, 30, 41, 73–4, 210; in New York City during war, 207, 211–16, 272, 294; and 'Palestine exchange,' 216, 273, 297–8, 314–15; and Paraguyan passports, 225, 295–8, 320; on personal impact of Holocaust, 373; personality of, 17–18, 19, 30–1, 76, 92–3, 213–14; and Political Warfare Mission in USA, 213–14, 363–4; postwar returns to Germany, 372–4; returns to London (March 1945), 364, 367; reunited with daughters in New York (February 1945), 352, 363–4, 375; second marriage to Lotte Philips, 372; secures place on *Gripsholm* for daughters, 349–51; tour of Palestine (1926), 33; truth/rational argument as paramount for, 18, 23, 25, 29, 30, 33, 80, 375; as victim of Cuban visa scam, 215, 295; war medals of, 1, 19, 159, 283,

350, 373, 375; 'Between Heaven and Earth' (article), 42; *A Critical Journey through Palestine* (1927), 33–5; *Prelude to Pogroms* (tract, 1919), 21–3; *see also* Wiener Library (Jewish Central Information Office)

Wiener, Amalie (Alfred's mother), 66

Wiener, Eva (*see* Plaut, Eva)

Wiener, Margarete (Grete, maternal grandmother of author): and Alfred's attempts to obtain visas (1940-43), 98–9, 210, 214–16, 295–8; arrest and deportation of (20 June 1943), 158–60, 165, 267–9; arrival in Switzerland (24 January 1945), 328–9, 347–8; at Belsen, 299–313, 314–15; birth of children, 25, 42; as 'citizen' of Paraguay, 216, 217, 224–5, 292, 297–8, 314, 315, 316, 319–20, 322; conflict-related relief work, 24; death of (25 January 1945), 329, 347–8, 383; deteriorating health at Belsen, 312, 313, 315, 325, 328; family life in Berlin, 25–6, 32, 39, 76; farewell letter from sister Trude, 277–8; financial problems after outbreak of war, 95–6, 128–9, 130–1, 134, 145–7; grave of in Kreuzlingen, 348, 379; and incriminating material at family home (1940), 125–8; intellectual/ academic life, 24–5, 27, 69, 129; and Jewish Central Information Office, 88, 125–8; and Jewish community's refugee work in Amsterdam, 73, 88, 89, 90, 96, 139–40; Judaism of, 25, 70–1, 308; letter to Ruth on her sixteenth birthday, 287–90; life in Amsterdam (1930s), 66–71, 72–3, 88–90, 162, 163; life in Nazi Germany (1933-34), 39–42; loss of German citizenship (1939), 94–5; marries Alfred (1921), 24; and 'Palestine exchange,' 216, 272–3, 282–3, 297–8, 314–15; passes Belsen medical exam, 326; personality of, 68, 326; preparations for deportation, 156–7; released from Belsen on exchange, 315, 316–17, 323–9, 347; remains in Amsterdam

(1939), 93–8; role played in Alfred's work, 33, 67, 88, 95, 129; summons to Belsen (January 1944), 292; tour of Palestine (1926), 33; train journey to Switzerland (21-4 January 1945), 327–9; as trapped in Holland (May 1940), 99, 210; truth/rational argument as paramount for, 24–5; turns down offer to hide Mirjam, 155–6; in wartime Amsterdam, 125–9, 130–1, 132, 133–7, 145–58, 163–4; wartime work for van Tijn/Jewish Council, 129, 130–1, 146, 154–5, 163–4; at Westerbork, 269–71, 272, 273–8, 282–92

Wiener, Mirjam (see Finkelstein, Mirjam)

Wiener, Ruth (see Klemens, Ruth)

Wiener Library (Jewish Central Information Office): Alfred keeps alive postwar, 367–9; in Amsterdam, 73–7, 86, 88, 91–3, 95, 125–8, 210–11; Britain withdraws funding (1945), 367, 376; and broader problem of racism, 76, 374; James Callaghan's support for, 368–9; and David Cohen, 74, 91–2, 95, 126; and Eichmann trial, 369; FBI investigates, 212; intelligence work during war, 1, 207–10, 211–14, 293–5, 363–4; key importance of in Holocaust studies, 370; moved to London, 92–3, 125–6, 207; name change to Wiener Library, 208; New York office, 211–14, 293–5, 363–4; postwar work, 368–70, 374; role in Nuremberg trials, 369; and Grete Wiener, 88, 125–8; Wiener Library Board, 368

Yad Vashem Holocaust archive, 338–9

Yalta conference (February 1945), 342, 343

Yangiyul, Uzbekistan, 256, 258–9

Zhangiztobe, eastern Kazakhstan, 185–6

Zhdanov (Soviet ship), 264

Zielenziger, Kurt, 126–7

Zionism, 32–5, 57, 80, 84, 87, 213–14

Zöpf, Wilhelm, 291